# THE WORLD'S MOST EVIL
# SERIAL KILLERS

# THE WORLD'S MOST EVIL
# SERIAL KILLERS
## CRIMES THAT SHOCKED THE WORLD

## EDITED BY
## RICHARD BROWN

**WITH CONTRIBUTIONS FROM
CHARLOTTE GREIG, AL CIMINO, JO DURDEN SMITH,
PAUL ROLAND, JOHN MARLOWE AND VICTOR MCQUEEN**

SIRIUS

**SIRIUS**

This edition published in 2023 by Sirius Publishing, a division of
Arcturus Publishing Limited,
26/27 Bickels Yard, 151–153 Bermondsey Street,
London SE1 3HA

ISBN: 978-1-3988-0737-2
AD008659UK

Printed in China

# CONTENTS

# INTRODUCTION

Serial killers are some of the most terrifying criminals around. They strike again and again and the murders only end when they are caught. The FBI estimates that there are between 25 and 50 active serial killers operating in the United States at any one time. Their numbers peaked in 1994, when there were more than 150 such criminals operating. They have a particular hold on the popular imagination and have spawned countless books, films and television series based on their gruesome deeds – sometimes to the delight of the killers themselves. But the various myths and sensationalist stories that have arisen about the serial killer are only part of the story. The truth is often far more disturbing.

Serial killers can prove enormously difficult to detect. While most murders are committed by people the victims knew well, serial killers often roam further

*Ted Bundy used his undoubted charm to gain his victims' trust and lure them to their doom. He decapitated many of his victims and kept their severed heads in his apartment as souvenirs.*

afield. Their victims may seem almost to be chosen at random, linked only by proximity to a highway, to the killer's home, or sharing some characteristic that could easily be overlooked by an unprepared detective.

What drives someone to kill? Most of the people featured in this book share common traits – unhappy childhoods, anger at the world around them and a shocking lack of empathy which makes it hard for them to understand ordinary people. Yet it would be a mistake to see all serial killers as insane monsters. Sometimes they can be almost impossible to detect. They can appear charming and friendly, as Ted Bundy seemed to so many of his victims, and can even lead respectable lives and be loved by their communities, as was the case with John Wayne Gacy.

Serial murder has a long and bloody history. Cruel-hearted aristocrats like Countess Elizabeth Báthory used their wealth and power to inflict all manner of atrocities on their unfortunate subjects. Jack the Ripper terrorized Victorian London and, despite his identity never being revealed, he has become perhaps the most famous of all serial killers.

Serial killers come in all shapes and sizes. They come from all over the world. In this book you will find murderers from the USA, Russia, Great Britain, Brazil, Japan and Germany, among other countries.

There are women as well as men, and women make up nearly one-fifth of all serial killers today. Many are on the lookout for profit. Poison is often the weapon of choice, and it is often the immediate family who is most at risk.

There are disorganized killers, whose uncontrollable rages lead them to murder. These villains often claim that they were possessed by an evil spirit

*Serial killers are some of the most terrifying individuals on the planet.*

or perhaps the devil himself, but usually the truth is only that they cannot control their emotions and allow their worst impulses to run riot.

Others see themselves as cold-blooded executioners, enacting their sentence on those they deem unfit for this world. They plot out every step of the kill and take pleasure in seeing their deadly schemes come to fruition.

Then there are the angels of death, the nurses, doctors and carers who trade on the trust bestowed on their profession to keep their deadly deeds hidden.

For some of these vile individuals, even murder does not provide enough of a thrill. They first torture and mutilate their victims and occasionally even feast on their flesh. They turn their houses into horrifying dungeons filled with the tools of the trade, yet somehow keep prying neighbours away for years or even decades.

Serial killers don't always work alone. Partners are often roped into the crimes, and you will see examples of faithful spouses who don't just condone the evil excesses of their other half, but actively participate in torture, murder and all manner of atrocities. In other deadly duos, it is not lovers but friends who get in on the action, joining in for the thrill of the kill. Others like Charles Manson bring whole cults along with them.

Finally there are the mass killers or spree shooters, who gun down vast numbers of innocents and terrify entire communities in sudden, shocking bursts of violence, often ending their own lives in the process. An unhappy fact of life in modern America has been the persistence of mass shootings. There have been more than 300 such crimes every year since 2015 resulting in thousands of deaths and countless injuries.

You will find here a collection of the most vile, hateful and inhuman crimes ever committed. It is the sad truth that as long as people exist, there will be those who kill again and again.

*Many followers joined Charles Manson's bloody cult.*

THE BERNER ST VICTIM

CHAPEL HORRORS. WHEN WILL THEY END?

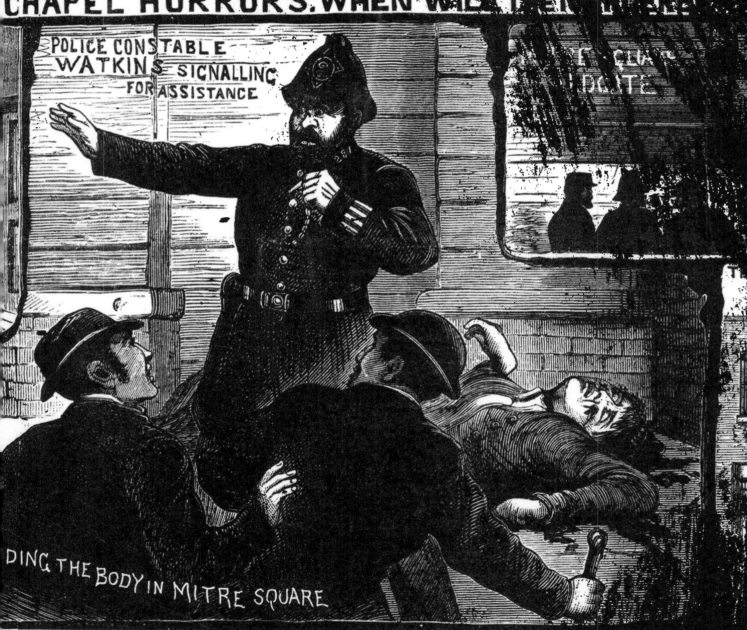

POLICE CONSTABLE WATKINS SIGNALLING FOR ASSISTANCE

DING THE BODY IN MITRE SQUARE

# A HISTORY OF MURDER

Throughout history, there have been men and women who killed, raped and tortured. Sometimes their reigns of terror lasted years or even decades before they were stopped. These killers could be high-ranking aristocrats or professionals eager to abuse their authority. Others came from the poorest strata of society. What they have in common is that their horrible deeds made their way into the popular psyche and gave rise to legends that persist to the present day.

# ELIZABETH BÁTHORY

When Countess Elizabeth Báthory, aged 15, married Count Nádasdy in around 1576, it was an alliance between two of the greatest dynasties in Hungary. For Nádasdy, the master of Castle Csejthe in the Carpathians, came from a line of warriors, and Elizabeth's family was even more distinguished: It had produced generals and governors, high princes and cardinals – her cousin was the country's prime minister. Long after they've been forgotten, though, she will be remembered. For she was an alchemist, a bather in blood – and one of the models for Bram Stoker's Dracula.

She was beautiful, voluptuous, savage – a fine match for her 21-year-old husband, the so-called 'Black Warrior'. But he was forever off campaigning, and she remained childless. More and more, then, she gave in to the constant cajolings of her old nurse, Ilona Jó, who was a black witch, a satanist. She began to surround herself with alchemists and sorcerers; and when she conceived – she eventually had four children – she may have been finally convinced of their efficacy. For when her husband died, when she was about 41, she surrendered to the black arts completely.

There had long been rumours around the castle of lesbian orgies, of the kidnappings of young peasant women, of flagellation, of torture. But one day after her husband's death, Elizabeth Báthory slapped the face of a servant girl and drew blood; and she noticed that, where it had fallen on her hand, the skin seemed to grow smoother and more supple. She was soon convinced that bathing in and drinking the blood of young virgins would keep her young forever. Her entourage of witches and magicians – who were now calling for human sacrifice to make their magic work – agreed enthusiastically.

*Countess Báthory pursued a grisly beauty regime.*

*Local servant girls arrived at the Báthory castle hoping that servitude would be relatively benign.*

Elizabeth and her cronies, then, began scouring the countryside for children and young girls, who were either lured to the castle or kidnapped. They were then hung in chains in the dungeons, fattened and milked for their blood before being tortured to death and their bones used in alchemical experiments. The countess, it was said later, kept some of them alive to lick the blood from her body when she emerged from her baths, but had them, in turn, brutally killed if they either failed to arouse her or showed the slightest signs of displeasure.

Peasant girls, however, failed to stay the signs of ageing, and after five years Elizabeth decided to set up an academy for young noblewomen. Now she bathed in blue blood, the blood of her own class. But this time, inevitably, news of her depravities reached the royal court; and her cousin, the prime minister, was forced to investigate. A surprise raid on the castle found the countess in mid-orgy; bodies lying strewn, drained of blood; and dozens of girls – some flayed and vein-milked, some fattened like Strasbourg geese awaiting their turn – in the dungeons.

Elizabeth's grisly entourage was taken into custody and then tortured to obtain confessions. At the subsequent trial for the murder of the eighty victims who were actually found dead at the castle, her old nurse, Ilona Jó, and one of the countess's procurers of young girls were sentenced to be burned at the stake after having their fingers torn out; many of the rest were beheaded. The countess, who as an aristocrat could not be arrested or executed, was given a separate hearing in her absence at which she was accused of murdering more than 600 women and children. She was then bricked up in a tiny room in her castle, with holes left only for ventilation and the passing of food. Still relatively young and curiously youthful, she was never seen alive again. She is presumed to have died – since the food was from then on left uneaten – four years later, on 21 August 1614.

# WILLIAM BURKE AND WILLIAM HARE

In early 19th century Edinburgh even the dead did not rest easy. No sooner were corpses interred in the city's cemeteries than they were likely to be dug up in the dead of night by 'resurrectionists' – grave robbers who profited from selling cadavers to the local medical schools.

The golden age of scientific discovery was dawning and the Scottish capital's surgeons were keen to supply their eager students with suitable specimens. However, they were forbidden to do so by an antiquated law which supported the Church's assertion that the act of dissection condemned the soul of the deceased to eternal damnation. It was said that only those whose bodies were intact would enter the kingdom of heaven on the Day of Judgment. As a consequence anatomists were forced to limit their examinations to the corpses of executed criminals and vagrants.

*Burke (left) had a chip on his shoulder about finding work, while Hare was always looking for get-rich-quick schemes.*

*In the days before refrigeration, murder was more lucrative than 'bodysnatching' since a fresh corpse earned top dollar.*

Contrary to popular belief, comparatively few criminals were executed at the turn of the century. Instead, transportation to the colonies had become the preferred punishment for all crimes apart from treason and murder, so fresh specimens from the scaffold were in short supply. Consequently, the only question asked of those selling cadavers was, 'Can you obtain another?' And if so, the fresher the better.

As the grisly trade increased, grieving relatives were forced to consider paying for the installation of 'mort safes' – iron, cage-like contraptions built over and around the graves of the newly deceased, for fear they might be disinterred at dead of night. But few could afford such measures.

While the more enlightened medical men lobbied unsuccessfully for a change in the law, two of their fellow citizens forced the issue by murdering at least 17 people, often their neighbours, in order to procure fresh cadavers. Ironically, neither of Britain's most notorious bodysnatchers personally robbed a grave during their brief criminal careers. They were either too frightened or too workshy to dirty their hands in the kirkyard.

At the time of the murders, which took place between November 1827 and October of the following year, itinerant Irish immigrant William Burke was 36 years old. He considered himself ill-used by society, with no prospect of finding gainful employment and no will to look for it. After abandoning his wife and two children in County Mayo, he emigrated to Scotland where he drifted aimlessly through a succession of labouring jobs. He ended up in Edinburgh where he settled down with Helen (Nell) McDougal, whom he had met while lodging at her home in Maddiston. Helen left her two children and her common-law husband to travel with Burke, who was said to be crudely handsome but sullen and quick-tempered. The couple found cheap lodgings in Tanner's Close in the West Port, a rat run of squalid tenements, gaslit streets and ale houses, where the inhabitants could drink themselves senseless for a shilling.

## A FRIGHTFUL SCHEME

With no work, and no hope of finding any, Burke reluctantly endured the company of his landlord, fellow Irish immigrant William Hare, who was generous with his rental income. Hare would buy drinks for anyone who would listen to his idle boasts and his plans to get rich without doing a day's honest work. Little is known of Hare's background, but according to contemporary accounts he was a repulsive, vindictive man who was given to fits of idiotic laughter, when his reptilian features would distort into a hideous mask, giving the impression of a fairground freak. Burke tolerated him so long as he bought the drinks, but he also half hoped that one of Hare's mad schemes might one day make them both rich. In the winter of 1827 they hit on a scheme that promised to do just that.

One of Hare's lodgers, an elderly soldier named Donald, had died suddenly after a long illness. While waiting for the body to be collected, Hare complained long and bitterly to Burke. The old man's rent remained unpaid and there were no known relatives that could be badgered into settling the account. Then it occurred to him that the medical colleges would pay for the corpse, perhaps even more than he was owed. They would split the money equally and be rich men by nightfall. No one would miss the old man or enquire into the cause of his death and there was no risk of being caught – but they would have to act quickly. So they swiftly removed the body from its coffin, hid it elsewhere in the house and replaced it with firewood. After the coffin had been collected they went in search of Professor Munro, the principal anatomist at Edinburgh University Medical School, but by chance they were misdirected to the classrooms of Professor Robert Knox, his colleague. Knox's assistants assured them that they would receive a good price and they were asked to return after dark. When they did so, carrying the still-warm corpse in a sack, Knox's assistants gave them just over £7, more than two weeks' wages for the average skilled labourer.

## MERCY KILLINGS

Any fears the two Irishmen might have had were soon dissolved by the keg of whisky they consumed that night. Emboldened by their success and excited by the prospect of more easy money, they were soon looking for their next subject. They did not have long to wait.

A few days later another of Hare's lodgers, Joseph the Miller, fell ill. Although his condition was clearly not life-threatening, Burke and Hare saw no necessity in prolonging the man's agony. They plied him with whisky until he lost consciousness, then one of them pinned his arms and legs down while the other covered his nose and mouth until all signs of life were extinct. Unwittingly, the pair had invented a new method of murder, one which would be named after its creator – 'burking'. It was crude, cruel but foolproof because it left no marks on the body. At first glance it appeared that the victim had died of drink or natural causes.

If Burke and Hare had been careful they could have continued enriching themselves in this way for years. But they drank the wages of sin as soon as they collected them and they also became impatient. They no longer wanted to wait for another ailing lodger to come their way. Instead, they went in search of their victims – those who no one would miss, such as tinkers wandering the cobbled streets and drunks sleeping in doorways.

During the following 11 months Burke and Hare committed 15 more murders without arousing suspicion. Their victims included prostitutes, beggars and the homeless. Many of them had come down to the capital from the Highlands, and from isolated villages, in search of work and so would have no family in Edinburgh to enquire after their whereabouts. One morning, Burke even had the gall to approach a pair of policemen, who were taking an inebriated woman to the police station so that she could sleep off her over-indulgence. He lied that he knew her and offered to take her home. That evening he had another £10 to spend on drink.

By this time several of Dr Knox's students were beginning to talk openly about how their eminent professor was able to offer his class a regular supply of fresh specimens when his colleagues had to make do with a badly decomposed cadaver or, more often, none at all. Their disquiet grew when the body of a local prostitute was delivered to the school. Those who had seen her on the previous day reported that she had looked lively and had been none the worse for drink. But no one dared raise the matter directly with Dr Knox. However, soon afterwards several students voiced their concerns when the body of a well-known local character known as 'Daft Jamie', a mentally retarded youth with a club foot, was placed on the dissecting slab. It was a matter of seconds before they started questioning how this young man had died so suddenly and conveniently within the reach of Burke and Hare, who by now were known to be the sole suppliers of specimens to Dr Knox. The professor confirmed their suspicions by first taking a scalpel to the club foot and then to Jamie's face, in order to eradicate his identifiable features. It was as good as a confession.

And still the students kept silent, fearing scandal and, quite possibly, the closure of the school. Knox, or someone else in authority, may even have raised the possibility that they might all be named as accomplices if the matter became public.

## THE LAST VICTIM

On the morning of 29 October 1828, Burke sat drinking his morning draught in the local tavern when he overheard an old woman, Mary Docherty, talking to the barman in a thick Irish accent. He engaged her in conversation and then claimed that he came from the same part of the old country as herself. They might even be related, he told her. With these words he lured Mary back to his house in Tanner's Close, where she met his wife Helen and a couple who were lodging with them, James and Ann Gray. A party was held in order to celebrate the happy chance meeting and the drinking and dancing continued long after the Grays left. They had gone to stay the night with William Hare and his common-law wife Margaret, giving up their room to Mary Docherty just as Burke had hoped. At around midnight another occupant of the house was passing the Burkes' door when he thought he heard two men arguing and a woman's stifled cries of 'Murder!' and 'Get the police!', but

*Among Edinburgh's floating population, there was no shortage of candidates for Burke and Hare's final ministrations.*

when he hurried into the street he could not see a policeman. On returning to the house all was quiet, so he assumed it was a domestic quarrel and he went to bed.

The next morning the Grays returned to Burke's rooms and were surprised to learn that Mary had gone. They were told that she had been turned out of the house in the early hours by Helen, who had claimed that the old woman and her husband were becoming too friendly for comfort. If the Grays found the explanation absurd they did not say so, but their suspicions were aroused when Burke warned Ann not to go near the bed. He later yelled at her when she started towards it to fetch some potatoes stored underneath. As soon as they were alone in the room the Grays looked under the bed and were horrified to see the body of the old woman. As they raced from the house they ran into Helen, who asked them where they were going in such a hurry. James accused her of murder and told her that they were going to fetch the police, which sent her into a panic. She begged them not to do so. Then she offered to share the profits with them if they kept silent, which only infuriated them further. However, by the time the police were summoned the body had vanished. Without it, there were no grounds for arresting William and Helen Burke.

But then a neighbour informed the police that two men had been seen carrying a large tea chest from the house only an hour or so before. When questioned, William claimed that Mrs Docherty had left at 7 o'clock that morning, whereas Helen asserted that the old woman had departed at 7 o'clock that evening. The discrepancy in their stories was sufficient to have them brought in for further questioning. Word soon went around the West Port that murder most foul

had been perpetrated at Tanner's Close and someone suggested that the authorities should pay a visit to the dissecting rooms of Dr Knox. There they found a body which was identified by James Gray as being that of Mary Docherty.

By nightfall William Hare and Margaret were also in custody. Their conflicting and inconsistent statements convinced the authorities that they were guilty, but there was no physical evidence and there were no eyewitnesses. All of the evidence was circumstantial. The Lord Advocate believed that most of the guilt lay with Burke, so in order to force the issue and secure a conviction, he offered Hare immunity if he testified against Burke and Helen. Hare seized the chance to save his own skin and he confessed to the crimes, which now included the killing of Daft Jamie and the prostitute Mary Paterson, bringing the total number of victims to 15.

## BURKE'S TRIAL AND EXECUTION

The trial of William Burke began on Christmas Eve 1828, with Helen named as his accomplice in the killing of Mary Docherty. The prosecution case relied almost entirely on the eyewitness testimony of William and Margaret Hare, the statements made by the Grays – which affirmed that the body of an old woman had been hidden in the house but was then spirited away – and the testimony of the lodger who had heard a woman crying 'Murder!' earlier that evening. Helen Burke's solicitor argued that she had been the woman who had cried out in horror when she had witnessed the old woman's death. He went on to say that the fact that she had been seen in the company of several of the victims did not prove that

*Edinburgh's citizens queued up to witness the execution of William Burke in 1829.*

she was implicated in their deaths. It was a poor defence, but it sowed the seed of reasonable doubt.

On Christmas morning the jury returned with its verdicts. Burke was guilty, but the case against Helen was 'not proven', a uniquely Scottish verdict which implied that the accused had escaped imprisonment only because there was insufficient evidence to secure a conviction. On hearing the sentence Burke embraced Helen and wept.

'You are out of the scrape,' he said.

In the following weeks Burke made two formal confessions, which were published in broadsheets and sold by hawkers on the street corners of the city. Damned by his own words and abandoned by his accomplice, William Burke resigned himself to his fate. On 28 January 1829 he was led through the jeering crowds who surged around the scaffold on the Lawnmarket. They called for Hare and Dr Knox to share his fate.

## THE AFTERMATH

Remarkably, the eminent anatomist escaped prosecution, but was hounded by stone-throwing crowds at his home and at the medical college. The popularity of his classes dwindled significantly in the weeks and months after the trial. He applied for vacant posts at Edinburgh University Medical School, but he was rejected twice.

Eventually he left for London, where he obtained a position at a cancer hospital. He died in 1862. Although Burke swore that Knox had known nothing of the method by which the corpses were obtained, it seems implausible that a renowned anatomist would not have recognized the signs of a violent – or at least unnatural – death when dissecting the bodies.

The body of William Burke was taken down from the scaffold and delivered to the medical college, where it was dismembered in full view of the students who had attended the dissection of his victims. His skeleton was then put on public display in the college museum, together with his death mask and several items made from his tanned skin. It proved an effective deterrent. The incidence of grave robbing rapidly declined and the practice was all but eradicated by the Anatomy Act of 1832, which permitted the regular supply of dead bodies for dissection.

Hare did not escape justice, however. Angry mobs pursued him and the two women, driving them out of Scotland and harassing them whenever they attempted to settle down. Margaret is thought to have eventually returned to Ireland, it was rumoured that Helen had gone to Australia and William Hare was last heard of in Carlisle. It is not known if there is any truth in the story that he was thrown into a lime pit by an angry mob, forcing him to end his days as a blind beggar on the streets of London.

# JACK THE RIPPER

Now that London's famous fogs have disappeared – and with them the gas-lamps, the brick shacks, the crammed slums, the narrow streets and blind alleyways of the city's East End – it's hard to imagine the hysteria and terror that swept through the area when The Whitechapel Murderer – later known as Jack the Ripper – went to work. Already in 1888 two prostitutes had been murdered. So when the body of another was found, her throat cut and her stomach horribly mutilated, on 31 August, she was immediately assumed to be the brutal killer's third victim. And brutal he was: 'Only a madman could have done this,' said a detective; the police surgeon agreed. 'I have never seen so horrible a case,' he announced. 'She was ripped about in a manner that only a person skilled in the use of a knife could have achieved.' A week later, the body of 'Dark Annie' Chapman was found not far away, this time disembowelled and with its uterus removed; and a fortnight after that, a letter was received by the Central News Agency in London which finally gave the killer a name. It read (in part):

'Grand job, that last job was. I gave the lady no time to squeal. I love my work and want to start again. You will soon hear from me, with my funny little game... Next time I shall clip the ears off and send them to the police just for jolly.'

It was signed: 'Jack the Ripper.' Five days later, he struck again – twice. The first victim was 'Long Liz' Stride, whose body, its throat cut, was discovered on the night of 30 September by the secretary of a Jewish Working Men's Club whose arrival in a pony trap seems to have disturbed the Ripper. For apart from a nick on one ear, the still-warm corpse was unmutilated. Unsatisfied, the Ripper went on to find another to kill. Just 45 minutes later – and 15 minutes' walk away – the body of Catherine Eddowes, a prostitute in her 40s, was found. Hers was the most mutilated so far. For her entrails had been pulled out through a large gash running from her breastbone to her abdomen; part of one of her kidneys had been removed and her ears had been cut off. A trail of blood led to a ripped fragment of her apron, above which had been written in chalk: 'The Juwes are The men That Will not be Blamed for nothing.' By this time 600 police and plain-clothes detectives had been deployed in the area, alongside amateur vigilantes, and rumours were rife. The Ripper was a foreign seaman, a Jewish butcher, someone who habitually carried a black bag; and there were attacks on anyone who fitted this description. He could even be – for how else could he so successfully avoid apprehension? – a policeman run mad. There was plenty of time now for speculation. For the Ripper didn't move again for more than a month – and when he did, it was the worst murder of all. His victim was

25-year-old Mary Jane Kelly; and her body, when it was found in the wretched hovel she rented, was unrecognizable: there was blood and pieces of flesh all over the floor. The man who found her later said: 'I shall be haunted by [the sight of it] for the rest of my life.' This time, though, there was a clue. For Mary Jane had last been seen in the company of a well-dressed man, slim and wearing a moustache. This fitted in with other possible sightings and could be added to the only other evidence the police now had: that the killer was left-handed, probably young – and he might be a doctor for he showed knowledge of human dissection.

After this last murder, though, the trail went completely cold. For the Ripper never killed again. The inquest on Mary Jane Kelly was summarily closed and investigations were called off, suggesting to some that Scotland Yard had come into possession of some very special information, never disclosed. This has left the problem of the Ripper's identity wide open to every sort of speculation. The finger has been variously pointed – among many others – at a homicidal Russian doctor, a woman-hating Polish tradesman, the painter Walter Sickert, the Queen's surgeon and even her grandson, Prince Albert, the Duke of Clarence. The theory in this last case is that Albert had an illegitimate child by a Roman Catholic shopgirl who was also an artist's model. Mary Jane Kelly had acted as midwife at the birth, and she and all the friends she'd gossiped to were forcibly silenced, on the direct orders of the prime minister of the day, Lord Salisbury.

The probable truth is that the Ripper was a man called Montagu John Druitt, a failed barrister who

had both medical connections and a history of insanity in his family. He'd become a teacher, and had subsequently disappeared from his school in Blackheath. A few weeks after the death of Mary Jane Kelly – when the killings stopped – his body was found floating in the river.

*The Whitechapel Murders appalled the public.*

# LIZZIE BORDEN

Lizzie Borden, so the old rhyme goes, took an axe and gave her mother 40 whacks; when she saw what she had done, she gave her father forty-one. The truth is, though, that the number of whacks which despatched Abbey Borden and her rich husband Andrew in Fall River, Massachusetts, in 1892, numbered 19 and ten respectively – and daughter Lizzie, much to the delight of the courtroom which tried her, was finally acquitted.

But was she really guilty? She certainly had a motive. For Abbey was in fact 32-year-old Lizzie's stepmother, and she resented her deeply, particularly after her father, usually very tight with his money, bought Abbey's sister a house and gave the deeds to his wife. Lizzie was also given to what her family had come to call 'funny turns'. One day, for example, she announced to her father that Abbey's bedroom had been ransacked by a burglar. He reported it to the police, who soon established that Lizzie had done the ransacking herself.

As for her father, whom she loved, the repressed spinster may even have had a motive for his murder too, apart from his meanness with money and the fact that, with both him and her stepmother dead, she would finally inherit it. For three months before his death in August, when outhouses in the garden were twice broken into, he'd convinced himself that whoever was responsible had been after Lizzie's pet pigeons. So he'd decapitated them – yes, with an axe.

Suffice it to say that at about 9.30 am on 4 August, while dusting the spare room, Abbey Borden was struck from behind with an axe and then brutally hacked at even after she was dead. There were only two people in the house at the time, Lizzie and the maid Bridget who was cleaning the downstairs windows. Slightly less than an hour and a half later, Andrew Borden returned, to be told by his daughter that his wife was out. A few minutes later, after Bridget had gone upstairs to her room in the attic, he too was struck down while dozing on a settee in the living-room.

It was Lizzie who 'found' the body of her father, and the neighbours she immediately called in found the body of his wife upstairs. They did their best to comfort her. But she seemed curiously calm, and she was happy enough to talk to the police as soon as they arrived. Trouble was that, both then and subsequently, she began giving conflicting accounts of her whereabouts during the morning; and it wasn't long before the police, who found a recently cleaned axehead in the basement, came to regard her as the chief suspect. Only the day before the murders she'd tried to buy prussic acid in Fall River, they discovered, and when that had failed, she'd told a neighbour she was worried that her father had made many potentially vengeful enemies, because of his brusque manner.

After the inquest she was arrested – and vilified as a murderess in the newspapers. But by the time her trial took place in New Bedford in 1893 the tide had begun to turn. Bridget and her sister played down her hatred of her stepmother; and though Bridget confessed that Lizzie had burned one of her dresses on the day after her parents' funeral, she said that there had been no bloodstains on it. Lizzie herself was demure and ladylike in the dock – she even fainted halfway through the proceedings. And in the end the jury agreed with her lawyer, an ex-governor of the State, that she could not be both a lady and a fiend.

After the trial, now rich, she returned to Fall River and bought a large house, in which she died alone in 1927. Bridget the maid returned to Ireland – with, it's said, a good deal of money from poor Andrew Borden's coffers. There's since been a suggestion that Lizzie became a killer during one of her 'funny turns' – caused by temporal-lobe epilepsy.

*Lizzie Borden 'gave her mother 40 whacks'.*

# DR HAWLEY HARVEY CRIPPEN

r Hawley Harvey, later Peter, Crippen is one of the most famous – and most reviled – murderers of the 20th century. Yet he was a small, slight man, intelligent, dignified, eternally polite and anxious for the welfare of those around him. With his gold-rimmed spectacles, sandy whiskers and shy expression, he was, in fact, more mouse than monster. His problem was his wife.

Crippen was born in Coldwater, Michigan, in 1862, and studied for medical degrees in Cleveland, London and New York. Around 1890, his first wife died, leaving him a widower; three years later, when working in a practice in Brooklyn, he fell in love with one of his patients, a 17-year-old with ambitions to be an opera singer, called Cora Turner. She was overweight; her real name was Kunigunde Mackamotzki – she was the boisterous, loose daughter of a Russian-Polish immigrant. But none of this mattered to Crippen. He first paid for her singing lessons, and then he married her.

In 1900, by now consultant physician to a mail-order medicine company, Crippen was transferred to London to become manager of the firm's head office

and Cora came to join him. On arrival in London, though, she decided to change her name once again – this time to Belle Elmore – and to try out her voice in the city's music halls. She soon became a success and acquired many friends and admirers. She bleached her hair; became a leading light in the Music Hall Ladies Guild; and entertained the first of what were to be many lovers.

*Dr Crippen is one of the most reviled murderers of the 20th century.*

Increasingly contemptuous of her husband, whom she regarded as an embarrassment, she forced him first to move to a grand house in north London that he could ill afford, and then to act as a general dogsbody to the 'lodgers' she soon moved in.

Crippen took such consolation as he could with a shy secretary at his company called Ethel Le Neve. But in 1909, he lost his job, and his wife threatened to leave him, taking their life savings with her. By the beginning of the following year, he'd had enough. On 19 January, he acquired five grains of a powerful narcotic called hyoscine from a chemist's in New Oxford Street; and the last time his wife was seen was 12 days later, at a dinner for two retired music-hall friends at the Crippens' home. Two days after that, as it turned out, Crippen began pawning her jewellery, and sent a letter to the Music Hall Ladies Guild, saying that she'd had to leave for America, where a relative was seriously ill. Later he announced that she'd gone to the wilds of California; that she had contracted pneumonia; and, in March – after Ethel had moved into his house – that she had died there.

Two actors, though, who'd been touring in California returned to England and, when told, said they'd heard nothing at all about Cora's death. Scotland Yard took an interest and Crippen was forced to concede that he'd made up the story: his wife had in fact left for America with one of her lovers. Though this seemed to satisfy the detectives, he then made his first big mistake: he panicked, settled his affairs overnight and left with Ethel the next day for Europe, after persuading her to start a new life with him in America. When the police called again, it was to find them gone. They began a thorough search of the house. What remained of his wife – rotting flesh, skin and hair – was found buried under the coal cellar.

Unaware of the furore of horror created by this discovery in the British press, Crippen – his moustache shaved off, under an assumed name, and accompanied by Ethel, disguised as his son – took a ship from Antwerp to Quebec in Canada. But they were soon recognized by the captain who, aware of a reward, used the new invention of the wireless telegraph to send a message to his employers. Each day from then on, in fact, he sent via the same medium daily reports on the doings of the couple which were published in the British newspapers.

Meanwhile, Chief Inspector Dew of Scotland Yard took a faster ship and arrested Dr Crippen and 'son' Ethel when they reached Canadian waters.

Huge, angry crowds greeted them when they arrived back a month later, under arrest, in England. The newspapers had done their job of transforming the pair of them into vicious killers. But Crippen always maintained that Ethel had had absolutely no knowledge of the murder, and when they were tried separately, she was acquitted. Crippen, though, was found guilty and was hanged in Pentonville Prison on 23 November 1910. Before he died, he described Ethel as

'my only comfort for the past three years. . . As I face eternity, I say that Ethel Le Neve has loved me as few women love men. . . Surely such love as hers for me will be rewarded.'

It is not known whether she was rewarded, or indeed what became of her, though one story recounts that she ran a tea-shop in Bournemouth, under an assumed name, for 45 years…

# BÉLA KISS

**B**éla Kiss was 40 years old when he moved with his young bride Maria to the Hungarian village of Czinkota in 1913. A plumber by trade, but obviously well-to-do, he bought a large house with an adjoining workshop and settled down to a quiet life, growing roses and collecting stamps. From time to time he would drive into Budapest on business, but otherwise his was an uneventful life. No one in the village ever thought to tell him that whenever he was away his wife was often seen out with a young artist called Paul Bihari.

Nor did anybody particularly remark on the fact that when he returned from the big city he started bringing oil drums back with him. Everyone, after all, knew that war was coming, and that fuel was likely to be scarce. When Kiss's wife and the artist Bihari ended up disappearing from Cinkota, the villagers took it for granted that they'd eloped. Why, Kiss even had a letter from his wife that said as much.

Besides, poor man, he was clearly distraught at what had happened. He withdrew from village life – and it only became clear much later what the oil drums, which he continued from time to time quietly to bring back from Budapest, along with the occasional woman overnight guest, were really for…

*Béla Kiss was the talk of the town in Cinkota, Hungary, and considered quite a catch. Women queued up to meet him when he announced in 1912 that his wife had left him after an affair with an artist.*

*Kiss marched off with the army, but did he move on to the Foreign Legion?*

After war came in August 1914, the reclusive Kiss was conscripted. While he served in the army, his house remained empty, its taxes unpaid; and then, in May 1916, news arrived that he'd been killed in action. His house was sold at auction for the unpaid taxes, and bought by a local blacksmith, who found seven oil-drums behind sheets of corrugated iron in the workshop. One day he opened one of them. It was full of alcohol – as were the rest of the drums. But in each one floated the body of a naked woman. When police subsequently searched the garden, they found the pickled bodies of another 15 women, aged between 25 and 50, and that of a single young man. All of them had been garrotted.

It wasn't long before police in Budapest picked up Kiss's trail. He'd been placing advertisements in a newspaper, giving a post-office box number and claiming to be a widower anxious to meet a mature spinster or widow, with marriage in mind. Both the name and the address he'd given the newspaper proved false. But one of the payments he'd made to it had been by postal order, and when the signature on it was published in the press, a woman came forward and said it was that of her lover, Béla Kiss – and she produced a postcard sent from the front to prove it. When a photograph of Kiss was found and published in its turn, he was recognized as a frequent – and sexually voracious – visitor to Budapest's red-light district. He'd apparently been using the savings he'd persuaded his victims to withdraw – in advance of their marriage – to feed his constant need for sex.

Kiss was, of course, dead. So the case was closed. But then a friend of one of his victims swore she'd seen him one day in 1919 crossing Budapest's Margaret Bridge. Five years later a former French legionnaire told French police of a Hungarian fellow-soldier, with the same name as that used in Kiss's ads, who'd boasted of his skill at garrotting. In 1932, Kiss was again recognized, this time in Times Square in New York. Had he swapped his identity with a dead man at the front and got away with it?

# CARL PANZRAM

As the moment of his execution approached, when serial killer Carl Panzram was asked whether he had any last words, he is reported to have turned to his executioner and said: 'Hurry it up, you Hoosier bastard! I could kill ten men while you're fooling around!' It was probably not much of an exaggeration.

Much of what we know about Panzram comes from his autobiography, published 40 years after his death. It is a well-written and articulate account of his life; not at all what one would expect from someone with limited formal education. The man who would come to murder dozens was born to a Prussian immigrant couple on 28 June 1891 on a Minnesota farm near the Canadian border. He and his six siblings were raised in poverty, a situation made worse when his father deserted the family. This shameful act took place when Carl Panzram was seven years old. A year later the boy was arrested for the very adult crime of being drunk and disorderly. He was soon committing burglary, and at the age of 11 was sent to the Minnesota State Training School, a reform institution. Panzram's claims, made late in life, that he was beaten and sexually abused, are probably true. That he also committed his first

*Making up for a childhood of deprivation, Carl Panzram became a career criminal, beginning with theft before graduating to rape and murder.*

murder there, the victim being a 12-year-old boy, has not been verified. In July 1905, he burnt one of the school's buildings to the ground. Evidently, he wasn't a suspect in the destruction, as he was released just a few months later.

## MURDER IN MIND

He enrolled in another school, but was soon in conflict with one of the teachers. The dispute was elevated to such a point that Panzram brought a handgun to class, intending to murder the instructor in front of his fellow students. The scheme collapsed when the gun fell to the floor during a struggle. He left the

school and the family farm, and started 'riding the rails'. Any feeling of freedom the 14-year-old might have felt in this transient lifestyle probably came to an end when he was gang-raped by four men. For the rest of his 39 years, Panzram was enraged by the pain and humiliation he had suffered through the incident. As part of some warped idea of revenge, he went on to forcibly sodomize more than a thousand boys and men.

Mere months after having left the Minnesota State Training School, Panzram was again in reform school, again for having committed burglary.

He soon escaped with another inmate named Jimmie Benson. They remained together for a time, moving around the American Midwest, causing havoc, burgling houses and stealing from churches before setting them on fire.

After they split up, Panzram joined the United States Army. It was a strange choice of profession, one for which he was ill suited. During his brief stint in service, he was charged with insubordination, jailed numerous times for petty offences and, ultimately, was found guilty on three counts of larceny. Panzram received a dishonourable discharge and on 20 April 1908 was sentenced to three years of hard labour at the United States Disciplinary Barracks at Fort Leavenworth in Kansas.

In prison, the 16-year-old Panzram was beaten and chained to a 50-pound metal ball which he was made to carry. He dreamed of escape, but found it impossible. It was only after serving his three-year sentence that he finally got out. Panzram returned to his old transient lifestyle, moving through Kansas, Texas, California, Oregon, Washington, Utah and Idaho. He committed burglary, arson, robbery and rape. In his autobiography, Panzram writes that

he spent all his spare change on bullets and for fun would take shots at farmers' windows and livestock.

Another story involves a railway policeman whom Panzram raped at gunpoint. He forced two hobos to witness the act and then recreate it themselves.

He was arrested many times and served a number of sentences under a variety of assumed names. After his second incarceration and escape from Oregon State Prison, Panzram made his way to the east coast. Ending up in New Haven, Connecticut, in the summer of 1920, Panzram burgled the home of former United States president William H. Taft, the man who had once signed the paper sentencing him to three years in prison at Fort Leavenworth.

The haul from the Taft mansion far exceeded previous burglaries. After fencing the goods in Manhattan's Lower East Side, Panzram bought a yacht. He then sailed the East River, breaking into the yachts of the wealthy moored along his route. He took to hiring unemployed sailors as deckhands. In the evenings, he would drug his crew, sodomize them, shoot each in the head with a pistol stolen from the Taft house and throw their bodies overboard. After about three weeks, Panzram's routine came to an end when his yacht was caught in an August gale and sank. He swam to shore with two sailors, whom he never saw again.

## HEART OF DARKNESS

Following a six-month sentence for burglary and possession of a loaded gun, Panzram stowed away on a ship bound for Angola. While in the employ of the Sinclair Oil Company he sodomized and murdered a young boy. He later hired six locals to act as guides and assist in a crocodile-hunting expedition. Once downriver, with crocodiles in sight, he shot all six and fed the men to the beasts. After travelling along the Congo River and robbing farmers on the Gold Coast, he made his way back across the Atlantic.

Following his return to the United States, Panzram continued where he left off, committing robbery, burglary and sodomy. These 'routine' crimes were punctuated by the murders of three boys; each was raped before being killed.

On 26 August 1923, Panzram broke into the Larchmont, New York, train depot and was going through the stored baggage when he was confronted by a policeman. He was sentenced to five years in prison, most of which was served at Clinton Prison in upstate New York. True to character, Panzram made no attempt to become a model prisoner. During his first months at Clinton he tried to firebomb the workshops, clubbed one of the guards on the back of the head and, of course, attempted to escape. This final act had consequences with which he would struggle for the rest of his life.

The incident began when Panzram failed in his attempt to climb a prison wall. He fell nearly 30 ft (10 m), landing on a concrete step. Though his ankles and legs were broken and his spine severely injured, he received no medical attention for 14 months. The months of agony Panzram endured intensified his hatred and he began to draw up elaborate plans to kill on a mass scale. One scheme involved blowing up a railway tunnel, then releasing poison gas into the area of the wreck.

*Prisoners at Fort Leavenworth Penitentiary where Panzram served time.*

# ONE-MAN CRIME WAVE

When he was finally released from Clinton, in July 1928, Panzram emerged a crippled man. However, his diminished capacity did nothing to prevent his return to crime. During the first two weeks of freedom, he averaged approximately one burglary each day. More seriously, on 26 July 1928, he strangled a man during a robbery in Philadelphia. By August, Panzram was again in custody. Perhaps realizing that he would never again leave prison, he confessed to 22 murders, including those of two of the three boys in the summer of 1923.

On 12 November, he went on trial for burglary and housebreaking. Acting in his own defence, he used the courtroom as a stage from which to scare the jury and threaten witnesses. By the end of the day he had been found guilty on all counts and was sentenced to a total of 25 years in prison.

On 1 February 1929, he arrived at the United States Penitentiary at Leavenworth, Kansas. It was an area of the country he knew well; 20 years earlier he had served time at the nearby military prison. Standing before his new warden on that first day, Panzram warned, 'I'll kill the first man that bothers me.'

True to his word, on 20 June 1929, Panzram took an iron bar and brought it down with force on the head of Robert Warnke, his supervisor in the prison laundry. When the other prisoners attempted to escape, Panzram began chasing them around the room, breaking bones.

He was tried for Warnke's murder on 14 April 1930. Again, he undertook his own defence, smugly challenging the prosecutor to find him guilty. It wasn't a difficult challenge. When the judge sentenced Panzram to hang, he was threatened by the condemned man.

On 5 September 1930, Panzram was hanged. Many organizations had worked to prevent the execution, much to Panzram's annoyance. Nine months before his death, he wrote to one such organization, the Society for the Abolishment of Capital Punishment: 'The only thanks you and your kind will ever get from me for your efforts on my behalf is that I wish you all had one neck and that I had my hands on it.'

*Panzram's sadism knew no bounds. In Angola, he hired six locals to act as guides and assist in a crocodile hunting expedition. Once downriver, with the crocodiles in sight, he shot all six and fed the men to the beasts.*

N.Y.C. POL

4 176354

8 1 17 7

# FOR THE LOVE OF THE KILL

Many serial killers take great pleasure in the act of killing itself. Often they fantasize about it from an early age. Then it becomes an obsession and they prepare themselves to commit the deadly deed. Once they have killed their first victim, it's never enough: their bloodlust becomes insatiable and they leave a string of bodies in their wake.

# ED KEMPER

Ed Kemper earned the 'Co-ed Killer' sobriquet for the murder of six young female students in California in the 1970s. However, he began his homicidal career by murdering his grandparents and ended it by murdering his mother and her best friend.

His parents split in 1957, when Kemper was nine. Missing his dad, he became emotional and clingy. Fearing he might become a homosexual, his mother tried toughening up young Ed by making him sleep in the basement with a heavy table over the trapdoor leading to it. A visit from his father put a stop to that, but Ed continued to complain that his mother was 'an alcoholic and constantly bitched and screamed at me'.

Clearly this had an effect on him. He buried alive the family cat, then dug it up, cut off its head and stuck it on the end of a stick, keeping this grisly relic in his bedroom. Asked why he had done it, he said it had transferred its affections to his two sisters and he killed the cat 'to make it mine'. On a visit to New York, he tried to jump off the top of the Empire State Building, but was restrained by an aunt.

At school Kemper was an outcast. He would annoy the other kids by sitting and staring at them. Although he was a big child, he was branded a weakling and a coward, and excluded from their games. His little sister Allyn was upset when he started cutting up her dolls. Soon he began to fantasize about killing people – largely women – cutting them up and keeping their body parts as trophies.

Kemper's mother could not cope with his disturbed behaviour and sent him to live with his dad, who had remarried. When his stepmother found him no easier to handle, his father took him to live with his own parents on their isolated farm in California's Sierra Nevada mountains. There, his grandfather taught him to shoot, but was otherwise dull company. His grandmother was bossy.

'My grandmother thought she had more balls than any man and was constantly emasculating me and my grandfather to prove it,' said Kemper. 'I couldn't please her. It was like being in jail. I became a walking time bomb and I finally blew.'

## KEMPER'S FIRST KILLS: A FAMILY AFFAIR

One day, in August 1964, he was going out of the house with his rifle when his grandmother told him not to shoot any birds. He turned and shot her twice in the head. When his grandfather returned from a shopping trip to Fresno, he shot him too.

Kemper was just 15 and did not know what to do next. So, he phoned his mother who told him to call the local sheriff. Kemper told the sheriff that he had killed his grandmother because he wondered what

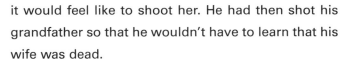

*Ed Kemper picked up hitchhikers before brutally slaying them.*

it would feel like to shoot her. He had then shot his grandfather so that he wouldn't have to learn that his wife was dead.

Diagnosed as a paranoid schizophrenic, Kemper was sent to the Atascadero State Hospital, a secure facility for the criminally insane. It specialized in sex offenders and Kemper attended group therapy sessions with rapists. They had been caught because their victims had testified against them. It was better, he soon learned, not to leave the victims alive.

At the age of 20 Kemper was released to a halfway house and complained that he did not get help from his parole officer to help him reintegrate into a society which had changed radically in the five years he had been away. He was still steeped in the Second World War values of his father and the conservative 1950s' ethos concerning discipline and conformity. Now, people his age were taking on the police in civil rights and anti-Vietnam war demonstrations.

'When I got out on the street it was like being on a strange planet,' he said. 'People my age were not talking the same language. I had been living with people older than I was for so long that I was an old fogey.'

He reserved particular contempt for hippies, especially the long-haired young women who hitched rides in cars with strangers.

After three months, Kemper was released into the custody of his mother who was then an administrative

assistant at the University of California at Santa Cruz and living in the nearby town of Aptos.

'She was Mrs Wonderful up on the campus, had everything under control,' he said. 'When she comes home, she lets everything down and she's just a pure bitch; busts her butt being super nice at work and comes home at night and is a shit.'

In short, they did not get on any better than they had before.

'She loved me in her way and, despite all the violent screaming and yelling arguments we had, I loved her too,' he said. 'But she had to manage your life… and interfere in your personal affairs.'

She wanted him to go to college and get a degree. He preferred to hang out at local bars, particularly one called the Jury Room that was frequented by off-duty cops. He applied to join the police, but was rejected because, at 206 cm (6 ft 9 in), he was too tall.

Instead, he got a job manning a stop-go sign for a state roadworks gang. He bought a motorcycle with his wages but soon crashed it, injuring his head. With the insurance payout, he bought a 1969 Ford Galaxie.

His job gave him the money to move out of his mother's place, along with a good knowledge of the back-country roads which he cruised in his spare time, picking up young female hitchhikers and trying to make himself pleasant and agreeable.

'At first I picked up girls just to talk to them, just to try to get acquainted with people my own age and try to strike up a friendship,' he said.

Soon he began fantasizing about raping the young women he picked up, but was afraid he would get caught. Clearly, he would have to murder them afterwards. This would also satisfy the bloodlust he'd had from childhood.

## PLANNING FOR ACTION

Kemper put a great deal of effort into planning his crimes. He had learnt to spot potential victims at a distance so that he did not have to turn back or make any sudden manoeuvres that would draw attention to his car. He already knew that there were more hitchhikers on the roads at weekends and that young women were more likely to get into his car when it was raining. When he had finished with them, he would dump their bodies in some remote spot – he had come across many while working with the road gang.

Kemper decided that nothing must connect him to his victims. He resolved to keep none of their possessions, nor any of the weapons he had used in the commission of the crime. It was also necessary to be in control at all times, so he would never go out on the hunt for prey when he was upset or angry, particularly after a row with his mother. Ultimately, however, he broke all of these rules. Even so, the police had no clue to the identity of the Co-ed Killer until he gave himself up.

## KILLING FOR KICKS

Early in 1972, he began buying knives and borrowed a 9 mm Browning automatic from a friend. Then it was time to get out on the road.

His first two victims were 18-year-old Fresno State college co-eds, Mary Ann Pesce and Anita Luchessa, who he picked up on the afternoon of 7 May 1972 with the intention of killing them. When he pulled off into a wooded side road near Alameda, they asked him what he was doing. In reply, he pulled the gun from under his seat.

Intending to take them back to his apartment to rape them, he put Anita in the boot of the car. Meanwhile, Mary Ann was placed in the front passenger's seat with her hands handcuffed behind her back and a plastic bag over her head. When she struggled Kemper panicked and stabbed her, then slit her throat. Then he went around to the back of the car and opened the boot. As Anita got out, he stabbed her repeatedly until she fell back into the boot. He threw the knife in after her. Satisfied they were dead, Kemper's only regret was that he had not raped them first.

Back at his apartment, he photographed and then dismembered their naked bodies. He then had oral sex with Mary Ann's severed head. The remains of their bodies were dumped in the boondocks, though he kept their heads for some time. Later, he would return to Mary Ann's dumping ground.

*Victim Aiko Koo decided to hitchhike after tiring of waiting for a bus.*

'Sometimes, afterward, I visited there… to be near her… because I loved her and wanted her,' he said. A few months later, her head was found by hikers and she was identified from dental records. Neither Anita Luchessa's head nor her body was ever found and the trail of the killer soon went cold.

But he was not far away. From the contents of the girls' handbags, he had their addresses and liked to drive past their houses, imagining the grief their families were suffering inside.

Following a motorcycle accident, he broke his arm and had to have a metal plate inserted. During his convalescence, Kemper spent time trying to get his juvenile record deleted. Having a conviction for murder made it difficult to buy a gun.

On 14 September 1972, 15-year-old Aiko Koo was waiting for the bus in University Avenue in Berkeley when a Caucasian male stopped and picked her up. In the car, he pulled a gun. Out in the mountains, he taped Aiko's mouth and pinched her nostrils until she suffocated, then he raped her dead body and put it in the boot.

He stopped for a beer and could not resist opening the boot to gloat over the body.

'I suppose as I was standing there looking, I was doing one of those triumphant things, too, admiring my work and admiring her beauty, and I might say admiring my catch like a fisherman,' he said. 'I just wanted the exaltation over the party. In other words, winning over death. They were dead and I was alive. That was the victory in my case.'

After visiting his mother, he dismembered Aiko in his apartment, dumping her body in the Sierra Nevada mountains. Again, he kept her head for a few days, storing it in the boot even when he went for an assessment by court psychiatrists. For Kemper, cutting off his victims' heads was the best bit.

'I remember it was very exciting,' he said. 'There was actually a sexual thrill… It was kind of an exalted triumphant-type thing, like taking the head of a deer or an elk or something would be to a hunter. I was the hunter and they were the victims.'

## THE CO-ED KILLER'S FINAL VICTIMS

After his motorcycle accident Kemper was unable to work, so he returned to live with his mother and to the Jury Room where the cops were discussing the missing girls. On the evening of 7 January 1973, he drove up to the Santa Cruz campus, where he picked up 19-year-old Cindy Schall and pulled a gun on her. Forcing her into the boot, he shot her in the head.

His mother was out when Kemper got home, so he hid Cindy's body in a cupboard in his bedroom. In the morning, when his mother had gone to work, he sexually assaulted Cindy's corpse then dismembered it in the bathroom. Leaving the head in his closet, he put the other body parts in bin bags and threw them over a cliff in Monterey. The next day, one of the bags washed ashore and enough of Cindy's body was recovered for her to be identified – or so Kemper learnt in the Jury Room. In panic, he dug the bullet out of Cindy's head and buried her head in the garden.

On 8 January 1973, he had a row with his mother. Fuming, he returned to Santa Cruz campus where he picked up 24-year-old Rosalind Thorpe and 23-year-old Alice Liu. While driving, he pulled a gun and shot both of them. He drove home with their bodies in the boot. After his mother had gone to bed, he cut off

their heads, then raped Alice Liu's headless corpse. Their bodies were dumped in a canyon in northern California.

From the cops in the Jury Room, he learnt that a full-scale hunt was on. Knowing that he was bound to get caught, he decided to spare his mother the guilt and shame. In the early morning of 21 April 1973, Kemper crept into her bedroom and slit her throat. He cut off her head and raped her headless corpse. Then he cut out her larynx and shoved it down the garbage disposal unit.

'It seemed appropriate,' he said, 'as much as she'd bitched and screamed and yelled at me over so many years.'

He decided to tell her work colleagues that his mother had gone away. To make this more plausible, he made out that she had gone with her friend Sally Hallett, who he had already murdered as part of his cover story. Then he got into his car and made a run for it. But when he reached the town of Pueblo, Colorado, Kemper realized that flight was futile. Stopping at a phone booth, he called the police and confessed. They thought it was a crank call at first, until he got through to a cop he knew from the Jury Room.

In custody, Kemper made a full confession. The public defender's insanity plea was rejected by the jury, who found him guilty on eight counts of murder on 8 November 1973. Ed Kemper was sentenced to life imprisonment with no possibility of parole.

*Even in court, it was hard to read
what was on Kemper's mind.*

# DAVID BERKOWITZ

On 17 April 1977, a letter was found on a Bronx street in New York from a postal worker called David Berkowitz. It was addressed to a police captain and read in part:

'I am deeply hurt by your calling me a woman-hater. I am not. But I am a monster… I am a little brat… I am the Son of Sam.'

Nearby was a parked car in which Berkowitz's latest victims, a young courting couple, had been arbitrarily gunned down. Valentina Suriani had died immediately; Alexander Esau died later in hospital, with three bullets in his head.

No one, of course, knew then that the 'Son of Sam' was the pudgy 24-year-old Berkowitz. But for nine months he'd been terrorizing the late-night streets of Queens and the Bronx. He'd killed three people and wounded four, seemingly without any motive at all. New York City Mayor Abe Beame had held a press conference to announce: 'We have a savage killer on the loose.'

The first attack had come out of the blue on 29 July 1976 at about one o'clock in the morning, when two young women, one a medical technician, the other a student nurse, were sitting chatting in the front seats of an Oldsmobile parked on a Bronx street. A man had walked up to them, pulled a gun out of a paper bag and fired five shots, killing one of them and wounding the other in the thigh. Four months later, the same gun had been used, again after midnight, against two girls sitting outside a house in Queens. A man had walked up to them and asked directions; then he'd simply opened fire. Both young women had been badly wounded, and one of them, with a bullet lodged in her spine, paralysed.

In between these two shootings, there had been yet another one – it turned out later from forensic evidence – using the same .44. Another young couple had been sitting in front of a tavern – again at night and once more in Queens – when someone had fired shots through the back window. The man had been rushed to hospital, but had recovered; the woman had not been hit.

The panic really began, though, with the mysterious killer's fourth and fifth attacks. On 8 March 1977, a young Armenian student, Virginia Voskerichian, was shot in the face at close range only a few hundred yards from her home in Queens, and instantly killed. Forty days later, with the deaths of Valentina Suriani and Alexander Esau and the discovery of the letter, it became clear that the killings weren't going to stop. More than that, the killer now had a name – and it was a name to stir up nightmares. The 'Son of Sam' wrote:

'I love to hunt. Prowling the streets, looking for fair game – tasty meat.'

Restaurants, bars and discos in Queens and the Bronx were by now closing early for lack of business. People stayed home and kept off the streets at night, despite the deployment of 100 extra patrolmen and the setting-up of a special squad of detectives. For no one had any idea when 'the Son of Sam' might strike again, and the nearest description the police had been able to come up with was that he was a 'neurotic, schizophrenic and paranoid' male, who probably believed himself possessed by demons...

He could, from that description, be any man at all – that was what was so frightening. He could even be a policeman himself – which might explain why he'd proved so elusive. This idea began to take hold when he struck yet again in the early hours of a late-June morning, shooting through the windscreen of a car in Queens and wounding another young couple. All the police could do in response to the gathering panic was once more to beef up foot-patrols in anticipation of the anniversary of his first murder a year before.

Nothing happened, though, on the night of 29 July 1977; and when he did strike again, it wasn't in his usual hunting-ground at all – but in Brooklyn. In the early hours of 31 July, he fired through the windshield at a pair of young lovers sitting in their car near the sea-front at Coney Island. The woman died in hospital; the man recovered, but was blinded.

*Deputy Sheriff Craig Glassman holds up two letters by the 'Son of Sam' which helped lead to his identification in 1977.*

This time, though, the 'Son of Sam' had made a mistake. For a woman out walking her dog at about the same time not far away saw two policemen ticketing a car parked near a fire hydrant and then, a few minutes later, a young man jumping into the car and driving off. As it happened only one car, a Ford Galaxie, was ticketed that night for parking at a hydrant – and it was registered to a David Berkowitz in Yonkers.

When approached the next day by the police officer in charge of the search, Berkowitz instantly recognized him from the TV, and said,

'Inspector Dowd? You finally got me.'

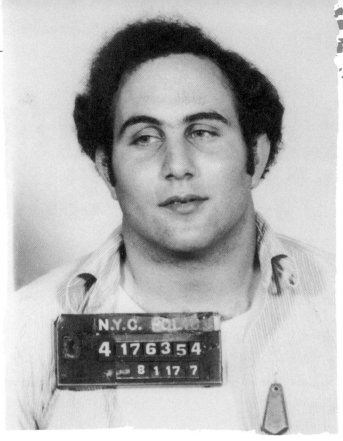

As a figure of nightmare, Berkowitz was something of a let-down: an overweight loner with a moronic smile who lived in squalor, was pathologically shy of women and probably still a virgin. He later said he heard demons urging him to kill, among them a 6,000-year-old man who had taken over the body of a dog he had shot. On the walls of his apartment he'd scrawled a series of demonic slogans:

'In this hole lives the wicked king'; 'Kill for my Master'; and 'I turn children into killers'.

Berkowitz was judged sane, and was sentenced to a total of 365 years in prison. His apartment became a place of pilgrimage for a ghoulish fan-club; and he himself has since made a great deal of money from articles, a book and the film rights to his life.

*Berkowitz seemed to choose his victims at random.*

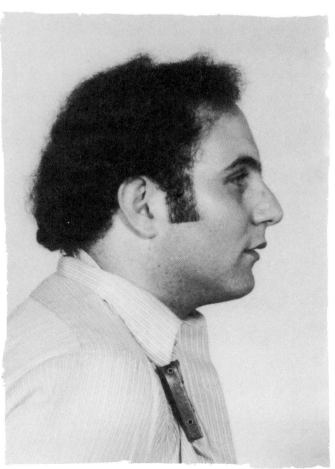

# LOREN HERZOG AND WESLEY SHERMANTINE

California's Central Valley is an agricultural area of the state that has little to do with Los Angeles and Southern California, or San Francisco and the Bay Area. In the 1970s, as well as producing fruit and vegetables, it became known for the production and distribution of crystal meth. With it came an attendant wave of crime.

Loren Herzog was born to a middle-class family in the town of Linden on 8 December 1965. He was a good-looking young man, who was rarely without a girlfriend. In the 1980s, he married and started a family, but there was another side to him. The words 'Made and Fueled by Hate and Restrained by Reality' were tattooed along his left leg and 'Made the Devil Do It' appeared on his right foot.

His friend Wesley Shermantine, born on 24 February 1966, came from a well-off family who spoiled him. The two friends went through elementary and high school together. While Herzog

*California's Central Valley is an agricultural area. In the late 1970s, as well as providing fruit and vegetables, it was known for producing crystal meth and the wave of crime that came with it.*

was docile and compliant, Shermantine was loud and aggressive. He would fight with other boys, or intimidate them, and answer back to teachers. Herzog claimed to have been bullied by Shermantine since nursery school and to have lived in fear of him ever since. Nevertheless, the bond between them endured, because if anyone else tried to bully mild-mannered Herzog, Shermantine would intervene in his defence.

The Shermantine clan had quite a reputation in the area. They relished conflict and those who accused them of intimidation or assault usually dropped the charges. Wesley's mother was a prime example. When one of her husband's customers was late paying a bill, she took a bulldozer and knocked down the debtor's house. The victim did not file a complaint and though the police knew who was responsible the matter ended there.

Mrs Shermantine was also a drinker and often heaped verbal abuse on her children, although she was not above hitting them too. But a particular punishment was devised for Wesley. He was made to stand still while his parents shot at his feet, even for trivial offences.

At 16, when Shermantine got his driving licence, his parents bought him a new car. The first thing he did was go around to pick up Herzog and they drove around San Joaquin County showing off the shiny vehicle. Both boys had a love of the outdoors and Wesley's father had taught them how to hunt. This was commonplace for boys brought up in rural California, though Shermantine would sometimes talk about the 'ultimate kill' – hunting humans. They also collected guns and knives.

As they grew up they began drinking heavily in the nearby Linden Inn, where they soon progressed to crystal meth. They then became drug dealers and earned a reputation as a couple of thugs. Shermantine's sister Dolly said Herzog had entered her bedroom one night when he was drunk and raped her. No one in the family would listen to her. Later she said Wesley had raped her too, but that also fell on deaf ears.

# CRYSTAL METH-FUELLED KILLINGS

By the time they left high school in 1984 both Shermantine and Herzog were addicted to crystal meth. They had graduated from snorting the powder to smoking it and those around them noticed the change in their behaviour. Their increasing consumption brought them into contact with high-level drug dealers and prostitutes, who were offered drugs free or at a knock-down price for their services. The women were then supposed to do whatever the men demanded once they got high. It is thought that this was when they started killing. If a woman refused them, she would be killed and disposed of by being dropped down an old well. This killing spree was said to have started in September 1984, though some suspected that Shermantine started killing on his own two years earlier.

That September, Herzog and Shermantine went up to the new casino at Lake Tahoe, but they lost all their money and ran out of meth. They knew no one they could score off up there, so after they had scraped together enough money for a drink they set off back to San Joaquin County. On the way, they came across 41-year-old Henry Howell, a drunk driver who had pulled over to sleep it off.

According to Herzog, Shermantine pulled over, took a rifle from the boot of the car, shot Howell dead and then robbed him – though it might have been Herzog himself who had pulled the trigger. The body was found soon enough, but there were few clues on which to build an investigation.

A couple of months later, on the night of 26 November, Herzog and Shermantine were taking a drive after drinking and getting high on meth when they saw a 1982 Pontiac parked on a rural road, with two men in it. They pulled up behind and the two of them got out with shotguns. Shermantine then blasted one of the men, killing him. Herzog said that after that Shermantine pulled the other man from the car and then killed him using his friend's gun. It was thought unlikely that Shermantine would have switched guns like that, so they must have killed one man each. The two then celebrated the killings with more beer and meth.

When the bodies were found the next day, the victims were identified as 31-year-old Paul Cavanaugh and 35-year-old Howard King. At the time, the investigation seemed to stutter to a halt, but the killers had left behind a crucial clue – a tyre print from Shermantine's truck, which would eventually be used in evidence against them.

The killers' next victim was 19-year-old Kimberly Billy, who went missing from Stockton, ten miles from Linden, on 11 December 1984. It is thought that Herzog approached her and then Shermantine raped and killed her, after which her body was dropped down one of the mine shafts that pockmarked the surrounding area.

Some months later, on 29 August 1985, 16-year-old JoAnn Hobson disappeared from San Joaquin. No one suspected that the Speed Freak Killers, as they became known, were involved until Shermantine, then on death row, wrote to her parents saying that Herzog and an accomplice named 'Jason' had killed her and thrown her body down a well.

He later wrote to a reporter, saying that they would find JoAnn's body with that of an unidentified pregnant black woman. Shermantine also said that Herzog hung out in Modesto, 25 miles from Linden, and it was thought that they may have killed others in that area. Of course, the letters could have just been a cruel hoax, designed to distress JoAnn's family.

# MURDER ANNIVERSARY CELEBRATION

The following month, Herzog and Shermantine wanted to celebrate the anniversary of their first murder together. High on booze and meth they drove into Stockton, where they met 24-year-old Robin Armtrout, who supported her drug habit with prostitution. In a field outside Linden they all did drugs. Herzog said that Shermantine started stabbing Armtrout while he was having sex with her. Others think that it was Herzog who killed her. They left her naked and mutilated body face down in a creek. Although they had left biological evidence, Herzog and Shermantine were never considered serious suspects and were not even interviewed.

Although 16-year-old Chevelle 'Chevy' Wheeler seemed to have grown out of her rebellious phase, on 7 October 1985 she told friends she was going to skip school and hang out with a boy at Valley Springs in Calaveras County. She was overheard talking to a 'Wes', so it was clear that her date was with Wesley Shermantine. They had started seeing each other several months earlier and Shermantine supplied her with drugs. Her parents did not approve, particularly when they saw that he carried a gun.

When Chevy did not return home that day, Shermantine turned up at the Wheelers' house and asked where she was. He appeared to be smirking. The Stockton police investigated and when they interviewed Shermantine he denied seeing Chevy on 7 October. Nevertheless, they got a search warrant for Shermantine's car and the family's hunting cabin in Calaveras County. There they discovered drops of blood that matched Chevy's blood type. It was the best they could do as DNA profiling had not been introduced back then. Later DNA testing confirmed that it was Chevy's blood and Herzog then admitted that he was with Shermantine when he stabbed her to death. Again her body was disposed of in a mine shaft.

## FAMILY MEN

By the mid-1980s Herzog was married with three children and was said to be a good father. Shermantine was also married, and had fathered two boys, but he was said to have physically abused his wife and children, although his wife only asked for a divorce when he was on death row. Meanwhile, the families socialized and occasionally the two men would go off on a hunting trip, fuelled with drink and crystal meth.

Although Shermantine had been the prime suspect in the disappearance of Chevy Wheeler, they began killing again in the summer of 1986. No one is sure how many people they murdered in the next 12 years. When they were finally arrested in 1999, Herzog told the police that the body count was 24 – though he said Shermantine was to blame.

On 3 June 1986, 31-year-old Sylvia Lourdes Standley was abducted in Modesto. She was raped and murdered and her body was consigned to a mine shaft or cave. The following year, 16-year-old Theresa Ann Bier disappeared after going to a store in Fresno. The same fate befell her. Two more murders took place in 1988. On 18 October, 18-year-old Gayle Marks disappeared from Stockton and then, on 19 November, nine-year-old Michaela Garecht was seized in Hayward. The description given by a witness to the abduction fitted Herzog.

Michaela was never seen again. Later from death row Shermantine said that Herzog was responsible, but then withdrew the accusation.

The Speed Freak Killers then appear to have taken a break. They may have been busy with family responsibilities. It was nearly five years before 47-year-old Phillip Martin went missing from Stockton on 30 September 1993. Fuelled by crystal meth, Herzog and Shermantine were thought to have subjected him to a lengthy torture session before killing him and disposing of his body.

Then on a hunting trip to Utah in 1994, when the game grew scarce, Herzog said that Shermantine lined up another hunter in his sights and shot him dead. Shermantine denied it, blaming Herzog. Circumstantial evidence indicates that they may have killed others outside California.

## HIGH-PROFILE MURDER

In 1997, in the small town of McCloud, California, 320 km (200 miles) north of Linden, two people went missing. First Karen Knechtel Mero disappeared from her front porch, though it was not reported for some months. At first it was thought that she had left of

*A bounty hunter holds a map to the locations of the bodies of the Speed Freak Killers' victims sent to him by Wesley Shermantine.*

her own accord, until it was realized that she had not taken vital medication. Then on 4 June 1997, 15-year-old Hannah Zaccaglini also disappeared.

When Herzog and Shermantine were arrested, it was discovered that they had been on a hunting trip in the area at the time. Two more men were arrested for the abduction and murder of Hannah Zaccaglini, but Herzog and Shermantine remained suspects in the Karen Mero case.

Although Shermantine and Herzog had somehow got away with killing Chevy Wheeler – someone known to them – the Speed Freak Killers were about to make the same mistake again. Twenty-five-year-old Cyndi Vanderheiden was the daughter of John Vanderheiden, owner of the Linden Inn. She had worked there as a cook and a barmaid and had also learned to drink there. In her twenties, she moved

on to marijuana and crystal meth and had a bad time with money and men, but by 1998 she had straightened out. She returned home, worked as a computer technician and saved money.

On Friday 13 November 1998, she dropped by the Linden Inn for a drink. Shermantine and Herzog were there, already a little high, and Herzog invited Cyndi to sit with them, which she accepted. She knew them from the bars in the area and, while others shunned them because of their wild talk, she considered their murderous boasts empty braggadocio. For a time, Herzog had even been the lover of Cyndi's sister Kim.

The Speed Freak Killers had been rejected by several women that evening and were determined to even up the score. Although Cyndi had been free of crystal meth for some time, the alcohol lowered her inhibitions and she agreed to meet them in a nearby cemetery for a smoke.

At first things were pleasant enough. Then Shermantine made his move on Cyndi. When she refused his overtures, he punched her repeatedly then forced her to give him oral sex at knifepoint. Afterwards he cut her throat. The two men loaded her body into the boot of Shermantine's car and dropped her body down a decommissioned mine in Calaveras County and then they returned home to their families like any other evening.

The following morning John Vanderheiden grew concerned when he saw his daughter's car parked outside the cemetery, which was an infamous drug haven. A quick ring around her friends established that no one had seen her since the Linden Inn the previous evening, when she had been sitting with Herzog and Shermantine, two notorious thugs.

After a couple of days, her parents filed a missing person's report, but given Cyndi's troubled background the police took little notice at first. However, when they learned that she had been seen with Shermantine – still the prime suspect in the disappearance of Chevy Wheeler 13 years earlier – they put him and his sidekick Herzog under 24-hour surveillance.

Meanwhile, the Vanderheidens plastered the area with missing persons' posters, offering a $20,000 reward, and organized a hunt that attracted over 500 people.

## ADVANCES IN DNA PROFILING

While the killers tried to maintain a low profile, the police reopened the Chevy Wheeler case that had been cold for over a decade. In the meantime, there had been considerable advances in forensic science. DNA profiling had first been used in Britain in 1986, but large samples were needed. However, during the early 1990s methods of amplification were developed

that allowed reliable profiles to be built from small or badly degraded samples. Even so, it was still an expensive process and the Department of Justice Crime Lab in Washington, DC, discouraged police departments from sending samples unless they had a firm suspect.

The police upped the surveillance on Herzog and Shermantine's homes and also increased the pressure on them. When the two men were called in for interviews, Shermantine refused but Herzog complied. He was clearly uncomfortable during the interview. Although he admitted seeing Cyndi on the night of her disappearance, he said he had only talked to her for a short time. Witnesses, however, said they had been together for an extended period, but he could not be cajoled into a confession and the police had to let him go.

Meanwhile, Shermantine had fallen behind on the repayments for his car and it had been repossessed. This gave the police the opportunity to make a forensic examination of the vehicle. They found spots of blood on the passenger headrest and in the boot, which provided them with enough evidence to bring Shermantine in. Under interrogation, he said that he had not talked to Cyndi on the night she had gone missing, but witnesses said that he had. This, along with the blood found in the car and the cabin, was enough for the police to arrest Shermantine for the murders of Chevy Wheeler and Cyndi Vanderheiden.

While there was little evidence against Herzog, the police picked him up and read him his rights. Waiving his right to see a lawyer, he told investigators what had happened to Cyndi, saying that he had begged Shermantine not to kill her but had not intervened because he was afraid of him. Herzog went on to clear up a number of missing persons' cases in the Central Valley from the 1980s and 1990s, along with the murder in Utah in 1994, blaming Shermantine in each case. He also admitted being with Shermantine when he killed Chevy Wheeler.

Despite Herzog's confession, Shermantine continued to deny everything – even when he was told DNA profiling matched blood found in his car with that of Cyndi Vanderheiden. When pressed, he turned on Herzog.

## EQUALLY GUILTY

The two men were tried separately. Shermantine's lawyers blamed Herzog, but on 14 February 2001 Shermantine was found guilty on four counts of first-degree murder, including those of Chevy Wheeler and Cyndi Vanderheiden. Shermantine now faced the death penalty, but the district attorney offered him life without parole if he revealed where the two women's bodies were. He agreed – provided he received the $20,000 reward the Vanderheidens had offered. He said he was going to use the money to compensate the victims' families under a restitution order made by the judge, with the remainder going to his two sons. The Vanderheiden and Wheeler families rejected the deal and Shermantine was sentenced to death.

The only substantial evidence against Herzog was his confessions. However, when forensic investigators reconstructed the murders of King and Cavanaugh, it showed that two shooters had been involved. Herzog's attorney's defence that his client was only guilty of 'having the world's worst friend' did not work. He was found guilty on three counts of first-degree murder and was sentenced to life imprisonment, though with the possibility of parole.

In jail, Herzog was stabbed and his life was constantly under threat. An appeal court found that the questioning that had elicited his confession had violated his Fifth Amendment rights against self-incrimination and a new trial was ordered. He was offered a plea bargain – a sentence of 14 years if he pleaded guilty to the voluntary manslaughter of Cyndi Vanderheiden. Taking into account the time he had already served, he was paroled in 2010, but the only accommodation that could be found for him was a trailer in the grounds of the High Desert State Prison, miles from the nearest town, where he was kept under tight security.

On 16 January 2012 he was found hanged from a homemade noose. A few days before a bounty hunter had contacted him, telling him that he was dealing with Shermantine in an effort to find the remains of Chevy Wheeler and Cyndi Vanderheiden. Shermantine then provided a hand-drawn map showing a location he called 'Herzog's Boneyard'. The authorities found human bones there, belonging to three women and a foetus.

Next Shermantine revealed that Chevy Wheeler had been buried in the backyard of his parents' house. Her remains were quickly found. Then he told the authorities the location of the mine shaft in Calaveras County where he had dumped Cyndi Vanderheiden.

# RANDY STEVEN KRAFT

While still at large, Randy Steven Kraft was initially known as the Southern California Strangler. Then as the death toll mounted, he became the Freeway Killer. However, there were two other contenders for the soubriquet. One was Patrick Kearney, also known as the Trash Bag Killer, who started his murderous career in 1962 and continued until he was arrested in July 1977, claiming as many as 43 lives. The other was William Bonin, who killed more than 21 young men and boys between May 1979 and his arrest in June 1980. Meanwhile, Kraft continued killing until 14 May 1983.

At around 1.10 am that day, two California Highway Patrol officers noticed a Toyota Celica weaving down Interstate 5 in Orange County. Suspecting the driver was drunk, they pulled the car over. The driver was Kraft, who got out, dumping the contents of a beer bottle as he did so. Officer Michael Sterling noticed that Kraft's jeans were unbuttoned. He admitted that he had been drinking, but denied being drunk. A roadside sobriety test showed that was not the case.

The other patrolman, Sergeant Michael Howard, approached the vehicle and found a man slumped in the passenger seat. There were beer bottles at his feet. His body was cold and he was clearly dead. He had been bound, strangled and his pants had been pulled down. There were tranquilizers and various prescription drugs in the car. The dead man was 25-year-old US Marine Terry Lee Gambrel, who was stationed at the El Toro air base and who had ingested enough of the prescription tranquilizer Ativan, mixed with alcohol, to kill him. Human blood was also found. It was not Gambrel's. Pictures of naked young men in various pornographic poses were also discovered and, in the boot of the car, was a ring binder containing coded notes that, it was soon discovered, referred to Kraft's murder victims. It was his scorecard.

Searching the home Kraft shared with his gay partner Jeffrey Seelig, the police found various items of clothing in the garage that did not appear to belong to the couple. One jacket belonged to a murder victim from Michigan who had been killed in December 1982. The couch in the apartment matched one in the Polaroids found in Kraft's car – three of the naked men posed there had been found dead. Fibres from the sofa matched those on a corpse found in Anaheim in April 1978, and Kraft's fingerprints matched those found at a murder scene in December 1975.

Initially Kraft was charged with the murder of Terry Gambrel. When Kraft pleaded not guilty, he was immediately charged with four more murders. Another charge of a torture-slaying followed a week later.

## SEND IN THE MARINES

From the age of 20, Kraft was openly gay, sharing an apartment with a male friend from college and visiting gay bars. In 1966, he was arrested for lewd conduct, after propositioning an undercover policeman in Huntington Beach, but he got off with a warning for a first offence.

The Vietnam war was under way and he briefly joined the US Air Force, though was quickly discharged ostensibly on medical grounds. Back on the gay scene, he told friends: 'There's a part of me that you will never know.' Fourteen years later they would discover what he meant. His sexual preference was for fit and healthy Marines. Otherwise, young boys would do.

In March 1970, Kraft picked up 13-year-old runaway Joseph Fancher on Huntingdon Beach. He took him home, plied him with booze, marijuana and pills, and showed him pictures of men having sex. When Fancher was semi-conscious, Kraft stripped and sodomized him.

After Kraft went to work the following day, Fancher escaped barefoot. Patrons of a nearby bar called an ambulance. After having his stomach pumped, Fancher led the police back to Kraft's apartment, where they found his shoes, illegal drugs and photographs of Kraft having sex with various men. However, the search had been done without a warrant, so the matter went no further.

After enrolling at Long Beach State University, Kraft moved in with classmate Jeff Graves. Nevertheless, he continued cruising gay bars for sex with strangers – preferably Marines.

His first murder victim was thought to be 30-year-old Wayne Dukette, whose naked body was found dumped alongside the Ortega Highway on 5 October 1971. He had gone missing on 20 September and the body was so badly decomposed it was not possible to accurately determine the cause of death, though a high level of alcohol was noted. Dukette worked at a gay bar on nearby Sunset Beach named 'The Stable'. The first entry on Kraft's scorecard read 'Stable'.

*When they looked in the boot of Kraft's car, they found a ring binder containing coded notes referring to his victims. It was his scorecard.*

On Christmas Eve 1972, 20-year-old Marine Edward Moore was seen leaving Camp Pendleton. Two days later his body was found beside the 405 Freeway at Seal Beach, apparently dumped from a moving vehicle. He had been bound, strangled and bludgeoned. There were bite marks on his genitals and one of his socks had been forced up his rectum.

Six weeks later, the naked body of an unidentified man was found beside the Terminal Island Freeway in the Wilmington district of Los Angeles. About 18 years old, the victim had been strangled a day or two before he was found. He had a brown sock stuffed into his anus. There was an entry on Kraft's scorecard saying simply 'Wilmington'.

Two months later, the body of 17-year-old Kevin Bailey was found beside a road in Huntington Beach. Though fully clothed, except for his shoes and socks, he had been sodomized and castrated.

The next victim, also unidentified, was dismembered and the body parts scattered along the coast from Sunset Beach to San Pedro. It showed signs of bondage. The hands were not found.

The body of another 20-year-old was found alongside 405 Freeway at Seal Beach on 30 July. He had disappeared bar-hopping two days before. He was fully clothed but barefoot. His body showed signs of torture. He had been hung upside down, beaten and strangled. There were bite marks on his stomach and penis and, again, one of his socks was found inside his anus.

Twenty-three-year-old art student Vincent Cruz Mestas was also found clothed and barefoot with a sock in his anus when his body was recovered from a ravine in the San Bernardino mountains 113 km (70 miles) inland on 29 December. His hands were missing and plastic sandwich bags covered the bloody stumps. An object the size of a pencil had been forced up his penis before he died.

On 1 June 1974, the naked body of 20-year-old Malcolm Eugene Little, an unemployed truck driver from Alabama, was found propped up against a mesquite tree alongside Highway 86. He had been castrated and a branch rammed 15 cm (6 in) up his rectum.

A branch 122 cm (4 ft) long and 75 mm (3 in) in diameter had been shoved up the anus of 19-year-old James Dale Reeves whose body, naked except for a bloody T-shirt, was found in Irvine on 29 November 1974. He had disappeared while out cruising on Thanksgiving Day.

The naked body of 18-year-old Marine Roger Dickerson was discovered in a dead-end street in Laguna Beach on 22 June. There were bite marks on his penis and left nipple. Last seen in a bar in San Clemente, he told friends that he got a ride to LA. He had been sodomized and strangled.

The body of 25-year-old Thomas Paxton Lee was found by oilfield workers in the harbour at Long Beach on 3 August, fully clothed. The waiter and sometime gay hustler had last been seen in Wilmington the previous night. He had been strangled. Twenty-three-year-old Gary Wayne Cordova was also found fully clothed except for his shoes and socks on 12 August. His body had been dumped down an embankment near Cabot Road and Oso Parkway in Laguna Hills. He had disappeared while hitchhiking. The cause of death was an overdose of Valium and alcohol. As Lee and Cordova's bodies did not show the killer's trademark mutilations, they were not attributed to him at first.

The body of 17-year-old John William Leras was found floating in the surf at Sunset Beach on 4 January 1975. A wooden stake had been rammed up his rectum. He had last been seen getting off the bus near Ripples Bar on his way to try out the new roller skates he had got for Christmas at the nearby rink. The police found two sets of footprints where his body seemed to have been carried from a car park to the water. He had been strangled.

Twenty-four-year-old Craig Victor Jonaites was found next to the Golden Sails Hotel-Bar on the Pacific Coast Highway near Loynes Drive in Long Beach, fully clothed except for shoes and socks. In fact, he was wearing two pairs of trousers, one over the other. The cause of death was strangulation.

## EVENING UP THE SCORE

Clearly a serial killer was at work. A task force was set up and an FBI profiler was called in. But the murders continued. On 29 March 1975, the head of 19-year-old Keith Crotwell was found near the Long Beach Marina. He was last seen getting into a black and white Mustang. The owner was Randy Kraft. He was questioned and told police he had dropped the youth alive and well at an all-night café. The police wanted to charge him with murder, but the LA

County prosecutors would not proceed due to lack of evidence.

After this, Kraft stopped killing for a while. Then, on 3 January 1976, the naked body of 22-year-old Mark Hall was found tied to a sapling at the east end of Santiago Canyon. He was last seen leaving a New Year's Eve party in San Juan Capistrano two days before. He had been sodomized. His legs had been slashed with a knife. His eyes, face, chest and genitals were burnt with a cigarette lighter. A cocktail swizzle stick had been jammed through his penis with such force that it ruptured the bladder. His genitals had then been cut off and stuffed into his rectum, along with dirt and leaves.

In the midst of this spree, Kraft left Jeff Graves and moved in with 19-year-old Jeff Seelig. He then began killing teenagers. The bodies of six of them were dumped in bin bags. But the arrest of Trash Bag Killer Patrick Kearney in 1977 muddied the waters. Kearney typically shot his victims and denied using torture on them.

With Kearney in jail, the murders continued. The body of 19-year-old Marine Scott Hughes was found beside the 91 Freeway in Orange County on 16 April 1978. His genitals had been mutilated. So were those of 23-year-old Roland Young, who was found dead in Irvine, less than eight hours after being released from jail.

The body of another Marine, 23-year-old Richard Keith, was found on the northbound lane of I-5 on 19 June. The body had been pushed from a moving car, so it was suspected that two killers were involved. The victim had been bound and tortured.

Twenty-one-year-old Michael Inderbeiten, a truck driver from Long Beach, was found on 18 November, just feet from where Edward Moore had been dumped six years earlier. His eyes had been burned with a cigarette lighter. He had been sodomized and castrated.

The bodies of more than a dozen victims were dumped along the highways of southern California in 1979. They had been bound, tortured, sodomized, castrated and strangled. More murders continued in 1980, 1981 and 1982. They all showed the trademarks of the same killer.

The police tried to match the victims to Kraft's coded scorecard. Forty-five corresponded, though they could find no match for known victims Eric Church and Terry Gambrel. There were 65 entries on the lists, making a death toll of 67, 22 of whom had not been recovered or identified. Kraft was found guilty of 16 murders, one count of sodomy and one of emasculation.

During the penalty hearings, the defence claimed that abnormalities in Kraft's brain meant he could not control his emotions and impulses, while the prosecution insisted: 'There is nothing wrong with Mr Kraft's mind other than that he likes killing for sexual satisfaction.'

Kraft was sentenced to death. As it was suspected that he had an accomplice, the police were preparing to question his lover Jeff Graves when he died of an AIDS-related illness in 1987. Dennis McDougal, author of *Angel of Darkness*, reported that small-time criminal Bob Jackson confessed to murdering two hitchhikers with Kraft, though the authorities could not substantiate the claims.

Kraft sued McDougal for $62 million, for unjustly portraying him as a 'sick, twisted man' and damaging his prospects for future employment. The California Supreme Court dismissed the lawsuit as frivolous in June 1994.

# DALE HAUSNER AND SAMUEL DIETEMAN

ale Hausner was born in Nebraska in 1973. To those who knew him, the idea of him as a serial killer was unthinkable. He was polite, timid and shy. He worked as a custodian at Sky Harbor International Airport in Phoenix, Arizona, and spent his spare time working as a boxing photographer. Mary Ann Owen, a Las Vegas photographer who had known him since 1999, said 'He doesn't even look like he would know which end of the barrel the bullet would come out of.'

In 1994, Hausner suffered an immense personal tragedy. His two sons, aged two and three, drowned in a creek during a car accident when his wife, Karen, fell asleep at the wheel. He became severely depressed. When his wife threatened to leave him, he drove her to the desert and pulled out a gun. She obtained a restraining order against him and left Hausner to live alone. He threatened to shoot her, but in the end thought better of it. Hausner turned to joy-riding with his brother Jeff. It was his brother who introduced him to Samuel Dieteman in early 2006.

Dieteman was born in 1976. He had two daughters. His wife left him in 2001 and, as his family claim, he developed a drug addiction. When his apartment

*Phoenix, Arizona, the hunting grounds of the 'Serial Shooters'.*

was repossessed he moved in with his mother and stepfather, but they eventually threw him out because of his alcoholism. Hausner offered him a place to stay. The two men, sharing the history of their broken lives, soon became friends. They set up a small-scale shoplifting and fencing business: Dieteman would steal alcohol, CDs and other small items, and Hausner would sell them to his coworkers. Eventually, Hausner stopped showing up to boxing fights. Clement Vierra, who met Hausner in 2004, said 'It was really pretty strange because he was really involved with boxing.' But the truth was that by mid-2005, Hausner had another hobby.

The two men began to see crime as a form of entertainment. Dieteman described his relationship with Hausner as 'just random, senseless destruction.' They started shooting dogs and horses for recreation and set trash cans on fire as well as engaging in other various acts of violence such as breaking car windows and puncturing tires with their BB guns. On one occasion, they pulled up to a woman on the street, armed with the BB gun. Hausner said to her

*The killers began their shootings with BB guns before progressing to real guns and live ammunition.*

'Are you working? Do you need a ride?' When she said no, he shot her in the chest with the BB gun. Soon they would progress to murdering people for their thrills. In January 2006, the Phoenix police linked the killing of several animals to the murders of three people in the area. It seemed that the serial killers did not discriminate between species.

# DRIVE-BY SHOOTINGS AND RECREATIONAL VIOLENCE

The first body turned up in May 2005. It was 56-year-old Reginald Remillard who had been shot in the neck while he slept at a bus stop. One year later, in July 2006, the 'Serial Shooters' would take their last victim – 22-year-old Robin Blasnek. Over this short period, the two killers were responsible for eight murders and at least 29 other shootings in the Phoenix area.

They described their killings as 'RV', short for 'random recreational violence.' Murder was a game for the two partners. During the nights they would drive around the streets of Phoenix in Hausner's Toyota Camry looking for victims walking or cycling alone. Their method was the drive-by shooting. Once they had found an innocent pedestrian they would open fire from behind with a .22 rifle or a .410-gauge shotgun. Hausner and Dieteman would take turns at the wheel and on the trigger. When they were arrested, a video of *America's Most Wanted* was found in their apartment. Hausner and Dieteman kept track of their killings with a map marked by red and blue dots.

At his trial, Dieteman said: 'My favourite thing is, you know, when somebody is walking away … it gives me, you know, a couple of extra seconds to aim. I don't have to worry about them looking.'

*Mug shots of Samuel Dieteman (left) and Dale Hausner (right) from the Arizona Department of Corrections.*

Even the killings were not enough to keep the pair entertained. On 8 June 2006, they set fire to two Walmart stores. Sometimes they decided just to beat their victims rather than shoot them. Hausner was not just in it for the entertainment. He believed that he was helping with social cleansing. Hausner had a deep hatred for illegal immigrants, homeless people and prostitutes, while Dieteman had no ideological purpose behind his participation.

They gloated over their killings and closely followed the news on their own killings and the progress of other serial killers in the country. A police wire-tap captured their conversation:

Dieteman: 'On the 5 am news, it was when they first said "Phoenix and Mesa Police have now officially linked the … death of a young Mesa woman to the serial killer, which now brings their total to six."'

Hausner: 'It's higher than that! What about the guy I fucking shot on 27th Avenue in the yard.'

They were keeping score. The 'Serial Shooters' wanted the police and the public to know just how many they had killed. They seemed proud of their

*Dale Hausner holds up six fingers, referencing the six counts of murder the jury convicted him of in Phoenix, 26 March 2009.*

notoriety. A wire-tap in their apartment before their arrest recorded the two men's conversation. Upon hearing that police were looking to link similar shootings in neighbouring states, Hausner said: 'So we're being copycatted, Sam? We're pioneers, Sam? We're leading to a better life for everybody, Sam?'

## INVESTIGATION AND IMPRISONMENT

Their joy in the murders would be their downfall. In July, Dieteman began bragging about the shootings to a drinking partner of his, Ron Horton. His friend duly reported him to the police. They began trailing the pair. They tapped their phone lines. 'We were on him 24/7, because if this turned out to be our suspect, we were not going to let another incident happen.' Soon they had accumulated enough evidence to pursue a trial. The two were arrested on 3 August

2006. Hausner's two-year-old, terminally ill daughter was in the apartment at the time.

As they went to trial, their partnership quickly broke up. Dieteman pleaded guilty to two murders and was sentenced to life imprisonment without parole. Dieteman's statements labelled Hausner as the ringleader. Consequently, Hausner was found guilty of six of the eight murders and a total of 80 criminal charges including aggravated assaults, cruelty to animals and arson. Hausner's comment on Dieteman was: 'I don't see Sam as a cold-blooded killer but if they've got evidence saying he is, there's not much I can do to refute that.'

Hausner was sentenced to death: one death sentence for each of his six murders. However, he was not prepared to wait out his time on death row. On 19 June 2013, he was found dead in his cell. He had committed suicide by overdosing on antidepressants that he had been secretly hoarding.

# ALEXANDER PICHUSHKIN

In June 2006, Moscow police found a chess board with dates written on 61 of its 64 squares. Alexander Pichushkin was only too willing to explain its significance. He was trying to break the record set by the prolific Russian serial killer and cannibal, Andrei Chikatilo, who had murdered a minimum of 52 women and children and eaten their body parts. Each covered square on the board represented a victim. He was caught with just three to go before completing his horrific game. In 2007, he was convicted of 48 murders although he claimed to have been responsible for over 60 murders. His crimes were so terrible they led to a serious consideration of reinstating the death penalty.

## A CHILDHOOD ACCIDENT

Alexander Pichushkin was born in 1974 in Mytishchi, a small city on the outskirts of Moscow. A year after his birth his father left. He said himself that he had a 'difficult life' because he had never known his father. He spent much of his childhood in Bitsevsky Park (or Bitsa Park), a sprawling and densely wooded area where locals would hang out, smoke and drink alcohol.

As a young child he was known to be friendly and sociable, but early on in his young life an accident would change this. When he was four years old he fell off a swing and was struck in the forehead by the seat. The injury damaged the frontal cortex in his brain – an area that is used to regulate impulses and limit aggression. Soon after the accident he became hostile and aggressive and he was transferred to a school for those with learning disabilities. He was soon beset by bullying from children from his old school who referred to him as 'that retard'.

Encouragement from his grandfather led him to the game of chess. Pichushkin was fascinated by chess and soon became an outstanding player. He began to participate in regular exhibition games, usually against older men in Bitsa Park, with great

*Moscow's Bitsa Park, where Pichushkin preyed on his victims.*

success. He was also an animal lover – his neighbour, Svetlana Mortyakova, once found him in tears over the death of his cat. Towards the end of his school days, Pichushkin's grandfather died which came as a great blow to him and he began to drink heavily to dull the pain. Psychologists would later suggest that Pichushkin's murders were prompted by anger at his grandfather for 'abandoning' him.

Around this time, he also developed a disturbing passion for filming young children and watching the footage, which allegedly gave him a feeling of superiority. Pichushkin began to take a camera with him if he knew he would come into contact with children. On one occasion, he held a child upside down by one leg and spoke into the camera: 'You are in my power now … I am going to drop you from the window … and you will fall 15 metres to your death.'

Pichushkin was obsessed by Andrei Chikatilo. He committed his first murder while he was still a teenager during the serial killer's trial in 1992. Pichushkin pushed a boy out of a window and remembered the experience fondly. When questioned by the police, he said, 'This first murder, it's like love, it's unforgettable.'

He treated murder as a game: the 64 squares on his chessboard functioned as his motivation to achieve a set target. His life, otherwise, was very dull. He worked as a supermarket shelf-stacker and lived in an apartment with his mother near Bitsa Park. The setting was important to Pichushkin because the size of the park, spanning some ten kilometres and covered in forests, provided the ideal location for a determined serial killer to practise his art.

For Pichushkin, murder was the only change to his dull routine. He targeted elderly homeless men – similar to those he had spent his teenage years playing chess against – and lured them to his house with the offer of free vodka. He often talked to his victims about his dog as a way to befriend them. Usually they were elderly men, but when the opportunity arose, he had no qualms about killing women and children. Not all of his victims were killed in this cold, calculating manner. He was motived to kill his neighbour, Valery Kulyazhov, because the man had told him 'to take away his enormous, mongrel mutt.' Pichushkin could not tolerate an insult to the one thing he loved most in the world – his dog.

Shortly after his arrest he stated that, 'In all cases I killed for only one reason. I killed in order to live … For me, life without murder is like life without food for you.'

He always attacked his victims from behind. He did not like to get blood on his clothes. Psychoanalyst Tatyana Drusinova said he was 'detached from human beings … Human beings were no more than wooden dolls, like chess pieces, to him.'

In 2001 people began vanishing from Bitsa Park. Maria Viricheva was a shop clerk from Tatarstan. In 2001, she entered a secluded part of the forest with Pichushkin, lured by the promise of black market goods. Pichushkin grabbed her by the hair and threw her down a well 9 m (30 ft) deep. Unbeknown to Pichushkin she survived the ordeal, but, unbelievably, police refused to investigate. Pichushkin was allowed to roam free and become more brazen in his attacks. Viricheva finally came forward to identify her attacker years later after his arrest for his other crimes.

In October 2005, one of Pichushkin's victims was found along one of the park's footpaths. The skull had been smashed and a vodka bottle driven into the brain. By June 2006, police had found 13 more bodies, all killed in the same way. They dubbed the killer the 'Bitsa Park Maniac'.

Pichushkin's last victim was Marina Moskalyova. Moskalyova had told her son of her plans to go on a date with a co-worker, and even left the man's phone number – this man's name was Alexander Pichushkin. This was the police's first major lead. Next, when they discovered the dead body of Moskalyova they also discovered her metro ticket in the pocket of her jacket. They were able to identify Pichushkin from the security cameras at the metro station walking alongside Moskalyova. Pichushkin was arrested on 15 June 2006 for Moskalyova's murder. He told police: 'I kept thinking whether to kill her or take caution. But finally I decided to take a risk. I was in that mood already.'

Soon Pichushkin was confessing to a bewildering array of crimes. Detectives checked his confessions against missing persons reports. They quizzed him on the locations of the murders and he recalled them with astounding accuracy. His victims included old men, young women and even a nine-year-old boy. Forty-three of the bodies he had disposed of by throwing them in the sewer pits of the park. He showed no hint of remorse.

His trial lasted six weeks. Like his old hero, Chikatilo, he was kept inside a glass cage for his own protection during the trial. Moscow prosecutor Yury Syomin stated, 'This is the first such case in Moscow. We are charging him with 52 murders. He insists that he killed 63, but there are no bodies, no murder weapons, no testimony, and not even records of people gone missing.'

*Alexander Pichushkin is led into the court room at Moscow's City Court, 29 October 2007, on the day of his sentencing.*

The jury only needed three hours to make their decision. Pichushkin was found guilty of 48 counts of murder and of three counts of attempted murder. He was sentenced to life imprisonment and during his first 15 years he was to be kept in solitary confinement.

Tamara Klimova, the wife of one of Pichushkin's alleged victims, told Russian media, 'He should be handed over to the public for punishment rather than allowed to live in prison at our expense.'

Pichushkin had one last thing to say. If he had reached his goal of 64 murders, it would not have been enough.

'I never would have stopped, never. They saved a lot of lives by catching me.'

# HIGHWAY HUNTERS

America's highways have proved prime hunting grounds for serial killers. The victims are usually women with no one available to come looking for them when they disappear. The anonymity of the open road can allow killers to escape detection for years while providing a ready supply of victims. As the number of cars and roads increases, serial killers will continue their rampages along the country's endless highways.

# THE ZODIAC KILLER

On a frosty December night in 1968 in Vallejo, California, Stella Borges was driving her mother-in-law and daughter along Lake Herman Road. When her car approached the Benicia water pumping station, the headlights picked out a station wagon parked in a nearby exit. As Borges got closer she realized, with mounting horror, that two bodies lay sprawled beside the car. She accelerated to 110 kp/h (68 mph) and raced towards the nearby city of Benicia to get help. Flashing her headlights and honking her horn she flagged down a police car. Just minutes later the police were on the scene.

Seventeen-year-old David Faraday was still breathing, but unresponsive; he had a bullet wound in the head. His date for that night, 16-year-old Betty Lou Jensen, evidently ran for her life away from the gunman. She made it 9 metres (30 ft). Shot five times in the back, she was already dead.

'I never saw so much blood on the side of the road in my life,' an ambulance attendant told reporters at the time.

Thus begins the most mysterious unsolved serial killer case in modern history. Although the world didn't know it yet, the two teenagers lying on the roadside in fresh pools of blood would later be identified as the first victims of the infamous 'Zodiac Killer'.

## THE ZODIAC'S GENESIS

One of the most extraordinary decades in US history was drawing to a close. The 1960s was a period of unparalleled social change and domestic division in the United States. The year that ended with the Zodiac's first murders saw the Army occupy three American cities and the National Guard patrol a dozen more in the wake of riots sparked by the assassination of Martin Luther King. Democrat candidate for the White House Robert Kennedy was gunned down two months later. Incumbent President Lyndon Johnson had already announced he would not stand for re-election, all too aware of how divisive his policy to widen the war in Vietnam had become. The liberal 'New Deal Coalition' that had brought the country through the challenges of the Great Depression, the Second World War and the Cuban Missile Crisis was unravelling.

Republican Richard Nixon was elected to the White House in November 1968. He promised to restore order and security to a country that had begun to feel as though it had lost its way. Nowhere was the division in US society more starkly seen than in the West Coast San Francisco Bay area. It was here that hippies proclaimed 1967 to be the 'Summer of Love'. Conservative America's bemusement with the 'flower children' had rapidly turned to mistrust and fear. Republican Governor of California Ronald

Reagan had already begun to crack down on the drug-taking, lovemaking and peacenik protests. In Death Valley, cult leader Charles Manson preached to his 'Family' about a coming civil war and the end of the world.

The very day after David Faraday and Betty Lou Jensen were murdered, *Apollo* 8 blasted off from the Kennedy Space Center on a mission to orbit the Moon. They took the famous 'Earthrise' photo of planet Earth viewed from space, and broadcast the creation story from the Book of Genesis to an enthralled nation. The astronauts signed off with the words 'good night, good luck, a Merry Christmas and God bless all of you – all of you on the good Earth'. Commander Frank Borman later received a telegram from a stranger that summed up the mood in the United States. It read 'Thank you *Apollo* 8. You saved 1968'.

On 21 July 1969, Neil Armstrong would take his famous 'one small step' on to the surface of the Moon. By then, back on Earth, the Zodiac killer had murdered again.

## INDEPENDENCE

The man who called Vallejo Police Headquarters in the early hours of 5 July 1969 spoke methodically and without emotion, as if reading from a script. He wanted to inform the authorities of a double murder, roughly 1.5 km (¾ miles) east on Columbus Parkway, in a public park. When asked for his identity and location, he declared that he was the killer not only of the two victims shot half an hour earlier, but also of Betty Lou and David in 1968. This was the first indication that the Vallejo police were dealing not with two unrelated crimes, but with a serial killer.

By the time of the call, police were already on the scene at Blue Rocks Spring, alerted by three teenagers who had come across the couple. Nineteen-year-old Mike Mageau was found slumped against the right rear tyre of a brown Corvair, bleeding heavily from gunshot wounds to the neck, leg and arm. Darlene Ferrin, 22, was in the driver's seat, suffering from multiple gunshot wounds, and barely alive. She was pronounced Dead On Arrival at the nearby Kaiser Foundation Hospital. The anonymous caller was wrong about the 'double murder', however: Mageau, despite his horrific injuries, survived.

The story Mageau told the police was the first glimpse into the character of the Zodiac killer. Mageau stated that a white male had approached the car shining a bright flashlight and, without saying a word, began firing 'again and again'. When he finally finished his murderous volley, he turned and walked back towards his own car. Mageau cried out in pain, and the assailant returned to fire two more shots into him, and two more into Darlene. He then walked back to his car and sped off at high speed. Mageau failed to get a good look at either the suspect or his car, but believed the man was 'beefy' with a large face and driving a light brown vehicle.

Whoever attacked Darlene and Mike took a huge risk: it was the night of 4 July, Independence Day in the United States, and thus a national holiday. Many people were out and about that night, heading to and from firework displays and parties. Any offender brazen enough to attack in such circumstances, and to even brag about it shortly afterwards, was likely to strike again. And so it proved.

> This is the Zodiac speaking. I am the murderer of the taxi driver over by Washington St + Maple St last night, to prove this here is a blood stained piece of his shirt. I am the same man who did in the people in the north bay a-rea. The S.F. Police could have caught me last night if they had

## 'THE MOST DANGEROUS ANAMAL'

*A chilling letter from the Zodiac Killer.*

In August 1969, three separate newspapers received almost identical letters claiming to be from the man who had attacked the four youngsters at Lake Herman Road and Blue Rocks Spring. The letters included information about the crime scenes that only the killer or the police could possibly know. The *Vallejo Times Herald*, *San Francisco Chronicle* and *San Francisco Examiner* also each received one-third of a 408-symbol cryptogram that the killer claimed would reveal his identity. The papers all published their part of the cryptogram, along with the killer's ominous threats to kill again.

Within a week the cryptogram was broken by a husband-and-wife team of local teachers, Bettye and Donald Harden. The message deciphered was as follows (complete with spelling and grammatical errors): 'I like killing people because it is so much fun it is more fun than killing wild game in the forrest because man is the most dangerous anamal of all to kill something gives me the most thrilling experence it is even better than getting your rocks off with a girl the best part of it is that when I die I will be reborn in paradice and thei have killed will become my slaves I will not give you my name because you will try to slow down or stop my collecting of slaves for my afterlife'.

A further 18 characters appeared to be gibberish, there only to pad out the code – if the killer meant anything by these letters then they have not, as yet, been deciphered. Although the included message had claimed that breaking the cipher would reveal the killer's identity, the actual text gave the police precious little to go on in terms of solving the case.

Indeed, the author suggested that he wanted to continue his 'collecting of slaves', which hinted that he intended to kill again. Tip-offs poured in to the police, and dozens of suspects were questioned, but the killer remained at large.

# BLOODSHED AT BERRYESSA

Summer had faded into autumn when students Cecelia Shepherd and Bryan Hartnell took a trip out to the idyllic shores of Lake Berryessa, around 80 km (50 miles) north of Vallejo. It was Cecelia who first noticed that a man seemed to be watching them on that September evening. Bryan, without his glasses on, only became aware of a problem when the man was practically upon them, holding a gun. He was wearing a bizarre costume: a square hood with clip-on sunglasses covered his head, and a bib came down over his chest. On it was sewn the same 'crosshair' symbol that the Zodiac signed his letters with.

The man told the two youngsters that he just escaped from prison and needed money and a car in order to get to Mexico. Hartnell offered his wallet and car keys, and tried to keep the assailant calm. But the man ordered Cecelia to tie Bryan up and, once she had done so, he tightened the binds and tied her up, too. As they lay helpless on the ground, he took out a knife that police would later estimate to be 25–30 cm (10–12 in) long. He used it to stab Bryan six times in the back, then Cecelia a total of ten times as she writhed and spun in desperate terror. He then calmly walked away, taking neither the car keys nor the wallet.

*Donald Harden hard at work decoding the Zodiac Killer's message.*

Bryan and Cecelia managed to free themselves and, eventually, summon help from a fisherman out on the lake. But by the time an ambulance had made it out to the remote spot each of the victims had been bleeding heavily for more than an hour. Cecelia died in hospital two days later. She was 22 years old. Bryan, incredibly, survived. The police who questioned him at his bedside already knew who was responsible for the attack: it was the latest atrocity by the Zodiac killer.

This time, the Zodiac not only rang the police to take credit (from a pay phone traced to downtown Napa); he also left a taunting message written with a marker pen on the door of Bryan Hartnell's white Kharmann Ghia car. It gave the dates of the previous attacks, along with the date and time of this one: 'Sept 27 – 69 – 6:30'. The Zodiac added 'by knife' to signal the change in his weapon of choice.

Though he couldn't describe the face of his attacker, Bryan could at least furnish the investigating officers with some fresh details about the elusive Zodiac. The man was wearing pleated, old style trousers, black or dark blue and a dark blue 'windbreaker' style jacket. He was heavy-set, and 1.7–1.8 m (5.5–5.9 ft) tall. He

spoke in a drawl that Bryan described as 'distinctive', but he couldn't place the accent. Bryan glimpsed greasy dark brown hair through the eyeholes of the man's mask.

The police also discovered footprints that were made by a distinctive 'Wing Walker' boot, size 10 ½. They lifted a palm-print from the telephone the man had used in Napa, but the technician smudged it during the lifting process, ruining its evidential value. The Zodiac had struck in daylight, in staggeringly theatrical fashion, and he had – just, only just – got away with it. His next attack would bring terror to the very heart of West Coast 1960s America: San Francisco.

## PRESIDIO HEIGHTS ATTACK

On Saturday 11 October 1969, San Francisco cab driver Paul Stine picked up a fare at the corner of Mason and Geary Streets in Union Square, San Francisco. His passenger asked to be taken to an area near the Presidio at the northern tip of the peninsula. It is not known whether the man who climbed into his cab sat in the rear or the front seat with Stine. What is known is that the man he picked up was the Zodiac killer.

It was just before 10 pm when Stine arrived at the destination that he'd entered in his log, the corner of Washington and Maple Street. For reasons unknown, he then proceeded one block further west, to the junction of Washington and Cherry Street. Nobody reported hearing the gunshot that then blew apart Stine's head. Three teenagers noticed the cab parked opposite their house, and watched a man in the front seat rifle through the dead driver's pockets, taking his wallet, ID and the keys to his cab. The body of Paul Stine was slumped in the murderer's lap, meaning that the killer must have been covered in blood as he calmly walked away north, towards the park.

The witnesses described a white man in his early forties, around 1.7 m (5 ft 6 in) tall, of heavy build, wearing dark brown trousers and a navy blue or black 'Parka' jacket. He had reddish-blond hair cut in a 'crew-cut' style and was wearing glasses. But instead of that description, the police officers who raced to the scene were told to be on the look out for a black male. When a patrol car passed a white man in glasses casually strolling towards the park minutes later, it didn't stop. Only when the description was corrected did it screech to a halt and speed back in pursuit. But by then it was too late: despite the use of police dogs and search lights, the suspect had melted into the night.

It was an agonizingly close near-miss. The Zodiac would give a detailed, mocking account of it in a series of letters to the *San Francisco Chronicle*, claiming that the police even stopped and talked to him at one point. In the first of his letters, sent two days after the murder, he enclosed a bloodied piece of Paul Stine's shirt to ensure that the journalists and police knew that he was a killer rather than a crank or hoaxer. The police thus had to take seriously his next ominous threat: 'School children make nice targets'.

## THE DEATH MACHINE

The Zodiac's 13 October letter to the *San Francisco Chronicle* was read aloud to the nation's news media by San Francisco Police Department Captain Martin Lee: 'I think I shall wipe out a school bus some morning, just shoot out the front tyre and then pick off the kiddies as they come bouncing out'.

WANTED

SAN FRANCISCO POLICE DEPARTMENT

NO. 90-69          WANTED FOR MURDER          OCTOBER 18, 1969

ORIGINAL DRAWING          AMENDED DRAWING

Supplementing our Bulletin 87-69 of October 13, 1969. Additional information has developed the above amended drawing of murder suspect known as "ZODIAC".

WMA, 35-45 Years, approximately 5'8", Heavy Build, Short Brown Hair, possibly with Red Tint, Wears Glasses. Armed with 9 MM Automatic.

Available for comparison: Slugs, Casings, Latents, Handwriting.

ANY INFORMATION:
Inspectors Armstrong & Toschi
Homicide Detail                    THOMAS J. CAHILL
CASE NO. 696314                    CHIEF OF POLICE

*The Zodiac Killer from 1969.*

Zodiac's message has never been decoded. There have been countless attempts and claims to have broken the code, but none has been widely accepted as successful.

On 20 December 1969, exactly one year after the murders of David Faraday and Betty Lou Jensen, the Zodiac posted a further letter to the prominent lawyer Melvin Belli, along with another swatch of Paul Stine's bloody shirt. He claimed to have now killed eight, and stated that the 'death machine' was taking longer to prepare than he had imagined. He wished Belli a 'happy Christmass [sic]' and asked him for help in controlling 'this thing in me'.

There were several further communications which purported to be from the Zodiac, though most are now considered to be fakes. A greetings card sent to the *Chronicle* urged people to wear 'Zodiac' buttons (badges), and a map of the Mount Diablo area was sent with another cipher that claimed to reveal where a bomb had been planted. This communication claimed that the Zodiac's body count had by now risen to 12. Again, the cipher has never been broken. On 27 October 1970, *Chronicle* reporter Paul Avery received a Halloween card that seemed to threaten his life and also appeared to claim that the Zodiac's running total of victims had reached 14. Despite the claims, however, no further murders were definitively linked to the killer.

The threat caused panic across California, and particularly in San Francisco. Buses changed routes daily, marked and unmarked police cars followed ahead or behind them, and fixed-wing aircraft patrolled overhead. The Police instructed school bus drivers to keep their buses moving 'at all costs' and advised passengers to lie on the floor in the event of an attack. The authorities were deluged with calls from members of the public across the United States offering tips and outlining suspicions and fears.

After a couple of weeks, the danger appeared to have subsided. But then the Zodiac wrote another letter, on 10 November. He began by claiming to have now killed seven people – two more than the police had thus far associated with him. Then, enclosing detailed diagrams to back up his claim, he outlined his plan to carry out a terrorist attack on schoolchildren by using a bomb he described as 'the death machine'. He also sent another cryptogram, containing 340 mysterious characters. To this day the

## THE ZODIAC'S LEGACY

Why did the slaughter suddenly stop? It is yet another mystery in this most mysterious of cases. Some have suggested that the Zodiac killer was arrested and jailed for some unrelated crime, and this ended his career. Others posit that he died, or moved away from the San Francisco area to assume another identity elsewhere. Perhaps, others argue, he simply grew bored and ended his reign of terror because it no longer amused or thrilled him. There's one more theory, perhaps the most troubling of all – that the later Zodiac letters are true, and that the body count provided in them is accurate. In one letter the author wrote 'when I commit my murders they shall look like routine robberies, killings of anger and a few fake accidents etc'. Could the Zodiac really have killed, as he went on to claim, a total of 37 people without the police even realizing the deaths were murders?

The first serial killer to attain legendary status was Jack the Ripper, and like Jack 'The Zodiac Killer' evaded capture. Perhaps this explains why these two killers remain so fascinating to researchers today. Between them, they helped to define what we think of as the 'classic serial killer': an evil genius who taunts the authorities and remains forever one step ahead of them. Countless films and books have been inspired by the Zodiac's trademark method of sending cryptic messages that only the brightest minds could crack. Although in truth such individuals are incredibly rare, they have given birth to an entire mythology, one that remains 'box office' to this day.

Few crimes remain vivid in the collective memory of the United States of America, the home of the serial killer. An estimated 85 per cent of all the world's serial killers operate in the States, for reasons that remain hotly debated by experts. Even those with far higher body counts than the Zodiac's five are soon forgotten, and yet he remains the killer that most intrigues, fascinates and horrifies all those who read about him.

Unlike in the case of Jack the Ripper, there remains the possibility that The Zodiac Killer is still alive, still out there somewhere; that he could still, even now, kill again – or be caught. In 2005, William Speer was convicted of murdering 14-year-old Linda Harmon after DNA taken at the scene of the crime was finally matched to him. Speer had remained free since committing the crime 37 years earlier, in 1968.

But in 2004, the San Francisco Police Department officially closed the Zodiac Killer case (although it has remained open with The California Justice Department). It was the first time in their history that they had closed an unsolved homicide case. 'The police shall never catch me, because I have been too clever for them,' the Zodiac wrote in a letter to the *San Francisco Chronicle*. While the case has since been re-opened by the San Francisco Police Department, tragically, it appears as though the killer's prediction has been right.

# PATRICK KEARNEY

Preying on young men in California from 1965 to 1977, Patrick Wayne Kearney was first known as the Freeway Killer. But as there were two other Freeway Killers – Randy Kraft and William Bonin – operating at around the same time, he came to be distinguished by the trademark method by which he dumped the dismembered bodies of his victims in trash bags.

Kearney had got away with murder for years until 17-year-old John LaMay went missing. On the evening of 13 March 1977, LaMay told his next-door neighbour that he going to see a guy called Dave he had met in a gym in downtown Los Angeles. He was gay and, since same-sex sexual intercourse had been decriminalized the previous year, many gay people had flocked to the Golden State.

When LaMay did not come home the following day, his mother called the El Segundo police. As usual in such cases, the police marked him down as another teenage runaway. But five days later his remains were found beside a highway near Corona. His body had been skilfully dismembered, drained of blood and washed. Then the parts had been packed into industrial trash bags and sealed with nylon filament tape. The head was missing, but a birthmark identified the remains as those of John LaMay.

'Dave' was identified as David Hill. Friends of LaMay supplied an address for him. He lived in an apartment owned by Patrick Kearney in Redondo Beach near Los Angeles.

The eldest of three sons, Kearney had been born in East Los Angeles. A thin and sickly child, he had been bullied at school. From the age of eight, he was fantasizing about killing people. When he was 13, his father taught him how to kill pigs by shooting them behind the left ear. He later used this technique to slaughter animals unsupervised and found pleasure in rolling around in the blood and guts.

He lived in Texas for a while, joining the US Air Force briefly there and having a short marriage. Then he moved back to California where, with a near genius IQ of 180, he went to work as an engineer at the Hughes Aircraft Company.

## KILLING AS AN ACT OF REVENGE

While in Texas in 1962, Kearney met David Douglas Hill, a younger man from Lubbock. They became lovers. Hill had served in the army, but was discharged after being diagnosed with a personality disorder. Returning to Lubbock, he married his high-school sweetheart. This marriage too was short-lived. After meeting Kearney, he divorced and moved to California in 1967. They lived together, eventually moving to Redondo Beach.

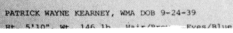

## RIVERSIDE COUNTY SHERIFF
# BULLETIN
OFFICIAL PUBLICATION OF SHERIFF'S DEPARTMENT, COUNTY OF RIVERSIDE, CALIFORNIA
BERNARD J. CLARK, SHERIFF

TUESDAY, JUNE 14, 1977

## ARREST FOR MURDER

PATRICK WAYNE KEARNEY, WMA DOB 9-24-39

DAVID DOUGLAS HILL, WMA DOB 12-23-42
Ht. 6'2", Wt. 175 lb., Hair/Brown, Eyes/Brown
453-58-4702

*A wanted poster of Patrick Wayne Kearney (left).*

Kearney went out to work while Hill kept house. But their relationship was tempestuous. Hill would frequently walk out and stay with friends, or have a one-night stand. Sometimes he would flee to Lubbock, but somehow they always got back together. While Hill was gone, Kearney would be seized with a murderous rage. He too would go out for sex.

Kearney would cruise gay bars or pick up hitchhikers in his Volkswagen. At just 165 cm (5 ft 5 in) and with a slight built, he liked bigger men, blond and arrogant, like those who had bullied him as a child. And he had a foolproof way of subduing them. Out on the open road, he would suddenly pull out a .22 pistol and shoot his victim in the head while keeping one hand on the steering wheel.

Alone with the body, he would undress it and sodomize the corpse. Sometimes he would take revenge for his childhood bullying by beating the dead and violated body. Then he would cut it up with a hacksaw, cleaning up thoroughly afterwards.

Inspired by reading up on Dean Corll, he put the body parts in trash bags and dumped them beside the freeway.

With other Freeway Killers on the loose, the police were confused, but eventually began to recognize Kearney's distinctive signature. While Bonin and Kraft tortured their victims before strangling or stabbing them, Kearney always shot his man then dumped the remains in trash bags. The cops began to call his the 'fag in a bag' murders.

With an address for 'Dave', the police visited Kearney's home and interviewed Kearney and Hill, who appeared unperturbed. The detectives helped themselves to a few carpet fibres. For once, Kearney had been careless. A few carpet strands had got stuck to the tape he had used to seal the bags in which he had put LaMay. The fibres matched. Building a case, the police returned to get samples of pubic hair from Kearney and Hill, as well as some hairs from their dog. Thus alerted, Kearney destroyed the cuttings he had kept from the coverage of Dean Corll.

When the police visited a third time, they found that the couple had gone. But they had left behind a hacksaw with traces of blood and tissue. There was blood residue invisible to the naked eye in the bathroom, too. A search of Kearney's office at Hughes Aircraft found the same trash bags and nylon filament tape as the killer used. Posters were printed with Kearney and Hill's pictures on them.

Kearney and Hill had fled to El Paso, Texas. But with their photographs circulating, it was clear that they could not escape. They returned to California and at 1.30 pm on 1 July 1977 they walked into Riverside County Sheriff's office. They indicated the wanted poster on the wall with their pictures on it.

'That's us,' they said.

They were arraigned on two murders and the bail was set at $500,000 each. Questioned about six other murders, Kearney co-operated fully with the police. They asked him about picking up Marines, plying them with booze and pills, castrating them and leaving things jammed into their anuses – the signature of Randy Kraft.

'I am not the Wooden Stake,' he said.

He did not torture, strangle or stab, he said. He killed cleanly with a bullet to the head.

# A LONG LITANY OF DEATH AND DISMEMBERMENT

The investigation into the Trash Bag Murders had been going on since 13 April 1975, when the body of 21-year-old Albert Rivera had been found in a heavy-duty trash bag near Highway 74, east of San Juan Capistrano. However, Kearney admitted committing his first murder in the spring of 1962. He did not know the victim's name, only that he was 19 and white. The boy had been persuaded to take a ride with him on his motorcycle. In a secluded spot near Indio, California, Kearney shot him and had sex with his dead body, then mutilated it. He did not know if it had ever been found. He also killed the boy's 16-year-old cousin who had seen them ride away together, along with another unknown victim, an 18-year-old named Mike.

The first murder on the charge sheet, though, was of a man known only as George. It happened at Christmas 1978, after Hill had moved into Kearney's apartment in Culver City. They had been visiting a friend of Hill's in Tijuana. Kearney had shot the man between the eyes while he was sleeping, then sodomized his dead body in the bathroom. While dismembering the corpse he also took the precaution of removing the bullet. The body was then buried behind his garage. When Kearney took the police there they dug up a body and found it had a single bullet hole in its skull – and no bullet.

Kearney did not kill again for over a year, fearing that the police would be investigating George's disappearance. But no one came knocking on his door. As he had seemingly got away with murder, he began his killing spree in earnest.

On 26 June 1971, he killed 13-year-old hitchhiker John Demichik. Then came 17-year-old James Barwick, another hitchhiker. Both bodies were found in 1973. The following year five-year-old Ronald Dean Smith Jr was killed. Albert Rivera, a homosexual prostitute, was next. After being shot in the head, he had been taken back to Kearney's house, sodomized, cut up and stuffed in trash bags. Later, in 1975, 20-year-old Larry Gene Walters, a hitchhiker, was shot at Kearney's house, sodomized, then dismembered and put into trash bags to be dumped in various locations.

*Patrick Kearney was known as the 'Trash Bag Killer' due to his tendency to dispose of the mutilated corpses of his victims in trash bags.*

Kenneth E. Buchanan was killed on 1 March 1976. Kearney shot him in the back of the head. But after he had sodomized him, he found that the 17-year-old loner was not dead. He came round, so Kearney shot him another three times. Three weeks later, Kearney picked up 13-year-old hitchhiker Oliver Peter Molitor and played 'doctor' with him to lure him into sex. He then killed the boy, cut him up and buried the pieces in several places at the Palos Verdes landfill.

Fifteen-year-old Larry Armedariz was killed on 19 April 1976. His body was never found. Neither was that of 13-year-old Michael Craig McGhee, who was killed on 11 June 1976. Kearney said he had picked up McGhee when he was hitchhiking from Inglewood Avenue near Lennox to Torrance. He befriended the boy and invited him on a camping trip to Lake Elsinore that weekend.

'I disposed of the body... You aren't going to find him,' Kearney told the police.

The body of 23-year-old John 'Woody' Woods was found a year after he was killed on 20 June 1976. The body of 17-year-old Larry Epsy was found that August. Later that month 20-year-old Wilfred Lawrence Faherty was killed. His body was found the same day. Also in August 1976, 20-year-old hitchhiker Randall 'Randy' Lawrence Moore was killed. Twenty-year-old hitchhiker Mark Andrew Orach was shot in the head on 6 October 1976.

In the autumn of 1976, 17-year-old Robert 'Billy' Benniefiel accepted a lift from Kearney when his bicycle broke down. He was shot in the back of the head. Kearney then took his body back to his house and sodomized him, dismembered him and dumped his body parts in several different locations. It was never found. Also that autumn, 27-year-old soldier David Allen was shot in the head and left at the side of the road.

In November 1976, 19-year-old hitchhiker Timothy B. Ingham was picked up on the eastbound carriageway of Highway 79 near Indio and killed. His remains were thrown down a ravine and his personal possessions were given to friends of Kearney's in Mexico.

On 23 January 1977, 28-year-old prostitute Nicholas 'Nicky' Hernandez-Jimenez was killed and dismembered. Then in February 1977 Arturo Romos Marquez was shot and dismembered. His body was only found after Kearney confessed. Finally, John LaMay was killed in March. Following Kearney's 25 confessions, 18 murder charges were filed.

During this mayhem, nobody noticed anything odd about Kearney. His supervisor at Hughes Aircraft referred to him as a 'model worker'. However, a local hardware store owner noticed that he kept buying butcher's knives.

# HOPING FOR A QUICK CONVICTION

So what happened to John LaMay? When he arrived at Kearney's apartment, Hill was not in. Kearney invited LaMay to stay until Hill returned. While he was watching TV, Kearney shot him in the back of the head. After he had sodomized and dismembered the body, he dumped the remains in the desert. Other missing bodies also seem to have been disposed of there.

'Things disappear very rapidly in the desert,' he said. 'You can put a small animal on an ant hill and it disappears right in front of your eyes.'

However, this made little sense if you dumped body parts in sealed trash bags.

In the end, Kearney was caught due to his own carelessness, but he had had a few close calls earlier. Once, he had a flat tyre and found the spare tyre was flat, too. He had to call a tow truck to get his car to the service station where a new tyre was fitted. The whole time a victim's remains sat on the back seat.

On another occasion, he had got out to inspect a dump site and locked his keys in the car. It took him hours to open the door using a wire coat hanger. Afterwards, however, he felt an even greater sense of relief and empowerment.

Kearney took full responsibility for the murders. He said that all the killings had taken place while Hill was away and he knew nothing about them. After hearing three hours of evidence, the Riverside County Grand Jury refused to indict David Hill. The district attorney admitted that the evidence against

Hill was weak and probably not sufficient to take him to court. But the publicity surrounding the case was such that he had to be smuggled out of jail and moved back to Lubbock, Texas.

Kearney's attorney advised him to plead not guilty by reason of insanity. Instead, he pleaded guilty to the first three charges and asked to be sentenced immediately as California was about to reintroduce the death penalty. He was sentenced to life, but with the possibility of parole in just seven years.

'This defendant has certainly perpetrated a series of ghastly and grisly crimes,' said Judge Breckenridge. 'I can only hope the community release board will never release Mr Kearney. He appears to be an insult to humanity.'

There were more hearings. While he seems to have committed around 32 murders, he was charged with only 21 of them. Convicted in every case, he was given a life sentence for each of them. Seven of his victims remained unidentified.

*Patrick Kearney, with David Hill behind him (centre) –*
*Kearney took full responsibility for the murders.*

# RANDALL WOODFIELD

No one expected things to turn out badly for Randy Woodfield. At high school in Newport, Oregon, he got good grades and was the star of the football team there and at Portland State University (PSU), even trying out for the Green Bay Packers. Yet he ended up in jail for life for murder, with another 90 years for a string of other crimes. And that's not to mention the other murders and felonies he no doubt committed but was never prosecuted for – the authorities reasoned that they had their man, and didn't need to waste further time and public money in court.

Born in 1950 in Salem, Oregon, to a middle-class family, Woodfield seems to have been overshadowed by his two older sisters – one who became a doctor, the other an attorney. Nevertheless, everything seemed set fair for young Randy until he was 11, when he began exposing himself to women. He also had anger issues, but the therapists his parents employed found they couldn't help him. At college he joined the Campus Crusade for Christ and the Fellowship of Christian Athletes. But the flashing continued and he graduated to petty theft and burglary. It was hoped that he would grow out of it. He didn't.

*Randall Woodfield was drafted by the NFL to play for the Green Bay Packers, but they had to let him go after a series of arrests for indecent exposure.*

Meanwhile, his misdemeanours were covered up to keep him in the football team. Things got more difficult when he was arrested for breaking into a girlfriend's apartment and trashing her bedroom in 1970. Three years later, he got a suspended sentence for indecent exposure. The Packers sent him home after a series of similar offences.

# HE HAD IT ALL, BUT IT WASN'T ENOUGH

In 1975, a man carrying a knife forced women to perform oral sex on him before stealing their handbags. Policewomen were sent out as bait and on 3 March Randy Woodfield was arrested after stealing marked money from one of the officers. He served four years of a ten-year sentence.

Though he had trouble holding down a job – and holding on to a girlfriend – Woodfield was still brimming with self-confidence. He was seen cruising around Portland in a gold 1974 'Champagne Edition' Volkswagen Beetle and took unmistakable pride in his physique. He was especially fond of sending naked photos of himself to women. In late 1979, Woodfield was photographed with his muscles abundantly oiled for inclusion in *Playgirl* magazine.

The year following his release, his former classmate 29-year-old Cherie Ayers was raped and murdered, having been savagely beaten around the head and stabbed in the neck. They had met up at a class reunion and Woodfield was an immediate suspect. During interrogation, detectives found his answers 'evasive' and 'deceptive'. Although the semen found on the victim did not match his blood type, subsequent DNA analysis proved a link. By then Woodfield was incarcerated for life. He was also linked to the murders of Darcey Fix and Doug Altic, who had been shot dead in Altic's apartment. Woodfield had a connection to the murdered woman. One of his closest friends – a teammate from PSU's track team – had dated Fix. Again, Woodfield was questioned, but police had nothing concrete tying him to the murders.

On 9 December 1980, a young man wearing a false beard held up a petrol station in Vancouver. Four nights later, a man answering the same description held up an ice-cream parlour in Eugene, Oregon. The next night he robbed a drive-in restaurant in Albany. A week later, he robbed a chicken restaurant in Seattle, forcing a waitress to masturbate him in a toilet cubicle. Twenty minutes later, he robbed another ice-cream parlour. The culprit quickly became known as the I-5 Bandit as the crimes were taking place up and down Interstate 5, which runs parallel to the Pacific coast for 2,250 km (1,400 miles) from the Canadian to the Mexican borders, through Washington state, Oregon and California. All of the I-5 Bandit's crimes took place close to interstate exits.

He hit a Vancouver petrol station a second time on 8 January 1981. This time, after he had emptied the till, he forced the attendant to expose her breasts. Four days later, he wounded a woman grocery clerk with gunfire in Sutherlin, Oregon. Two days after that, still wearing a false beard, he broke into a home in Corvallis, Oregon, where he forced two sisters, aged eight and ten, to strip and fellate him.

Four days later, he raped two women, Shari Hull and Beth Wilmot, in an office building, then shot them in the back of the head as they lay face down. Beth somehow survived. On 26 and 29 January, he committed robberies in Eugene, Medford and Grant's Pass, during which he fondled a female customer and a clerk.

On 3 February 1981, 37-year-old Donna Eckard and her 14-year-old stepdaughter Jannell Jarvis were raped and murdered together in bed at their home in Mountain Gate, California. Jannell had also been sodomized. The same day, a female clerk was kidnapped, raped and sodomized after a holdup in nearby Redding. The next day, an identical crime was reported in Yreka. The bandit went on to rob a motel

*Randall Woodfield committed a series of murders along the I-5, which runs from California up to Washington.*

in Ashland the same night. A fabric store in Corvallis was hit five days later, where the bandit molested the clerk and her customer before departing. He also committed three more sexual assaults on 12 February during robberies in Vancouver, Olympia and Bellevue, Washington.

The I-5 Bandit struck again in Eugene on 18 and 21 February, with another sexual assault in Corvallis on 25 February. But by then the police were on his tail after former girlfriend Julie Reitz was found dead at her home in Beaverton, Oregon, on 15 February.

Woodfield had organized a Valentine's Day party at the Marriott Hotel in downtown Portland. No one showed up. At 2 am, Woodfield turned up on Reitz's doorstep a few miles away. They had a glass of wine

and were about to have a cup of coffee when he raped and shot her. Her mother found her body at the bottom of the stairs at 8.30 am. Woodfield had been working as a bouncer at the Faucet Tavern in Raleigh Hills where he let the 18-year-old in with a fake ID. 'Randy was fired from the bar,' said his colleague Chuck Heath later. 'His thing was young girls. He was always bringing underage girls into the place. Then he asked me to go with him to small claims court and lie. I realized he was kind of weird.'

## TRIED, CONDEMNED, INCARCERATED – AND UNREPENTANT

Detective Dave Kominek of the sheriff's office in Marion County, Oregon, was working on the murder of Shari Hull. He quickly put a case together against

Woodfield. Having already served a prison sentence for preying on women, Woodfield was acquainted with some of the victims and he matched the physical description provided by witnesses. Then Marion County detectives put together a payphone call log that showed Woodfield using phonecards to make calls within a few miles of various murders.

One survivor, 21-year-old Lisa Garcia, then picked his photograph out of a lineup. When his apartment was searched, tape of the same brand as that used to bind the victims was found. In his racquetball bag, there was a spent .32 bullet that matched those found in the victims.

On 9 March 1981, Randall Woodfield was charged with Hull's murder, Garcia's attempted murder and two counts of sodomy. Woodfield, employing a public defender, entered a plea of not guilty. A week later, indictments were rolling in from various jurisdictions in Washington and Oregon, including multiple counts of murder, rape, sodomy, attempted kidnapping, armed robbery and possession of a firearm by an ex-convict.

In the summer of 1981, Woodfield went on trial in the Hull and Garcia cases. Lisa Garcia testified against him. The prosecutor Chris Van Dyke (son of actor Dick Van Dyke) said he was ready with 'armloads of evidence, overwhelming evidence'. He also characterized the accused as 'an arrogant, cold, unemotional individual… probably the coldest, most detached defendant I've ever seen'.

The flimsy defence alleged mistaken identity, even suggesting that Garcia had identified Woodfield because she had been hypnotized by a detective. Woodfield eventually took the stand. He spoke softly, standing with his arms crossed. Crime writer Ann Rule, then a reporter, said: 'Randy Woodfield had

been touted in the media as a massively muscled professional athlete. The man in person seemed strangely diminished, not a superman after all…. He looked, if anything, humbled – a predatory creature brought down and caged in mid-rampage.'

In court, he admitted having owned a .32 pistol, but said that when he'd learnt that as a parolee it was a violation to own a firearm, he threw the gun in a river.

On 26 June 1981, the jury took just three-and-a-half hours to find him guilty on all counts. He was sentenced to life imprisonment plus 90 years. That December, he was given another 35 years when a jury in Benton County, Oregon, convicted him of sodomy and weapons charges tied to another attack in a restaurant toilet.

As it seemed unlikely that he would ever be released there was little point in pursuing further prosecutions. He admitted nothing. However, DNA evidence later linked him to the murders of Fix, Jarvis, Eckard, Altig, and Reitz.

An officer following the I-5 case listed other victims. Twenty-one-year-old Sylvia Durante had been strangled in Seattle and dumped beside the highway in December 1979. Three months later, 19-year-old Marsha Weatter and 18-year-old Kathy Allen had vanished while hitchhiking along I-5. Their corpses had been found in May, after the eruption of the Mount Saint Helens volcano nearby. At least four women had died around Huntington Beach, California, while Woodfield was sunning himself in the area. All were killed in his trademark style.

Interviewing him in connection with unsolved crimes in July 2005, cold-case supervisor Paul Weatheroy said: 'I remember that his hair was perfect, feathered and combed; he had a perfectly even tan, nails manicured. He was very charismatic, which makes sense because he would lure victims and get them to let their guard down.'

They found common ground when Woodfield learnt that Weatheroy's son was a high school football star in Portland who went on to play for the Air Force. 'He loved talking about sports,' said Weatheroy. 'His high school career, playing in college, his time with Green Bay....'

According to Ann Rule, Woodfield even kept in his wallet a carbon copy of the airline tickets the Packers sent him back in June 1974.

Jim Lawrence, another detective in Portland's cold case unit, was struck most by Woodfield's utter lack of accountability or remorse – even decades later and in the face of indisputable evidence.

'If you're talking about somebody moving toward some form of rehabilitation, they had to at some point acknowledge they are responsible for their own behaviours,' said Lawrence. 'That is not Randy Woodfield.'

Combing the files, he came to a report of Woodfield's father visiting him in jail.

'It was a really short meeting,' Lawrence said. 'When the dad walked out, he told the detectives, "He's not the son I know."'

And if he was paroled tomorrow? 'He would re-offend, there's no doubt about it,' said Lawrence. 'Even to this day, he is still a stone-cold killer.'

Jennifer Furio, who published *The Serial Killer Letters* in 1998, included a couple from Woodfield. In them he was still blaming a mysterious 'Larry Moore' for the murders.

'Read the police report first filed by Det. Kominek, lead "Dick" who hypnotized the victim-witness, who helped police draw the composite drawing of "I-5 Killer" suspect!! Go figure,' wrote Woodfield.

'Now ask yourself why they would fight my defense counsel, to keep [Larry Moore] out of my trial for murder. Because they KNOW they messed up, and arrest this mass-murderer 4-5 weeks after my arrest in the "I-5 Bandit" crime spree. Even the blood-type evidence doesn't match my type (B Neg.), so Judge throws state's blood evidence out of court! But my jury had a right to hear how the first blood test revealed (A/B) typing, and after my arrest, it changes to a plain (B) type. No "negative" enzyme can be detected. Maybe (Larry Moore's) blood type is (A/B)?

'The 1986 "Break-In" at D.A. offices, stinks of an "Inside" corruption case! Only my file is ransacked – so go figure Jenny. They only charged me because of a "Line-Up" identification by [Lisa Garcia]. But she never ONCE picked me out of color, close-up photos! Or did she describe me in any police report! Even the ambulance attendants testified for me, they state Ms. Garcia was slightly wounded, with scalp wound, but clear thinking to describe a shorter, sandy-haired fella matching the mass-murderer (Larry Moore).'

The closest Woodfield came to admitting what he had done was when he joined MySpace in 2006. In his profile, he wrote: 'I spend the remainder of my days in prison because I have committed a murder along with many other crimes. I once tried out for the Green Bay Packers. The only reason I didn't make it is because the skills I had to offer they didn't need at the time.'

# LARRY EYLER

arry Eyler was known as the Interstate Killer or the Highway Killer because he dumped his victims' bodies along the interstate highways from south-east Wisconsin to north Kentucky. They were young men who had been sexually abused before being strangled or stabbed repeatedly. Often, they had been bound and sometimes their bodies had been mutilated or dismembered. After Eyler's conviction for just one of his numerous murders, the judge said: 'If there ever was a person the death penalty is appropriate for, it is you. You are an evil person. You truly deserve to die for your acts.'

The crimes were spread out across a number of jurisdictions, so he had killed at least ten men before the police realized that a serial killer was at work. The perpetrator was clearly gay. Although homosexuality was largely decriminalized at the time, it was not widely accepted in the Midwest. This meant that the police were not trusted by the gay community, allowing the killer to go about his monstrous business with impunity.

## THERE'S A KILLER ON THE ROAD

Eyler's first known victim was 19-year-old Steven Crockett, whose mutilated corpse was found in a cornfield outside Kankakee, Illinois, 64 km (40 miles) south of Chicago on 23 October 1982. He had been stabbed 32 times – four times in the head – and had been dead for 12 hours when discovered.

Then on Christmas Day 1982, the body of barman John R. Johnson was found 56 km (35 miles) away near Lowell, Indiana. He had gone missing from Chicago's seedy Uptown district a week after Crockett had been killed, but the police in Illinois and Indiana had no reason to think that the two crimes were related. The FBI's Violent Criminal Apprehension Program (ViCAP), which records and correlates information on violent crime, was not begun until 1985.

The following day, a 26-year-old named Edgar Underkofler disappeared from Rantoul, Illinois. His body was not discovered until 4 March 1983, in a field close to Danville, Illinois. His shoes had been removed and he was wearing white socks which were not his.

On 28 December 1982, two more mutilated bodies were found in Indiana. Twenty-three-year-old Steven Agan had left his mother's home in Terre Haute on 19 December to go and see a movie. He did not return. His body was found 48 km (30 miles) away in a wooded area outside Newport in Vermillion County, close to Indiana State Road 63. His throat had been slashed and there were more frenzied cuts across the abdomen and chest as if the killer wanted to open him up. In more than ten years in forensic pathology, Dr John Pless at Bloomington House said he had never seen such mutilation.

It did not seem that Agan had been killed where the body was found. At an abandoned farm nearby, traces of his flesh were found on nails hammered into the wall. Police speculated that Agan had been hung upside down and cut open like a deer being dressed. Like Underkofler, who was found later, he was wearing white socks that were not his.

The same day, Dr Pless had to perform another autopsy, on 21-year-old John Roach from Indianapolis whose body had been dumped along Interstate Highway 70 in Putnam County some 48 km (30 miles) from his home. He had disappeared three days before Christmas and had been the victim of a frenzied knife attack. Pless noted similarities between the three Indiana cases and called the state police to suggest a central investigation, rather than leaving the matter separately to the local police. They ignored his advice.

Two days later, 22-year-old David Block, who had just graduated from Yale, disappeared while visiting his parents in Chicago. His Volkswagen was found locked on the Tri-State Tollway near Deerfield to the north of the city. When his skeletal remains were found near Zionsville, Indiana, some 240 km (150 miles) to the south, on 7 May 1984, decomposition and exposure to the elements made it impossible to determine the cause of death.

While the police still refused to link these cases, Indianapolis' gay newspaper *The Works* set up a hotline and published a profile of the killer.

'This man is not openly gay yet,' it said, 'but he knows that he is, and when the urge hits him he can only absolve this tendency by committing a murder.'

Even when the police did take an interest, the clientele of gay bars were suspicious and refused to co-operate.

On the night 21 March 1982, 26-year-old Jay Reynolds, the owner of a Baskin-Robbins ice-cream shop in Lexington, Kentucky, had left his wife and nine-week-old son to close up his store. The next day, his body was found at the bottom of an embankment alongside US Highway 25, south of the city. He had been stabbed to death.

On 8 April 1983, the body of 28-year-old Gustavo Herrera was found buried under debris on a building site. A father of two, he often hung out in gay bars. His right hand had been cut off and was found nearby. A week later, the body of 16-year-old Ervin Gibson was found with the corpse of a dog covered

*Larry Eyler was told by the judge: 'You are an evil person. You truly deserve to die for your acts.'*

*Photos of one of Larry Eyler's crime scenes in Indiana.*

with rubbish and branches in woods a couple of miles west of the Herrera dump site. His overalls had been pulled down and he had been stabbed numerous times. Both bodies had been found near exit ramps from I-94.

The body of 18-year-old Jimmy Roberts, a Chicagoan, was found floating in a creek to the south of the city on 9 May. His trousers had been pulled down and he had been stabbed more than 30 times. However, the police did not associate it with the other killings because none of the previous victims had been found in water, nor had any of them been black.

That same day the body of Daniel Scott McNieve was found in a field in Henderson County on State Road 39, a mile south of I-70. It was taken to Bloomington Hospital where Dr Pless recognized the handiwork of the killer of Steven Agan and John Roach. He drew this to the attention of the state police who, this time, took notice.

The Central Indiana Multi-Agency Investigative Team was set up under Lieutenant Jerry Campbell. A force of 50 officers compiled a list of unsolved murders of young men and boys. By 6 June, they had a suspect. A caller from Indianapolis had named 31-year-old Larry Eyler. Years before, on 3 August 1978, Eyler had picked up hitchhiker Mark Henry near Terre Haute. Pulling into a dark side street, he pulled a butcher's knife and forced Henry to strip. He handcuffed him, but Henry broke away. Eyler pursued him and stabbed him through the lung. Henry played dead and, after Eyler had gone, found refuge in a nearby house.

After the police and medics had turned up, Eyler gave himself up, handing over the keys to the handcuffs. He was arrested and, in his pickup, the police found a sword, three knives, a whip and a canister of tear gas. Eyler was bailed and charges were dropped after he gave $2,500 compensation to Henry and paid $43 in court costs.

Three years later, Eyler was arrested for drugging a 14-year-old boy and dumping him in a coma in the woods near Greencastle, Indiana. The boy survived and his parents dropped charges when he left the hospital after several days with no lasting damage.

## BUILDING A PROFILE

Born in Crawfordsville, Indiana, in 1952, Eyler had a difficult early life. His father was an alcoholic who used to beat his wife and children. Larry's parents split when he was two. His mother remarried three times, each time to an abusive alcoholic. Eyler spent some time in a children's home. As an adolescent he came out as gay, though he still tried dating girls. On the gay scene, it was noted that he had a sadistic streak and a violent temper.

He failed to graduate from high school and dropped out of college. Working as a decorator and a liquor store clerk in Greencastle, Indiana, on Saturdays, he lived supposedly platonically in a condominium in Terre Haute with a 40-year-old library science professor named Robert David Little, who he'd met in 1975. He also had a long-term masochistic relationship with John Dobrovolskis who lived with his wife Sally, two children and three foster children in Greenview, Illinois. Dobrovolskis' wife tolerated her husband's sexual aberrance and Eyler often lodged with them on weekdays, paying a third of the rent. He also drove to Chicago to visit the gay scene there.

With no other suspect, the Indiana police concentrated their surveillance on Eyler. While they followed him, the skeletal remains of another victim, found in Ford County, Illinois, on 2 July 1983, was added to the list.

On the night of 30 August 1983, 28-year-old Ralph Carlisle left his girlfriend in Chicago's Uptown and went out on the town. The following day, his body was found in Lake Forest, near where Gustavo Herrera and Ervin Gibson had been discovered that April. His trousers had been pulled down and he had been stabbed in the torso 17 times, practically disembowelling him. There were handcuff marks on his wrists and the killer had left footprints.

Carlisle had lived just two doors down from Herrera, while Crockett and Johnson lived not far away. The Illinois police realized that they had a serial killer on their hands. Reviewing their files, they came across the case of Craig Townsend who had been abducted from Uptown on 12 October 1982, and was found drugged, beaten and dumped semi-conscious near Lowell, Indiana. This led the Illinois police to join the Indiana task force. FBI psychologists then came up with a psychological profile of the killer that fitted Eyler.

The Chicago police were now on the lookout for Eyler and spotted him cruising Uptown on 30 September 1983. He picked up Daryl Hayward, offering him $100 for sex – specifically bondage. However, the tail lost him when he drove south on I-90 into Lake County, Indiana.

Near Lowell, Eyler stopped and persuaded Hayward to have sex with him in an abandoned yard. They were making their way back to Eyler's pickup when State Trooper Kenneth Buehrle stopped to issue a ticket for parking illegally beside the state highway. When Buehrle radioed in Eyler's details, he was told to arrest him.

Once in custody, Eyler was charged with soliciting for prostitution. It was also noticed that the soles of his boots resembled plaster casts taken from the Carlisle crime scene. A bloodstained knife was found in his pickup. Nevertheless, he was released.

The investigation continued, though. Handcuffs were found in Little's apartment. Phone records

*A Ford pickup truck of the type driven by the Interstate Killer.*

led the police to Dobrovolskis' home. Eyler was there. Questioned by the police, he explained their unconventional relationship and admitted that he liked to bind his partners before sex.

Then a dismembered corpse, drained of blood, was found near Highway 31 at Petrified Springs Park, in Kenosha County, Wisconsin. It proved to be that of 18-year-old Eric Hansen, a street hustler from St Francis, Wisconsin, last seen alive in Milwaukee on 27 September. An identified skeleton was found in Jasper County, Indiana, on 15 October. Notches on the bones showed the victim had been stabbed.

Four days later four more bodies were found on a deserted farm near Lake Village, Indiana. Detectives found a pentagram and an inverted cross inside the abandoned building. Two were identified as 22-year-old Michael Bauer and 19-year-old John Bartlett. The other two remain unidentified.

Surviving victims came forward. Ed Healey from West Virginia said that Eyler had handcuffed him for sex, then beat him and threatened him with a shotgun, while Jim Griffin from Chicago said that Eyler had beaten him and threatened him with a knife. Forensic evidence was also mounting, with blood found on Eyler's boots and knife matching Carlisle's blood type, though DNA fingerprinting was not available then. But at a preliminary hearing on 23 January 1984, Eyler's attorney David Schippers

managed to get the bulk of the evidence ruled as inadmissible and Eyler was released.

On 21 August 1984, the janitor of an apartment house on West Sherman Street, Chicago, found the building's dumpster full of bin bags containing body parts. A witness recalled seeing Eyler, who lived at 1618 West Sherman, putting rubbish bags into the dumpster that night. Fingerprints were found, along with blood and more bin bags in his apartment. The body belonged to 16-year-old Daniel Bridges. A male prostitute from the age of 12, he had been bound to a chair before being beaten and raped, then stabbed to death. Eyler had then dismembered Bridges' body in his bathroom.

When the case finally came to court on 1 July 1986, Eyler pleaded not guilty. He was convicted of murdering Bridges and sentenced to death by lethal injection. He also got 15 years in prison for aggravated kidnapping and five years for attempting to conceal his victim's death. Appeals dragged on for another three years.

Eyler admitted another 20 murders, receiving a further 60 years on each count. He also testified against Robert Little, who he said was his accomplice in the murder and mutilation of Steven Agan. Little was acquitted. Eyler died in jail on 6 March 1994 from complications related to AIDS.

# HERB BAUMEISTER

The I-70 has been the killing ground of so many serial killers that it has become known as 'America's Sewer Pipe'. One killer who dumped the bodies of nine gay men along the stretch between Indianapolis and Columbus, Ohio, in the 1980s became known simply as the 'I-70 Strangler'. No suspect was ever apprehended, despite the widespread publicity the murders have generated, including their being featured several times on the television show *America's Most Wanted*.

However, in October 1998, authorities announced that they strongly suspected that Indianapolis businessman and serial killer Herb Baumeister could have been the I-70 Strangler. The remains of 11 other victims were scattered around the wooded area behind his ranch in Westfield, Indiana. But by the time they were unearthed, he was dead.

## AN UNUSUAL LITTLE BOY

Born in 1947, Baumeister was the son of a doctor. As a child, he seemed normal enough, but by the time he reached adolescence it was plain that something was not quite right. He would fall into strange reveries and ponder what it was like to taste human urine. When he found a dead crow in the road, he took it to school and dropped it on his teacher's desk when she wasn't looking. His father took him for psychological tests. He was diagnosed

with schizophrenia, though there was no record of treatment for the condition.

He dropped out of college and his father got him a job as a copyboy on the *Indianapolis Star*. Though he tried to fit in, he was generally considered an oddball. In 1971, he married college graduate Juliana Saitor in the United Methodist Church in Indiana. They were both Young Republicans and both yearned to own their own business one day. Six months after they were married, Baumeister spent two months in a psychiatric hospital.

Baumeister got a well-paid job at the Bureau of Motor Vehicles and Juliana quit working as a high-school journalism instructor to become a stay-at-home mother. Over the next five years, they had three children. But Baumeister was a closet homosexual. Juliana said; over the 25 years of their marriage, they only had sex six times. She had never even seen her husband naked. Seemingly ashamed of his skinny body – in front of a woman, at least – he put his pyjamas on in the bathroom before coming to bed.

His behaviour at the Bureau of Motor Vehicles became increasingly odd. He sent Christmas cards showing himself and another man dressed in drag. Nevertheless, he was promoted to program director and his employment was only terminated when, bizarrely, he urinated on a letter addressed to the governor. The ever-loyal Juliana went back to work

to support the family, while he got a job in a thrift shop. Around that time, the body of 17-year-old Eric Roetiger was found dumped along Interstate 70.

Baumeister found himself in trouble with the police over an auto-theft and a hit-and-run while he was drunk. He beat the rap. Then his father died and he borrowed $4,000 from his mother to open a thrift shop of his own in conjunction with the Children's Bureau of Indianapolis. With Juliana's help, in the first year it earned $50,000. Soon they opened the second in their Sav-A-Lot thrift-store chain. Meanwhile, the body of 27-year-old Steven Elliot was found along I-70 in 1989 and that of 32-year-old Clay Boatman in 1990. Six more would follow.

## GOING UP IN THE WORLD

Now a successful business couple, the Baumeisters moved into the $1-million mock-Tudor Fox Hollow Farm in the fashionable Westfield suburb, some 32 km (20 miles) from Indianapolis. It had four bedrooms, an indoor swimming pool in the basement, a riding stable and 7.5 hectares (18-and-a-half acres) of grounds. The Strangler then ceased dumping his victims along the I-70.

Unbeknown to his wife, Baumeister secretly frequented gay bars in Indianapolis. In the summer, when Juliana and the kids were away at his mother's lakeside condominium, he would invite young men back for a 'cocktail and a swim' at Fox Hollow Farm. During sex, he would strangle them, then burn their bodies and scatter their bones in the grounds.

Ten men went missing over two years, leaving no clues as to their whereabouts. The police took little interest, so the mother of 28-year-old Alan Broussard went to see private detective Virgil Vandagriff. Her son had last been seen leaving a gay bar called Brothers on 6 June 1994. Vandagriff was not greatly concerned. There could be an innocent explanation for his disappearance. Nevertheless, he had posters printed asking for information from anyone who had seen Alan.

Then Vandagriff discovered that a detective named Mary Wilson at the missing person's bureau was working on the disappearance of other gay men of similar ages and physical appearance. He also came across an article in the gay lifestyle magazine *Indiana Word* about 31-year-old Jeff Jones who had disappeared in July 1993. Vandagriff was researching these cases when 34-year-old Roger Goodlet vanished after he had left his mother's house to visit a gay bar.

'The fates of these three men were too close to ignore,' said Vandagriff. He was convinced a serial killer was at work.

A friend of Goodlet's, who knew him from the gay scene, saw one of Vandagriff's posters and got in touch, saying that he had been picked up by a man who called himself Brian Smart. They had gone to Smart's sprawling estate for a drink and a swim.

After swimming naked in the basement pool, Smart said: 'I just learned this really neat trick. If you choke someone while you're having sex it feels really great. You really get a great rush.'

Indicating the carotid arteries in his neck, he said: 'You just want to pinch these two veins. And it's such a great buzz. You should see how someone looks when you're doing it to them. Their lips change colour – that's how you can tell it's working.'

Smart raved about erotic asphyxiation.

'Do it to me,' he begged. He lay back on a couch and masturbated while being throttled.

When it came time to swap roles, the informant feigned unconsciousness while being throttled. Finding the man he had just choked still alive, Smart grew agitated and admitted that, sometimes, there had been accidents. When he asked about Roger Goodlet, his host grew defensive. Nevertheless, he managed to persuade Smart to give him a lift back to Indianapolis. He told the police about the incident, but they treated him like he was crazy.

Vandagriff took his informant to meet Mary Wilson. She was also investigating the disappearance of 20-year-old Richard Hamilton, 21-year-old Johnny Bayer and 28-year-old Allan Livingstone who had gone missing the previous year, as well as other persons dating back to the early 1990s. All of them were gay.

There was little they could do with the information that Vandagriff's informant had brought them. There were many places in the Westfield area that matched the informant's description and Brian Smart proved to be a pseudonym. All they could do was hope that he would turn up again on the gay scene.

## SPIRALLING OUT OF CONTROL

Meanwhile, the fortunes of the Sav-A-Lot stores were in a steep decline. Baumeister was frequently drunk and fired employees on a whim. The Children's Bureau withdrew its support and Juliana was contemplating divorce. Then their son, 13-year-old Erich, found a human skeleton in the backyard. Baumeister insisted that it had belonged to his father's medical practice. He had come across it when he had been clearing out the garage and had thrown it away.

On 29 August 1995, Vandagriff's informant spotted the man he knew as Brian Smart again in a gay bar and took down his licence-plate number when he left. The car was registered to Herbert R. Baumeister of Fox Hollow Farm, Westfield, Indiana.

Mary Wilson and Lieutenant Thomas Green approached Baumeister in his shop. They told him that they were investigating the disappearance of several young men and asked for permission to search his home. When he refused, they petitioned his wife who was co-owner of the property. They told Juliana that her husband cruised gay bars and

that they suspected him of being a serial killer. She refused to believe them.

'The police came to me and said, "We are investigating your husband in relation to homosexual homicide,"' she recalled. 'I remember saying to them, "Can you tell me what homosexual homicide is?"'

Wilson then tried to get a search warrant. But Westfield is in Hamilton County, outside the jurisdiction of the Indianapolis police, the city being in Marion County. And the authorities in Hamilton County refused to co-operate.

The Sav-A-Lot stores were failing and the Baumeisters filed for divorce. Juliana began to fear

*Campers were treated to an unhappy surprise when they discovered the body of Herb Baumeister in Pinery Provincial Park, Ontario.*

for her husband's sanity and felt released from any duty of loyalty to him. In June 1996, when he was away, she got in touch with Mary Wilson and told her about the skeleton Erich had found.

Wilson visited Fox Hollow Farm with two detectives from the Hamilton County Sheriff's office. On a brief inspection of the Baumeisters' estate, they found numerous fragments of charred bones and teeth. Over the next three months, they found the remains of an estimated 11 men, only four of whom were positively identified.

All the victims used the same bars that Baumeister visited and disappeared at times when his wife and kids were away. Meanwhile, 49-year-old Baumeister himself disappeared. On 3 July 1996, campers found his body lying beside his car in Ontario's Pinery Provincial Park. He had a bullet hole in his forehead and a .357 Magnum in his hand. He left a suicide notice that mentioned his failing business and marriage, but nothing about the murders.

An FBI profiler said that Baumeister's cavalier manner of openly dumping his victims' corpses on his own land indicated that he had killed many times before. Baumeister had insinuated to a potential victim that he had killed 50 to 60 people, though he may have been bragging. He was known to have travelled on the I-70 from Indiana to Ohio around the time of the highway killings, which stopped in 1991, around the time that Baumeister bought Fox Hollow Farm.

In 1998, investigators concluded that Baumeister probably killed 60 men in all after linking him to nine other men whose bodies were found dumped along the I-70 in Indiana and Ohio between 1980 and 1990. Baumeister's wife provided credit card receipts, phone call records, and even gave the police the use of the car that her husband had used on those business trips.

Baumeister's photo matched the police sketch drawn from descriptions provided by witnesses who thought they had seen the I-70 Strangler. One eyewitness identified Baumeister's picture as the same man who had given his friend Michael Riley a lift home from a bar one evening in 1988. Riley was found dead the next morning.

'We'll never know for sure, of course, if he was indeed the same man,' said Virgil Vandagriff. 'Everything points to him – even the fact that the roadside killings ended at the same time he bought his house and now had a place with plenty of room to dump his bodies with a lot less hassle.'

However, Vandagriff complained that, as a private detective, he did not always have the freedom or the money to follow his suspicions to their conclusion.

'I would have taken the Baumeister case a lot further than I feel the police did,' he said. 'While there were many fine moments in the investigation... I think there were certain loose ends that should have been tied up.'

For example, while Baumeister was active in Fox Hollow Farm, his older brother in Texas was found dead in his pool.

# PORTRAIT OF A SERIAL KILLER

Vandagriff found time to write a report called *Who Is A Serial Killer?* which offers an insight into the Baumeister case. Describing the typical serial killer, he said: 'He is typically white, male, between the ages of 25 and 35. He is often married, has children and has full-time employment. The majority of the time he will kill white victims.... His intellect ranges from below average to above average. He does not know his victims nor have any particular hatred for them.

'Of the four main types of killers – the psychotic, the missionary motive type, the thrill killer and the lust killer, Baumeister fits the last category. The lust killer, the most common type, gets turned on by the killings. They usually torture their victims. The more heinous their action the more they become aroused.

'Serial killers experience certain traumas in life. These are many. Among them are those suffered by Baumeister: poor body image (witnessed by the fact he didn't want his wife to see his lanky body nude) and phobias (over-concerned about what his co-workers thought of him at the *Indianapolis Star* and at the BMV).

'Herb also had feelings of what is called disassociation, including separation of feelings (able to kill and then go on to live a normal life with his children) and daydreaming...

'Often, there is trauma re-enforcement; in Herb's case this translates as loss of employment and financial stress brought on by the decline of the Sav-A-Lot stores. Facilitators, such as alcohol and drugs, seem to have served as accessories to Herb's crimes.... In short, Herbert Richard Baumeister was the consummate serial killer.'

*Herb Baumeister dumped the bodies of his victims along the I-70 between Indiana and Ohio.*

# ANGELS OF DEATH

Medical professionals swear an oath to do no harm. We rely on them to take care of us when we are at our most vulnerable. But behind the friendly façade there sometimes lurks an unscrupulous killer. And unsuspecting victims often thank their murderers for their care, not realizing the terrible danger they are in. Behind the mask of the medical profession, these killers can go undetected for many years on the graveyard shift, racking up huge body counts along the way.

# DONALD HARVEY

Claiming some 87 victims, Donald Harvey is possibly America's most prolific serial killer. Working as a hospital orderly, he murdered patients in what he claimed were mercy killings. However, he also let his murderous ways spill out into his personal life.

On the surface there was little clue in his early life that Harvey would turn out a serial killer. His mother said that he had 'always been a good boy' and the principal of his elementary school said: 'He was always clean and well dressed with his hair trimmed. He was a happy child, very sociable and well-liked by the other children. He was a handsome boy with big brown eyes and dark curly hair… he always had a smile for me. There was never any indication of any abnormality.'

However, it appears that his parents had an abusive relationship. His father dropped him when he was just six months old, before the soft spot had closed. He suffered another head injury at the age of five when he fell off the running board of a truck. Although he did not lose consciousness, there was a cut 10–13 cm (4–5 in) long on the back of his head.

From the age of four he was sexually abused by his Uncle Wayne. A neighbour also sexually abused him, but Harvey did not mind this as the old man gave him money.

*Donald Harvey suffered a couple of serious head injuries when he was young. He was also sexually abused by his Uncle Wayne.*

At high school, his classmates saw him as a teachers' pet who would rather have his nose stuck in a book than play sports. He did well academically, initially. But learning came too easily. He grew bored and dropped out. He had his first consensual sexual encounter when he was 16. The following year he began an on-off sexual relationship with James Peluso that lasted for 15 years.

With little direction in life, Harvey left Booneville, Kentucky, and moved to Cincinnati, where he got a job in a factory. In 1970, he was laid off. His mother asked him to visit his ailing grandfather who was in Marymount Hospital in London, Kentucky. Spending time there, he got to know the staff.

One of them asked Harvey if he wanted a job as an orderly. Unemployed at the time, he jumped at the chance. Though he had no medical training, his duties included passing out medication, inserting catheters and changing bedpans. The job meant he spent time alone with patients. Around that period, he claimed he was raped by his roommate.

## AN ANGRY YOUNG MAN

While Harvey made out that he was a mercy killer, his first murder was motivated by anger. He later told Dan Horn of the *Cincinnati Post* that when he went to check on 88-year-old stroke victim Logan Evans in his private room, the patient rubbed faeces in his face. Harvey lost control.

'The next thing I knew, I'd smothered him,' he said. 'It was like it was the last straw. I just lost it. I went in to help the man and he wants to rub that in my face.'

Harvey put a sheet of blue plastic and a pillow over the old man's face and listened to his heartbeat with a stethoscope until he was dead. He disposed of the plastic and cleaned him up, dressing Evans in a fresh hospital gown. Then he had a shower before notifying the nurse on duty of Evans' death. Harvey had no fear of getting caught.

'No one ever questioned it,' he said.

The following day he said he accidentally killed 69-year-old James Tyree when he used the wrong-sized catheter on him. When Tyree yelled at him to take it out, Harvey silenced him with the heel of his hand. Tyree then vomited blood and died.

Three weeks later came the first of what could be considered mercy killings. Forty-two-year-old Elizabeth Wyatt told him she wanted to die, so he turned down her oxygen supply. Four hours later, a nurse found her dead.

The following month, he killed 43-year-old Eugene McQueen by turning him on his stomach when he knew he wasn't supposed to. McQueen drowned in his own fluids. Harvey told the nurse merely that McQueen looked bad and she told him to continue with his duties. Consequently, Harvey gave McQueen a bath even though he was already dead. For as long as he worked at Marymount, the staff teased Harvey for bathing a dead man.

He accidently killed 82-year-old Harvey Williams when a gas tank proved faulty. But the next death at his hands was premeditated murder. Eighty-one-year-old Ben Gilbert knocked him out with a bedpan and poured its contents over him, saying that he thought Harvey was a burglar. Harvey retaliated by catheterizing Gilbert with a female-sized 20-gauge catheter instead of the smaller 18-gauge used for men. He then straightened out a coat hanger and shoved the wire through the catheter, puncturing Gilbert's bladder and bowel. Gilbert went into shock and fell into a coma. Harvey disposed of the wire and

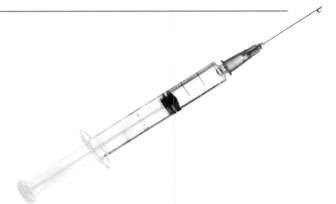

*Donald Harvey attempted to dispose of the syringe he used to kill Milton Sasser by flushing it down the lavatory.*

replaced the 20-gauge catheter with an 18-gauge. Ben Gilbert died four days later.

Harvey began a seven-month relationship with Vernon Midden, a married man who had children. He was an undertaker who taught Harvey the tricks of the trade and introduced him to the occult. When the relationship went sour the following January, Harvey fantasized about embalming him alive.

## KILLING AS AN ACT OF KINDNESS?

Maude Nichols had been so neglected that her bedsores crawled with maggots. When she arrived at Marymount, Harvey fixed her up with a faulty oxygen tank. He simply neglected to turn on the oxygen for 58-year-old William Bowling, who had difficulty breathing and subsequently died of a heart attack.

A faulty oxygen tank also did for 63-year-old Viola Reed Wyan after his attempt to smother her was interrupted. She had leukaemia and Harvey complained that she smelt bad. Ninety-one-year-old Margaret Harrison was despatched with an overdose of Demerol, morphine and codeine that was intended for another patient.

Harvey decided that 80-year-old Sam Carroll had suffered enough and he was given a faulty oxygen tank. Maggie Rawlins was smothered with a plastic bag. Both 62-year-old Silas Butner and 68-year-old John V. Combs were killed with faulty oxygen tanks after attempts to smother them had failed. Ninety-year-old Milton Bryant Sasser was killed with an overdose of morphine which Harvey had stolen from the nurse's station. Harvey tried to dispose of the syringe by flushing it down the lavatory, where it was found by a maintenance man. Harvey left Marymount Hospital soon after. He was still only 18.

Harvey then had his first heterosexual encounter. He got drunk with the daughter of the family he was staying with and they ended up naked. Nine months later she had a child, naming Harvey as the father, though he rejected any responsibility.

Depressed, Harvey tried to kill himself by setting fire to the bathroom of an empty apartment. He was arrested and fined $50. Then he was arrested on suspicion of burglary, though the police really wanted to question him about his involvement with the occult. During the interview, he admitted killing 15 people at Marymount Hospital, but they did not believe him.

He briefly enlisted in the US Air Force, but was discharged after trying to commit suicide. A further suicide attempt landed him in a Veterans' Administration Hospital after his parents would not take him in.

In 1972, he started work at the Cardinal Hill Convalescent Hospital in Lexington, Kentucky. It is not thought he killed anyone there. For ten months he lived with Russell Addison. This was followed by a five-year relationship with Ken Estes.

In September 1975, he became a nursing assistant at the VA Hospital in Lexington. He tampered with the oxygen supply for Joseph Harris, possibly resulting in his death. Harvey also claimed he had a hand in the deaths of James Twitty, James Ritter, Harry Rhodes and Sterling Moore.

To be initiated into the local occult group, Harvey had to hook up with a woman, so they could then swap partners with another couple. This resulted in the conception of another child, though Harvey denied any responsibility once again. He also acquired a spirit guide named Duncan, a doctor during his lifetime, who now directed him to kill from beyond the grave.

## POISONOUS RELATIONSHIP

In 1980, Harvey began dating Doug Hill. When they fell out, Harvey attempted to poison him by putting arsenic in his ice cream. In August, he moved in with Carl Hoeweler. When he found Carl was fooling around with other men, he put small doses of arsenic in his food to prevent him going out. Fearing that Carl's 'fag hag' friend Diane Alexander was trying to split them up, he gave her hepatitis-B serum stolen from the hospital. He also tried unsuccessfully to infect her with AIDS.

His 63-year-old neighbour Helen Metzger was also considered a threat and murdered with arsenic in her food, though Harvey contended he did not mean to give her a lethal dose. Her family got sick from leftovers served at the funeral. Carl's 82-year-old father Henry was also despatched by arsenic. Carl's

*Donald Harvey awaits his sentence from the judge after pleading guilty to 24 counts of murder.*

brother-in-law Howard Vetter was killed accidentally, Harvey claimed, when he left wood alcohol in a vodka bottle. Harvey also murdered another neighbour, Edward Wilson, who he thought was a threat to his relationship with Carl Hoeweler. Wilson was despatched with arsenic in his Pepto-Bismol bottle.

Harvey killed Hiram Profitt accidentally, giving him the wrong dose of heparin. Former boyfriend James Peluso, then 65, asked Harvey to help him out if ever he could not take care of himself. Harvey put arsenic in his daiquiri.

After he joined the neo-Nazi National Socialist Party, Harvey was fired from the VA Hospital in 1985 for carrying a gun in his gym bag. Body parts which he intended to use in occult practices were also found. The following year, he started a new job at Daniel Drake Memorial Hospital in Cincinnati.

After six weeks, he smothered 65-year-old Nathan J. Watson with a bin bag after several thwarted attempts. Watson was semi-comatose and was fed through a gastric tube and Harvey said he didn't think

anyone should live that way. He also believed Watson to have been a rapist.

Four days later, 64-year-old Leon Nelson was despatched the same way. A week after that 81-year-old Virgil Weddle was killed with rat poison. Cookies stolen from him were used in rites for Duncan. Rat poison was also used to kill Lawrence Berndsen the next day.

Harvey put cyanide in 65-year-old Doris Nally's apple juice. Sixty-three-year-old Edward Schreibesis got arsenic in his soup, though arsenic failed to kill Willie Johnson. Eighty-year-old Robert Crockett succumbed to cyanide in his IV. Sixty-one-year-old Donald Barney had cyanide injected in his buttocks, while 65-year-old James T. Wood was given cyanide in his gastric tube. Eighty-five-year-old Ernst C. Frey got arsenic the same way.

Eighty-five-year-old Milton Canter got cyanide in a nasal tube. Seventy-four-year-old Roger Evans ingested it in his gastric tube. Sixty-four-year-old Clayborn Kendrick got it the same way. More cyanide was injected into his testes.

Cyanide was given to 86-year-old Albert Buehlmann in a cup of water and to 85-year-old William Collins in orange juice. Seventy-eight-year-old Henry Cody had it fed through his gastric tube.

Following his break-up with Carl, Harvey was treated for depression and tried to kill himself by driving off a mountain road, injuring his head. Sixty-five-year-old Mose Thompson and 72-year-old Odas Day were despatched with solutions of cyanide, while 67-year-old Cleo Fish got it in her cranberry juice. Two other patients were given arsenic but survived, while 47-year-old Leo Parker succumbed to cyanide in his feed bag.

Eighty-year-old Margaret Kuckro got it in her orange juice, as did 76-year-old Stella Lemon. Sixty-eight-year-old Joseph M. Pike and 82-year-old Hilda Leitz were despatched with the adhesive remover Detachol. Forty-four-year-old John W. Powell was killed with cyanide in his gastric feeding tube. An autopsy was performed and the pathologist smelt bitter almonds – the characteristic aroma of cyanide. Three laboratories confirmed its presence and the Cincinnati Police Department was notified.

Harvey came under suspicion because of his sacking from the VA Hospital. He called in sick the day that staff were given polygraph tests. When questioned, he admitted killing Powell, saying he felt sorry for him and denied killing anyone else.

Pat Minarcin, then an anchor at WCPO-TV in Cincinnati, figured that if he had killed once he might have done it on other occasions. Digging into Harvey's past, he managed to link him to 24 murders, filling a half-hour special report.

Court-appointed defence attorney Bill Whalen cut a plea bargain. If the death penalty was taken off the table, he said, Harvey would confess to all the murders. In August 1987 in Ohio, Donald Harvey pleaded guilty to 24 counts of murder and was sentenced to three concurrent terms of life. That November in Kentucky he pleaded guilty to another nine murders, giving him another life sentence plus 20 years. In the end, the self-styled Angel of Death pleaded guilty to 37 murders, though he admitted many more.

Incarcerated in Toledo Correctional Institution, he was found badly battered in his cell on 28 March 2017 and died two days later. Fellow inmate James Elliott was charged with his murder.

# GENENE JONES

There are 'Angels of Death' – nurses who work with old people and kill them as they approach the end of their lives. Then there are 'Death Nurses' who kill babies and young children who have hardly started theirs. Genene Jones fell into the second category, killing maybe as many as 50 infants.

Born in Texas in 1950, she was immediately given up for adoption. Her new parents, Gladys and Dick Jones, had three other adopted children, two older than Genene, one younger. They lived in a comfortable four-bedroom house in the suburbs of San Antonio. Her adoptive father Dick ran a nightclub until, when Genene was ten, he was arrested. A safe had been stolen from the house of a man who was in Jones' nightclub at the time of the burglary. When the safe turned up, Jones was suspected. He confessed, but claimed that the theft was a practical joke and charges were dropped. The nightclub then foundered. He opened a restaurant which also failed. Then he took to erecting billboards.

Through the resulting family tribulations, Genene felt overlooked and began calling herself the 'black sheep' of the family. To get attention, she feigned illness. At school she was shunned for being aggressive and manipulative. She was also short and overweight, which did not help.

Her closest companion was her younger brother Travis, two years her junior. When he was 14, he was making a pipe bomb that blew up in his face and killed him. A traumatized Genene screamed and fainted at the funeral.

A year later, her adoptive father died of cancer and her mother took to drink. To escape the family tragedies, Genene sought to marry. Underage, her mother would not allow it. Eventually, when she graduated, she married a high-school dropout who, after seven months, enlisted in the US Navy. She then began a series of affairs with married men. The couple divorced after four years while her husband was in hospital after an accident. The divorce papers indicate that it had been a violent relationship.

## NO LOVE LIKE A MOTHER'S LOVE

Claiming that she had always wanted children, Genene Jones had two, but left them to be brought up by her mother, while she enrolled at beauty school. Fearing that hair dyes might give her cancer, Jones changed course. Having a penchant for medicine and doctors, she trained to become a Licensed Vocational Nurse, or LVN.

Her first job at San Antonio's Methodist Hospital lasted just six months. She was fired for making decisions that she was not qualified to take. Another

*Genene Jones at a pre-trial hearing in 1984 – she was convicted of killing one infant, Chelsea McClellan, and nearly killing another, Rolando Santos, earning her a total of 159 years in prison.*

job lasted little longer. Then she was hired by Bexar County Medical Center Hospital to work in their paediatric unit.

The first child she took care of had a fatal intestinal condition. When he died shortly after surgery, Jones broke down. She brought a stool into the cubicle where the body lay and sat staring at it. The other nurses could barely understand this. She hadn't known the child long and her grief seemed excessive.

Needing to be needed, she took care of the sickest children on the long 3–11 pm shift. It soon became known as the 'Death Shift'. Jones skipped classes on the proper handling of drugs and, in her first year, made eight elementary nursing errors, some concerning the dispensing of medication. Never liking to admit mistakes, she was bossy, telling other nurses what to do.

Foul-mouthed and always bragging about her sexual conquests, Jones was disliked by colleagues who regularly applied for transfers to get away from her. However, the head nurse Pat Belko protected her, even when she turned up for work drunk. She also upset new nurses by predicting which babies were going to die.

'Tonight's the night,' she would say. In one week, seven children died, often from conditions that should not have been fatal. Jones took a special interest in children that were near death and liked to be there when it happened, taking special pleasure informing and commiserating with the parents.

There were also numerous cases of children slipping into critical conditions in her care, then reviving during dramatic medical interventions. One child had a seizure three days in a row, but only on Jones' shift.

'They're going to start thinking I'm the Death Nurse,' Jones quipped.

Others thought so too, but Pat Belko sought to quash rumours that she was doing something to the children. This was just spiteful tittle-tattle from jealous colleagues, she maintained.

When Dr James Robotham became medical director of the paediatric unit, he took a more hands-on approach, leaving less for junior nurses to do. However, Jones ingratiated herself and basked in the attention he gave her.

She also sought attention by her old ruse of feigning illness, referring herself to the outpatients' unit 30 times in two years. This behaviour is now recognized as Munchausen Syndrome.

Then, a six-month-old baby named Jose Antonio Flores went into cardiac arrest while in Jones' care. He was revived, but went into arrest again the next day during her shift and died from internal bleeding. Tests on the corpse indicated an overdose of a drug called heparin, an anticoagulant. No one had prescribed it.

At the news of his son's death, the child's father had a heart attack. After helping the father to the emergency room, Jones seized the dead baby and made off down the corridor with the family in pursuit. She gave them the slip and delivered the dead child to the morgue. Nobody could explain this bizarre behaviour.

Being treated for pneumonia, Rolando Santos began having seizures, cardiac arrest, and extensive unexplained bleeding. This started, then intensified on Jones' shift. In a coma, blood came up into his throat and his blood pressure dropped dangerously. But after he was removed from the paediatric ICU and put under 24-hour surveillance, he survived.

Another child was sent to the paediatric unit to recover from open-heart surgery. Although he progressed well at first, on Jones' shift his condition deteriorated and he soon died. Jones grabbed a syringe and squirted fluid over the child in the sign of a cross, then did the same again on herself. Grabbing the dead baby, Jones began to cry.

Two resident physicians treating a three-month-old boy named Albert Garza suspected that Genene had probably given him an overdose of heparin. When they confronted her, she got angry, but after their intervention the child recovered. Following this incident tighter control was applied to the use of heparin, making nurses more accountable.

While Genene's health was deteriorating, at least according to her own account, she refused to take the drugs she had been prescribed. Again, she seemed to be angling for attention. Her former ally Dr Robotham began to express concerns about Jones. However, in November 1981, the hospital administration had a meeting and decided that Robotham was over-reacting. They were not willing to invite the attention a formal investigation would garner. Nevertheless, Dr Robotham continued to keep an eye on the records of drug use on the 3–11 pm shift.

While the use of heparin was being monitored, 11-month-old Joshua Sawyer, who suffered a cardiac arrest after inhaling smoke during a fire at his home, was prescribed Dilantin, an anticonvulsant. While the doctors expected him to recover, Jones told his parents that it would be better to let him die as he would be suffering from brain damage. Suddenly, he had two more heart attacks and died. Tests showing a lethal dose of Dilantin in his blood were overlooked.

Finally, a committee was formed to look into the high mortality rate headed by Dr Robotham and Pat Belko. They decided not to put the blame on one nurse but to replace the LVNs on the unit with

*One baby on Jones' watch died after an overdose of heparin, despite the drug never being prescribed for the child.*

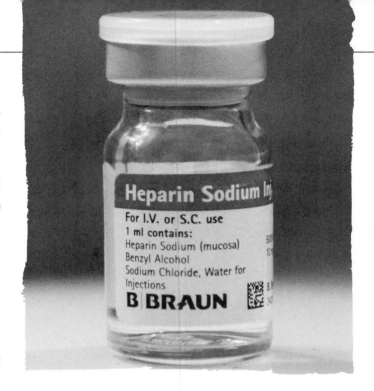

registered nurses, or RNs. That meant Jones would be transferred away from the paediatric unit. She promptly resigned.

## A NEW LIFE IN A NEW TOWN, BUT THE DEATHS CONTINUE

In 1982, Dr Kathleen Holland opened a paediatric clinic in Kerrville, Texas. She hired Genene Jones, believing that she had been the victim of the male medical establishment at Bexar. Dr Holland had testified on Jones' behalf in the investigation and helped her move to Kerrville. However, she found she had bought into trouble. Children at the clinic began having seizures. In two months seven had to be transferred by ambulance to Kerr County's Sid Peterson Hospital, where the staff grew suspicious. In one case Jones was seen to inject something into the child. However, all recovered.

The first suspicious seizure happened on 17 September 1982, the very day the clinic first opened. The child was Chelsea McClellan, who had been born prematurely and was suffering from breathing problems. She was the clinic's first-ever patient. She had stopped breathing while in Jones' care, but she had placed an oxygen mask over the baby's face and they rushed her to an emergency room at the nearby Sid Peterson Hospital. To everyone's relief, the child recovered and Jones was showered with praise.

Nine months later, Chelsea returned to the clinic for a routine check-up and to have two inoculations. When Jones gave her the first, the child began having breathing difficulties. She had a seizure and her mother asked Jones to stop, but she went ahead and gave Chelsea the second injection anyway. She stopped breathing and was rushed to the Sid Peterson Hospital, but died in the ambulance on the way.

Jones allegedly said: 'And they said there wouldn't be any excitement when we came to Kerrville.'

She sobbed over the child's body and lovingly wrapped it in a blanket before presenting it to the parents. The cause of death was given as SIDS – sudden infant death syndrome, or cot death.

A week after the funeral, Chelsea's grief-wracked mother Petti visited her daughter's burial site to find Jones kneeling at the foot of the grave, sobbing and wailing the child's name over and over as if Chelsea had been her own.

'What are you doing here?' asked Petti.

Jones stared at her blankly, as if in a trance, and walked away without a word. When she was gone, Petti McClellan noticed that Jones had left a small token of flowers, but had also taken a bow from Chelsea's grave.

Meanwhile, a committee had been formed at the Sid Peterson Hospital to investigate the deaths. They asked Dr Holland if she used succinylcholine, a powerful muscle relaxant. She said she kept some in her office but did not use it. The committee notified the Texas Rangers.

Jones then claimed that she had taken an overdose of doxepin, a drug used to fight anxiety, and had her stomach pumped. In fact, she had taken just four tablets, faking a coma, and was in no danger. Then a bottle of succinylcholine went missing and Dr Holland fired Jones.

# CAPTURED, BUT NO REST FOR HER VICTIMS' FAMILIES – YET

On 12 October 1982, a grand jury in Kerr County investigated the death of Chelsea McClellan and the eight other children from Dr Holland's clinic who had developed emergency respiratory problems. Chelsea's body was exhumed and succinylcholine was found in the tissue. Her death had been caused by an injection of the muscle relaxant.

In February 1983, another grand jury was convened in San Antonio to look into the 47 suspicious deaths of children at the Bexar County Medical Center Hospital that had occurred while Genene Jones had been there. Chelsea's parents began a lawsuit against Jones and Holland, alleging wrongful death. Meanwhile, Jones married a 19-year-old boy, seemingly to deflect rumours that she was a lesbian.

The Kerr County grand jury indicted Jones on one count of murder and several charges of injury to seven other children who had been injected with muscle relaxants. Then the San Antonio grand jury indicted her for injuring Rolando Santos by deliberately injecting heparin. She remained a suspect in ten infant deaths at the hospital.

There were two separate trials. The prosecution alleged that the motive was Munchausen Syndrome by Proxy – a psychological disorder where a caregiver indulges in attention-seeking behaviour by manipulating the health of their patients. Jones liked the excitement and the attention the sick children brought her. The children were at her mercy. They couldn't tell on her, so she was free to create the situation over and over again. There was no doubt that, over time, her actions had escalated and that she had taken more risks.

The first jury took just three hours to find Jones guilty of murdering Chelsea McClellan. She was given the maximum sentence of 99 years. Later, she was given another 60 years for injuring Rolando Santos. She had the possibility of parole, but the McClellans fought to keep her inside.

However, she was due for mandatory release in 2018 to avoid prison overcrowding. To prevent this, fresh charges were brought for the murder of Joshua Sawyer. The Bexar County District Attorney said that more murder charges would be levelled against her to prevent her release. In January 2020 Jones made a plea bargain with prosecutors by accepting guilt for the death of Joshua Sawyer in return for all other ongoing investigations against her being dropped.

# BEVERLEY ALLITT

On 23 February 1991, just two days after Beverley Allitt had started work as a nurse on Children's Ward Four at Grantham and Kesteven Hospital in Lincolnshire, seven-week-old Liam Taylor was brought in with a chest infection.

His doctor did not think his condition was serious but in hospital it could be properly monitored. The staff nurse said that newly enrolled state nurse Allitt would take good care of him, but when they returned two hours later they were told that he had taken a turn for the worse.

'I was feeding him and he suddenly threw up,' said Allitt. 'It went all over me. I had to go and change my uniform.'

The child was so sick, she said, that he had stopped breathing for a moment.

'He was choking on his vomit,' she said. 'If he'd been at home, you'd probably have lost him.'

The couple were upset but took an instant liking to the young nurse who was so frank with them and they were relieved and grateful when Allitt volunteered for an extra night shift to look after him. However, early in the morning Allitt called for an emergency resuscitation team as Liam had stopped breathing. The doctors managed to revive him, but there was bad news. The specialist told Liam's parents that, if their child survived, he would have severe brain damage.

'Normally, in children who have respiratory failure, their condition can be stabilized in a matter of minutes,' Dr Charith Nanayakkara said. 'In Liam's case, it took an hour and fifteen minutes.'

The chaplain was called to christen the child. Liam's parents then agreed to switch off the life support system, but Liam did not die – not immediately anyway. His parents took turns holding him until he finally perished seven and a half hours later.

The doctors could not understand how he had died. A post-mortem concluded that Liam had suffered an 'infarction' of the heart – that is, the muscles of the heart had died. This usually happened in patients in middle age or beyond, after a lifetime of heavy smoking or drinking, so the pathologist could not explain how it had happened to a tiny child.

## INSULIN IN BLOOD

Then on 5 March, just three days after Liam had been buried, 11-year-old Timothy Hardwick was admitted to Ward Four. He had been born with cerebral palsy and had suffered an epileptic fit. Again Allitt seemed to lavish care on the child and initially the doctors were pleased with his progress. Suddenly, when the ward was particularly busy, Timothy unexpectedly died. Given his chronic condition, no further investigation was made and no one called the police.

In the same bed just five days later, 14-month-old Kayley Desmond stopped breathing while in the

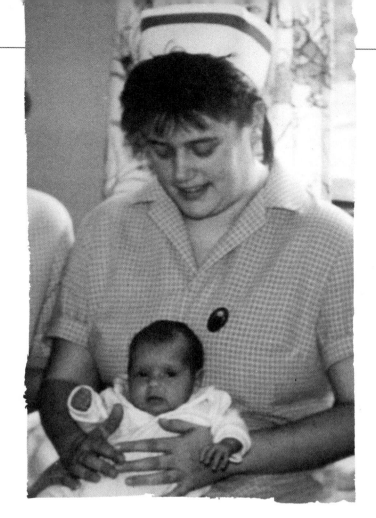

Sue Phillips, the mother of Becky and Katie Phillips, who were also on the ward, said: 'I heard Bev Allitt say: "I think I know what's wrong with him. He's hypoglycaemic."'

Paul was put on a glucose drip and quickly recovered.

'I thought how clever the nurse was to have realized what was wrong with him so quickly,' Sue Phillips said.

He had two more unexplained attacks of hypoglycaemia, a critical lack of sugar in his body. After the third attack, he was rushed to the Queen's Medical Centre, with Allitt in the ambulance, where the lab discovered that he had a high level of insulin in his blood.

## PARENTS' GRATITUDE

The following day five-year-old Bradley Gibson was admitted suffering from pneumonia and during the night he complained of pain in the arm where his antibiotic drip was attached. He was attended by Allitt. On the second occasion, he suffered a cardiac arrest. For half an hour, the emergency resuscitation team battled to save him – successfully – and he too was taken to the Queen's. His parents went to the local newspaper, the *Grantham Journal*, to praise the doctors and nurses who had saved their son and the paper ran the story under the headline 'Our Miracle'. Three national newspapers picked up on it.

The day after that, two-year-old Yik Hung 'Henry' Chan was admitted after he had plunged from a bedroom window on to the patio below, suffering a

care of Allitt. Then her heart stopped beating. She was revived and rushed to the intensive care unit at the Queen's Medical Centre in Nottingham, amid concern that she might have suffered brain damage when starved of oxygen. It was assumed that this had occurred when, as a bad feeder, she had inhaled milk and stopped breathing. No one spotted that under her right armpit there was a needle puncture with a small bubble of air behind it, as if someone had injected her ineptly. It was only seen when her X-rays were re-examined later. Nevertheless, Kayley made a full recovery.

Another ten days passed before five-month-old Paul Crampton was admitted to the ward with mild bronchitis. Responding well to treatment, he was due to be discharged four days later when suddenly he took a turn for the worse.

fractured skull. Although he was dizzy and complaining of bad headaches, his condition quickly improved and the doctors were thinking about sending him home. However, when attended by Allitt the child started vomiting. Other staff saw he was blue, so the emergency team were called and he was revived with oxygen. When this happened a second time, Henry, too, was rushed to the Queen's.

Four days later, it was the turn of identical twins Becky and Katie Phillips. Becky had been admitted for observation after suffering from acute gastroenteritis. She was untroubled for the first two days because Allitt had been off duty. When she returned, Becky's mother Sue Phillips recognized her immediately, because they had been to Grantham College of Further Education together. Strangely, though, Allitt did not acknowledge her.

When Becky returned home she fell ill again and was taken back to hospital. The doctors suspected that the problem was with the milk the twins were being fed. Whereas the hospital used ready-mixed baby's milk, Sue mixed her own from powder. That evening Becky screamed and her eyes rolled in her head. Allitt did not want Sue to take Becky home but nevertheless she was discharged. However, despite a midnight rush to A&E, she died in the night. No reason could be found, though the doctor in A&E thought she might have contracted meningitis. The death certificate said 'infant death syndrome' – cot death.

As a precaution, Katie was sent to hospital for observation, only to be cared for by Allitt, who now offered Sue seemingly genuine words of comfort. Seeing Sue was tired, Allitt told her to go home and get some rest.

'You go. I will look after her,' said Allitt. 'She will be all right with me.'

Within half an hour of reaching home, Sue got a call saying Katie was having trouble breathing. She suffered a cardiac arrest, but Allitt was on hand to call for 'resus'. Emergency treatment saved Katie's life, but the same thing happened again two days later. Rushed to the Queen's, she was found to have suffered brain damage. She had cerebral palsy, paralysis of the right side and damage to her eyesight and hearing. What's more, five of her ribs were broken. This was put down to frantic efforts to resuscitate her. But Katie's mother Sue was so grateful to Allitt for saving her daughter's life that she asked her to be her godmother. As it was, the hospital's chaplain became Katie's godparent.

## QUESTIONS RAISED

A few days later, six-year-old Michael Davidson was admitted after being accidentally shot with an airgun. After minor surgery to remove the pellet, Allitt helped prepare an intravenous antibiotic. When it was administered, the child stopped breathing. His face turned black and his back arched. CPR from Dr Nanayakkara had him breathing again before the emergency team arrived and after being resuscitated he recovered and was eventually discharged.

That same day two-month-old Christopher Peasgood was admitted with breathing difficulties. While he was put in an oxygen tent, Allitt suggested that his parents, who had lost a child to cot death two years earlier, should go and have a cup of tea. When they returned they found the emergency team in action. The boy was blue. A nurse had discovered that the alarm indicating he had stopped breathing had been turned off. Nevertheless, Allitt assured

*Beverley Allitt had been to Grantham College of Further Education with Sue Phillips. Allitt told Phillips she would look after her daughter Katie. 'She will be all right with me.'*

Christopher's parents that he would be all right, but he suffered another cardiac arrest during the night. Fearing that he was dying, the child was christened. The doctors wanted to send him to the Queen's but feared he might not survive the journey. However, Christopher's parents agreed to the move, figuring they had nothing to lose, and in the intensive care unit there he quickly recovered.

Christopher King was a month old when he was admitted for an operation, but he became inexplicably ill before going to surgery and had to be revived with oxygen. The operation was a success, but he had to be resuscitated four more times before he was sent to the Queen's. His mother Belinda was a nurse and she swore that she would never take Christopher back to Ward Four.

Seven-week-old Patrick Elstone had been playing and laughing when his parents had dropped him off for a check-up, but in Allitt's care he had stopped breathing – twice. He was rushed to the Queen's, but not before he had suffered brain damage. By then, the doctors at the Queen's were beginning to ask the question: Why were so many children coming into their care from Ward Four?

## LIGNOCAINE FOUND

Asthmatic 15-month-old Claire Peck had been admitted to the ward on 18 April. She was put on a nebulizer that cleared her airways and she was discharged two days later, but after a coughing fit she returned on 22 April. Her mother Susan found Nurse Allitt unfriendly, even hostile, and the Pecks had been ushered away while their daughter was being treated. Left alone with the child, Allitt suddenly cried out: 'Arrest! Arrest!'

Doctors came running and revived the child, but as soon as she was left alone with Allitt the same thing happened again. This time the doctors could not save her. Susan Peck, holding the dead child, noticed that everyone else was upset but Allitt just sat there staring.

The authorities at first suspected that legionnaires' disease was responsible, so although no virus was found the ward was meticulously scrubbed. Initially a post-mortem showed that Claire had died from natural causes, but Dr Nelson Porter, a consultant at the hospital, was unhappy with the number of heart cases that had occurred in Ward Four over the previous eight weeks and ordered further tests. Lignocaine, a drug that was used to treat adults suffering from cardiac arrest, was found in Claire's body. It was never given to babies.

The police were called in and it was discovered, by checking the rotas, that Allitt was the only person who was present every time there was a medical emergency. Also, notes covering Paul Crampton's

stay were missing. Allitt was suspended, but the parents of the Phillips twins had so much faith in her that they hired a private detective to clear her name.

## MUNCHAUSEN'S SYNDROME

After Allitt's arrest a missing ward diary was found in her home. She was charged with four counts of murder and eleven counts of attempted murder, to which she pleaded not guilty at Nottingham Crown Court on 15 February 1993. In the court case, which lasted two months, the prosecution easily showed that Allitt had the means and the opportunity to commit the crimes – but what of the motive? Consultant paediatrician Professor Roy Meadow told the court that Allitt exhibited all the symptoms of Munchausen's Syndrome and Munchausen's Syndrome by Proxy. In the first condition, the sufferer seeks attention by self-harm or faking complaints. Allitt's extensive medical record confirmed that. Even while she had been out on bail she had been admitted to hospital complaining of an enlarged right breast. It was discovered that she had been injecting herself with water. She attended the court for just 16 days, absenting herself for the rest of the time due to mysterious illnesses.

The second condition is usually exhibited by mothers, where they seek medical attention by complaining that their offspring is suffering from fictitious complaints or by inflicting actual abuse. Professor Meadow said that to suffer from both Munchausen's Syndrome and Munchausen's Syndrome by Proxy was extremely rare, but he came across around 40 cases of the proxy condition a year.

Allitt was found guilty on all charges. In Children's Ward Four at Grantham and Kesteven Hospital in Lincolnshire, she had administered potentially lethal injections or attempted to suffocate 23 children in her charge, killing four and leaving a further nine irreparably damaged – all in just 59 days.

# DANGER SIGNS SINCE CHILDHOOD

In court, it became clear that Beverley Allitt should never have been allowed to become a nurse because she had shown disturbing symptoms of a mental disorder from an early age. One of four children, she sought attention by wearing dressings and casts over supposed wounds that she would allow no one to examine. Growing overweight as an adolescent, her attention-seeking became aggressive and her parents regularly had to take her to hospital for treatment for fictitious ailments. These included pain in her gall bladder, headaches, urinary infections, uncontrolled vomiting, blurred vision, minor injuries, back trouble, ulcers and appendicitis, resulting in the removal of a perfectly healthy appendix. The scar was slow to heal as she kept picking at the wound.

While training as a nurse she had a poor attendance record, frequently being absent with supposed illnesses. She was also suspected of odd behaviour, including smearing faeces on the walls of the nurses' home. Her boyfriend accused her of being aggressive, manipulative and deceptive. She falsely claimed to be pregnant and told people he had AIDS and she had accused a friend of his of rape, though she did not go to the police.

When Allitt returned to the dock for sentencing, the judge told her:

You have been found guilty of the most terrible crimes. You killed, tried to kill or seriously harmed thirteen children, many of them tiny babies. They had been entrusted to your care. You have brought grief to their families. You have sown a seed of doubt in those who should have faith in the integrity of care their children receive in hospital. Hopefully, the grief felt by the families will become easier to bear, but it will always be there. You are seriously disturbed. You are cunning and manipulative and you have shown no remorse for the trail of destruction you have left behind you. I accept it is all the result of the severe personality disorder you have. But you are and remain a very serious danger to others.

He gave her 13 concurrent terms of life imprisonment, which meant she would serve a minimum of 30 years and would only be released if she was considered to be no danger to the public. Committed to Rampton Secure Hospital, she admitted three of the murders and six of the attempted murders. Her earliest possible parole date is 2032, when she will be 64. Meanwhile, the families and the victims whom she disabled will have to live a lifetime with what she has done.

# KRISTEN GILBERT

Kristen Gilbert was known as a skilled nurse who remained calm in medical emergencies. She won the admiration of those that worked alongside her at the Veterans Administration Medical Center in Northampton, Massachusetts. But in 1990, after she returned from maternity leave, it was noted that the rate of cardiac arrests on Ward C was three times greater than it had been over the previous three years. Patients were dying of cardiac arrest even though they had not suffered from heart complaints previously. So many of them were under the care of Kristen Gilbert that her co-workers began to call her the 'Angel of Death'. At first, it was a joke.

Born Kristen Heather Strickland in Fall River, Massachusetts, in 1967, she showed signs as a teenager of being a pathological liar. For one, she made unfounded claims about being a distant relation of the infamous Lizzie Borden, who reputedly despatched her mother and father with 40 whacks in Fall River in 1892, though she was acquitted.

Former boyfriends accused her of being strange and controlling. They said she even resorted to verbal and physical abuse, or tampering with their cars. When all else failed, she would fake suicide attempts.

Graduating from high school a year and a half early, she enrolled in Bridgewater State College and majored in pre-med, though she later transferred to Greenfield Community College to be closer to her future husband, Glenn Gilbert. While working as a home health aide, she once badly scalded a child with learning difficulties, though no action was taken against her. No one suspected that it might have been deliberate. Then in 1988 she became a registered nurse and eloped with Glenn Gilbert. Their marriage was full of rows, however, and on one occasion she chased him around the house with a butcher's knife.

Soon after their marriage, Kristen got a job at the Veterans Administration Medical Center in Northampton, Massachusetts, working on Ward C. Well liked, she remembered birthdays and organized gift exchanges during the holidays. She distinguished herself early on and was featured in the magazine *VA Practitioner* in April 1990.

## DEATHS START TO CLIMB

Everything changed after the birth of her first child, when she was switched to the 4 pm to midnight shift. Deaths during her shifts then began to climb, though she still showed skill and confidence during these emergencies. However, one doctor refused to let her treat any more of his patients.

After the birth of her second son in 1993, the Gilberts' marriage ran into difficulties. She had taken a fancy to James Perrault, a security guard at the hospital.

The VA hospital in Northampton, Massachussetts, where Kristen Gilbert committed her crimes.

Under VA rules, security had to be on hand during any medical emergency, so when there was a cardiac arrest on Ward C he would be called, giving her the chance to impress him with her medical skills and flirt with him. They would also have drinks together after her shift ended.

When they became lovers, it was alleged that an AIDS patient suddenly died of a heart attack so that she could leave early to go on a date with Perrault. Gilbert's husband Glenn then found his food tasted odd and was convinced that she was trying to kill him. Soon afterwards, Kristen moved out of the marital home to be closer to Perrault and she then filed for divorce.

The high mortality rate on Ward C put all the nurses under suspicion. While the authorities were searching for some explanation, it was noted that stocks of the drug epinephrine – a synthetic form of adrenaline – were going missing. It was a heart stimulant that could cause cardiac arrest if injected unnecessarily. Three fellow nurses then reported their suspicions to the authorities.

## HOAX BOMB CALLS

While the matter was under investigation, Gilbert bought a device to disguise her voice and then called the hospital to say that bombs had been planted there. Staff and patients, many of whom were sick and elderly, had to be evacuated. No explosives were found, but the hoax calls always occurred on Perrault's shift.

It was not long before the police linked Gilbert to the calls. Perrault was then summoned before a grand jury, where he testified against his lover. At that point, Glenn Gilbert asked investigators to come to his house and search Kristen's former pantry, where they found the Handbook of Poisoning. Meanwhile, Gilbert was temporarily placed in a psychiatric ward at Arbour Hospital for the third time in a month.

She later turned up at Glenn Gilbert's house and threatened him with her car keys. A court order then confined her to Bayside Medical Center. When she was released, she was arrested on a charge of making bomb threats. She was then sentenced to 15 months at Danbury Federal Prison and treated for psychiatric problems.

## PATIENTS' BODIES EXHUMED

While she was in prison, investigators began to exhume some of the bodies of those who had died on her shift. They were found to contain epinephrine, though the deceased patients had no history of heart complaints.

In November 1998, aged 30, she was indicted for the murders of four men and the attempted murders of three others. However, the United States attorney said that 37 men had died during her shifts between January 1995 and February 1996. Her potential body count was much greater. In the seven years she had worked at the VA hospital, 350 patients had died on her shifts and she was thought to have been responsible for 80 of the deaths.

In all the prosecution brought 70 witnesses and 200 pieces of evidence against her.

The witnesses included her ex-husband, who said she had confessed to the murders.

Perrault also testified against her, saying that she had told him during a telephone conversation: 'I did it. You wanted to know, I killed all those guys by injection.'

The defence maintained that she had only said that after suffering psychiatric problems following the break-up of their tempestuous affair. There were no witnesses to Gilbert administering the drug, so all the evidence was circumstantial.

'The four murders were especially cruel and heinous,' said US Attorney David Stern, citing the case of 41-year-old Kenneth Cutting, who was blind and had multiple sclerosis. Gilbert had asked a supervisor if she could leave work early if he were to die. He died 40 minutes later and empty ampoules of epinephrine were found nearby. Prosecutors maintained that Gilbert was also on duty when 37 of the 63 patients on Ward C died and that she tried to cover her tracks by falsifying medical records.

Explaining why Gilbert was standing trial in just seven cases, Assistant US Attorney Ariane Vuono told jurors: 'These seven victims were veterans. They were vulnerable. They were the perfect victims. When Kristen Gilbert killed them, she used the perfect poison.'

Lawyers for Gilbert argued that the patients died of natural causes. They said Gilbert had been falsely accused by her co-workers, who were upset that she was having an extramarital affair.

*Hoax bomb calls always seemed to occur during Glenn Perrault's shift. His wife, Kristen, was the one behind them.*

*Gilbert seemed to be an exemplary employee but when she changed shifts, the death rate went up*

'She was scorned by her peers and her co-workers,' defence attorney David Hoose told the jury. 'You must understand how rumours about what was going on in Kristen Gilbert's life affected, coloured and tainted everyone's opinions of what was going on in Ward C.'

## LIFE IMPRISONMENT

Despite her lawyers' pleas, in March 2001 Kristen Gilbert was found guilty of three counts of first-degree murder, one count of second-degree murder and two counts of attempted murder. While there was no death penalty in the state of Massachusetts, the crimes had taken place on federal property, so she faced the prospect of execution – ironically, by lethal injection. Assistant US Attorney William Welch called Gilbert a 'shell of a human being' who deserved to die for the cold and calculating way she murdered her victims.

The defence argued that she did not need to die, because it would be punishment enough to lead a life 'where you can't walk out into a field, or see snow or play with a puppy'. Her father and grandmothers also pleaded for her life, saying a death sentence would be devastating to them and Gilbert's two sons.

'It is easier to incite good and decent people to kill when their target is not human but a demon,' said defence attorney Paul Weinberg. 'Kristen Gilbert is not a monster, she is a human being.'

This won little sympathy from the relatives of the victims.

Claire Jagadowski, widow of 66-year-old Stanley Jagadowski, told the judge: 'I still listen for his key in the door. Now I have to face old age alone.'

Gilbert herself declined to take the stand and wept softly when the decision was handed down.

After six hours' deliberation, the jury decided against the death penalty, though the decision was not unanimous. Instead, the judge sentenced her to four consecutive terms of life imprisonment without possibility of parole, plus 20 years. There was no audible reaction in the courtroom. Her parents wept and the victims' families sat stone-faced.

'It's a very bittersweet day when you think your daughter is going to get life imprisonment instead of the death penalty,' said Gilbert's father, Richard Strickland.

Gilbert dropped her appeal after the US Supreme Court ruled that she risked the death penalty on retrial. Her life sentence would be served at the Carswell Federal Medical Center in Fort Worth, Texas.

# HAROLD SHIPMAN

**H**arold Shipman is almost certainly the most prolific serial killer in British history. A public enquiry in 2002 reported that over his career he had probably killed 215 people, mostly women, all of whom had been his patients. For Shipman was a doctor who killed, apparently, simply because he could. His victims were mostly elderly or infirm – they would die sometime, so why not when he dictated? He was caring, after all: a trouble-taker, a pillar of the community always ready to go out of his way to help. So why on earth would anyone suspect him of using the home visits he made to inject his victims with enough heroin or morphine to stop them breathing? No one ever thought to doubt his word and covering his tracks was simplicity itself: all he had to do was doctor his victims' medical records, if that was necessary, and write a fake cause of death, as their personal GP, on the death certificate. There was no need at all, he'd announce, for a post mortem.

Occasionally Dr Shipman would be mentioned in his patients' wills, of course, but that seemed only natural. They mostly didn't have a great deal of money in the first place; sometimes they had no living family and the doctor, who always worked alone at his surgery in Hyde, Greater Manchester, was the personification of kindness. Then, though, in 1998, he got greedy. For one of his patients, Kathleen Grundy, a woman in her eighties, left him over £380,000. Questions were asked, and the will turned out to have been forged by none other than Shipman himself. He was sentenced to four years in prison.

It was this that triggered a full-scale enquiry. For unlike a great many of his patients – who'd been cremated, along with the evidence in their bones and blood – Kathleen Grundy had been buried. So her body was disinterred and it was found to contain enough heroin to have killed her. Shipman's records were then seized and searched; relatives of dead patients were interviewed and police began the grisly business of recovering and testing as many corpses as they could locate. The list of those murdered via injections began to rise; and so, to the horror of relatives, friends and patients alike, did the roster of probables.

Shipman, who turned out to have a history of drug addiction, was tried on 15 counts of murder, all of which he denied; and in January 2000, he was sentenced to life on each count, with the judge adding that, in his case,

'life would mean life.'

When the subsequent enquiry reported that he had probably been guilty of another 199 murders, he had nothing to say except, again, that he was innocent; at the beginning of 2003, he launched an appeal against his sentence, on the grounds that his legal team hadn't been allowed to conduct their own post-mortems and that the jury had been wrongly instructed. It seems oddly apt that one of the solicitors involved in his appeal also acted for Slobodan Milošević.

On 13 January 2004, the eve of his 58th birthday, Shipman was found hanged in his prison cell.

*Dr Harold Shipman, the most prolific serial killer in British history.*

# KIMBERLY CLARK SAENZ

On April 2008, inspectors of the Texas Department of Health Services were alerted to problems at the DaVita Dialysis clinic in Lufkin, Texas. A member of the emergency services sent an anonymous letter saying: 'In the last two weeks, we have transported 16 patients. This seems a little abnormal and disturbing to my med crews. Could these calls be investigated by you?'

Reviewing the clinic's record, it was found that there had only been two emergency calls in the previous 15 months, but they had been called out 30 times that month – seven for cardiac problems. Four people had already died. On 1 April, Clara Strange and Thelma Metcalf died after suffering cardiac arrest. On the 16th, Garlin Kelley suffered cardiac arrest and died two days later at the hospital, while Graciela Castañeda lost consciousness during treatment.

On 22 April, Cora Bryant suffered cardiac arrest and died three months later at the hospital. The following day, Marie Bradley suffered a severe drop in blood pressure. Then on 26 April, Opal Few died after suffering cardiac arrest and Debra Oates experienced multiple symptoms and a severe drop in blood pressure.

Concerned about the mortality rate, DaVita sent in a new supervisor from Houston named Amy

*Kimberly Saenz abused her position as a nurse for years before she was finally arrested.*

Clinton who promptly took charge. When 34-year-old Kimberly Saenz arrived on shift at 4.30 am on 28 April, she was distressed to find that she had effectively been demoted. She was in tears. Previously, she had the run of the place. Her job as a nurse was to move from patient to patient, injecting medication into the dialysis lines and ports with a syringe. Now she was to clean up after patients, wiping up blood and vomit.

At around 6 am, Marva Rhone and Carolyn Risinger came into the clinic. Like other patients

*Bleach was the weapon of choice for Kimberly Saenz.*

with failed kidneys, they spent hours on the dialysis machine cleansing their blood three times a week. It was a matter of life and death.

Two other patients, Lurlene Hamilton and Linda Hall, sitting nearby, noticed that Saenz was nervous. They saw her squat down and pour bleach into her cleaning bucket. Then they saw her draw up the caustic liquid into a syringe. At the very least, they thought this insanitary. But then they said they saw her inject the contents of the syringe into the dialysis lines of Rhone and Risinger.

Hamilton told Amy Clinton what she and seen, adding: 'I'm a little nervous right now, and I'm worried because she's assigned to me.'

Linda Hall also reported that Saenz had filled a syringe and injected Rhone's 'saline' line. Both witnesses said they saw Saenz dispose of the syringes in the DaVita sharps containers. Shortly after, Rhone and Risinger experienced a dramatic drop in blood pressure.

After speaking to Hamilton and Hall, Clinton asked Saenz whether she had administered any medication that day. Saenz said no. When asked about the bleach, Saenz explained that she 'was drawing up bleach to mix for her containers' that she had on the floor. Three syringes collected from the sharp container tested positive for bleach. She then acknowledged using a syringe to extract the bleach from its container because she was concerned about

being precise and following procedures. A solution of bleach was commonly used to sterilize equipment in the clinic, but she adamantly denied ever injecting bleach into a patient.

Saenz was sent home. The following day the clinic was closed as an investigation was carried out. A meeting was called to inform the employees. All of them turned up except for Saenz. Co-worker Werlan Guillory phoned her and asked: 'Where are you? Are you coming to the meeting?'

Saenz said she could not make it.

'I'm a chaperone at my daughter's field day,' she said.

Guillory expressed concern that Saenz might lose her job, but Saenz simply responded: 'Okay.'

After the meeting, Guillory went to find Saenz. He said she was uncharacteristically unkempt and acted as if she did not recognize him. She was crying and told him she 'didn't kill those people'. This was unexpected as, at that point, no one had made any allegations that someone was killing patients. Guillory described Saenz as seeming 'like she had lost all the hope in the world'.

## A CHEQUERED PAST

Saenz had held her entry-level position as a Licensed Vocational Nurse (LVN) at the clinic for nine months by then. Previously, she had been fired from another hospital in Lufkin for stealing the opioid Demerol, which was found in her handbag. She had also been arrested for public intoxication and criminal trespass, and the police had been called for domestic disturbances involving her husband, Mark Kevin Saenz. He filed for divorce and had obtained a restraining order against Saenz in June 2007, just a few months before she began at DaVita. An examination of the records revealed that 84 per cent of the time patients had suffered from chest pain or cardiac arrest, Saenz had been on duty.

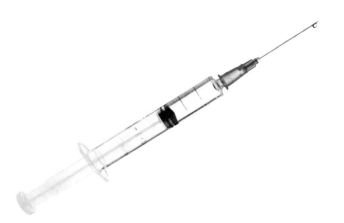

Questioned by Lufkin police officers, Saenz was noticeably upset that two patients had accused her of giving them another patient's medication. Asked why she had not attended the meeting, Saenz said she was scared to go to work because DaVita 'can't tell us what's going on, and I'm doing everything by the book, and I'm scared because I have a licence'. She added: 'If I'm doing something wrong, I want to know that I'm doing something wrong 'cause I don't want to kill somebody.'

When asked whether she had administered any medications during her shift on 28 April, Saenz said: 'I did give [Rhone] some saline, only because she said she was cramping.'

She said she opened her saline line because her nurse wasn't there. This was recorded on the patient's chart, but the patient's blood pressure didn't really go down that much, and then she said she felt nauseous.

The officers asked Saenz if she had any theories about the underlying cause of the injuries. She mentioned a 'bleach loop' and wondered whether 'our machines are hooked up and they have some bleach in them.'

She went on to explain the clinic's 'bleaching procedures' – a medicine cup was used to pour bleach into a container where it was diluted. Sponges were then soaked in the liquid and used to wipe the chairs. Although Saenz understood the policy was to use a medicine cup to measure the bleach, when pushed by the officer on whether she had ever used a syringe, Saenz acknowledged doing so.

'Sometimes I do when I can't find the little medicine cups,' she said. 'There wasn't any cups up there that

*Kimberly Clark Saenz admitted that she filled syringes with bleach rather than using the measuring cup.*

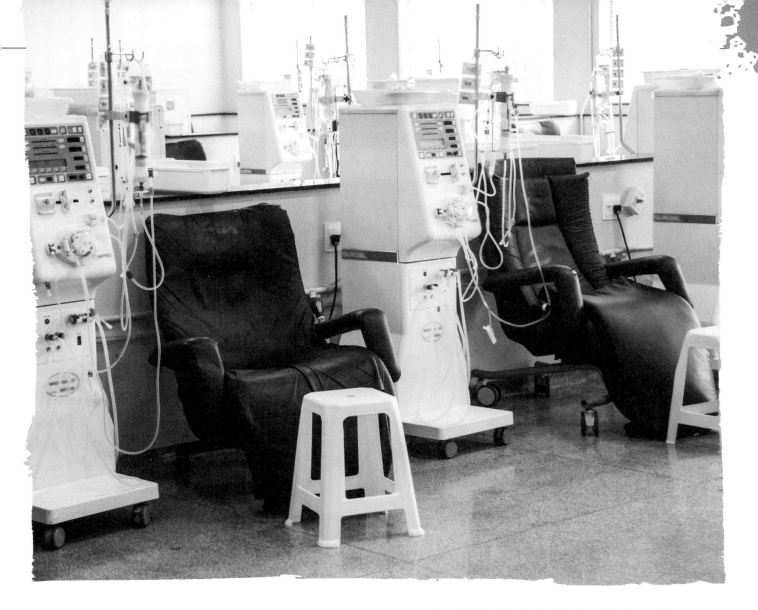

day. But if you use a syringe, 10 cc, then you're going to have to, you know, put it in the receptacle. So I took my bleach and I just poured it and then I pulled up to 10 cc, 'cause I knew that would be like 10 ml.'

Other than Saenz's own statement, there was no evidence that the supply of measuring cups was depleted. Saenz further explained the monitors at the facility made her nervous, and she wanted to ensure that she was precisely following procedures.

Tests by the US Food and Drug Administration showed the presence of bleach in the dialysis lines, and the victims tested positive for bleach also. Saenz was indicted on five counts of murder and

*Saenz described a 'bleach loop' in the dialysis machines.*

five counts of aggravated assault for the injuries to other patients. The deadly weapon Saenz used, the indictment said, was sodium hypochlorite – bleach. Even while she was out on bail, Saenz had applied for other healthcare jobs in violation of her bail conditions.

She swore an affidavit that she had no previous felony record. But documents filed by Angelina County District Attorney Clyde Herrington listed about a dozen instances of wrongdoing. They included allegations Saenz overused prescription drugs, had substance abuse and addiction problems, was fired at least four times from healthcare jobs and put false information on an employment application.

Investigators found internet searches on Saenz's computer about bleach poisoning in blood and whether bleach could be detected in dialysis lines. Saenz told the grand jury she had been concerned about the patients' deaths and looked up bleach poisoning references to see 'if this was happening, what would be the side effects'.

Saenz did not take the stand in her own defence at the trial. But a recording of the testimony she gave before a grand jury was played, where she said she felt 'railroaded' by the clinic and 'would never inject bleach into a patient'.

The defence insisted that Saenz had no motive to kill.

'Kimberly Saenz is a good nurse, a compassionate, a caring individual who assisted her patients and was well liked,' said defence attorney T. Ryan Deaton. He argued that Saenz was being targeted by the clinic's owner for faulty procedures at the facility, including improper water purification, and suggested that officials at the clinic fabricated evidence against her.

# TROUBLE IN THE WORKPLACE

Before the trial, Deaton fought for the jury to have access to a US Department of Health and Human Services report from May 2008 that was heavily critical of DaVita's practices. But the report was ruled inadmissible by District Judge Barry Bryan.

According to the report, from 1 December 2007 to 28 April 2008, when Saenz had been there, the facility had 19 deaths compared to 25 for the whole of 2007.

Those numbers put the facility at a mortality rate of seven per cent, which was above the state average.

The clinic was also not keeping proper records of adverse occurrences, the report stated. From 1 September 2007 to 26 April 2008, there was a total of 102 DaVita patients transported by ambulance to local hospitals during or immediately following dialysis. Of those, 60 did not have a complete adverse occurrence report.

The report went on to say that, based on record reviews and nursing staff interviews, the clinic 'did not demonstrate competence in monitoring patients during treatment alerting nurses or physicians of changes to a patient's condition and following the physician's orders for the dialysis treatment'.

However, the prosecution described claims that Saenz was being set up by her employer as 'absolutely ridiculous'. They described her as a depressed and disgruntled employee who complained about specific patients, including some of those who died or were injured.

Clinic employees reported Saenz was not happy with her employment at DaVita. Several people reported Saenz was frustrated when DaVita had reassigned her to the lesser position of patient care technician. Saenz herself considered administration of medications much less stressful and felt she was being treated unfairly by DaVita. During her shift on 28 April, Saenz was described as 'teary-eyed' in reaction to her lesser assignment.

In addition to Saenz's displeasure with her demotion, she expressed her aversion to some of the DaVita patients. One employee testified Saenz specifically voiced her dislike of Strange, Metcalf, Kelley, Few, Oates, Rhone and Risinger, all of whom either died or were injured during treatment that April. The records substantiated that during each of the alleged incidents, Saenz was at the DaVita facility functioning either as a patient care technician or as a nurse responsible for preparing medications for each patient.

# TAKEN OFF THE STREETS – FOREVER

The prosecution also maintained that there were more victims, but detectives could only obtain medical waste from two weeks prior to 28 April 2008, so there was inadequate evidence to raise further indictments against Saenz. Nevertheless, an epidemiologist from the Centers for Disease Control and Prevention statistically connected Saenz to other adverse health events to patients.

'The only days there were deaths in April, she was there,' said prosecutor Clyde Herrington. 'Dialysis patients are sick, but every source of information we can find says it is very unusual for patients to die during dialysis treatment.'

He pointed out that the state did not have to prove motive to get a conviction. However, the prosecution had talked to a registered nurse who studied more than 100 healthcare killers. The most common method they used was injecting a patient with some type of medication or substance.

'Criminal behaviour is something we've been trying to understand since Cain killed Abel,' Herrington said. 'Only when the healthcare killer confesses do we know motive.'

Speculating, Herrington said he believed that Saenz was a troubled woman with marital problems who lashed out because of job dissatisfaction.

'From talking to some of the folks who worked with her, it sounded like her husband didn't want her to quit [the clinic],' Herrington said. 'She was depressed. She was frustrated, and I think she took those frustrations out on the patients.'

On 30 March 2012, Kimberly Saenz was convicted of killing five patients and deliberately injuring three others. She faced the death penalty. Addressing the jury, another of Saenz's attorneys, Steve Taylor, asked for leniency, saying: 'She's never getting out no matter what you do.'

He reminded jurors Saenz had been free on bail during the trial and prosecutors had failed to show she would present a future danger – one of the questions jurors are required to answer when deciding a death penalty.

'Society is protected,' said Taylor. 'You will never see her again.'

The prosecution made no real effort to urge the jurors to impose the death penalty.

'I know you'll reach a verdict that's just and in accordance with the law,' said Herrington after showing the jury photographs of some of the victims on a large screen in the courtroom. Ultimately, they chose to impose a life sentence for each of the murders, plus 21 years' imprisonment for each of the aggravated assaults. The Court of Appeals of Texas in San Antonio confirmed the trial court's verdict.

# UNCONTROLLABLE URGES

There are serial killers who do the deed for pleasure. These people are often highly organized and calculating. And then there are those who find they just can't stop themselves. These criminals talk of a beast lurking inside them that makes them commit the most gruesome crimes. The most innocuous events can set them off, and once the blood starts flowing, they find themselves on the path of evil that will only lead to more and more death.

# JOHN WAYNE GACY

Twenty-five-year-old John Wayne Gacy was a married man with two children and was an upstanding member of the Junior Chamber of Commerce in Waterloo, Iowa, when, in 1968, he lured a 15-year-old boy into the back room of the Kentucky Fried Chicken outlet he was running. He handcuffed the boy and tried to bribe him into performing oral sex. When the youth refused, Gacy attempted to penetrate him anally, but his victim escaped.

The young man reported Gacy to the police and he was arrested. While awaiting trial, another youngster came forward with a similar accusation. Pleading guilty to sodomy, Gacy expected a suspended sentence. Instead, he was sentenced to ten years' imprisonment and his wife divorced him. A model prisoner, he was released after 18 months. He moved back to Chicago, his hometown, where he lived with his widowed mother.

Gacy had had a troubled childhood in the Windy City. His father had been an abusive alcoholic who beat his wife and assaulted his children. On one occasion, Gacy's father struck him over the head with a broomstick, knocking him unconscious. At the age of 11, he was hit on the head by a swing, which caused a blood clot on his brain, though this was not diagnosed until he was 16. Gacy's father also beat him with a razor strop when he was caught fondling a girl. Nevertheless, he remained fond of his father, though he never managed to become close to him.

A congenital heart condition meant that Gacy could not play sports with other children. He was labelled a sissy and told he would probably 'grow up queer'. Later, when he realized that he was attracted to men, he was thrown into turmoil over his sexuality. His heart condition also meant that he put on a lot of weight.

Dropping out of school, he went to Las Vegas where he worked as a janitor in a funeral parlour. Returning to Chicago, he went to business school and immersed himself in community work. Then, in 1964, he married Marlynn Myers, whose parents owned a string of Kentucky Fried Chicken outlets in Waterloo and his father-in-law offered him the position of manager in one of them. His wife petitioned for divorce in 1968 after a succession of unseemly incidents and assaults.

## TAKING WHAT HE WANTED BY FORCE

Within a year of his release, Gacy had picked up another youth and tried to force him to have sex. He was arrested, but the case was dropped when the boy did not turn up at court. The police had not informed the authorities in Iowa of his arrest, so he was discharged from his parole there, too. His mother helped him to buy a house in the suburb

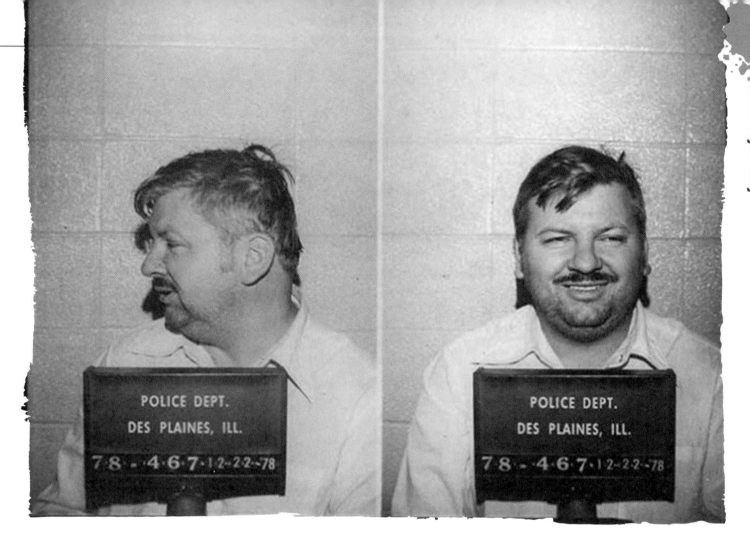

of Des Plaines, where he remarried in 1972 and set up a construction firm. Although Gacy limited his homosexual encounters to times when his wife was out of town, the strain on his marriage was too much and the couple separated in 1976.

For Gacy, sex was rarely consensual. He pulled a gun on a youth who had come to him for work, threatening to shoot him if he did not have sex. The boy called his bluff, even though Gacy said that he had killed people before. This may well have been true. According to Gacy's own account, in January 1972 he had picked up a boy at a bus terminal and killed him. Nevertheless, his young employee in this instance escaped unmolested.

Gacy then developed a simple formula to ensnare victims. He would flash what appeared to be a police

*Gacy had a troubled childhood. His father was an abusive alcoholic who beat his wife and assaulted his children.*

badge, pull a gun and tell his victim he was arresting him. Otherwise, he would invite teenage boys home, ply them with alcohol and then introduce them to his 'magic handcuffs'. Once manacled, he would sexually abuse his victims over a number of days. When he tired of his captives, he murdered them and buried them in the crawlspace underneath his house.

In 1977, Gacy was accused of sexually abusing a youth at gunpoint. Gacy admitted to having participated in brutal sex, but claimed that the boy had been a willing partner and was now trying to blackmail him. He was released with a caution.

*John Wayne Gacy was a pillar of his community and entertained audiences as Pogo the Clown, but lurking beneath this jolly exterior was something more sinister.*

By this time, Gacy was a successful contractor and a leading light in the local Democratic Party and was even photographed with the First Lady, Rosalynn Carter. And he entertained at children's parties, appearing as Pogo the Clown. He also hung out at notorious gay bars, picking up male prostitutes and ex-jailbirds as well as teenage runaways.

Gacy got tired of digging holes in his crawlspace, though there was a pressing need for more room to bury his victims. He hired one of his employees named David Cram to do the digging for him. Cram also stayed in the spare bedroom in his boss's house. One night, Cram came home from work and found Gacy drunk and in his clown costume. They had a few drinks and then Gacy tricked Cram into putting on his handcuffs. Gacy then turned nasty. He began spinning Cram around the room screaming: 'I'm going to rape you.' But Cram managed to push Gacy

over, grabbed the key to the handcuffs and escaped.

Others also survived. In December 1977, Gacy abducted Robert Donnelly at gunpoint, tortured and sodomized him at his home, then let him go. Three months later, he picked up 27-year-old Jeffrey Rignall at one of his hangouts. He invited the young man to share a drink in his car. Once inside the sleek black Oldsmobile, Gacy held a rag soaked with chloroform over Rignall's face. When Rignall woke up, he was naked and strapped to a homemade rack in Gacy's basement. Gacy was also naked and showed Rignall a number of whips and more sinister sexual devices, explaining how he intended to use them. Gacy also told Rignall that he was a policeman and would shoot him if he raised any objection.

He beat his defenceless victim mercilessly. The abuse and torture went on for hours. At times, it was so painful that Rignall begged to be allowed to die. Gacy would chloroform him again, then wait until he came around before he began the torture all over again. Eventually, Rignall said that if Gacy let him go he would leave town and tell no one what had happened. He blacked out again, and woke up fully dressed by a lake in Chicago's Lincoln Park. There was money in his pocket but his driver's licence was missing.

In hospital, it was discovered that he was bleeding from the anus. His face was burnt and his liver was damaged by the chloroform. The police were sympathetic, but had little to go on. Rignall could not give them the name, address or licence plate of his assailant. But Rignall was determined. He rented a car and drove the route he thought Gacy had taken him, which he vaguely remembered through a haze of chloroform. Eventually, he found the expressway turn-off Gacy had taken. Waiting there, he struck lucky when Gacy's black Oldsmobile swept by. He noted down the licence plate number and followed the car to where it parked in the driveway of 8213 West Summerdale Avenue. Rignall even checked the land registry and found that the house belonged to John Wayne Gacy. Then he took the information to the police.

When they followed up on Rignall's leads, the Chicago Police Department found that Gacy's suburban home was just outside their jurisdiction, meaning they could not press felony charges against him. However, Gacy agreed to give Rignall $3,000 towards his medical bills and the matter was dropped. Despite this brush with the law, Gacy did not give up his campaign of abduction, sexual abuse and murder.

# ATTRACTING THE AUTHORITIES' ATTENTION

In December 1978, Mrs Elizabeth Piest reported to the local police that her 15-year-old son Robert was missing. She had gone to collect him from the pharmacy where he had a part-time job, but Robert asked her to wait as he was going to visit a contractor who had promised him a summer job. He did not return and his parents spent the rest of the night driving around the streets looking for him, before reporting his disappearance.

The pharmacist told the police that the contractor concerned might have been John Gacy, who had recently refurbished his shop. The local police then phoned Gacy, but he denied all knowledge of the missing boy. Robert Piest was, in fact, lying dead on Gacy's bed as they spoke. Checking the records, the police discovered Gacy's earlier conviction for sodomy. They went to see him, but Gacy refused to come down to the precinct to discuss the matter and the police realized that they had no charge on which to hold him.

Instead, they put Gacy's house under 24-hour surveillance. Nevertheless, Gacy managed to put Piest's body in a trunk and smuggled it out to his car. He jumped behind the wheel and raced off at high speed, leaving the police standing. Having lost his tail, Gacy drove down to the nearby Des Plaines River, where he dumped Piest's body.

The police finally managed to get a search warrant, which was difficult as there was so little evidence to go on. In the house they found a receipt from the chemist for a roll of film made out to Kim Beyers, Robert's girlfriend. Although this wasn't enough to arrest Gacy, it was enough to justify putting him under further 24-hour surveillance. Meanwhile, checking back through the records in both Illinois and Iowa, they found details of his previous sexual offences.

Gacy must have thought he was untouchable and figured he could bluff this way through. He filed a civil lawsuit of $750,000 against the city of Des Plaines, alleging illegal search and seizure, harassment and slander. Then, one morning, he invited in two of the cops stationed outside his house for breakfast. As they sat down to eat, the policemen noticed a peculiar smell. Gacy had inadvertently switched off the pump that drained the basement. Water flowing under the house disturbed the soil where Gacy had buried 29 of his victims over the years and now the stench came up.

Armed with another warrant, the police discovered a trapdoor in the floor of a cupboard. When they opened it, they reeled back from the smell of rotting flesh that rose from the crawlspace below. A brief examination revealed a mass of human remains in a sea of stinking black mud. Gacy was immediately arrested and charged with murder.

# INFAMY AND CELEBRITY

Sixteen bodies were found in the crawlspace, while another 11 had been buried in the ground around the house. Four more bodies – including Robert Piest's – were found in the Des Plaines River. Eight of them have never been identified. The youngest of his victims was nine; the oldest were full-grown men. John Wayne Gacy admitted killing 33 young men and boys over the previous seven years after having forced them to have sex with him. He was tried for mass murder in 1980.

One of those who testified against him was Jeffrey Rignall. His testimony did not last very long because he broke down while telling the court the details of his rape and torture. Rignall was so upset that he began to vomit and cry hysterically and was eventually removed from the courtroom. Gacy

*The body count grows as investigators carry another corpse from Gacy's house. He was convicted of 33 murders and sentenced to death, but had to wait 14 years before the penalty could be carried out.*

*Gacy began painting on Death Row. This far from benign image was auctioned after his execution.*

exhibited no sign of emotion throughout Rignall's harrowing account.

The defence sought to show that Gacy was insane. The jury disagreed and convicted Gacy of the murder of 33 young men. He was given 12 death sentences and 21 whole life sentences.

Despite his known homosexuality, on death row Gacy received fan mail from women. He studied law books and filed numerous appeals. Though he had confessed, Gacy later denied his guilt and set up a premium-rate telephone number that featured a 12-minute recorded statement declaring his innocence.

While imprisoned at the Menard Correctional Center, Gacy took up studying the visual arts. His paintings were shown to the public in an exhibition at a Chicago gallery. Many of his pictures depict him in costume as Pogo the Clown. Others depict fellow serial killers Ed Gein and Jeffery Dahmer. Gacy was allowed to profit from their sale, with one painting fetching nearly $10,000. Some people bought his pictures with the sole intention of destroying them.

In October 1993, Gacy's final appeal was thrown out by the US Supreme Court and his death sentence was set for 10 May 1994. Gacy's last meal included a bucket of Kentucky Fried Chicken. Prison officers said he was 'chatty... talking up a storm'. In the press interview shortly before his execution, Gacy told a reporter: 'There's been 11 hardback books on me, 31 paperbacks, two screenplays, one movie, one off-Broadway play, five songs, and over 5,000 articles. What can I say about it?' Even though he was

contributing to one more article, he quickly added: 'I have no ego for any of this garbage.'

Gacy was executed by lethal injection just after midnight on 10 May. His last words were 'Kiss my ass.' The following month, 25 of his paintings were burnt on a bonfire at an event in Naperville, just outside Chicago, attended by family members of nine of his victims.

Gacy's house at 8213 West Summerdale Avenue in Norwood Park, just east of Chicago's O'Hare International Airport, was torn apart in 1978 in an effort to find more evidence. The following year the site was cleared. One demolition worker said: 'If the devil's alive, he lived here.'

The empty lot attracted ghost hunters and other ghouls. A new house was built on the site, but it still attracted tourists and the occasional TV crew. A neighbour said: 'If you've got two guys in a car, or an out-of-state plate, it's probably Gacy.'

# TED BUNDY

Ted Bundy had the power to charm women. Many of them paid with their lives. He claimed his sexual impulses were so strong that there was no way he could control them. During his first attacks, he maintained that he had to wrestle with his conscience. But soon he began to desensitize himself. He claimed not to have tortured his victims, but said that he had had to kill them after he had raped them to prevent them from identifying him.

Bundy had been a compulsive masturbator from an early age and later became obsessed by sadistic pornography. After glimpsing a girl undressing through a window, he also became an obsessional Peeping Tom. His long-time girlfriend Meg Anders described how he would tie her up with stockings before anal sex. This sex game stopped when he almost strangled her. For years, they maintained a more or less normal sexual relationship, while Bundy exercised his craving for total control with anonymous victims, whom he often strangled during the sexual act.

## BIZARRE LEANINGS

His attitude to sex was often ambivalent. Although he desired the bodies of attractive young women, he would leave their vaginas stuffed with twigs and dirt and sometimes sodomize them with objects such as aerosol cans.

Some of the bodies, though partly decomposed, were found with freshly washed hair and newly applied make-up, indicating that he had kept them for necrophilia. In only one case did he admit to deliberately terrorizing his victim – or rather victims. He kidnapped two girls at once so that he could rape each of them in front of the other, before killing them.

*Bundy always protested his innocence, right up to his execution.*

# RANDOM ATTACK

Bundy's first victim was Sharon Clarke of Seattle. He had broken into her apartment while she was asleep and smashed her around the head with a metal rod. She suffered a shattered skull, but survived. She could not identify her attacker and no motivation for the attack has been given.

Then young women began to disappear from the University of Washington campus nearby. Six vanished within seven months. At the Lake Sammamish resort in Washington State, a number of young women reported being approached by a young man calling himself Ted. He had his arm in a sling and asked them to help get his sailboat off his car. But in the parking lot they found that there was no boat on the car. Ted then said that they would have to go to his house to get it. Sensibly, most declined. Janice Ott seems to have agreed to go with him though. She disappeared. A few hours later, Denise Naslund also disappeared from the same area. She had been seen in the company of a good-looking, dark-haired young man who fitted Ted Bundy's description. The remains of Janice Ott, Denise Naslund and another unidentified young woman were later found on waste land, where they had been eaten and scattered by animals.

Witnesses at the University of Washington came forward, saying that they had seen a man wearing a sling. Some other bodies were found, again disposed of on waste ground.

# TOO MANY LEADS

The police had two suspects. Ex-convict Gary Taylor had been picked up by the Seattle police for abducting women under false pretences. Then there was park attendant Warren Forrest, who had picked up a young woman who consented to pose for him. He took her to a secluded part of the park, tied her up and stripped her naked. He taped her mouth and fired darts at her breasts. Then he raped her, strangled her and left her for dead. But she survived and identified her attacker. Both were in custody though, and the attacks continued. Bundy's girlfriend called anonymously, giving his name, but the tip-off was overlooked among the thousands of other leads the police had to follow up.

# CASTING HIS NET WIDER

Bundy began to travel further afield. On 2 October 1974, he abducted Nancy Wilcox after she left an all-night party. He raped and strangled Melissa Smith, daughter of the local police chief. Her body was found near Salt Lake City. He took Laura Aimee from a Halloween party in Orem, Utah. Her naked body was found at the bottom of a canyon.

In Salt Lake City a week later, he approached a girl named Carol DaRonch. Bundy pretended to be a detective and asked her for the licence number of her car. Someone had tried to break into it, he said. He asked her to accompany him to help identify the suspect. She got into his car, but once they were in a quiet street he handcuffed her.

She began to scream. He put a gun to her head. She managed to get out of the door and Bundy chased after her with a crowbar. He took a swing at her skull, but she managed to grab the crowbar. A car was coming down the street. Carol jumped in front of it, forcing it to stop. She jumped in and the car drove away.

Carol gave a good description to the police, but Bundy continued undeterred. He tried to pick up a young French teacher outside her high school. She declined to go with him. But Debbie Kent did. She disappeared from a school playground where a key to a pair of handcuffs was later found.

## FURTHER ATTACKS

The following January in Snowmass Village, a Colorado ski resort, Dr Raymond Gadowsky found that his fiancée, Caryn Campbell, was missing from her room. A month later, her naked body was found in the snow. She had been raped and her skull had been smashed in. Julie Cunningham vanished from nearby Vail and the remains of Susan Rancourt and Brenda Bell were also found on Taylor Mountain.

The body of Melanie Cooley was found only about ten miles from her home. Unlike the other victims, she was still clothed, though her jeans had been undone, convincing the police that the motive was sexual.

The Colorado attacks continued with Nancy Baird, who disappeared from a petrol station, and Shelley Robertson, whose naked body was found down a mine shaft.

## BAD BREAK FOR BUNDY

A Salt Lake City patrol man was cruising an area of the city that had recently suffered a spate of burglaries. He noticed Bundy's car driving slowly and indicated that he should pull over. Instead, Bundy sped off. The patrolman gave chase and caught up with him. In his car were found maps and brochures of Colorado. Some coincided with the places girls had disappeared.

Forensic experts found a hair in Bundy's car that matched that of Melissa Smith. A witness also recognized Bundy from Snowmass Village. He was charged and extradited to Colorado to stand trial. However, few people could believe that such an intelligent and personable young man could be responsible for these terrible sex attacks, even though Carol DaRonch picked him out of a line-up.

Bundy was given permission to conduct his own defence. He was even allowed to use the law library for research. There he managed to give his guard the slip, jumped from a window and escaped. He was recaptured a week later.

Bundy still protested his innocence and managed to prolong the pre-trial hearings with a number of skilful stalling manoeuvres. Using the time he gained to lose weight, he cut a small hole under the light fitting in the ceiling of his cell. He squeezed through the one-foot-square hole he had made and got clean away.

## SHOCKING VIOLENCE

He travelled around America before settling in Tallahassee, Florida, a few blocks from the sorority houses of Florida State University. One evening, Nita Neary saw a man lurking in front of her sorority house. She was about to phone the police when a fellow student, Karen Chandler, staggered from her room with blood streaming from her head. She was screaming that she had just been attacked by a madman. Her roommate Kathy Kleiner had also been attacked. Her jaw was broken. Margaret Bowman had been attacked sexually and strangled with her own pantyhose.

Lisa Levy had also been sexually assaulted. Bundy had bitten one of her nipples off and left teeth marks in her buttocks. Then he beat her around the head.

She died on the way to hospital. In another building, Cheryl Thomas had also been viciously attacked, but she survived.

The police had only a sketchy description of the attacker. But Bundy had plainly got a taste for killing again. While making his getaway, he abducted 12-year-old Kimberly Leach, sexually assaulted her, strangled her, mutilated her sexual organs and dumped her body in the Suwannee River Park.

## DESPERATE MEASURES

Bundy was now short of money. He stole some credit cards and a car, and sneaked out of his apartment where he owed back rent. But the stolen car was a giveaway. He was stopped by a motorcycle cop and arrested. At the police station, he admitted that he was Ted Bundy and that he was wanted by the Colorado police.

*Ted Bundy reacts to news of his death sentence.*

*Victim of Ted Bundy, 12-year-old Kimberly Leach.*

The Florida police began to tie him in with the Tallahassee attack. When they tried to take an impression of his teeth, he went berserk. It took six men to hold his jaw open. The impression matched the teeth marks on murdered student Lisa Levy's buttocks.

Again Bundy conducted his own defence, skilfully using the law to prolong the court case and his personality to charm the jury. But the evidence of the teeth marks was too strong. He was found guilty of murder and sentenced to death. At 7 am on 24 January 1989, Bundy went to the electric chair. He is said to have died with a smile on his face. On death row, Bundy made a detailed confession. He also received sacks full of mail from young women whose letters dwelt on cruel and painful ways to make love. Even on death row, he had not lost his fatal charm.

# GARY RIDGWAY

On 15 July 1982, two boys riding their bicycles around Kent, Washington, peered into the waters of the picturesque Green River. There, caught on a snag, was the body of a woman, naked but for a pair of jeans wrapped tightly around her neck. It was the body of 16-year-old Wendy Lee Coffield, the first official victim of a terrifying sexual predator who became known as the Green River Killer.

Gary Ridgway was born in 1949 in Salt Lake City, Utah. The middle child in a family of three boys, he struggled at school and his childhood was marked by his domineering and violent mother. At the age of 13, he was still a bed-wetter. His father drove a city bus and regularly voiced his vehement disapproval of the prostitutes who worked along his route – an attitude his son Gary was also to adopt.

By 1980, Ridgway had already clocked up two failed marriages and had begun to frequent prostitutes along the very strip his father used to drive. He was arrested on soliciting charges on a number of occasions, and was once accused of having tried to choke a prostitute.

In July and August 1982, five females aged between 16 and 31 were found in or near the mouth of the Green River. Most were prostitutes; all had

*Gary Ridgway was found to have an IQ of just 82. As a boy he was a bed-wetter and his mother used to belittle him in front of his family.*

been raped and strangled to death. The police wasted no time in linking the deaths and pronouncing them the work of a serial killer. By April 1983, the body count had risen to 20.

That summer, a dozen or so more women disappeared. Under mounting pressure, and inundated with tips, the police team solicited advice from all quarters, including serial killer Ted Bundy, who from his prison cell helped to form a profile of the Green River Killer.

It was all to no avail. Months, then years, passed, with more women meeting brutal deaths. Ridgway, one of numerous individuals of interest to the police, was twice given polygraph tests, in 1984 and 1986. He passed both. In 1987, his house was searched and

DECEASED

GREEN RIVER VICTIMS

*Police Lieutenant Dan Nolan stands beside a display of the Green River Killer's victims, many of whom were left in the forest and picked clean by scavengers. Ridgway may have killed many more women than he was arraigned for.*

a DNA sample taken. After police searched his locker at work, co-workers joked that he was 'Green River Gary'. No one gave any serious thought to the notion that he might be the serial killer.

By 1986, the killing seemed to have stopped. Bodies were still being found, but the victims had died several years earlier. By 1991, the police unit investigating the case had been reduced to a single person. The case was all but dormant. But new DNA testing methods led to a breakthrough in 2001. A connection was made between semen found on the bodies of several of the victims, and the DNA taken from Ridgway in 1987. He was arrested and charged with the murders of Marcia Chapman, Cynthia Hinds, Opal Mills and Carol Ann Christensen, four of the women whose bodies had been found with his DNA.

On 5 November 2003, Gary Ridgway pleaded guilty to the aggravated first-degree murder of 48 women. His plea was part of a bargain to spare him the death penalty. He also agreed to cooperate in locating the remains of his victims.

Ridgway claimed that all of his victims had been killed in and around the Seattle area, though he disposed of some of them elsewhere in an attempt to confuse police. He also admitted to occasionally contaminating the dump sites with gum, cigarettes and written materials that belonged to others, to throw investigators off the scent. He confessed to killing 44 women between 1982 and 1984, but claimed to have killed only four thereafter – in 1986, 1987, 1990 and 1998.

Ridgway was given 48 life sentences. Since sentencing, he has confessed to yet more murders – a total of 71, although some speculate the true figure is closer to 150. It was a price, he claimed, worth paying for the betterment of society:

'I killed so many women I have a hard time keeping them straight. I wanted to kill as many women that I thought were prostitutes as I possibly could.'

*Green River killer Gary Ridgway cries in court as he listens to testimony from relatives of his victims. Devoted husband Ridgway avoided the death penalty by agreeing to help police find the bodies of those who were still missing.*

# ANDREI CHIKATILO

Even as the USSR retreats into history, there is something almost surreal in the grouping of the words 'Soviet serial killer'. Rightly or wrongly, the phenomenon often seems so much a symptom of the West. How incredible, then, that a serial killer from the Soviet Union was more prolific and, one might claim, more sadistic than any of his Western contemporaries. Andrei Chikatilo is thought to have raped and killed at least 52 people of both sexes. He mutilated their bodies, often in ways reminiscent of Jack the Ripper.

Andrei Romanovich Chikatilo was born on 16 October 1936 in Yablochnoye, a village in what is now Ukraine. As a child he suffered terribly, growing up with the after-effects of the Ukrainian famine. His mother often told him a story that he'd had an older brother, Stepan, who had been kidnapped and then consumed by starving neighbours.

No documentary evidence supports the existence of this sibling.

After the Soviet Union entered the Second World War, when he was 4, his father went off to fight. Chikatilo was left alone with his mother, sharing her bed each night. A chronic bed-wetter, he was beaten for each offence. As the war progressed, he was witness to the Nazi occupation and the massive devastation and death caused by German bombing raids. Dead bodies, not an uncommon sight, were things he found both frightening and exciting.

The end of the war brought little happiness to the Chikatilo household. His father, who had spent much of the conflict as a prisoner of war, was transferred to a Russian prison camp.

## OUTSIDER

Awkward and overly-sensitive, Chikatilo withdrew from other children. He was considered a good student, but failed his entrance exam to Moscow State University. In 1960, after finishing his compulsory military service, he found work as a telephone engineer. It was during this period that Chikatilo, now 23 years old, attempted his first relationship with a woman. He found himself unable to perform sexually, a humiliation that his prospective girlfriend spread among his acquaintances. As a result, he developed elaborate fantasies of revenge in which he would capture the woman and tear her apart.

When Chikatilo married, in 1963, it was through the work of his younger sister, who made the arrangement with one of her friends. He suffered from chronic impotence, yet managed to father a son and daughter.

Late in life it was discovered that he had suffered brain damage at birth, which affected his ability to control his bladder and seminal emissions.

In 1971, after completing a degree in Russian literature through a correspondence course, he managed to get a teaching position at a local school. Though a poor instructor, Chikatilo continued in the profession for nearly a decade, often dodging accusations that he had molested his students.

In 1978, having accepted a new teaching position, Chikatilo moved to Shakhty. Living alone, waiting until his family could join him, he began to fantasize about naked children. Chikatilo bought a hut off a shabby side street from which he would spy on children as they played, all the while indulging in his solitary practices. Three days before Christmas, he managed to lure a 9-year-old girl, Yelena Zabotnova, into his lair. He had intended to rape the girl, but found himself unable to achieve an erection. He then grabbed a knife and began stabbing her, ejaculating in the process. He later disposed of the girl's body by dumping it into the Grushovka River. Chikatilo was a suspect in the crime; several witnesses had seen him with the girl and blood was discovered

on his doorstep. However, another man, Alexsandr Kravchenko, confessed to the murder under torture. Kravchenko was subsequently executed.

Chikatilo's good luck did not transfer to his new school. In 1981, he was dismissed after molesting boys in the school dormitory. Through his membership of the Communist party, he was soon given a position as a supply clerk at a nearby factory.

Though he did not kill again until the 3 September 1981 murder of Larisa Tkachenko, Chikatilo had begun a series of murders that lasted until the month of his capture, 12 years later.

Chikatilo most often preyed on runaways and prostitutes who he found at railway and bus stations. Enticing his victims with the promise of cigarettes, alcohol, videos or money, he would lead them into nearby forests. The corpse of one young female runaway, discovered in 1981, is typical of the horrific scenes Chikatilo would leave behind. Covered by a newspaper, she was lacking her sexual organs. One breast was left bloody by a missing nipple. Chikatilo later admitted that he had bitten and swallowed it, an act which caused him to ejaculate involuntarily.

His male victims, all of whom ranged in age from eight to 16, were treated in a different manner. It was Chikatilo's fantasy that each was being held prisoner for some undisclosed crime.

He would torture them, all the while fantasizing that he was a hero for doing so. Chikatilo would offer no explanation as to why, more often than not, he would remove the penis and tongue while his victim was still alive.

Many of his early victims had their eyes cut out, an act performed in the belief that they would provide

*Chikatilo always professed his guilt once he was captured.*

*The body of Tanya Petrosan, 32, who was murdered in 1984.*

One story had it that boys and girls were being mauled by a werewolf. It was not until August 1984, after Chikatilo had committed his 30th murder, that the first news story was printed in the local party daily.

## SUSPICIOUS BEHAVIOUR

On 14 September 1984, there was a break in the case when an undercover officer spotted Chikatilo approaching various young women at the Rostov bus station. When questioned, Chikatilo explained that, as a former schoolteacher, he missed speaking with young people. The explanation did nothing to allay suspicions and the officer continued to trail Chikatilo. Eventually, the former teacher approached a prostitute and, after having received oral sex, was picked up by the police. His briefcase, when searched, was found to contain a kitchen knife, a towel, a rope and a jar of petroleum jelly.

So certain were the authorities that they had their serial killer that the prosecutor was asked to come and interrogate Chikatilo. However, any celebration was cut short when it was discovered that Chikatilo's blood type did not match that of the semen found on the victims' bodies. This discrepancy, which has never been satisfactorily explained, is most often considered the result of a clerical error. After two days, Chikatilo was released, having admitted to nothing more than soliciting a prostitute.

There is the possibility that Chikatilo would have remained under interrogation for a longer period had it not been for the fact that he was a member of the Communist party.

a snapshot of his face. The practice all but stopped when, upon investigation, Chikatilo realized this to be an old wives' tale.

There can be little doubt that Chikatilo was greatly aided in his crimes by the state-controlled media of his time. No-one knew what was going on. Reports of crimes like rape and serial murder were uncommon, and seemed invariably to be associated with what was portrayed as the hedonistic West.

While close to 600 detectives and police officers worked on the case, staking out bus and train stations, and interrogating suspects, those living in the areas where the bodies were found were entirely unaware that there might be a serial killer in their midst. Still, with over half a million people having been investigated, there were bound to be rumours.

*Police photographs of Chikatilo carrying the black bag which contained the knives used on his victims.*

This association would quickly come to an end weeks after his near-capture when he was arrested and charged with petty theft from his workplace. Chikatilo was expelled by the party and sentenced to three months in prison.

After his release, Chikatilo found new work in Novocherkassk. His killing began again in August 1985 and remained irregular for several years. By 1988, however, he seemed to have returned to his old ways, murdering at least nine people.

And yet it appears he took no life during the calendar year that followed. In 1990, he killed nine more people, the last being on 6 November, when he mutilated Sveta Korostik in the woods near the Leskhoz train station.

With the station under constant surveillance, Chikatilo was stopped and questioned as he emerged from the area where the body would later be discovered.

On 14 November, the day after Sveta Korostik's body was discovered, Chikatilo was arrested and interrogated. Within the next 15 days, he confessed to and described 56 murders. The number shocked the police, who had counted just 36 killings during their investigation.

## CRAZY OUTBURSTS

Chikatilo finally went to trial on 14 April 1992. Manacled, he was placed in a large iron cage in the middle of the courtroom. It had been constructed specially for the trial, primarily to protect him from the families of his victims. As the trial got under way, the mood of the accused alternated between boredom and outrage. On two occasions Chikatilo exposed himself, shouting out that he was not a homosexual.

Chikatilo's testimony was equally erratic. He denied having committed several murders to which he'd already confessed, while admitting his guilt in others which were unknown. Claiming other murders as his own seemed less bizarre than other statements. At various points Chikatilo announced that he was pregnant, that he was lactating and that he was being radiated. On the day the prosecutor was to give his closing argument, Chikatilo broke into song and had to be removed from the courtroom. When he was brought back and offered a final opportunity to speak, he remained mute.

On 14 October 1992, six months after his trial had begun, Chikatilo was found guilty of murdering 21 males and 31 females. All of the males and 14 of the females had been under the age of 18.

Throughout the trial, Chikatilo's lawyer had made repeated attempts to prove that his client was insane, but a panel of court-appointed psychiatrists dismissed the claim. An appeal having been rejected, on St Valentine's Day, 1994, Chikatilo was taken to a special soundproof room and executed with a single gunshot behind his right ear.

# ROBERT CHARLES BROWNE

In 1991, 13-year-old Heather Dawn Church was abducted from her home in Black Forest, Colorado, while she was babysitting. Two years later her skull was found in nearby mountains. Fingerprints had been found on the window ledge of her bedroom. They matched those of Robert Charles Browne, who had served time in Louisiana for car theft in 1987. When he was finally arrested in March 1995, he denied the murder, but pleaded guilty in court to avoid the death penalty. He was sentenced to life without parole and that seemed to be the end of that.

However, he sent a cryptic letter to the prosecutors. 'Seven sacred virgins, entombed side by side, those less worthy, are scattered wide,' the letter read. 'The score is you 1, the other team 48. If you were to drive to the end zone in a white Trans Am, the score could be 9 to 48.'

He attached a hand-drawn map listing numbers of victims in different states – seven in Texas, nine in Colorado, 17 in Louisiana, three in Mississippi, five in Arkansas, two each for California, Oklahoma and New Mexico, and one in Washington state. Cold-case investigators across those states went to work and found that many of his assertions were credible, though it was thought that he was claiming 49 murders in order to challenge Gary Ridgway's record.

*Robert Charles Browne admitted to at least 48 killings across the USA.*

'It's possible he's exaggerating, but I don't think you can conduct business assuming he's exaggerating,' El Paso County Sheriff Terry Maketa said. 'We'll continue to pursue leads.'

Deputies complained that Browne was taunting them, but former FBI and CIA agent Charlie Hess, a sheriff's department cold-case investigator, set up a correspondence with him.

'We started by writing a very direct letter to Robert indicating who we were,' said Hess. 'It became obvious with Robert that most things were a negotiation: If I can have a single cell I'll tell you this. If I can have this, I can give you three murders,' said Hess. 'All of the things he asked for were reasonable, within the law, within the rules of DOC [Department of Corrections].'

Hess added: 'He told me outright, "Get me a private doctor, I'll give you three murders."' Hess complied and Browne gave up details that only the killer could have known.

On 27 July 2006, Browne pleaded guilty to first-degree murder and received another life sentence for the murder of 15-year-old Rocio Delpilar Sperry on 10 November 1987 at an apartment complex in Colorado Springs. He strangled her. Afterwards, he dismembered her body in the bathtub, 'just popping' her joints apart, as he remembered. He said he had dumped her body in a rubbish bin. It was never found.

She was the wife of a soldier and the mother of a three-month-old girl. Her husband lost custody of his baby daughter after his family blamed him for the murder of his teenage wife. He later said that Browne's guilty plea had brought him a measure of peace after two decades of grief.

'Last week was the first time I had a dream about my wife,' he said. 'It was her face, and there was a bright light behind it. I woke up and I felt good. I feel I can move on.'

Heather Church's father Mike said: 'I can identify with him and I'm so very thankful for the closure that he has with his family and his daughter.'

# A YOUNG MAN WITH A SHORT FUSE

Robert Browne was born in 1952 in Coushatta, Louisiana, a town of fewer than 3,000 inhabitants some 80 km (50 miles) south-west of Shreveport. He was the youngest of nine children, including three sets of twins. His parents ran the local dairy.

'He came from a tough family,' said the sheriff. 'They came up during some hard times.'

His high school teacher said that Browne was competitive and had a temper, but wasn't too different from most kids.

'I remember him being kind of a loner, but not somebody you would expect to do this. He wasn't one that had a lot of friends, but he had friends,' he said. 'He did have a hot temper. In a pickup basketball game, if somebody fouled him or hit him, he'd fly off the handle.'

Although he had an IQ of 140, Browne dropped out of school and at the age of 17 joined the US Army and served in South Korea where, he claimed, he killed a man in a fight over a prostitute. The murder remained unverified. Serving from 1969 to 1976, he attained the rank of sergeant before being dishonourably discharged for a drug offence.

Browne had a series of six wives or 'what he would consider a wife', according to El Paso District Attorney John Newsome. All six were similar in appearance – petite, weighing between 43–57 kg (95–125 lb) – and all six were still alive when he was convicted for murder.

One of them, Rita Morgan, met Browne when she was 16 and he was still serving overseas. They exchanged letters. When they next met she was recently divorced with two boys, and in her 20s. She was working as a waitress at the Cotton Patch in Coushatta. He remembered her right away, brought her flowers and asked her out.

'He made you feel comfortable, like you knew him,' Morgan said. In 1980 she became his fourth wife, but the marriage was not a week old before he changed. 'I could just kill you, and nobody would do anything about it down here,' he told her.

The man who had once held open the car door for her would knock her down for losing a set of keys. Though he apologized and said it would never happen again, she never knew what might send him into a rage. When her father tried to talk to him, Browne told him to mind his own business, and said that he would 'do whatever I want, whenever I want'.

Rita witnessed other violence. She said she saw Browne punch his mother for refusing to give him money. He choked her so hard that she had to go to hospital, and he once pointed a gun at her head. He pulled the trigger, but the gun didn't fire.

'It's not your day, is it?' he said. Then he asked her to take the gun and shoot him.

'Do it yourself,' she said.

After a rocky marriage where they separated regularly, she left for good when he hurt her son.

'That's what did it,' she said. 'He had no concern. You might hurt me, but the day it involved my children and you're not helping me.... He never even called up to the hospital.'

They divorced in 1984 after four years of marriage. Even so, their marriage had lasted longer than his other relationships and he had been killing women while they were together. Nor was he apologetic about it.

'Women are unfaithful, they screw around a lot, they cheat, and they are not of the highest moral value,' he told detectives. 'They cheat and they are users.'

## A MAN WITHOUT A PLAN

He told investigators he rarely if ever planned a killing, choosing his prey at random. He met his victims in everyday settings – a motel bar, a restaurant, a convenience store or apartment block where he worked. He said he never just went out 'looking for someone'. His motive? 'It was just disgust with the person and some of it just confrontation.'

Investigators were confused because he used different types of guns and strangled, stabbed and sometimes beat his victims. One died after he put a rag soaked in ant killer over her face while she slept, he said. Sheriff Maketa said Browne probably got away with his crimes because he never spent much time with his victims before killing them and was adept at disposing of their bodies.

His first known victim was 15-year-old Katherine Hayes who disappeared after leaving Fausto's restaurant in Coushatta on 4 July 1980. Hayes' body was found in October in Nantachie Creek. Browne said he had taken her to a house, had sex with her and strangled her with shoelaces.

Twenty-six-year-old Faye Self was reported missing 30 March 1983 after she left the Wagon Wheel bar on Louisiana Highway 1. She said she was going to pick up her daughter and had to get home because she had work the following day. However, she left her car at the bar. Browne told authorities that he went to Self's apartment, which was next to his. He said he placed a chloroform-soaked rag over her face and left to get rope to tie her up, but she died before he could have sex with her. He said he disposed of her body in the Red River, which was near the apartment building. Her body was never found. Her daughter Tiffany was just 11 months old when her mother disappeared. She had two older children.

Twenty-one-year-old Wanda Faye Hudson was found dead on 28 May 1983, in her apartment in Coushatta. She had been restrained with an ant pesticide that contained chloroform and stabbed multiple times with a screwdriver. Browne was living in the same block and had done maintenance work on Hudson's apartment, including changing the lock on her door the day before she died. At the time, the block belonged to his brother Donald and his father Ronald was a deputy on the team investigating the murder.

Twenty-two-year-old Melody Bush was found dead on 30 March 1984, in Flatonia Fayette County, Texas. Her body was found in a drainage ditch and the coroner ruled Bush died of acute acetone poisoning. This was puzzling as acetone, used as nail polish, paint remover and drain unblocker, would normally be vomited up before a lethal dose could be ingested. The police first suspected her husband Robert. The couple had been seen drinking and arguing in the Antlers Inn's Stag Bar at the back of the hotel in Flatonia, where she was last seen. However, the police never found any evidence to link him to the killing.

Melody was barefoot and so drunk she was having trouble walking when she left the bar. Browne variously claimed he had picked her up in the bar or at the side of the road – others said she left the bar alone. He said he had taken her back to his motel room. After they had sex, Browne told Hess: 'Then I used ether on her. Put her out. And then I used an ice pick on her. She was just acting like a slutty, low-life woman.'

He then said he returned to the bar, then visited a local truck stop with a bartender to have breakfast. When he went back to his motel room, her body was still lying on the bed. He loaded her body into his van and then drove north of Flatonia and dumped the body over a bridge. Melody's body was found in a culvert five days later. Browne told investigators in Colorado that at the time of Bush's murder, he was employed as a truck driver and delivered flowers. One of his routes took him through Flatonia.

He was in Texas again on 2 February 1984 when 17-year-old Nidia Mendoza went missing. Her remains were found four days later in a ditch. Browne had cut off her head and legs using a dull butcher's knife he found in his motel kitchenette.

Investigators concluded that she had left the Dames nightclub and gone back to the Embassy Suite, where they had sex. He then strangled her and cut her up in the bath.

'Mr Browne indicated he actually dismembered the body and put the pieces in a suitcase,' said Captain Gary Cox of the Sugar Land Police Department. 'He actually walked through the hotel with the suitcase, emptied the contents into the van, then went back to the room to get the additional body parts.'

The month following the murder of Heather Church, 21-year-old Lisa Lowe was reported missing on 3 November in Arkansas. She disappeared as she was going to a club in Forrest City. She dropped off her children at their aunt's apartment, and was going to walk the three or four blocks to the club. She never arrived.

Her badly decomposed body was found on 26 November in the St Francis River. She had been strangled. She left four young children, who were raised by their grandmother and aunts. Until Browne's confession, the main suspect had been their father, though no evidence had been found linking him to her death.

Other investigations are still ongoing.

'We don't like to call them cold cases,' said Hess. 'We like to call them unresolved cases. A cold case would indicate to me a case that is put on the shelf and forgotten. We don't forget them.'

# TIAGO HENRIQUE GOMES DA ROCHA

At the age of 26, Brazilian serial killer Tiago Henrique Gomes da Rocha was arrested on 14 October 2014 after being pulled over by the police when riding a motorcycle carrying stolen licence plates. He then confessed to killing 39 people over just three years. Fifteen of them were young women who looked like his girlfriend who would often take him to the Assembly of God church where she was a member. His favourite modus operandi was to ride up on his motorbike, shout 'robbery', then shoot and flee without taking anything.

Rocha began killing in 2011. At first, he targeted homeless people, gay men and prostitutes. Asked why he selected these groups in particular, he said: 'Nobody would care about them.'

In 2014, he turned his attention to young women. His first female victim was 14-year-old Bárbara Costa, who had been waiting for her grandmother in a public square on 18 January when a man riding a motorcycle shot her in the chest.

The following day, 23-year-old Beatriz Moura was also shot by a man on a motorcycle. He once again didn't take anything. In all, he killed 15 women, aged between 13 and 29, in seven months. The murders took place in Goiânia, a city of 1.3 million people and the capital of Goiás state some 320 km (200 miles) from the country's capital, Brasilia. His last victim, Ana Lidia Gomes, was also 14. He shot her dead as she left home.

It was only in August that year that the police realized that a serial killer was at work. A task force of 150 officers was formed to track him down after the families and friends of the murdered women staged a series of demonstrations to put pressure on the police and local government. They wore white and carried photographs of the victims.

Chief Police Detective Joao Gorski then told reporters: 'I believe he is a serial killer. In the beginning, he killed at random, but by the end he had established a pattern.'

## UNABLE TO FIGHT THE KILLER WITHIN

Had Rocha not been caught, the murders would have continued. Even the Sunday before he was arrested, he had tried to kill a woman but was foiled when his gun failed to go off. The woman later identified him as her would-be assassin.

Interviewed by the newspaper *Folha de São Paulo*, he said he regretted his crimes but had been 'moved

*Tiago Henrique Gomes da Rocha claimed to have killed 39 people in Brazil.*

by a greater power'. Rocha also said he killed because of the 'fury he felt against everything', which only subsided when he murdered.

'I wanted to say that I am remorseful, that I wanted to have a chance to pay for what I've done – to ask for forgiveness,' he told *Folha*.

During the interview Rocha sat with his eyes downcast, pausing frequently and giving short answers. He avoided personal questions but confirmed that he had problems in his childhood. He was asked twice about the number of victims. The first time he refused to answer. The second time, he said only: 'No comment.'

Nor could he explain why he killed so many people, simply saying: 'It was stronger than me, I can't explain,' adding that he was feeling 'bad, very bad' about the killings. *Folha* reported that he would often drink before the killings to give himself courage. He also dehumanized his victims in his mind's eye. When speaking to the police, he would refer to them only by number in the order that he had killed them.

'All the police officers who followed the interrogation were shocked by his coldness, not only with his modus operandi but also in the way he formulated his ideas,' said the chief interrogator, Commissioner Douglas Pedrosa, of the Goiás Civil Police. 'He identified each victim by a number – number 30, number 12.'

Asked for the name of the first woman he had murdered, he answered: 'It wasn't a woman. It was a man.'

According to the police, victim number one was 16-year-old Diego Martins Mendes. In 2011, Rocha approached Diego at a bus station, believing him to be gay. He then lured the youth into undergrowth with the promise of sex. The act was never consummated, according to Rocha. Instead, he strangled Diego. His body was never found.

Rocha's next victims were two more men. One was a former co-worker, who he stabbed. The other was a man who Rocha again thought was gay.

However, Commissioner Pedrosa said Rocha remembered every detail of his many crimes with relish.

'After admitting to a murder, he would stay there for some five minutes in a catatonic state,' Pedroso said. Rocha told police he was thinking about the crime – reliving it, even. At times, he would have a smile on his face.

'After, he would give details about the place and what he was feeling,' Pedrosa said. But he was not thinking about the victim, only the action he had taken. 'He didn't have details of the faces, he had details of the violence.'

Asked what motivated him to kill, he simply said: 'I am angry with the world.'

As well as being cold during interrogation, he was visibly bothered by female police staff. When a woman walked in he 'stopped talking, said he was bothered and that he wasn't going to talk anymore,' Pedrosa said.

Nevertheless, he was determined to get things off his chest. When his lawyer, Thiago Vidal, counselled him about his right to remain silent, Rocha pounded his fists on the interrogation table and insisted: 'No, I will talk. I have to get this from inside me.'

Vidal said he was concerned that the police were applying undue pressure and left the interview room 'perplexed'.

'At first I thought the police may have coerced him into confessing to a crime he didn't commit, but he narrated with richness of detail each of the deaths,' the lawyer told *Folha*.

While Rocha talked, the lawyer read through the police report detailing the confession from the previous two days. There were no discrepancies in his retelling of his grisly tale.

'He didn't hesitate,' Vidal said. 'Everything fits.'

In jail, Rocha attempted suicide using shards from a light bulb. He was put on suicide watch and kept in handcuffs.

Police chief Eduardo Prado said: 'We're monitoring him constantly. He doesn't love himself and he's already attempted suicide. He constantly asks for dental floss when I'm with him. When you ask him if it's so he can kill himself, he just laughs sarcastically.'

At his request, Rocha was visited by his mother, an aunt and four other relatives. They described him as a quiet young man with few friends. He lived with his mother and a brother, and rarely went out to social events at night. He had never met his father.

After graduating from high school, he worked for a couple of years in a private security firm, from where he stole the .38-calibre revolver that he used in the murders. The gun was found at his mother's home. Police confirmed that the gun was linked to the murders of six women that year. In the four months before he was arrested, Rocha had worked a night security shift in a large hospital in Goiânia.

Although Rocha said he felt remorseful about his crimes, his arrest had not sated his appetite for killing. In jail, he asked the police guarding his cell if he was allowed to murder other inmates.

Police chief Prado, one of those in charge of the investigation into the slayings, said: 'He asked whether he would face trial if he killed someone else in custody. He still wants to kill. We found this attitude very strange, as well as the disjointed things he's always saying.'

# A DIFFICULT MAN TO MANAGE

His behaviour continued to puzzle his captors. During the early hours of the morning he read 40 magazines from back to front in quick succession.

'It was a curious thing that he would read from the back forwards and very quickly, as if it were a task he was being made to do, reading aloud,' said Prado. But that did not lull his jailers into a false sense of security. 'Truly, when he is transferred to a long-term prison, that prison's management will have to have a very robust and more methodical control of the situation, which is actually highly dangerous.'

After a week in custody, Rocha began to open up. He said his rage started when he was sexually abused as an 11-year-old boy. That was when his urge to kill began.

'I had an ordinary childhood until I was 11. Then I was sexually abused by a neighbour,' he said. 'After that I felt like I was nothing. In a way I'm a victim here, too.'

His rage grew through his adolescence. When he reached adulthood, it peaked.

'When I was 22, I couldn't stop myself anymore. It was like I had to do it,' he said. That was when he killed his first victim – a homeless person.

Soon, he started targeting women and girls.

'I was rejected a lot in the past, so I directed part of my anger towards women,' he said.

The killings were random. Rocha said he shot many of his victims while speeding past them on his motorcycle. Some of the women were walking home when he shot them. Others were waiting at bus stops, he said.

'My mind went blank, but I would cry later,' he said, noting that he was emotionless when he randomly selected his targets.

*Tiago Henrique Gomes da Rocha terrorized the streets of Goiânia in central Brazil.*

He also admitted stabbing prostitutes and robbing stores. Footage from one stickup in a shop had helped police identify him.

Although Rocha's lawyers still insisted he had confessed to crimes he didn't commit after police interrogated him aggressively, Rocha confirmed that he was the killer in interviews with the media.

'I want to ask forgiveness,' he said.

Speaking to Brazil's *Jornal Nacional* news programme on TV Globo, Rocha said he was motivated by 'a great anger' and that killing was the only way to get it out of his system.

'I tried to do other things to get it out, but they didn't work,' he said. 'When the thing comes you have to do it. There's no way of explaining it.'

Speaking at a news conference, Chief of Police Deusny Aparecido said Rocha 'felt anger at everything and everyone. He had no link to any of his victims and chose them at random. It could have been me, you or your children.'

Despite his confession, Rocha was tried separately for each murder. The first conviction came on 16 February 2016. It was for the murder of 15-year-old student Ana Karla Lemes da Silva, who was shot in the chest. He was sentenced to 20 years.

On 2 March 2016 he was convicted of the murder of 22-year-old administrative assistant Juliana Neubia Dias. The young woman was killed while in a car with her boyfriend and a friend. Sentence: 20 years.

The third conviction, for another 20 years, was for the murder of 17-year-old Ana Rita de Lima. Then 20 more for the murder of 16-year-old student Arlete dos Anjos Carvalho. Then he got 22 years for the murder of 15-year-old Carla Barbosa Araújo in front of her older sister.

The murder of 14-year-old Bárbara Luíza Ribeiro Costa, shot in the chest while sitting in a car, earned him another 25 years. A further 25 years was handed down for the murder of 51-year-old photographer Mauro Nunes. During the sentence, the victim's son landed two punches on the defendant. Yet another 25 years was given for shooting 13-year-old Taynara Rodrigues da Cruz in the back.

Fourteen-year-old student Ana Lidia Gomes was shot four times on 2 August 2014 at a bus stop on her way to meet her mother. Sentence: 26 years. Twenty-three-year-old butcher Adailton dos Santos Farias was murdered in July 2014. Sentence: 25 years. Twenty-four-year-old journalist Janaína Nicácio de Souza was murdered in a bar. Sentence: 25 years and six months. Twenty-eight-year-old housewife Lilian Sissi was murdered as she left to pick up her children from school. Another 25 years.

The jail time continued to mount, month by month, until his 33rd trial on 20 September 2018, when Tiago Henrique Gomes da Rocha was sentenced to 21 years in prison for the murder of 26-year-old receptionist Bruna Gleycielle de Souza Gonçalves, who was killed at a bus stop on 8 May 2014. Altogether, the sentences came to more than 600 years.

In addition to the killings, the court sentenced him to 12 years and four months for twice robbing the same lottery agency. He was also sentenced to three years in prison for the illegal possession of a gun. On appeal this was reduced to a fine and a term of community service, though it is not clear how he will find the time to do that.

# EVIL WOMEN

While the stereotype of the serial killer is that of a lonely, antisocial man, women can prove just as deadly in their own right. Nearly one-fifth of all serial killers are female and their crimes can be even more gruesome and horrific than their male counterparts. That's why they call them deadlier than the male.

# NANCY 'NANNIE' DOSS

hen she became famous – or infamous – 'Nannie', or Nancy, Doss was 47 years old. She was not an old woman by any means, yet in Eisenhower's America she became known as 'the Giggling Granny'. It was a misleading nickname, because it hid a past that included a good deal of drinking, fraud, sexual promiscuity and murder.

Nancy Hazle, later Doss, was born in Blue Mountain, Alabama on 4 November 1905. Her parents were farmers. She experienced a childhood that was anything but pleasant because her irritable father forced her to spend most of her out of school hours working on the farm. Not only that, the daily grind of chores was accompanied by poverty. The biggest thrill of her early life came at the age of seven, when

*Grandmotherly pride: Nannie Doss' public image hid her dark secret for many years.*

she and her family boarded a train to visit a relative in another part of Alabama. However, this small vacation would be marred by an accident. When the train made an emergency stop Nannie was flung forward and hit her head on the iron bars of the seat in front. She claimed that she experienced blackouts for several months afterwards, followed by a lifetime of severe headaches. Later on, she would blame her murderous behaviour on this incident.

Nannie's contact with the opposite sex was limited to the classroom, because her father, James Hazle, did not want his daughters to get any romantic ideas. He feared that he would lose the bulk of his workforce if his daughters got married. So anything that might attract male attention was outlawed, including cosmetics, pleasing hairstyles and flattering dresses. He also forbade his daughters to attend any social gatherings.

Then in 1921, at the age of 15, Nannie went to work at the Linen Thread Company. No doubt her father thought the factory job would be good for the family, bringing in some badly needed money. However, it meant that James could no longer keep an eye on his daughter. She soon met a handsome local boy named Charley Braggs. When she brought him home to meet her parents, James must have realized that Nannie would one day get married. With such an attractive daughter matrimony was inevitable. In any case, Charley was a cut above most of the boys out there. For one thing, he doted on his mother, whom he supported through his work at the Linen Thread Company. That sort of filial devotion would certainly have appealed to James.

The couple were married four days after their first meeting. They moved in with Charley's mother. Nannie found her new mother-in-law a challenge right from the very beginning. She was a demanding woman who manipulated the couple by feigning ill-health. Young as she was, Nannie was forced to stay in at night in order to play cards with her mother-in-law at the kitchen table.

## CLANDESTINE OUTINGS

Two years into the marriage, when she was just 17 years old, Nannie gave birth to her first child, a daughter she named Melvina. By 1927, she was the mother of three more daughters. There was little chance of a social life for Nannie. She had to stay at home with her young children and her ageing mother-in-law. It is not surprising, then, that the young woman turned to drink. She began sneaking out to the local bars, where she enjoyed the attention of a variety of men. These clandestine outings were pretty easy to organize – Charley, the man who doted on his mother, had little time for his wife. He, too, was enjoying sexual dalliances with a number of partners. He would often disappear for days on end. However, these excursions were detrimental to his marriage and the family's finances.

In 1927, Nannie gave birth to her fourth child, Florine. Not long afterwards the two middle Bragg girls suddenly died. Seemingly healthy in the early morning, both were dead by noon. Though the deaths appeared suspicious the authorities took no action – but Charley suspected foul play. He left Nannie, taking Melvina with him. Months passed without any word from Charley, so when his mother died Nannie had no way of contacting him. Then suddenly, a little more than a year after he had disappeared, Charley came back. Melvina was with him, but so too was the woman with whom he had been living. Nannie was soon sent packing, together with Melvina and Florine. Her only option was to move back to her parents' house. She then took a job at a cotton mill. While Nannie's father might not have been very pleased with the situation, her mother enjoyed caring for her two granddaughters.

As always, Nannie enjoyed the attention she received from her male workmates. However, she set her sights higher when it came to matrimony. She began fishing for prospects by responding to personal advertisements that had been placed in the local newspaper. By this means she hooked a 23-year-old named Frank Harrelson. Like the men she came into contact with on a daily basis, he was a factory worker. What set him apart from the others was an element of sophistication – he wrote poetry – and his movie star good looks.

Nannie married Frank in 1929, after a brief courtship. She then moved to Jacksonville, Frank's home town, with her daughters. This might have been the stormiest of her five marriages, but it was also the longest. For 16 years Nannie put up with physical abuse and her husband's alcoholism, while she was struggling to raise Melvina and Florine. It probably came as something of a relief when both girls got married at a young age – at least they were out of the house.

## BECOMING A GRANDMOTHER

In 1943, at the age of 37, Nannie became a grandmother. Melvina had given birth to a son, Robert. Two years later, her eldest daughter went into labour for the second time. It was not an easy delivery, but Nannie sat at her bedside throughout the birth. She wiped her daughter's brow and provided words of encouragement. After enduring many hours of great pain, the expectant mother finally gave birth to a daughter.

Exhausted by the ordeal, Melvina's husband fell asleep in a chair close to the bed, while the new mother drifted in and out of consciousness. Their rest was broken when the baby girl died in Nannie's arms, less than an hour after her birth. The infant's death seemed such a mystery. Despite the difficult delivery, the newborn had appeared healthy and strong. That said, Melvina remembered having had some sort of vision while she had been in her semi-conscious state. Nannie had stuck a hatpin in the baby's head. Had it been a dream? A hallucination? Surely her mind had been playing tricks on her. Six months later, Melvina's son, Robert, also died under mysterious circumstances. He had been staying with Nannie at the time. Robert's death was recorded as asphyxia, though no one was ever able to determine the exact cause. A few months later, the grieving grandmother received $500 from a life insurance policy she had taken out on her grandson.

Only weeks later, in August 1945, Nannie's husband Frank also died. His final hours were spent in considerable pain, as one might expect – he had consumed a quantity of rat poison. Frank's widow was not a single woman for very long. It is quite possible that she married a man named Hendrix within a year of Frank's death. While the truth about Mr Hendrix remains unknown, Nannie certainly married Arlie Lanning, a labourer, in 1947.

For some reason Nannie appears to have been attracted to alcoholics and womanizers. Charley and Frank had both fitted this description and Arlie carried on with the tradition.

Needless to say, Nannie's latest marriage was no better than her previous failed attempts at wedded

*Widowed again: Nannie pictured beside the casket of her third husband Arlie, who died mysteriously in 1950.*

bliss. Leaving Arlie to drink himself into a stupor, Nannie would disappear from their Lexington, Kentucky, home for weeks at a time, often visiting sickly relatives.

The caring, generous Nannie became a well-respected and well-liked figure. She joined the Lexington Methodist Church and became a dedicated member of its ladies' auxiliary. Parishioners had a great deal of sympathy for Nannie. The poor soul was married to a man who drank and slept around. No one would ever have suspected that this generous caring woman had once behaved in much the same way. Arlie died of suspected heart failure in February 1950. He had been bedridden during the last days of his life, when he had displayed mysterious flu-like symptoms.

Two months later, tragedy again befell the 44-year-old widow. The house in which she and her late husband had spent their wedded lives had burned down. If there was any luck to be found it lay in the fact that Nannie had left the house just moments before the fire, taking her expensive television set with her.

According to Arlie's will, the house should have been inherited by his sister. However, Arlie's final wish did not prevent Nannie from cashing the insurance cheque for herself.

Bad fortune appeared to follow Nannie right through the first half of 1950. Now homeless, she moved in with Arlie's mother, but the old woman soon died. After that, she left Lexington behind for the small Alabama city of Gadsden, where she dedicated herself to the care of her ailing sister, Dovie. Despite

Nannie's care, though, the bedridden woman was dead by the end of June.

On the hunt for a new husband, Nannie turned to a new source, the Diamond Circle Club, a company catering to the lovelorn. After paying her $15 annual fee, the middle-aged widow started to receive monthly newsletters containing lists of prospective spouses. She settled on Richard L. Morton, a retired businessman from Emporia, Kansas. Tall, dark, handsome, and more than willing to flash the cash, Richard looked like the perfect partner. In October 1952 Nannie and Richard were married. Nannie realized the truth about her latest man just weeks after the wedding ring had been slipped on to her finger. Despite his displays of extravagance, Richard had no money. In fact, he was in debt to very nearly everyone he knew – everyone but a mistress who lived in the very same small Kansas city.

Two months into her marriage to Richard, Nannie was again going through the personal advertisements. She told her correspondents that she was a widow, a description that was a little premature. Nannie had already begun making plans to rid herself of Richard when news of her father's death arrived from Blue Mountain. Her widowed mother Louisa then left Alabama for Kansas. She had come to stay with her daughter and son-in-law, but her visit was destined to be a short one. Within 48 hours she was dead.

Three months later, Richard joined his mother-in-law in death.

## HUSBAND NO. 5

True to form, Nannie was not without a husband for long. In fact, she set a new personal speed record with her next spouse. Sam Doss proposed just weeks after she had buried Richard. Sam was a state highway inspector in Tulsa, Oklahoma. Honest and reliable, he had been among those corresponding with the 'widowed' Nannie during Richard's final months. He was like no other man Nannie had ever met. Not a drop of liquor touched his lips, he did not chase women and he would not think of raising a fist to his wife. Sam proved to be handy around the house and he enjoyed helping his new wife prepare the meals.

Just the man Nannie had been looking for, it seems. But the relationship was far from idyllic in her eyes. True, Sam had a good deal of money, but his wealth had been amassed through decades of frugal living. He even frowned on the gossip magazines and romance novels that Nannie devoured. They were a waste of time and cash, he thought. Eventually, Nannie rebelled. She moved back to Alabama, leaving her husband behind. Sam pursued her with letters. He pleaded for forgiveness and promised her a more luxurious lifestyle. The highway inspector even went so far as to transfer his savings into a joint account. Finally, he made certain that Nannie would continue

living in comfort even after his death – he took out two life insurance policies.

All this dramatic activity – the proposal, the wedding, the separation, the reconciliation, the financial arrangements and the life insurance policies – took place over the course of just three months. In September, Sam became violently ill after having eaten a tasty slice of his wife's prune cake. The ailing man took to his bed and was later taken by his doctor to the local hospital. There he stayed for 23 days, while he was treated for what had been diagnosed as a severe infection of the digestive tract. It was not until 5 October that he was finally well enough to return home. That evening, Nannie served Richard a roast pork dinner accompanied by a fresh cup of coffee.

He was dead before the following day had dawned.

None of Nannie's previous murders had attracted any suspicion of foul play. However, with Sam's death her luck had finally run out. The doctor who had cared for her husband during his hospital stay had been shocked to learn of his sudden death. An autopsy was ordered, which established that Sam had not died of a digestive tract infection. The cause of death had been a massive dose of arsenic.

When she was taken into custody, Nannie denied any knowledge of the arsenic. She spent her time reading cheap romantic fiction, such as *Romantic Heart* magazine, while investigators slowly began uncovering the trail of death she had left in her wake. When she was confronted with each new finding, Nannie just giggled. It was only when they took away her reading material that she finally confessed to Sam's murder.

'He wouldn't let me watch my favourite programmes on the television,' she complained, 'and

*Nannie Doss's police mugshot, taken in Tulsa in October 1954.*

publications, including *Life* magazine, sent along journalists to interview her. Charley Braggs, her first husband, also became a media star, but this time for the right reasons. As the only husband to survive marriage to Nannie he had a fascinating story to tell. He spoke quite openly about the troubled nature of their relationship, including the adultery. 'To tell you the truth, I was glad when she was off. It got to a point I was afraid to eat anything she cooked.'

'The Giggling Granny' died of leukaemia on 2 June 1965, several months short of what would have been her 60th birthday.

he made me sleep without the fan on the hottest nights. He was a miser and… well, what's a woman to do under those conditions?'

Nannie struck a deal with the police, in which she would tell them about her past husbands in exchange for the return of her magazine. All of her husbands had been 'dullards', she said. 'If their ghosts are in this room they're either drunk or sleeping.'

The bodies of Frank, Arlie and Richard were exhumed, together with those of her mother, her sister and her nephew. And then there was Arlie's mother. They had all died of arsenic poisoning or asphyxia. Despite the findings, Nannie was charged with the only murder that had taken place in Oklahoma – that of her last husband, Sam Doss. On 17 May 1955 she had no alternative but to plead guilty. The court sentenced her to life imprisonment. She escaped the electric chair only because of her sex.

Nannie became something of a celebrity when she was finally placed behind bars. Several leading

*A lucky escape: Charley Braggs was the only one of Nannie's five husbands to survive the marriage.*

# BETTY NEUMAR

The short, white-haired grandmother placidly followed Richmond County Sheriff Investigator John Faison into his car when he asked her to come with him. The woman was 76-year-old Betty Neumar. She was being investigated for a possible crime that had occurred nearly 20 years earlier.

Over the course of her life she had married five times. Her husbands kept dying in mysterious, violent ways. It was not until 2007 when Al Gentry, the brother of her fourth husband Harold Gentry, who had died in 1986, urged police to investigate the matter that authorities realized that perhaps this old lady had something to do with all these deaths. Let's face it, either Betty Neumar had the worst luck in marriage, or there was something going on.

## COAL-MINER'S DAUGHTER

Betty Johnson was born in 1931 to a coal-miner and his wife in Ironton, Ohio. Just a year after leaving high school in 1949, she married Clarence Malone. The marriage lasted less than two years. Betty filed a police report accusing her husband of abusing her. He died in 1970 from a single shot to the head, just outside his car repair shop. His killing remained

unsolved, though his brothers did not believe that Betty had anything to do with it.

Around 1951, she got married again, this time to James Flynn. The two had a child together, Gary, in 1952. Three years later James Flynn was dead. Betty gave a variety of explanations for his demise: he was an alcoholic, who had died in a truck, or had frozen to death, or been shot on a pier.

Her third husband was Richard Sills, a sailor. She moved to the Florida Keys with him and enrolled in beauty college in 1960. Sills died in 1965, another gunshot victim, this time apparently self-inflicted. The couple had been having an argument in their home in Big Coppitt Key, Florida, moments before Sills' fatal injury. Betty stated that during an argument the

*Betty Neumar: her men kept dying in mysterious, violent ways. There were five dead husbands in five states.*

drunken Sills had taken out a gun and shot himself in the side.

Her 11-year-old daughter, Peggy, had been in the room next door. When she came out, she saw the body of her stepfather. 'He was laying on the bed and he went into snorting and he rolled off the bed,' she later recalled. 'I asked the paramedic if he was dead; they said to get me out of there.'

Sills was shot twice. One bullet from his .22-caliber pistol pierced his heart, while another had sliced his liver. As the police had quickly ruled the death as a suicide, no autopsy was ever performed. But the two bullets would suggest that there was some doubt about suicide.

By 1985, Betty's son by James Flynn was dead as well – Gary Flynn's death once again was ruled as suicide. His passing netted Betty a $10,000 insurance pay-out. The relationship between Gary and his mother had never been ideal. After phone conversations with

*When Betty Neumar moved to the Florida Keys and enrolled in beauty college, her husband Richard was fated to die.*

her, he would often binge on drugs and alcohol. When they heard the news of his death, Gary's wife Cecilia and his stepson Jeff Carstensen rushed from Michigan to his house in Ohio to get hold of his cash before Betty could get there. They found $16,000 hidden under the mattress as well as a number of guns and ammunition.

Betty Neumar and her fourth husband, Harold Gentry, arrived at the house later that night, but they were too late.

## FOURTH TIME UNLUCKY?

It was the death of her fourth husband that would ultimately lead to Betty's downfall. In 1968 she had married Thomas Harold Gentry. For a time, it

*When Gary Flynn died, a cache of money, $16,000, was found under his mattress.*

seemed that she had finally settled down and found happiness. Gentry survived until 1986. Then he was found dead in their home in Norwood, North Carolina, with six gunshot wounds. At the time, any suspicious circumstances were ignored. On the day in question Betty had been with Gentry's brother, Al, in Augusta, Georgia. When she heard the news of Harold's death she showed no emotion. According to Al, 'If she had gotten out of that car with tears in her eyes and asked me why would anybody kill Harold, I would never have suspected her at all.' Her lack of emotion made him sure that Betty was somehow involved. He spent 22 years urging the police to investigate his sibling's murder more closely.

Betty's fifth husband was John Neumar, whom she had married in 1991. As with Gentry, the marriage proved long-lasting. Neumar was a wealthy man, worth more than $300,000 when they married. He was

also frugal and serious. His son said, 'Before he met her, he always saved his money. That's what he taught us.' But things changed and became strained. Betty had started up a get-rich-quick scheme that promised more than it paid out. She told investors they would receive $100,000 for every $100 they put towards the legal expenses of a rich European magnate who had died with no heirs. Even her husband's son, John Neumar, Jr., decided to invest $1,000. Of course, there was no European inheritance. In total, over 200 people were fooled. Seven defendants pleaded guilty to the scam in 1997, but Betty escaped without charges. Even so, debts began racking up. The Neumars were forced to declare bankruptcy after it emerged they had debts of more than $200,000 on 43 credit cards.

Did Betty see her husband's death as the solution to her financial problems? In 2007 Neumar died, apparently from natural causes. A coroner's report listed his cause of death as sepsis, ischemic bowel and ileus. Those were symptoms that could equally have indicated arsenic poisoning. Neumar's son,

*Al Gentry holds up photos of his murdered brother.*

John Neumar, Jr., only learned of his death after reading a local newspaper report. He contacted Betty about a funeral service, explaining that his father had already bought a burial plot. Much to his surprise, Betty had already had the body cremated. He said, 'I mean, it's just strange, why do you do that? I don't think my daddy ever said he wanted to be cremated.'

Among her neighbours, though, Betty continued to play the kindly grandmother next door. She ran beauty shops, attended church and raised money for charity. When her grandson, Jeff Carstensen, learned she had planned to buy him a $100,000 life insurance plan with herself named as beneficiary, he grew concerned. After all, the previous holders of life insurance policies which placed Betty as the beneficiary were now dead. Betty told him, 'People of our stature have insurance policies on each other. That way, if something happens to you, you take care of me, and if something happens to me, I take care of you.'

But Jeff had seen another side of his grandmother. At family functions there had been fist fights. She was frequently obscene and belittled relatives. Her public and private personas were starkly at odds. He decided to move back to Michigan for his own safety.

## DOZENS OF ALIASES

In 2007, the 77-year-old Betty was arrested and charged with three counts of solicitation to commit first-degree murder. Prosecutors alleged that she had hired three assassins to kill her husband Harold Gentry. At the time of her fourth husband's murder she desperately needed cash. Gentry had taken out life insurance. When he died, Betty received at least $20,000. It transpired, she had had dozens of aliases, driver's licences and passports which she had used to approach the alleged killers.

After her arrest, Al Gentry visited his brother's grave. His two-decade-long search for justice had ended. He thought it was finally over and speaking over the grave he said, 'Brother, we got her.'

New investigations were carried out into the deaths of her previous husbands but the authorities made no headway. County investigators hoped to exhume the body of Richard Sills. But the statute of limitations in Florida prevented further investigation of the murder. Richard Sills' brother, Michael, then turned to the Naval Criminal Investigative Service (NCIS) to look into the matter, as Richard had been a member of the Navy. They got no further. And in 2009 Georgia closed their investigation into the death of John Neumar, stating they had found no evidence linking Betty to the murder, much to the dismay of Neumar's family.

Betty denied all wrongdoing. She described her accusers as 'nuts'. 'Later on, it's going to eat their heart out,' she said. 'The hate and discontent that they are living in now will make them miserable.'

In the end, Betty Neumar never made it to trial. Soon after her arrest she was released after she posted $300,000 for bail. The legal process was slow. A date was never set for her trial. She would never return to jail.

On 13 June 2011 she died in a Louisiana hospital from cancer. Al Gentry felt cheated by her death. 'I'm numb,' he said. 'I wanted justice and we're not going to get it.' For her victims and their families, it felt like the case would never be over. Some of them were convinced that Betty might have faked her own death. Was it her final scam?

# AILEEN WUORNOS

any would say that the real-life exploits of Aileen Wuornos were sensational enough. Yet her case was still surrounded by a great deal of hyperbole.

In some media reports she was described as 'the first female serial killer', but that only demonstrates an ignorance of the facts. History is full of women who have committed multiple murders. Take Elizabeth Báthory, for instance, the 17th-century Hungarian countess known as the 'Bloody Lady of Cachtice'. She was convicted on 80 counts of murder, but some put her total at over 600.

To others, Aileen Wuornos was a 'lesbian murderer'. That is another false label, because it ignores the fact that she had displayed a marked preference for men as sexual partners. And at one time she had been someone's wife.

## TURMOIL

The turmoil that surrounded Aileen began before she was even born. Her mother, Diane, was 15 years old when she married Leo, Aileen's father.

A little more than a year into the marriage, in March 1955, Diane gave birth to a baby boy who was named Keith. Shortly afterwards, Leo was arrested and charged with a number of petty crimes. However, he managed to avoid going to jail by joining the army. Pregnant with Aileen, Diane saw Leo's departure as an open door through which she could flee the marriage.

After giving birth to Aileen on 29 February 1956 she returned to her parents' Troy, Michigan, home with her two children in tow. Four years later, she walked out of the door, leaving the two children for her parents to bring up.

Aileen would never see her father. In 1966, Leo was convicted of raping a seven-year-old girl and he was later diagnosed as a paranoid schizophrenic. He spent time in a number of mental hospitals before ending up in a Kansas prison cell. It was there that he hanged himself in 1969. Diane's parents then legally adopted Aileen and Keith and they were raised side by side with Diane's two younger siblings. The Wuornos couple did not look like grandparents. Indeed, Aileen maintained that for most of her childhood she thought they were her true parents. It was not always a happy environment. She and Keith suffered beatings from her grandfather.

## ON THE STREET

At the age of ten, Aileen began having sexual relations with Keith. Their encounters were witnessed by the neighbourhood boys. Within a year, she was having sex with boys other than her brother in exchange for cigarettes and small sums of money.

*Aileen Wuornos – her teenage dad dished out brutal beatings to her mother and hanged himself in his prison cell.*

She used the cash earned with her body to buy drugs and alcohol. In 1970, at the age of 14, Aileen became pregnant. She claimed that an older man, a neighbour, had raped her. When her grandparents found out, she was sent to a home for unwed mothers. On 23 March 1971, she gave birth to a baby boy. The child was taken away for adoption without her ever laying eyes on him.

Four months later, her grandmother died of liver failure. Her passing marked the end of Aileen and Keith's welcome in the Wuornos household. The two teenagers were told that they must leave the house immediately, never to return. They had no choice but to go their separate ways. Keith found a place to stay with friends in the neighbourhood, while Aileen turned to prostitution.

## ON THE MOVE

Three years passed before Aileen came into contact with the law. However, her crimes at this stage had nothing to do with cash for sex. She was charged with drunk driving, disorderly conduct and firing a gun from a moving vehicle. A further charge of failing to appear in court was added after she returned to Michigan.

Aileen spent so much time moving back and forth across the United States that she was never in any one place for long. Then in 1976, at about the time of her 20th birthday, she settled at Daytona Beach in Florida. Aileen had not been there long when she learned that the two most influential men in her life, her hated grandfather and her beloved brother, had died. While the old man had killed himself through gas inhalation, Keith's death was not of his own choosing. On 17 July, he had succumbed to throat cancer. As the beneficiary of his life insurance, Aileen received $10,000. Two months later, the money was gone. One of her purchases was a car, which she subsequently wrecked.

The only way was to go back to hitchhiking to pick up men. Then in September she was picked up by a wealthy retiree named Lewis Fell. Although he was 49 years her senior, the two were married before the end of the calendar year.

The event even made the society pages of the local newspaper. Fell proved to be a most generous man. He bought his bride a brand-new car and expensive jewellery. She now had every chance of leading a stable life.

However, the marriage was neither peaceful nor enduring. Aileen was not able to change her behaviour. She drank heavily and she would pick fights in the local bars. One bar room encounter led to her being jailed for assault.

Nine weeks after the wedding, Lewis filed for divorce. He claimed that his wife had struck him with his cane after he had refused to give her more money.

## ON THE GAME

Now that the marriage was over, Aileen returned to prostitution. She worked the exit ramps of the Florida highways. Without Keith to provide comfort and support, her behaviour became increasingly erratic.

In 1978, Aileen took a .22 calibre pistol and shot herself in the stomach. She was rushed to a hospital, where she received the very best in medical attention, but next to no counselling.

Aileen could never have been described as a beauty, but by now her average looks were fading with time, drink and drugs. As a result, her income from prostitution started to decline. Increasingly she turned to crime as a means of support. In May 1981, wearing only a bikini, Aileen held up a small supermarket in Edgewater, Florida. She was soon apprehended when her run-down getaway car overheated and broke down by the side of the highway. After being charged with armed robbery she spent most of the next two years in prison. Though much of her time was devoted to reading the Bible, Aileen did not emerge from jail a changed woman. Over the next two years, she was charged with attempting to pass forged cheques, speeding, grand theft auto, resisting arrest, obstruction and attempting to rob a boyfriend at gunpoint.

She once wrote that she turned to women as partners at the age of 28. The decision, she said, brought 'a world of trouble'. In the summer of 1986, while drinking in a Daytona gay bar, she met a 24-year-old motel maid named Tyria Moore. The two became lovers that same evening and they soon moved in together. Aileen encouraged Ty to quit her job, saying that she would support them both with her earnings as a prostitute.

The two adopted a transient lifestyle, which was a reflection of Aileen's success in trading sex for money. They bunked down in friends' apartments, abandoned trailers, motel rooms and, on occasion, the outdoors.

## LOADED PISTOL

Sex between the two women became a rare thing, yet they stayed together.

If money permitted, they would go to bars or rent motel rooms and just watch television. Though Ty seemed content to be supported by Aileen, she was concerned about her companion's safety. Aileen took to working the streets and exit ramps with a loaded, concealed pistol.

By the autumn of 1989, Aileen was finding it difficult to support herself and Ty. The lack of money was having an effect on their relationship. Ty returned to work by taking on occasional jobs as a motel chambermaid, which made Aileen worry that her companion would leave her. She would later write that under this pressure she spun out of control.

'Hypnotically entranced in our companionship, so deeply lost in its same-sex relationship, causing me then to do the unthinkable.'

Aileen was referring here to the events of 30 November 1989. It was on that evening that Aileen committed her first murder. The victim, Richard Mallory, was the 51-year-old owner of an electronics repair shop. Mallory was on his way to Daytona Beach for a weekend of partying when he met Aileen. She then came up with the idea that he could pay her for sex. Mallory apparently agreed, so they drove into the woods outside the city. They shared a bottle of vodka and chatted until dawn. Then, quite suddenly, Aileen pulled out her handgun and shot him four times in

*Richard Mallory was Wuornos' first victim – she told the court that she acted in self-defence after he had raped her.*

the chest and the back. She grabbed whatever money she could find, covered Mallory's body over with some carpeting and drove off in his car.

When she got home, Aileen told Ty what she had done. Ty did not believe the story until the news of the murder was reported in the media. Even then, she stuck by Aileen.

'I thought at that time: that, okay, she has all the frustration out of her system – for whatever reason she hated society – that she'll be okay. But obviously she wasn't. Obviously it was just the turning point, and she figured she got away with it once – she would keep doing it.'

## MORE MURDERS

Six months after the Mallory murder, in May 1990, Aileen was hitchhiking when she was picked up by a 43-year-old heavy equipment operator named David Spears. Aileen shot him six times and then stole his truck, which she later abandoned. Then on 6 June she flagged down her next victim, 40-year-old Charles Carskaddon. Aileen shot the man six times and then took his gun, money and jewellery. She drove off in his car. After putting some distance between herself and the body, she abandoned the vehicle. Now that she had no means of transport she began hitchhiking again.

She was soon offered a lift by 65-year-old Peter Siems, a former merchant seaman who had devoted his retirement to Christian outreach. The back of his car was loaded with Bibles, but this did not stop Aileen from murdering him.

Aileen then stole Siems' car, as she had done with her other victims. However, this time she chose to hold on to the vehicle. It was a foolish decision – one that would lead to her capture.

On 4 July, Ty was driving Siems' stolen car when she took a corner too fast and rolled the vehicle. She and Aileen panicked. They asked a witness not to call the police and then they fled the scene before the emergency vehicles could arrive. Although Aileen had wrenched the licence plates off the car and thrown them into the brush the authorities soon realized that they had found the car belonging to Siems. Added to that, the witness was able to provide extremely accurate descriptions of Aileen and Ty.

Over the next five months, Aileen killed three more men. It had become clear to the authorities that they were dealing with a serial killer. In November 1990 a number of newspapers across Florida ran a story about the killings. They included sketches of the

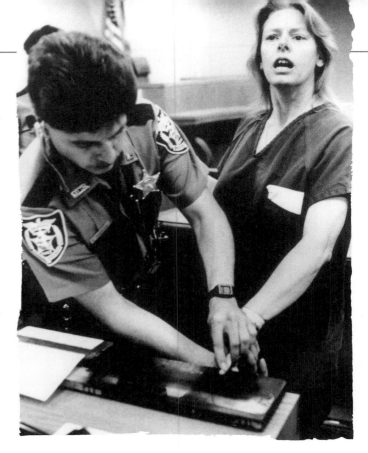

*Wuornos' killing spree ended when police identified her fingerprints on stolen goods.*

two women who had been seen walking away from Siems' stolen car.

As a result, Aileen and Ty were identified by a number of people. Sensing that the authorities were closing in on them, Ty made herself scarce while Aileen was buying alcohol. The younger woman travelled north out of the state to stay with her sister in Pittston, Pennsylvania.

## BREAKTHROUGH

As 1990 drew to a close, the authorities experienced a breakthrough when they came across pawn shop records of some of the items that had been stolen from Aileen's victims. On 6 January 1991, Aileen was arrested at the Last Resort biker bar in Florida. At the same time, Ty was tracked down to her sister's Pennsylvania home. She later helped the police out by getting Aileen to contact her at the motel at which she was staying. The telephone calls were then recorded. By 16 January, Aileen had become so fearful that Ty would be implicated in the murders that she confessed.

'The reason I'm confessing is there's not another girl,' she said. 'I did it. There is no other girl.'

Aileen admitted to killing seven men, though she claimed to have done so in self-defence. She maintained that all of them had either raped her or had intended to rape her.

A full year passed before she finally went on trial for the murder of Richard Mallory. Several people were called by the prosecution, including Ty. It was only then that Aileen realized she had been betrayed.

When her former lover took the stand she avoided all eye contact. The only witness for the defence was Aileen herself. Her testimony was erratic and unconvincing.

On 27 January 1992, the jury took less than two hours to find Aileen guilty of Mallory's murder. She addressed the jury as it was being led out of the courtroom.

'I'm innocent. I was raped. I hope you get raped. Scumbags of America!'

On the following day Aileen came out with several similar outbursts during the penalty phase of the trial. She was sentenced to death. Over the next two years, she pleaded guilty to two counts of murder and she entered no contest pleas on three more. Although she had confessed to murdering Siems, along with the others, she was not charged, because no body was ever found.

Then in July 2001, after more than ten years in prison, of which nine had been spent on death row, Aileen petitioned the court to put an end to the mandated appeals of her death sentence.

She testified that the murders had not been acts of self-defence, as she had originally claimed.

On 9 October 2002, Wuornos became the tenth woman to be put to death in the United States since the reintroduction of the death penalty in 1976. Two months before, she had begun writing a candid confession:

Dear Lord Jesus,
I know I've done some wicked things in my life, and Lord God, I know I deserve every bit of the rot of Hell.

*Wuornos began talks on selling her story to Hollywood almost as soon as she was arrested.*

# DOROTHEA PUENTE

Dorothea Puente ran the prettiest of boarding houses in Sacramento, California. The two-storey gingerbread Victorian house was situated at 1426 F Street, a lush, tree-lined thoroughfare in what had once been a grand neighbourhood. Dorothea's house stood out proudly from the others, which had fallen into disrepair. She took great pride in the look of her home. It was decorated with lace doilies and a variety of knick-knacks. The 59-year-old Dorothea also paid a great deal of attention to her own appearance. She spent a sizeable amount of money on silk chiffon dresses, Giorgio Armani perfume and at least one facelift.

## PRIM AND PROPER

Dorothea lived an orderly life, which was reflected in her orderly boarding house. Boarders lived on the ground floor, while Dorothea had the spacious second floor to herself. It was all quite proper. Her guests paid $350 per month. In exchange they received a private room and two very generous meals each day. If there was anything amiss it was the foul stench that appeared to be coming from her property. During the summer months the neighbours would complain to Dorothea. She would then come up with all sorts

*Dorothea Puente invented a variety of excuses to explain the foul stench that came from her property.*

of excuses: the sewer was blocked up; rats were to blame; she had been using a fish emulsion to fertilize her back garden.

She tried to eliminate the smell, or at least cover it up, by dumping a quantity of lime and gallon after gallon of bleach on to her back garden. The boarding house itself was sprayed constantly with air freshener. When three police officers came to call on the morning of 11 November 1988, she had perhaps already sprayed her house. They were looking for one of her boarders, a 51-year-old mentally disabled man named Alvaro Montoya. It was not that Alvaro was in trouble with the law – he just seemed to have vanished. His social worker was most concerned.

While Alvaro's room did not provide any clues as to his whereabouts, the officers noticed something

*The body count kept going up as police searched the house.*

unusual in Dorothea's back garden. In one corner of the property it appeared that the ground had been recently disturbed. Using shovels and spades, the three men began digging. Finally, they uncovered clothing and the remains of a human body. No one expressed more shock at the discovery than Dorothea.

Officials from the coroner's office arrived, as did a team of forensic anthropologists, supported by a work crew. Together, they worked to uncover the corpse. It appeared that the police officers had found the skeleton of a short female with grey hair. But that wasn't all. As the excavation continued, a second set of remains was uncovered – and these were much fresher.

## MORE CADAVERS

Just after this gruesome discovery had been made, Dorothea asked the detective in charge, John Cabrera, whether she might be permitted to go for coffee at the Clarion Hotel, just two blocks away. There was no problem with this request. After all, the boarding house owner was not under arrest. The detective did Dorothea the courtesy of escorting her through the gathered onlookers and then he returned to the garden.

As the afternoon progressed, the body count increased. Three more cadavers were found underneath a slab of concrete and another body had been buried beneath a gazebo. In the end, seven corpses – three male and four female – were found in Dorothea's back garden.

It went without saying that Dorothea would have to be questioned about the bodies that had been unearthed on her property. The only problem was that Dorothea had disappeared. She had never returned from her trip to the Clarion Hotel. Despite Dorothea's absence, a picture began to emerge. A note found in her quarters served as the key to what had been taking place. On this small piece of paper was written Alvaro's first initial, followed by those of six former boarders. Each of the initials was accompanied by a number, which was preceded by a dollar sign. The investigators had found a list of Social Security and disability benefits. Dorothea had been collecting money that had been intended for people who were dead. She became richer by $5,000 each and every month.

As they searched for the boarding house owner, the authorities began looking into her background.

What they found was not pretty. She had been born Dorothea Helen Gray in Redlands, California, on 9 January 1929. Both of her parents had died by the time she was nine – her mother in a horrible motorcycle accident – and she was sent to a number of homes. As a teenager, she turned to prostitution. She was able to earn a fair amount of money from her good looks.

## UNHAPPY UNION

Not long after the end of the Second World War, Dorothea met a 22-year-old soldier named Fred McFaul. They married in Reno. Though the couple had two daughters, their union was not a happy one. Dorothea lived an unrealistic fantasy life that required expensive clothing and evenings out.

She told people that she was the sister of the American ambassador to Sweden and that she counted Rita Hayworth among her closest friends.

In the midst of this fantasy life, she left her husband and daughters for the excitement of Los Angeles. There she became pregnant by another man. Though she miscarried, McFaul would not take her back. With the marriage at an end, their children were raised by others. Then in 1948, Dorothea served her first jail sentence. She was locked up for a total of four years after forging a number of cheques. Almost as soon as she was released, Dorothea wed for a second time. Though the marriage lasted for some 14 years, it was another disaster. It is likely that it only endured as long as it did because her husband, a merchant seaman, was often away.

Dorothea carried on working as a prostitute during both her marriages and in 1960 she was convicted of residing in a brothel. In 1968, she

married for a third time. Her groom, Robert Jose Puente, was just over half Dorothea's age. A year later, the marriage was over. As the 1970s began, Dorothea started to run the boarding house on F Street. After a few years, she ended up marrying one of her boarders, a 52-year-old named Pedro Angel Montalvo. The couple had not been married long when Dorothea was again arrested for cheque forgery. This time she avoided prison. She got away with five years' probation for the crime.

It is thought by the authorities that she committed her first murder in 1982. The victim, Ruth Munroe, made the mistake of starting a small lunchroom business with Dorothea. This happy, optimistic woman died from an overdose of codeine and Tylenol, a tragedy that the coroner dismissed as suicide. A mere month later, Dorothea was charged with drugging her boarders so that she could steal their more pricey possessions. It was a simple and obvious crime. As a result, she served three years in the California Institution for Women. Upon her release, Dorothea was told not to handle government cheques and to keep away from senior citizens. She violated both orders.

Still officially married to her fourth husband, the 56-year-old Dorothea became engaged to Everson Gillmouth, a man 21 years her senior. His body was found a few months later by fishermen who had been trying their luck in the Sacramento River.

## ATTRACTING CUSTOM

By this point, Dorothea had returned to running her boarding house. A string of social workers favoured her with boarders. They were oblivious to her lengthy criminal record. In the words of one of their number,

*They check in but they don't check out: one more victim leaves the boarding house.*

Dorothea had the 'best the system had to offer'. She was willing to accept into her boarding house the most difficult people that they had to place. However, she did not rely entirely on social workers for boarders. Dressed to the nines, Dorothea frequented the lesser bars of Sacramento. There she made conversation with lonely, down-and-out people, in a bid to encourage them to take a room at her boarding house.

All of these revelations came much too late. By November 1988 the authorities knew that they had to find Dorothea. But where was she?

## BOGUS STORY

The investigators were later able to piece together just what had happened. After Detective Cabrera had escorted her to the Clarion Hotel, Dorothea had spent some time in a bar on the other side of town. She had then boarded a bus for Los Angeles, where she had met a 59-year-old carpenter named Charles Willgues in a tavern. She gave him a fake name and an equally bogus story – a cab driver had driven

off with her suitcases. Dorothea tried to play upon the man's sympathy, but she did not get very far. When she suggested that they move in together, the carpenter declined. Later, in his apartment, Charles realized the true identity of the woman to whom he had been speaking. It was then that he called the police.

She was arrested the day after the bodies began to be pulled out of the ground. The former prostitute was later charged with nine counts of murder. It would take four years before Dorothea's case was ready to go to trial.

Her defence was extremely weak. Dorothea explained that the people whose bodies had been found in her back garden had all died of natural causes. She had buried them herself in order to hide the fact that she was operating a boarding house in violation of her parole. However, Dorothea's claims about natural deaths were countered by the concentrations of Dalmane, a prescription-strength sleeping pill, that were present in every one of the remains.

A friend of Alvaro Montoya took the stand to say that the dead man had complained that Dorothea had been plying him with drugs. The testimony of other witnesses indicated that the boarding house owner had been forcing drugs on her lodgers.

Dorothea was eventually found guilty on three counts of murder.

On 10 December 1993, she was sentenced to life imprisonment without the possibility of parole. She died in prison in 2011, at the age of 82.

# TRACIE ANDREWS

The earliest reports painted a picture that was as disturbing as it was gruesome. On the evening of 1 December 1996, Lee Harvey, a young English father, had been butchered beside his white Ford Escort. He had been stabbed 15 times and his throat had been slashed. The dead man was seen as a victim of road rage. 'He died in the arms of his fiancée,' reported *The Times*. His fiancée, Tracie Andrews, appeared at a news conference two days afterwards. The 27-year-old woman was a former model, so she was accustomed to being the centre of attention.

Sporting a black eye and a small facial cut, Tracie wept as she gave her account of the evening in question. It had begun as an 'ordinary night out'. She and her fiancé had shared a few drinks at the Marlbrook public house in Bromsgrove and then they had started out for their flat in nearby Alvechurch, Worcestershire. Not long into their drive Lee overtook a run-down Ford Sierra. The car he had passed was soon on his tail and the incident escalated to taunting, headlight flashing and a high-speed chase. At last, with his home in sight, Lee stopped. Both drivers got out of their vehicles and had a brief but fierce exchange. After the Sierra driver had returned to his car, his passenger then left the vehicle and attacked Lee. Tracie told the assembled reporters that she had confronted the man.

'I told him to F-off and he called me a slut and punched me. When I got up he was walking back to the car.'

The man, who had 'starey eyes' according to Tracie, was then driven away. Tracie attended to her fiancé, but she did not realize how serious his wounds were until a passing motorist approached with a flashlight.

'I tried to think of everything I should do,' she claimed to the press. 'I put my coat over him. I tried to stop the bleeding and comfort him.'

Tracie's story was horrifying, but it was by no

*Tracie Andrews demonstrates the 'starey eyes' of the man she had invented as the scapegoat for the crime.*

means unique. Seven months earlier, a man had been stabbed to death at the side of the M25 after an argument with another driver. Several days after that, another man had been shot and killed while he was a passenger in a car that was travelling along a London street. The authorities decided that the cause of both murders was 'road rage'.

Tracie was admitted to hospital on the day after her emotional appearance at the news conference. Initial reports suggested that she had collapsed from strain, but it was later revealed that she had attempted suicide by taking a large dose of aspirin, tranquillizers and paracetamol. She was discharged from hospital on 8 December but readmitted after doctors described her as being in a 'dangerously emotional state.'

Even though she was the mother of a five-year-old daughter, Tracie had left a suicide note in which she had written that she had nothing to live for – she only wanted to be with Lee. Then on 7 December, shortly after her release from hospital, Tracie was arrested. She collapsed and was taken back into medical care, where she remained in custody.

## MOUNTING EVIDENCE

In the meantime, the police continued their investigation. They descended on the small home that the couple had shared with two daughters from previous relationships. Roadblocks were set up and 650 motorists were interviewed in the search for the battered Ford Sierra. Dogs were then brought to the crime scene in the hope that they would be able to uncover the murder weapon. Tracie was still in police custody when, on 19 December, she was charged with murdering her fiancé.

The evidence that had been gathered by the police began appearing in the media. It appeared that Lee had been clutching a clump of Tracie's hair when he had died. A major inconsistency in the former model's story had also been found. She had told the police that the attack on Lee had occurred in front of his car, yet blood was found at the rear as well. Tracie was found to have had a history of violent behaviour. The 18-month relationship she had shared with her fiancé had been volatile and unstable and Lee had walked out on three separate occasions. The couple had even been seen arguing at the pub on their 'ordinary night out'. But Tracie stuck by everything that she had told the police. She even appealed for witnesses to come forward with information that would prove her innocence.

On 30 June 1997, Tracie's murder trial began at Birmingham Crown Court. The prosecution alleged that the argument that had begun in the Marlbrook public house had continued on the way home. At some point it had become so heated that Lee had stopped the car and both of them had got out. He was then stabbed 30 times – not 15, as the media had reported. Tracie had plunged a small, imitation Swiss Army knife into her fiancé's neck, face, head, chest, shoulder and back.

## LANDSLIDE OF INFORMATION

The evidence that had been leaked to the media provoked a landslide of information.

Two witnesses said they had seen Lee's Ford Escort travelling back from the public house, but no car had been following. The motorist who had come across the murder scene testified that Tracie had not been tending to her injured fiancé, nor had she been trying to get help from a nearby house. Instead, she was found covered in blood, standing next to the car. She made no mention of the shabby Ford Sierra or the murderous man with 'starey eyes'. Another person who had come upon the bloody scene – coincidentally, a former police detective – testified that Tracie had been suspected from the start. The dead man's fiancée had not been able to recall the make, the colour or the licence plates of the other vehicle, yet by the time the police arrived she was able to provide a detailed description. Added to that, the pattern of bloodstains on Tracie's clothing was consistent with an attack, but inconsistent with the marks that would have been created when cradling a dying man. It was also suggested that an elongated blood-stain found on the lining of a boot Tracie had been wearing had been created when hiding the bloody knife. It was alleged that the weapon had been disposed of during her six visits to a hospital lavatory.

Further evidence of a troubled relationship was presented. A policeman testified that on 19 October 1996 he had stopped Tracie as she was attempting to hit her fiancé. Just a few weeks later, Tracie had been seen biting and punching her fiancé in a nightclub. In neither case did Lee retaliate. He appeared to have been attempting to placate Tracie.

However, the defence put forward the possibility that Lee had been killed in a dispute over a drug deal. It was said that the dealer had followed Lee and Tracie out of the pub on the evening of the murder. The police were then accused of abandoning their hunt for the mysterious dark Sierra after only three days.

The defence described Tracie and Lee as a couple who 'had found glamour in each other, charm with each other.' Tracie's solicitor pointed out that she was wearing her engagement ring on the night of the murder, and had continued to wear it despite his death. 'She was committed to him,' he said. It was acknowledged that the relationship had been difficult at times, mainly because of an abortion. Tracie had recognized that adding a child to the relationship would have placed a further strain on a tenuous financial situation. The solicitor said that the abortion procedure had caused Tracie to lose her figure. Lee had made some unpleasant comments, but had later apologized and had paid for breast surgery.

Lee was presented as an immature, jealous man who could not accept his fiancée's past relationships. He was said to have hit Tracie 'once or twice'. Then a witness with a substantial criminal record was brought forward to testify that he had been threatened with a knife by the driver of a red Ford Granada three months before Lee's murder. Finally, the accused took the stand. Tracie denied that there had been any argument at the pub. She could not explain how her hair came to be found in the victim's hand, but added, 'My hair comes out easily anyway.' Tracie's solicitor had earlier suggested that the crime might have been racially motivated. Lee, who had dark skin, had been called a 'Paki bastard' by his killer, it was said. This theory was supported by Tracie.

## THE JURY DECIDE

On 27 July 1997, the jury of nine women and three men began its deliberations. While they were awaiting the decision, Tracie and her family had what was described as a 'premature celebration' – a party held in her parents' garden. In the end, the former model had nothing to rejoice about. On 29 July, the jury found her guilty of murder. She was subsequently

*Ray and Maureen Harvey, the parents of Lee Harvey, arriving at the trial of their son's murderer.*

sentenced to life imprisonment, accompanied by the recommendation of a 14-year minimum term. In October 1998, Tracie failed in an attempt to appeal her conviction.

Six months later, the one-time model wrote a letter to a friend in which she confessed to murdering Lee. Published in the 18 April 1998 edition of the *News of the World*, the letter tells of a night that was vastly different from the one that Tracie had described under oath in court.

According to Tracie's letter she and Lee had argued over an ex-lover, Andrew Tilston, the father of her daughter, when they were in the pub. During the ride home, the row had intensified to such an extent that Tracie had asked her fiancé to stop the car. She told him that she would rather walk the rest of the

way home. True to her word, she got out of the car and began to march along the road. However, she soon came across Lee's parked car. He had been waiting for her. When he told her to get into the car she refused. After telling him that their relationship was over, she demanded the keys to the flat. The argument then took a nasty turn when Lee accused his fiancée of sleeping around. Tracie countered by taunting him about Andrew Tilston. Lee then got out of the car and pulled out a knife. He grabbed her by the hair and said 'See if Andy wants to see you with a f***ed-up face.' During the ensuing struggle, Tracie wrote that she managed to bring Lee to the ground with her knee. The couple then wrestled until Tracie picked up the knife. Her letter continued,

> I must have stabbed him. Then he stood still and shouted, 'You f****** bitch,' then hit me so hard I fell again. I got up halfway and all I can remember is seeing red. I just went mad. Everything went like slow motion. I was shaking and had lost all control, all the abuse I had suffered and all the nasty things that had been thrown in my face, the way he had openly admitted to hating my relationship with my daughter and the fact that he had held the knife to me and was going to either slash my face or stab me, had just come to a head. I have never ever in my whole life lost control like I did this night.

Much of the remainder of the letter described Tracie's rather weak attempt at covering her tracks. She revealed the fate of the missing knife – it had been flushed down the hospital lavatory. Then she claimed that she had thought about admitting her guilt after the failed suicide attempt, but, as she said in her letter,

> My family, Lee's family, were going through a nightmare. How could I be the one to say, 'This is what happened – Lee was either going to slash my face or stab me, but I got the knife and it was me who killed him'. Please God tell me, how do you ever come to terms with something like this?

And so, ultimately, Tracie's letter was an excuse – a means of communicating the claim that she had killed Lee in self-defence. 'Lee', she went on to say, 'was a Jekyll and Hyde character'. The *News of the World* declined to reveal how it had come by the letter and whether any payment was involved. In any case, the letter failed to reach its desired effect: most people believed only a fraction of what Tracie had claimed.

Throughout her incarceration, Tracie proved to be a consistent source of fodder for the tabloids. She became friends with Jane Andrews, the woman who was convicted of stabbing her boyfriend to death in 2001. Despite Tracie's insistence that she should now be referred to as 'Tia Carter', the media have dubbed the pair the 'Andrews Sisters'.

# JUANA BARRAZA

The police in Mexico City made a fundamental mistake when hunting for *El Mataviejitas* ('The Old Lady Killer') – the serial killer who was murdering women over 60, strangling them with her bare hands or with cables, scarves and stockings. They assumed that the masculine figure seen leaving crime scenes dressed in women's clothing was a transvestite. In fact, she was a female professional wrestler known in the ring as *La Dama del Silencio*.

## EARLY LIFE

The real name of wrestling's 'Lady of Silence' was Juana Dayanara Barraza Samperio. She was born in 1956 in rural Hidalgo, Mexico, just north of Mexico City, to an alcoholic prostitute who left the child's father, a policeman, soon after she was born. The parent–child relationship was troubled. A silent child, Juana barely spoke as an infant. Being withdrawn hampered her at school and she never learned to read or write anything beyond her name.

When she was 11, her mother sold her to a man in exchange for three beers. He sexually abused her and she suffered miscarriages at the ages of 13 and 16, as well as giving birth to the first of her four children. After her mother died of cirrhosis of the liver, Juana left for Mexico City. There she had another three children from a series of failed marriages. Her eldest son died at the age of 24 after being beaten with a baseball bat by muggers.

Juana Barraza seems to have blamed her many misfortunes on her mother and criminologists believe this was the motivation for her murder spree.

## WRESTLING CAREER

During the 1980s and 1990s, Barraza toured Mexico while taking part in a form of wrestling known as *lucha libre*, or free fighting. The fighters wore masks and had cartoon-character names. They were identified as either *técnicos* – good guys who fought by the rules – or *rudos* – villains who broke them. Interviewed by a TV channel while attending a wrestling match a few weeks before her arrest, Barraza described herself as '*rudo* to the core'.

She was often seen in the front rows at the established arenas, selling popcorn. Organizing wrestling events for small-town fiestas, she occasionally took to fighting in the ring herself. She later told the police that she had picked the professional name *La Dama del Silencio* 'because I am quiet and keep myself to myself'.

Fairly low down in the rankings, she was getting just 300 to 500 pesos a fight – between £15 and £25 ($20-$33) – and began shoplifting and housebreaking to support her children. In 1996, she and a friend

*Wrestling masks on sale. In the '80s and '90s Barraza toured Mexico as a* lucha libre *wrestler and enjoyed her role as the villain.*

began stealing from elderly people. They dressed up as nurses to gain access to their homes and stole whatever they could when they got inside. However, her friend's lover was a corrupt cop who demanded a 12,000-peso (£480/$640) bribe from Barraza in return for not arresting her.

When Barraza retired from the ring in the year 2000, her financial situation grew worse. At the same time, a spate of brutal murders of elderly women began in Mexico City. The press dubbed the killer *El Mataviejitas*, assuming the perpetrator was a male – the female version is *La Mataviejitas*.

## THOUGHT TO BE A MAN

The first murder associated with Barraza was that of María de la Luz González Anaya on 25 November 2002. Once Barraza had gained entrance to her apartment, González made comments that Barraza considered derogatory. Infuriated, she beat González

before strangling her to death with her bare hands. Three months later, she killed again.

After a year, the police had enough evidence and witness statements to conclude that a serial killer was at work. The killer, they said, was a tall person with rough features who was posing as a city council nurse or a social worker to gain the victims' trust. In December 2003, the police released a wanted poster with two eyewitness sketches of the *Mataviejitas* – one slightly feminine and another more masculine.

Mexico City police had an eyewitness account that described the killer as 'a man, dressed as a woman, or a robust woman, dressed in white, height between 1.70 and 1.75 m [5ft 7in–5ft 9 in], robust complexion, light brown, oval face, wide cheeks, blond hair, delineated eyebrows, [and] approximately 45 years old'.

The Mexican Department of Justice also developed a psychological profile after examining cases of serial killers who targeted elderly women in France and Spain. This specified that the killer was 'a man with homosexual preferences, victim of childhood physical abuse, [who] lived surrounded by women, he could have had a grandmother or lived with an elderly person, has resentment to that feminine figure, and possesses great intelligence'. Consequently, the police announced that they were looking for a homosexual man, who was 'transvestite or transgendered'. They then arrested 49 transvestite prostitutes, who were all released when their fingerprints didn't match those at the crime scenes. Another red herring was the fact that at least three of the victims owned a print of an 18th-century painting by French artist Jean-Baptiste Greuze, *Boy in a Red Waistcoat*.

The police then came to believe that the killer was dead and checked the fingerprints of bodies in the morgue.

## OPERATION PARKS AND GARDENS

Meanwhile, Barraza continued approaching her victims on the street or knocking on their doors, pretending to be a city council nurse or a social worker. At first she had simply worn white clothes, but she later acquired a nurse's uniform. She would gain their trust by offering them a massage or help

in obtaining medicines and benefits. If her victims were distracted, she strangled them directly. If not, she would beat them, using moves she had learned in her wrestling career. Though she carried a bag with medical equipment, she usually strangled her victims manually or with a ligature taken from the victim's own home, which she would leave at the crime scene. Then she would rob them.

*Juana Barraza – when she was 11, her mother sold her to a man in exchange for three beers.*

The killing of 82-year-old Carmen Camila González Miguel on 28 September 2005 – mother of prominent Mexican criminologist Luis Rafael Moreno González – spurred the police into launching a special operation under the name of *Operación Parques y Jardines* – 'Operation Parks and Gardens'. Patrols in the areas where the killer was active increased and pamphlets

*Barraza had a shrine to Santa Muerte, a folk saint often worshipped by criminals in Mexico.*

were distributed advising old ladies to be wary of strangers. It was reported that the police even paid elderly women to act as bait in park areas they were keeping under surveillance.

# CAUGHT IN THE ACT

On 25 January 2006, Barraza entered the house of Ana María de los Reyes Alfaro in the Venustiano Carranza area of the capital by the simple device of asking for a glass of water. Once inside, she picked up a stethoscope that happened to be lying on the living room table and used it to strangle her elderly hostess. She was seen by a tenant as she left the apartment, shortly before he stumbled over the corpse of his landlady. He raised the alarm and she was arrested by a passing police patrol, who said she also confessed to three other killings.

Ismael Alvarado Ruiz, one of two policemen who made the arrest, said: 'My partner and I caught her by the arms and took her back to the patrol car. We went back to the house, and everything was scattered all around.'

Barraza was found in possession of a social worker's identification card and pension forms. She used them to gain entry to victims' homes by posing as a government employee who could sign them up to welfare programmes. A search of her home revealed a trophy room complete with newspaper clippings of the murders and mementoes, such as ornaments or religious items, taken from the victims. There was also an altar to Jesús Malverde and Santa Muerte (Saint Death), two folk saints often honoured by Mexican criminals.

# MEDIA CIRCUS

Her arrest was a media circus when she was paraded before the cameras. It is common practice in Mexico to let reporters interview suspects at the crime scene.

'Yes, I did it,' Barraza said, smiling for the television cameras. 'Just because I'm going to pay for it, that doesn't mean they're going to hang all the crimes on me.'

She also denied pretending to be a social worker.

'That's a lie. I wasn't carrying the documents they have there,' she said, maintaining that when she went to the victims' homes she offered to help with laundry or other household chores. But she offered no clues to her motive.

'You'll know why I did it when you read my statement to the police,' she said.

She was then posed beside a bust of the prime suspect, made during the hunt. With her cropped hair and distinctive mole, she bore a striking resemblance to the model. The police also released photographs of Barraza recreating the murder of Reyes for detectives, along with videoed excerpts of her police interrogation. All this was done before she had even been formally remanded in custody.

Barraza's fingerprints matched those found at ten murder scenes, along with one attempted murder. In the end, she was charged with 30 murders – though it was thought she had committed many more.

'I only killed one little old lady. Not the others,' Barraza told the court. 'It isn't right to pin the others on me.' Asked about her motive, she said simply: 'I got angry.'

Attempts to have her found not guilty by reason of insanity failed. She was pronounced guilty of 11 murders, plus 12 robberies. In each case, she was tied to the crime scene by fingerprint evidence. Although she was sentenced to 759 years in prison, under Mexican law she can only serve 50 years and will be due for parole in 2058, when she will be 102.

When she heard the sentence, she said: 'Let God forgive me and do not abandon me.'

# THE MADNESS OF MONSTERS

While all serial killers can be difficult to understand, there are some individuals whose acts seem to be so crazed that they are utterly beyond comprehension. Whether leading murder cults, drinking the blood of their victims or claiming they are possessed by devils and demons, these killers are the very personification of evil. You really wouldn't want to bump into any of them on a dark night.

# CHARLES MANSON

Charles Manson died in California State Prison in Corcoran in 2017 after serving 47 years for murder and conspiracy to murder, though he had not actually murdered anyone himself. But in 1969, on his orders, eight people were hacked to death in a meaningless orgy of violence that left America – and the rest of the world – reeling.

Born in 1934 in Cincinnati, Ohio, Manson was the illegitimate son of a teenage prostitute. Unable to support herself even through prostitution, his mother, Kathleen Maddox, left her son with his grandmother in McMechen, West Virginia. Later, he was sent to the famous orphans' home, Boys Town, in Nebraska, but he was soon kicked out for his surly manner and constant thieving. He became a drifter and was arrested for stealing food in Peoria, Illinois. Sent to Indiana Boys' School in Plainfield, he escaped 18 times. In 1951, he was arrested again for theft in Beaver City, Utah, and served four years in federal reformatories.

Released in November 1954, he married and was then arrested for transporting stolen cars across a state line. This time he served three years in Terminal Island Federal Prison near Los Angeles. In 1958, Manson became a pimp and was arrested under the Mann Act for transporting women across

*Charles Manson became one of the most hated figures in America.*

a state line for immoral purposes. Then he took to forging cheques, was caught and sentenced to ten years in the federal penitentiary on McNeil Island in Washington State.

## SCHOOL OF HARD KNOCKS

Being small, just 1.5 m (5 ft 2 in), he had a hard time in prison. He was raped repeatedly by other prisoners. This left him with a lifelong hatred of African Americans who picked on him. To survive, Manson became shifty, cunning and manipulative. Released in 1967, he discovered that he could use what he had learned in jail on the long-haired flower children who flocked to California at the time. His contempt for authority and convention attracted them to him and he developed a taste for middle-class girls who had followed fashion and dropped out of mainstream society.

His hypnotic stare, his unconventional lifestyle and the strange meaningless phrases he babbled made him appear the perfect hippy guru. He travelled with an entourage of young women – all his lovers – and docile males who would do anything he asked. These hangers-on he called the 'Family'. Patricia Krenwinkel was a typical recruit. A former girl scout, she had had a good education and a respectable job at a Los Angeles insurance company. She was 21 when she met Manson on Manhattan Beach. She walked out on her job and did not even bother to pick up her last pay cheque when she moved in with the Family on Spahn Movie Ranch, a collection of broken-down shacks in the dusty east corner of the Simi Valley where they hung out.

## ADDITIONS TO THE FAMILY

Twenty-year-old Linda Kasabian left her husband and two children and stole $5,000 from a friend to join the Family, where she saw her seamy life through a constant haze of LSD. Leslie Van Houten was just 19 when she dropped out of school. She then lived on the streets on a perpetual acid trip until she met Manson. A more pernicious influence was Susan Atkins, a 21-year-old topless dancer and bar-room hustler. She was a practising Satanist and brought devil worship to the suggestible minds of Manson's Family. Like the others, she had to share his sexual favours. Manson tried to satisfy his insatiable sexual appetite with his female followers, one or two at a time – or even with all of them together.

One of the few men in the commune was a 23-year-old former high-school athletics star from Farmersville, Texas, Charles 'Tex' Watson. Once he had been a top student. In Manson's hands, he became a mindless automaton.

## CONTROL FREAK

Surrounded by compliant sycophants, the drug-addled Manson began to develop massive delusions. His own name, Manson, became hugely significant: Manson, Man-son, Son of Man – that is, Christ, or so his demented logic demanded. He was also the Devil, or so Atkins told him.

Manson also dragged the lyrics of Beatles songs into his delusions. Unaware that a helter-skelter was a harmless British funfair ride, he interpreted the track 'Helter Skelter' on The Beatles' *White Album* as heralding the beginning of an inevitable race war. African Americans would be wiped out. Along with them would go the pigs – the police, authority figures, the rich and the famous, what Manson called 'movie people'.

Manson fancied himself as something of a rock star himself. He played the guitar – badly – and wrote a song whose lyrics consisted of the two words 'you know', repeated. Manson took his composition to Gary Hinman, a successful West Coast musician. Manson, Susan Atkins and Bobby Beausoleil – another Family member – badgered Hinman in an attempt to get the song recorded. Hinman humoured them, even letting them stay briefly at his expensive home. Manson then learned that Hinman had recently inherited $20,000. Naively believing that he kept the money at his house, Manson sent Atkins and Beausoleil to get it – and to kill Hinman for refusing to help Manson make 'You Know' a hit. Atkins and Beausoleil tied up Hinman and held him hostage for two days while they ransacked the house. The money was not there.

*Charles Manson and his followers carved an 'X' on their foreheads to show their rejection of society. Manson changed the cross to a swastika during his trial for the Tate and LaBianca murders.*

Eventually, out of frustration, they stabbed Hinman to death.

## THE WRITING ON THE WALL

To give this senseless murder some spurious significance, Susan Atkins dipped her finger in Hinman's blood and wrote 'political piggie' on the wall. The police found Beausoleil's fingerprints in the house and tracked him down. In Beausoleil's car, they found the knife that killed Hinman and a T-shirt drenched in Hinman's blood. Beausoleil was convicted of murder and went to jail without implicating Atkins.

Next Manson approached Terry Melcher. The son of Doris Day, Melcher was a big player in the music industry but, somehow, he failed to see the potential in Manson's material. On 23 March 1969, Manson drove his followers to Melcher's remote home in the Hollywood Hills to reconnoitre it. Melcher had moved out of the house in Cielo Drive in Benedict Canyon. But that did not matter to Manson. The people he saw at the house were 'movie types'.

On 8 August 1969, Manson sent Watson, Atkins, Krenwinkel and Kasabian to Benedict Canyon. Armed with a .22 revolver, a knife and a length of rope, they were ordered to kill everyone in the house and 'make it as gruesome as possible'.

The people now living at the end of Cielo Drive were indeed 'movie people'. The new tenant was film director Roman Polanski, although he was away shooting a movie in London at the time. His eight-months-pregnant wife, movie star Sharon Tate, was at home though. So was Folger's coffee heiress Abigail Folger, her boyfriend Polish writer Voyteck Frykowski and Sharon Tate's friend, celebrity hairdresser Jay Sebring.

## NO MERCY

Kasabian claimed she lost her nerve at the last minute and remained outside. But the others entered the estate. The first person they met was 18-year-old Steven Parent, who had been visiting the caretaker. Parent begged for his life, but Watson shot him four times, killing him instantly.

Inside the house, the three killers herded Sharon Tate and her guests into the living room. While they were being tied up, Sebring broke free, but was gunned down before he could escape. Realizing that they were all going to be killed, Frykowski attacked Watson. He was beaten to the ground. Then the girls stabbed him to death in a frenzy. There were 51 stab wounds on his body. Folger also made a break for it. She was out of the back door and halfway across the lawn before Krenwinkel caught up with her. She was knocked to the ground, then Watson stabbed her to death.

Sharon Tate was by then the only one left alive. She begged for the life of her unborn child. Atkins stabbed her 16 times. Tate's mutilated corpse was tied to Sebring's dead body. Then the killers spread an American flag across the couch and wrote the word 'pig' on the front door in Sharon Tate's blood.

The next day, Manson got stoned and read the lurid reports of the murders in the press. To celebrate, he had an orgy with his female followers. But soon he craved more blood.

*Members of Manson's 'Family' – all were spared the death penalty.*

## MORE MAYHEM

On 10 August, Manson randomly selected a house in the Silver Lake area and broke in. Forty-four-year-old grocery store owner Leno LaBianca and his 38-year-old wife Rosemary, who ran a fashionable dress shop, awoke to find Manson's pistol in their faces.

He took LaBianca's wallet and went outside to the car where his followers were waiting. With them was 23-year-old Steve Grogan. Manson sent Watson, Van Houten and Krenwinkel into the house with instructions to murder the LaBiancas, saying that he was going to the house next door to murder its occupants. Instead, he drove off.

Watson did as he was told. He dragged Leno LaBianca into the living room and stabbed him to death, leaving the knife sticking out of his throat. Meanwhile, Van Houten and Krenwinkel stabbed the helpless Mrs LaBianca. They used their victims' blood to write 'death to all pigs', 'Rise' and 'Helter Skelter' on the walls. Watson carved the word 'War' across LaBianca's stomach, again leaving the knife sticking in the dead man. Then the three killers had a midnight snack and took a shower together.

## NO JOKE

Although the killers thought of their senseless slayings as a joke, they knew that there was a danger that they might get caught and the Family began to break up. To support herself, Susan Atkins turned to prostitution and was arrested. In prison, she boasted to another inmate about the killings. Under interrogation, she told the police that Manson was behind them. He and several other members of the Family still at the Spahn Ranch were arrested, but they were released again due to lack of evidence.

Then on 15 October 1969 Manson was arrested again. This time he was charged. Most of the Family were in custody by then. Manson and his followers took the legal proceedings as a joke and showed no remorse. Basking in the publicity that surrounded the case, Manson portrayed himself as the most evil man on Earth and boasted that he had been responsible for 35 other murders. He, Beausoleil, Atkins, Krenwinkel, Van Houten and Grogan were all found guilty and sentenced to death. But in 1972, the death penalty was abolished in California and the sentences were commuted to life imprisonment.

# REVEREND JIM JONES

It's hard to know the point at which the Reverend Jim Jones went bad – the dynamics of power and its effects are hard to read. But little by little he turned from being an idealistic young pastor into a fire-and-brimstone flim-flam man – and from there it only got worse. By the end, near Port Kaituma in Guyana, he'd become a paranoid Messiah, preaching a demented millenarianism that was to kill almost a thousand men, women and children.

James Warren Jones was born in 1931 in the heart of America's Bible Belt, in Lynn, Indiana, and by the age of 12 he was already preaching impromptu street sermons to children and passers-by. When he was 18, he took a job in nearby Richmond as a hospital porter, so that he could pay his way through Indiana University as a religious-studies student. He got married to a nurse and, when he graduated, he started an outreach programme for poor blacks at an Indianapolis Methodist church.

From the outset he faced often violent opposition from racists both inside and outside his Methodist congregation. So in 1957 he bought a building and opened his own church, the People's Temple, in an Indianapolis ghetto, preaching a message of racial integration and equality. He and his wife adopted seven children, black, white and Asian and he took to describing himself as 'bi-racial,' pointing up his mother's Cherokee blood. He became, in effect, an 'honorary black,' and his style of preaching owed a lot to black holy-roller showmen like Father Divine.

In return he soon secured the undeviating loyalty of a black congregation that rapidly grew as he defied the threats and attacks of white bigots – some of which, it's been suggested, he made up. Like Divine, he became a faith-healer, putting on shows at the Temple in which the 'sick' were cured and the 'disabled' walked. Some of his church elders even began to claim that he'd raised people from the dead.

In 1963, at the height of American fears about nuclear warfare, he suddenly announced that he'd had a vision of a future holocaust in which only two places would be spared: Okiah, California, and Belo Horizonte, Brazil. (The 'vision' probably came from a 1960 magazine article.) He told his congregation to get ready by selling their houses and withdrawing their savings. Then he flew to Brazil to take a look, and on his return journey stopped over for a few days in the socialist republic of Guyana.

Brazil failed the test. So in 1965, he and 300 followers from Indianapolis settled in Redwood Valley near Okiah, California. They were hard-working, charitable and seemingly deeply religious. They took in problem children and orphans and impressed the local community enough for Jones to be appointed foreman of the county grand jury and the director of its free legal-aid services.

In 1970, Jones moved his tax-exempt People's Temple to downtown San Francisco, where his congregation's reputation as a willing and energetic army for good quickly followed him. The church's membership soon swelled to 7,500, both black and white; and the city turned over part of its welfare programme to it. Jones also carefully nurtured its public image, by making donations to the police welfare fund and awards to the press 'for outstanding journalistic contributions to peace and public enlightenment' in its name. He was even invited to President Carter's inauguration in Washington in 1976.

By 1976, though, defectors from the People's Temple were beginning to tell the press about Jones' obsession with sex: about how he preached sexual

abstinence, but treated female members of the church as his harem; about how he forced grown men to confess to imagined sins of homosexuality and browbeat married couples into divorce, so that they could then be reassigned to whoever he chose. There was worse: there were public beatings of children to make them show respect – a cattleprod was even used on the most recalcitrant; and there were sinister congregation-wide rehearsals – so-called 'White Nights' – for what Jones termed 'revolutionary mass suicide.'

By the following year, pressure from the press and public censure had become so intense that Jones put into effect his escape plan. Using the money provided by his congregation, he had already bought a lease on 8,000 hectares (20,000 acres) of jungle and swamp in Guyana, where a pavilion and dormitories had been built. In November 1977, he and a thousand

*Jim Jones (seated, centre) and his wife, Marceline (seated, left), his adopted family and his sister-in-law (seated, right) and her three children.*

loyal members of the congregation moved there. According to a 1978 report in the *San Francisco Chronicle*, the new community at Jonestown was surrounded by armed guards and subject to 'public beatings' and 'a threat of mass suicide.'

When California Congressman Leo Ryan read this, he made it his business to talk to the relatives of the people at Jonestown who were afraid they were being held there against their will. He then asked the federal authorities to intervene with the Guyanan government, and shortly afterwards flew to Jonestown himself with a team of newspaper and television journalists.

When they arrived at Jonestown, they found Jones holding court at the pavilion, with 1,000 American passports locked in a strongroom at his back. At first, the interviews with him and with members of the congregation went well. The armed guards were there simply 'to keep out the bandits;' and yes, Jones did have a number of mistresses, but the idea that his followers were not permitted to have sex was 'bullshit: thirty babies have been born since summer 1977.' The citizens of Jonestown still seemed fanatically devoted to their leader; the only sour note

that was struck was when Ryan offered to put under his personal protection anyone who wanted to leave.

The next day, when Ryan – who had stayed in Jonestown overnight – was picked up by the reporters, they found 20 congregation members who wanted to leave with him. There was a scuffle when one of the church elders tried to stab Ryan. So the press, Ryan and as many defectors who could get on board an earth-moving machine took off to the airstrip where their chartered plane was waiting. There they were later ambushed by armed guards. Ryan, three journalists and two of the defectors were killed.

Back at the settlement, Jones immediately gave orders for mass suicide. Babies had cyanide squirted into their mouths with syringes. Older children drank cups of Kool-Aid laced with poison from huge vats, followed shortly by their parents. When the Guyanese army arrived at the settlement the next day, they found whole families embraced in death, and the Reverend Jim Jones with a bullet through his brain.

After the mass suicide, a white professor who'd been a member of Jones' congregation in its Okiah days said that it had been based on the idealistic Oneida community, which also allowed multiple marriages. A dark hint of this – and a reminder of what it had become – was left in a suicide note, addressed to Jones, found at the scene. It said in part:

'Dad, I can see no way out, I agree with your decision. Without you the world may not make it to Communism. . .'

# PATRICK MACKAY

Few people who knew Patrick Mackay can have been surprised when he was arrested for murder in 1975. Seven years earlier Home Office psychiatrist Dr Leonard Carr had predicted that he would become 'a cold psychopathic killer'. Indeed, after quickly admitting the murder he had been arrested for, Mackay confessed to ten other killings over the previous two years.

Mackay's troubles began before he was born. His father Harold had kicked his mother Marion in the stomach when she was pregnant. Harold was a disturbed individual, having served in North Africa during the Second World War. He had been leading a patrol near Alexandria that had been ambushed. He was the only survivor and had been wounded. A metal plate inserted in his arm gave him trouble for the rest of his life.

In 1947, Harold's first wife died in childbirth. Three years later he took a job as a bookkeeper on a sugar plantation in what was then British Guiana, now Guyana. There he met and married Marion, a good-looking Creole woman. They returned to England where Patrick was born in 1952. Two sisters soon followed.

*In 1975, Patrick Mackay appeared at the Old Bailey charged with murdering five people. He used to spend evenings with his landlord, a priest, discussing the nature of evil and possession.*

In London, Harold took a dead-end job as an accountant. It made him enough money to buy a semi-detached house in Dartford, Kent. But he was disappointed with his lot in life. Consoling himself with drink, he became an abusive alcoholic.

'My father used to get violently drunk, shout, scream and always when he was like this beat me with the back of his hand and sometimes his fist,' recalled Mackay. 'He must have had a tremendous drinking problem, but of course he would never say so. I remember that my father never at all hit my two sisters when drunk, but only me and my mother. He would make a lot of filthy accusations towards her. This would take place usually Friday nights and Saturday nights. It was plain bloody regular.'

At school, Patrick took revenge on smaller children, particularly girls – including his younger sister. He stole and lied, and was an all-round troublemaker. There was no respite at home. The police were called regularly to restrain his father, who spent so much money on drink that the house began to deteriorate. At one point there was no hot water. The children and their clothes grew filthy. When his father was not abusing Patrick, he was regaling him with his reminiscences of the desert war, particularly the ambush and the gruesome manner of his comrades' deaths.

Patrick was ten when his father suddenly died. He refused to accept it. For years afterwards he lied, telling people Harold was still alive. He carried a picture of his father in his army uniform everywhere and claimed that he heard his voice.

He became violent and abusive towards his mother and sisters, threw tantrums and had fits, falling to the ground frothing at the mouth. In the autumn of 1963, Patrick's mother had a nervous breakdown and was admitted to hospital. Patrick was taken into care before being sent to a foster mother. However, his mother was eventually discharged and the children were returned to her.

# BECOMING A JUVENILE DELINQUENT

Patrick's violent rages were then taken out on animals. His pet dog was attacked remorselessly. He tortured his pet rabbit and tried to strangle a neighbour's cat. His tortoise was grilled alive on a bonfire and he played with dead birds that he may have killed himself. He also speculated aloud about his father's decaying bones.

He bullied younger children, threatened an old woman with a pitchfork and set fire to a neighbour's garden shed. The theft of some garden gnomes marked the beginning of his criminal record. In juvenile court for the first time at the age of 11, he had 21 charges taken into consideration and was given three years' probation.

Truanting from school, he would barricade himself in the house, or smash the place up. The police were called and he was referred to a psychiatrist. After further outbursts Patrick was sent to the adolescent unit of a nearby hospital, where it was noted that he took a doll to bed with him and kissed it goodnight. He ran away three times. Again, he found himself in the juvenile court for theft.

He was sent to an Approved School where he was caned regularly. One of the masters wrote: 'He is a potential murderer of women.'

After absconding several times, he found himself in a psychiatric unit. Having been discharged, in 1968 Patrick Mackay tried to strangle his mother. When the police arrived, they found him trying to commit suicide. He was sent to a mental hospital. Two days after his release he was charged with assaulting two boys. Mackay was sentenced to two years' probation. More assaults followed and a court sent him to Moss Side mental hospital in Manchester, certified as a diagnosed psychopath. He was discharged in 1970, returning home to continue abusing his mother and sisters.

Barely literate, he was found a job as a gardener's labourer with Kensington and Chelsea Borough Council. An aunt in west London took him in. He tried to strangle her. By then, he was a regular user of drink and drugs.

Returning to his mother, there was more domestic violence. When the police intervened, they found his bedroom was full of Nazi memorabilia. Sent back to mental hospital, Mackay absconded again. On his return, it was noted that he was violent and seemingly obsessed with death.

After another stretch in Moss Side, he was found another job, but was sacked after ten days, having only turned up twice. He stayed with friends, who he abused, and became more obsessed with the Nazis, even making himself a rudimentary uniform. His mother's mixed blood then became a concern. Failing to pick up his benefits, he supported himself instead by burglary.

# DEMON DRINK AND SAINTLY PRIESTS

In May 1973, Patrick Mackay was befriended by Father Anthony Crean, who lived in the village of Shorne, just outside Gravesend, in Kent. Father Crean took him to the pub and bought him drinks. One night, Mackay broke into Crean's cottage and stole a cheque for £30. He changed the £30 to £80 and cashed it. When Mackay was arrested, Father Crean tried to get the charges against him dropped, but the police insisted that the prosecution go ahead.

Mackay pleaded guilty and was fined £20 for breaking and entering with a two-year conditional discharge and was ordered to repay the £80 to Father Crean at £7 a week. Mackay went to see Father Crean and promised to repay him, a promise he never kept.

Unable to hold down a job and all too often drunk and abusive, Mackay found himself with nowhere to live. On 14 July 1974, the police found Mackay drunk and unconscious in the street and took him to St Thomas's Hospital in London.

The following day, he was arrested for chasing a tramp with a long metal pole and throwing bricks down a pedestrian subway. He then became abusive, claiming that he was a 'pure Aryan' and he would kill all 'Jewish bastards'. He later claimed to have been drunk and had no recollection of the incident. However, the police insisted that he was not drunk and that his behaviour was 'manifestly manic'.

While he was found guilty, sentencing was deferred for six months. Four days later he was back in court for being drunk and disorderly, and damaging a public lavatory. He was fined £15 and ordered to pay £10.44 for the damage he had caused. Two weeks later he was stopped riding a stolen child's bike, drunk, without lights at night. Unable to raise the £5 bail – or find anyone to post it for him – he spent three weeks on remand in Pentonville Prison, north London before being fined £25.

A kindly Anglican priest took him in as a lodger in his house in Finchley. He got a job as a gardener, which he liked. Back in court for sentencing in February 1974, he was given two months, once again suspended.

Some of the police involved in Mackay's later murder case think that he had probably killed five people by this time. Mackay admitted only one. After being arrested for murder in 1975, he said that in January 1974 he had thrown a tramp off Hungerford Bridge into the Thames. On average, three bodies a month are found in the river. None could be linked to the incident Mackay described. Lacking evidence, no charges were brought.

He found work as a groundsman, then as a keeper on Hadley Woods Common. In the evenings,

*Mackay claimed to have thrown a tramp off Hungerford Bridge.*

he would get drunk. After a drunken row with one of his few friends, he decided to kill himself, but a policeman stopped him and took him to Tooting Bec Hospital. There he admitted to having been under psychiatric care since the age of 17 and that he enjoyed the company of murderers and psychopaths.

It was concluded that Mackay was not mentally ill – that is, a schizophrenic or depressive. Rather, he had a psychopathic personality disorder. But that was no grounds for holding him. Instead, social services were informed and he was discharged.

Three days earlier, he had met 84-year-old widow Isabella Griffiths in Chelsea and helped carry her shopping. She invited him into her home at 19 Cheyne Walk, a tall house set back from the River Thames, and offered him a drink. When Mackay left, she gave him £5 and told him to drop in whenever he was in the area.

After being discharged from hospital, he went straight there. Mrs Griffiths opened the door, but kept it on a safety chain, saying that she did not want any shopping that day. He asked to come in. When she refused, Mackay pushed against the door hard enough to break the chain.

He throttled her and dragged her into the kitchen, then paused to listen to the news on the radio. According to his own account, he wandered around the house before he felt 'a strong compulsion to kill her outright'. In the kitchen, he found a large knife and stabbed Mrs Griffiths in the solar plexus. Sitting in the front room, he drank a bottle of whisky he had brought with him. Then he pulled the knife from his victim's body and thought momentarily of stabbing himself, but the suicidal feeling passed.

He closed Mrs Griffiths' eyes, crossed her arms and covered her body. Then he tidied up. After stealing a mahogany cigarette box, he locked up and left, throwing the knife into a garden.

The widow's body was not found for 12 days, when the police had to force entry into her home. The stab wound was not noticed until the corpse was in the mortuary. With little to go on, the murder remained unsolved for a year.

Back in Finchley, Mackay took to making model aircraft – black ones with swastikas on them. He also made toy monsters and burned their eyes out. Otherwise he would spend his evenings in a rambling discourse with his landlord, the priest, about the nature of evil and possession.

When Mackay and the priest eventually fell out, his aunt found digs for him. But in July 1974, he returned to Finchley and broke into the priest's home. Two days later Mackay was arrested and charged with burglary. Found guilty, he was sentenced to four months in Wormwood Scrubs. With nowhere to go when he was released, he was lodged in a hostel.

## OFF THE STREETS AT LAST, AT A HEAVY PRICE

Mackay had long paid for his excessive drinking by snatching elderly ladies' handbags. On 10 March 1975, he followed 89-year-old Adele Price home to Lowndes Square where she had a third-floor flat. He tricked his way in and throttled her.

'I felt hellish and very peculiar inside,' he said. 'This peculiar feeling I had for some days before and after each killing.'

Mackay watched television and fell asleep. He was awoken by Mrs Price's granddaughter who could not get in because he had secured the safety chain on the front door. When she returned, it had been taken off and Mackay had made his escape. The police only realized that Mrs Price had been murdered because Mackay had left her body in the bedroom and locked the door from the outside.

Two days later, Mackay walked off the platform at Stockwell underground station, hoping to be hit by a train, but alert staff turned the electricity off. The police took him to a mental hospital, but after five days' observation he was again discharged.

Following a spate of handbag snatching over the next two days, he took the train to Kent carrying two sharp kitchen knives. Mackay walked into Father Crean's cottage, saying he had come to discuss the money he owed him. Crean made for the front door.

Mackay grabbed him. They tussled. Crean said: 'Don't hurt me.'

'This seemed to get me even more excitable myself,' recalled Mackay, who started punching his former good samaritan.

Crean fled into the bathroom. Mackay grabbed an axe from under the stairs. He forced his way in. Pushing Crean into the bath, he stabbed him in the neck, then struck him on the head with the axe with such force that the priest's brain was exposed. Crean raised his hand to touch the wound, then died.

The body was discovered by the mother superior of nearby St Catherine's Convent, where Father Crean was chaplain. When considering possible suspects, the local police recalled the case where Father Crean had tried to prevent the prosecution of Mackay.

They quickly traced him to his probation hostel, and from there to the home of a friend, where he was arrested. In custody, he admitted ten other murders and was charged with five. Two of those charges were dropped due to lack of evidence. Convicted, he was still in jail over 40 years later; as he was convicted under a 'whole life tariff' he is unlikely ever to be released.

# RICHARD CHASE

At around 6 pm on 23 January 1978, 24-year-old laundry-truck driver David Wallin returned to his modest suburban home in north Sacramento to find his 22-year-old wife Terry, who was three months pregnant, dead and horribly mutilated. Screaming in horror, he ran to the house of a neighbour, who called the police.

It appeared that Terry Wallin had been attacked in the living room of her house while she was preparing to take the rubbish out. She had been shot with a .22 calibre firearm and had been stabbed repeatedly before and after she was dead. The perpetrator had then raped her corpse, cut off her left nipple and slashed open her belly. Some of her body parts were missing and there was a yoghurt carton beside her body which the killer appeared to have used as a cup to drink her blood. He had also collected dog faeces from the yard and forced them down her throat.

## PROFILE OF A KILLER

The local police called Russ Vorpagel, a veteran cop with the FBI's Behavioral Science Unit on the West Coast. He in turn contacted Robert Ressler, a pioneer in psychological profiling at the FBI's Training Academy in Quantico, Virginia. It was clear to both of them that such a killer was not going to be satisfied with one homicide. Unless he was caught quickly, he was bound to kill again. Ressler flew out to California as soon as he could.

Psychological profiling was in its infancy and normally the cases that got referred to the BSU were cold. This one gave them the chance to try out profiling techniques on a case that was hot. Ressler immediately came up with a profile of the suspect:

White male, aged 25–27 years; thin, undernourished appearance. Residence will be extremely slovenly and unkempt and evidence of the crime will be found at the residence. History of mental illness, and will have been involved in use of drugs. Will be a loner who does not associate with either males or females, and will probably spend a great deal of time in his own home, where he lives alone. Unemployed. Possibly receives some form of disability money. If residing with anyone, it would be with his parents; however, this is unlikely. No prior military record; high school or college dropout. Probably suffering from one or more forms of paranoid psychosis.

It proved extraordinarily accurate but was of no immediate use.

## ORGANS REMOVED

While the investigation got under way, there were more horrifying murders. Just four days after the slaughter of Terry Wallin, three bodies were found in another suburban house in north Sacramento, not far away. Thirty-six-year-old mother of three Evelyn Miroth, her six-year-old son Jason and 52-year-old family friend Daniel J. Meredith had all been shot with a .22 firearm. Evelyn had been babysitting her 22-month-old nephew David Ferreira, who was missing. It was assumed that the killer had abducted the child.

While Jason and Meredith had just been shot and were otherwise unmolested, Evelyn Miroth was found nude on her bed. She had been sodomized and there were multiple stab wounds all over her body, including cuts to the face and around the anus. As with Terry Wallin, her belly had been slashed open and organs removed. Blood, brains and faecal matter had been thrown into the bath.

In the playpen where David Ferreira would have been there was a blood-soaked pillow and an expended bullet, so detectives did not expect to find the child alive. Meredith's wallet and car keys were missing. The killer had used the keys to make his getaway in Meredith's red station wagon, which was found abandoned nearby with the driver's door open and the keys in the ignition. Ressler concluded that the killer was a 'disorganized' type and that he would live within half-a-mile to a mile from where he had left the car. He also believed that the perpetrator had committed 'fetish burglaries' in the area – that is, he had stolen jewellery of little marketable value or articles of women's clothing for autoerotic purposes.

Armed with an updated profile, 65 police officers began a manhunt in the immediate area. Ressler appeared to be on the right track when

*Aerial view of downtown Sacramento: Richard Chase became the 'Vampire Killer of Sacramento' after a murder binge in which he claimed six lives.*

*David Wallin looks at his wedding album, remembering his wife Terry who was killed by the 'Vampire of Sacramento'.*

it was discovered that a dog had been shot and disembowelled at a nearby country club.

A woman then came forward to say that she had seen a man she had known at high school in the shopping centre that Terry Wallin had visited on the morning of her murder. She had cashed a cheque there. He was thin and dishevelled, with sunken eyes, a yellow crust around his mouth and blood on his sweatshirt. He had tried to engage her in conversation and had pulled on the door handle of her car. She then took fright and drove away.

## BRAIN TISSUE IN FRIDGE

The man's name was Richard Trenton Chase. He had graduated from her high school in 1968 and lived just a block from where the station wagon had

been abandoned and a mile from both the shopping centre and the country club. The police phoned his apartment, but there was no answer. They knew that the killer had a .22 pistol so they staked out Chase's apartment and waited for him.

When he emerged, he was carrying a box. Seeing the officers, he made a dash for his truck but they gave chase and brought him down. As they grappled with him on the ground, a .22 pistol fell from the shoulder holster he was wearing. A quick search revealed Daniel Meredith's wallet in his back pocket and the box he was carrying was full of bloody rags.

His truck was a wreck and full of empty beer cans, newspapers and other litter. There was a 30 cm (12 in)

butcher's knife locked in the toolbox, along with a pair of rubber boots with blood on them. His apartment was also a mess. In it, the police found newspaper articles about Terry Wallin's murder, bloodstained clothing, pet collars and leads and food blenders with blood in them. In a kitchen drawer, there were knives taken from the Wallins' house and in the fridge they found dishes containing brain tissue and other body parts. On the wall of the apartment was a calendar with the word 'Today' scrawled on the days of the murders. The same word appeared on 44 days spread out over the rest of the year. Clearly, he intended to kill again.

Soon after Chase was arrested, it was found that he had committed another murder. The bullets from his gun matched the one taken from the body of 51-year-old Ambrose Griffin. On 28 December 1977, Griffin had just returned from the supermarket with his wife. They were unloading the groceries from their car when Chase drove by and fired two shots. One of them hit Griffin in the chest and killed him. Not only that but the decapitated body of the missing infant David Ferreira was eventually found not far from Chase's apartment.

Chase also fitted the description of a thief responsible for a number of fetish burglaries in the area and the collars and leads found in his apartment belonged to dogs and cats that had gone missing in the vicinity. He also had a criminal record. The previous August, he had been arrested near Lake Tahoe by an Indian agent. He had blood on his clothes but explained that he had been hunting rabbits. In his truck were a number of guns and a bucket of blood, which turned out to be bovine. However, his father rode to the rescue and he was released after paying a fine.

## BIT HEADS OFF BIRDS

Born in 1950, Chase was said to have been a sweet and co-operative child, though he wet the bed until the age of eight. When he was about 12, his parents fell out. His mother accused his father of being unfaithful, taking drugs and trying to poison her. Ressler described Mrs Chase as the classic mother of a schizophrenic – 'highly aggressive ... hostile ... provocative'. The fighting went on for ten years until the couple divorced and his father remarried.

Chase was unremarkable at school, lacked any ambition, had no close friends and was unable to keep girlfriends when they found he could not sustain an erection. He then began drinking heavily and smoking marijuana. Caught in possession, he was sentenced to community service. Unable to hold down a job, he dropped out of junior college and lived alternately with his mother and father, who supported him.

In 1972 he was arrested for drink driving and stopped drinking afterwards. The following year he was arrested for carrying a gun without a licence and resisting arrest. He was then thrown out of a party after trying to grab a girl's breast and, when two men restrained him after he returned, a .22 fell out of his waistband. The police were called and he was fined $50.

He got ill in 1976 after injecting himself with rabbit blood. Sent to a nursing home, he frightened other patients by biting the heads off birds he had caught in the bushes. He described his pleasure in killing small animals and was often found smeared with blood, so the staff called him Dracula. Apparently he believed he was being poisoned and his blood was turning into powder, so he had to drink another creature's blood to replenish it. Even so, Chase was discharged in 1977.

His mother then found him an apartment. At this point he became obsessed with flying saucers and thought a Nazi crime syndicate was out to get him. After his arrest at Lake Tahoe in August, his mental state rapidly disintegrated. The following month, he killed his mother's cat after an argument with her and in October he bought two dogs from an animal shelter for $15 each. Also in that month he tried driving out of a petrol station without paying his petrol bill for $20, but after being stopped and questioned he was allowed to drive on.

He soon bought more dogs and tormented a family who had placed an advertisement in a newspaper asking if anyone had seen their missing pooch. Meanwhile, police reports of missing pets backed up.

## ABLE TO BUY GUN

He then bought a gun, swearing on the form that he had never been in a mental institution. While he waited the ten days required before he was allowed to pick it up, he followed the doings of the Hillside Strangler in the newspaper and looked at small ads offering dogs for sale. Once he had the gun he shot at the side wall of the home of the Phares family. Next a bullet went through a kitchen window which, according to Ressler, parted the hair of Mrs Polenske. A few days later Ambrose Griffin was killed. He lived across the street from the Phares. Chase kept a cutting from the *Sacramento Bee* about the murder.

On 23 January, before he killed Terry Wallin, he tried to enter the home of a neighbour but when she saw him through the kitchen window he sat motionless on her patio, escaping before the police arrived. He then entered a nearby house, stole a few things, urinated on clothes in a drawer and defecated in a child's cot. An hour later he was at the shopping centre where he met the woman who had known him at high school. She did not recognize him until he asked her whether she had been on the motorcycle when her boyfriend, a friend of his, had been killed. She said she had not and asked who he was before making her escape. Immediately after that he left the shopping centre, entered the nearby Wallins' home and killed Terry.

## WORKINGS OF A KILLER'S MIND

Although Chase was unco-operative with the police, he confessed all to a prison psychiatrist, saying:

The first person I killed was sort of an accident. My car was broken down. I wanted to leave but I had no transmission. I had to get an apartment. Mother wouldn't let me in at Christmas. Always before she let me come in at Christmas, have dinner, and talk to her, my grandmother, and my sister. That year she wouldn't let me in and I shot from the car and killed somebody. The second time, the people had made a lot of money and I was jealous. I was being watched, and I shot this lady – got some blood out of it. I went to another house, walked in, a whole family was there. I shot the whole family. Somebody saw me there. I saw this girl. She had called the police and they had been unable to locate me. Curt Silva's girlfriend – he was killed in a motorcycle accident, as a couple of my friends were, and I had this idea that he was killed through the syndicate, that he was in the Mafia, selling drugs. His girlfriend remembered about Curt – I was trying to get information. She said she was married to somebody else and wouldn't talk to me. The whole syndicate was making money by having my mom poison me. I know who they are and I think it can be brought out in a court of law if I can pull the pieces together like I've been hoping.

## 'HIS EYES GOT ME'

On 6 May 1979 he went on trial on six counts of first-degree murder. The *Sacramento Bee* reported:

The defendant has a totally lustreless quality. Dull, limp brown hair, sunken opaque eyes, a sallow complexion and scarcely a spare ounce of flesh clinging to his bony frame. For the past four and a half months Richard Trenton Chase, just a couple of weeks short of his twenty-ninth birthday, has sat hunched in his chair, toying with papers in front of him or staring vacantly at the fluorescent lights of the courtroom.

The defence argued that he was not guilty by reason of insanity but the jury found him guilty on all counts and he was sentenced to death. While he was on death row in San Quentin, Ressler visited him. Ressler voiced his thoughts:

It was his eyes that really got me. I'll never forget them. They were like those of the shark in the movie *Jaws*. No pupils, just black spots. These were evil eyes that stayed with me long after the interview. I almost got the impression that he couldn't really see me, that he was seeing through me, just staring.

Again he admitted the murders. His excuse was that he was being poisoned via his soap dish. The toxin pulverized the blood so he had to drink more fresh blood to stay alive. Again he rambled on about the Nazis and UFOs, claiming that he had murdered in self-defence. He also claimed that his victims had left their doors unlocked, which invited him in. Otherwise he would not have entered their homes.

On death row, the other inmates taunted him and his paranoia got the better of him. He saved up his anti-depressant pills and killed himself with an overdose.

# RICHARD RAMIREZ

s the Night Stalker, Richard Ramirez terrorized Los Angeles for two years. He was a devil worshipper whose calling card was a hastily scrawled pentagram and he made his rape victims declare their love of Satan before he slaughtered them. At his first court hearing after being apprehended, he raised a hand with his trademark pentagram drawn on it and yelled: 'Hail, Satan.'

The Night Stalker's murderous career began on the night of 8 June 1984, when the mutilated body of 79-year-old Jennie Vincow was found spread-eagled on the bed of her one-bedroom apartment in the Glassell Park district of Los Angeles. She had been raped and her throat had been slashed so violently that she had almost been decapitated. Fingerprints were found, but in those days comparisons had to be done manually so matching them with any that might be on file was a monumental task.

Nine months later, on 17 March 1985, Maria Hernandez had just parked her car in her garage in the Rosemead condominium when she was confronted by a man with a gun. He shot her. The bullet ricocheted off her car keys, but the impact of the bullet was enough to knock her to the ground. The gunman kicked her viciously, then made his way into her apartment. From inside, Maria heard a gunshot.

*There seemed to be no pattern to the victims Ramirez singled out.*

She staggered to her feet, only to be confronted once more by the gunman running from the house.

'Please don't shoot me again,' she begged. The gunman froze, then took to his heels.

Inside the apartment Hernandez found her boyfriend, 34-year-old Hawaiian-born traffic manager Dayle Okazaki, lying on the kitchen floor, dead. He had been shot through the head.

## THE 'NIGHT STALKER' IS BORN

There was only one clue to the murder. Maria said that the gunman had worn a baseball cap bearing the AC/DC logo. The Australian band had recently

released an album called *Highway to Hell* which included a track called 'Night Prowler'. Although this was the *nom d'assassin* Ramirez would have preferred to have been known by, the newspapers instead dubbed him the Night Stalker.

The killer was not finished for the night. Less than an hour after killing Dayle Okazaki, he pulled 30-year-old law student Tsai Lian Yu from her car and shot her twice. She died before the ambulance arrived.

Ten days later, the killer entered the home of Vincent and Maxine Zazzara. Both of them were shot at point-blank range and Maxine's naked body was mutilated after death. She had been stabbed repeatedly and her eyes had been gouged out.

On 14 May 1985, Ramirez broke into a home in Monterey Park. He shot 66-year-old William Doi in the head while he lay sleeping. His disabled wife, 63-year-old Lillian, who was in bed next to him, was beaten around the head until she told the intruder where their valuables were hidden, after which he raped her.

A fortnight later, Carol Kyle was awoken in her Burbank apartment by a torch shining in her eyes. An armed man dragged her out of bed and raped and sodomized her. In the next room, Carol's terrified 12-year-old son had been locked in a closet. Her attacker ransacked the apartment and fled, leaving both Carol and her son alive.

Around the same time, two elderly women, 83-year-old Mabel Bell and her 80-year-old sister Florence Long, an invalid, were attacked in their home in the suburb of Monrovia. On 1 June, Florence was found lying on her bed in a coma. There was a huge wound over her ear and a bloodstained hammer was lying on the dressing table. Mabel was barely conscious on her bedroom floor in a pool of her own blood. An inverted pentagram, the encircled five-point star that is used in witchcraft, was scrawled in lipstick on Mabel's thigh. Another was drawn on Florence's bedroom wall. The police concluded that the two sisters had been left that way for two days. Six weeks after the attack, Mabel Bell died. Florence eventually regained consciousness and survived.

Then the Night Stalker's onslaught gained pace. On the night of 27 June, the killer slashed the throat of 32-year-old Patty Elaine Higgins in her home in Arcadia. The same fate befell 77-year-old Mary Louise Cannon five days later. Three days after that, again in Arcadia, Ramirez savagely beat 16-year-old Whitney Bennett with a tyre iron and throttled her with telephone wire. Somehow, she survived.

On 7 July, 61-year-old Joyce Lucille Nelson was found beaten to death in her home in Monterey Park and 63-year-old Sophie Dickman was raped and robbed in her apartment.

On 20 July, 68-year-old Max Kneiding and his 64-year-old wife Lela were shot and mutilated in their Glendale home. That same night 32-year-old Chainarong Khovananth was shot dead at his home in Sun Valley and his 29-year-old wife Somkid was raped and forced to perform oral sex. She was then beaten savagely and forced to swear in Satan's name that she would not cry out while he sodomized her eight-year-old son.

# A PATTERN OF BEHAVIOUR EMERGES

The police were mystified. While these crimes were related, the killer had no clear modus operandi. He killed with guns, hammers and knives. He raped orally,

*Richard Ramirez became known as the 'Night Stalker'.*

anally and genitally both children and women, young and old. Sometimes he mutilated the bodies after death, sometimes he let his victims live. Sometimes he stole; sometimes he didn't. However, there were some similarities between the crimes. The killer stalked quiet suburbs where homeowners were less security conscious. Entry was through an open window or an unlocked door. He made his attacks close to freeways, making escape easier. Pentagrams and other satanic symbols were commonly left by the killer, and his crimes were distinguished by their sheer brutality.

On the night of 5 August, Virginia Petersen was shot in the face in her Northridge home. The bullet entered the cheek just below her eye and went clean through the back of her head. Her husband Christopher then got a bullet in the temple. But he was a tough guy and flung himself at the intruder, who panicked and ran. Both miraculously survived to give a detailed description of their attacker.

Three days later, 35-year-old Elyas Abowath was shot dead at his home in Diamond Bar and his 28-year-old wife was beaten and raped. Again, she was forced to swear by Satan that she would not cry out.

The residents of Los Angeles were now on the alert. Locksmiths were doing a roaring trade and gun shops quickly sold out. But the killer simply travelled north to San Francisco. On the night of 17 August 1985, 66-year-old accountant Peter Pan was shot dead in his home in the suburb of Lake Merced. His 64-year-old wife Barbara was also shot as she fought off the attacker, but survived. An inverted pentagram was drawn in lipstick on the bedroom wall along with the words 'Jack the Knife'. At first, the police thought it was a copy-cat attack, but the bullets matched the small-calibre rounds found in the Los Angeles murders.

A week later, in the small town of Mission Viejo, 80 km (50 miles) south of Los Angeles, 29-year-old computer engineer William Carns was shot three times in the head and his fiancée Inez Erickson, also 29, was raped. The attacker announced that he was the Night Stalker and forced her to say 'I love Satan' during her ordeal.

Inez saw a rusty old orange Toyota drive off after the attacker left the house. This proved to be the vital clue that put an end to the reign of the Night Stalker. A sharp-eyed kid, James Romero III, had also spotted the orange Toyota and noted its licence plate. Two days later, the car was found in a parking lot in the Los Angeles suburb of Rampart.

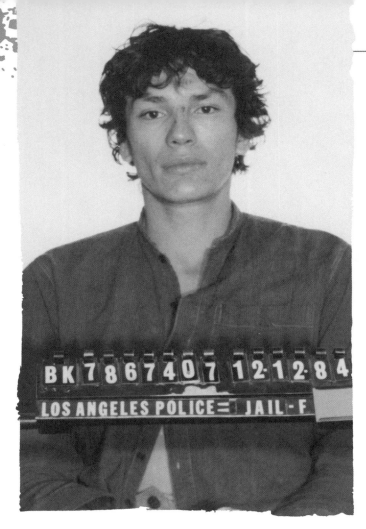

*Richard Ramirez – a sharp-eyed kid spotted his rusty old orange Toyota. Two days later, the car was found in the Los Angeles suburb of Rampart.*

A single fingerprint was found, and it was matched to those of 25-year-old Ricardo 'Richard' Ramirez, a petty criminal who had been arrested three times for marijuana possession. Soon his photograph was on the front page of every newspaper in California.

## THE PEOPLE VERSUS RICHARD RAMIREZ

Ramirez had been out in Phoenix, Arizona, to score some cocaine and was quite unaware of his new-found fame as he stepped down from the Greyhound bus at Los Angeles' main bus station at about 8.30 am on 31 August 1985. He was high. By then he had killed 13 people and he felt good. Surely, he must be Satan's favourite son.

He went into a local shop to buy a Pepsi. At the checkout he saw his own face splashed across the Spanish language paper *La Opinion*. The checkout clerk recognized him. So did the other customers. The game was up and Ramirez made a run for it.

Out on the street, someone cried out: 'It's the Night Stalker!'

Ramirez ran out on to the Santa Ana Freeway and tried to carjack a woman but was forced to flee by a crowd pursuing him. He ran for just over 3 km (2 miles). As he paused to catch his breath he was surrounded by the wail of police sirens. Desperate to get off the street, he knocked on a door at random. Bonnie Navarro opened it. Ramirez shouted 'Help me' in Spanish. She slammed the door in his face.

On the next block, he tried to pull a woman from her car, but bystanders again rushed to her rescue. Ramirez then jumped over a fence into a backyard where Luis Muñoz was cooking a barbecue. He hit Ramirez with his tongs. In the next yard, Ramirez tried to steal a red 1966 Mustang, but 56-year-old Faustino Pinon, who was working on the transmission, grabbed him in a headlock. Ramirez broke free and ran on, pursued by Pinon.

Angelina de la Torres was about to get into her gold Granada when she saw Ramirez running towards her screaming: 'I'm going to kill you.' She hit him with the car door. Her husband Manuel heard the fracas. He came out of the house with a metal pole in his hand and ran towards Ramirez. From the other side of the street 55-year-old construction worker Jose Burgoin and his two sons, Jaime and Julio, all ran after Ramirez. Now he had five men chasing him.

Manuel de la Torres caught up with Ramirez and struck him three times with the metal pole. Ramirez fell to the ground and Jose, Jaime and Julio jumped on top of him. Just then, a patrol car screeched to a halt in front of the group of men.

'Save me!' yelled Ramirez. As a patrolman handcuffed him, he said: 'Thank God you came. I am the one you want. Save me before they kill me.'

Safely in custody, Ramirez showed no contrition for his crimes. In fact, he relished them. He told the police: 'I love to kill people. I love watching them die. I would shoot them in the head and they would wiggle and squirm all over the place, and then just stop. Or I would cut them with a knife and watch their faces turn real white. I love all that blood. I told one lady one time to give me all her money. She said no. So I cut her and pulled her eyes out.'

On 20 September 1989, Richard Ramirez was found guilty on 13 counts of murder, five attempted murders, 11 sexual assaults and 14 burglaries. He was given 12 death sentences, along with a sentence of over 100 years' imprisonment. Sentencing him, the judge said that Ramirez demonstrated 'cruelty, callousness and viciousness beyond any human understanding'.

Asked if he had anything to say, Ramirez replied: 'I have a lot to say, but now is not the time or place. I don't know why I am wasting my breath. But what the hell, I don't believe in the hypocritical moralistic dogmas of this so-called civilized society. You maggots make me sick. Hypocrites one and all! You don't understand me. You are not expected to. You are not capable of it. I am beyond your experience. I am beyond good and evil.'

Peter Zazzara, the son of the murdered Vincent and Maxine, said after the trial: 'I don't know why somebody would want to do something like that. To take joy in the way it happened.'

Ramirez wasn't bothered. On his way to San Quentin where the gas chamber awaited, he said: 'Hey, big deal. Death comes with the territory. I'll see you in Disneyland.'

While he was on death row, many women wrote to Ramirez, some sending provocative pictures, pledging undying love and proposing marriage. In 1996 he married Doreen Lioy in San Quentin. She had written him some 75 letters in prison. She told CNN: 'I think he's a really great person. He's my best friend; he's my buddy.' Although she threatened to take her own life if Richard was executed, the marriage did not last and they divorced after a few years. In total, the trial cost $1.8 million and was California's most expensive legal proceeding until that of O.J. Simpson. It generated 50,000 pages of trial papers. Marshalling those meant that the first appeal did not even begin until 7 August 2006. Ramirez's lawyer then argued that his client was possessed by the devil and a helpless victim of his own sexuality, so he should not be sentenced to death.

'Life imprisonment without parole means he will never see Disneyland again,' he said.

The California Supreme Court upheld both the convictions and the death sentence. However, Ramirez escaped the gas chamber, dying of liver failure in 2013 at the age of 53. During his 23 years on death row, he never admitted to his crimes nor showed any remorse for what he had done.

# TSUTOMU MIYAZAKI

Many countries around the world look enviously towards Japan and ask the same question: how have they managed to create such an apparently harmonious and crime-free society? The crime rate in Japan is, by all modern standards, staggeringly low, and the rate of violent crime lower still. Fewer than one person is murdered for every 100,000 in the population, compared to 4.8 for the United States and 44.7 in Belize; only Iceland, with a population of 325,000, has a lower homicide rate than Japan, where 127 million live. Not only that, but the rate in Japan is actually falling, whilst in most other countries the already high homicide rate continues to climb. As a rule, then, Japan does not suffer from the curse of the serial killer. The exception to that rule was Tsutomu Miyazaki.

## THERE ARE DEVILS ABOUT

She was wearing a pink and white T-shirt with cats on it. Pink pumps. She had a pageboy haircut, and was 105 cm (3 ft 4 in) tall. On 23 August 1988, in Saitama, just north of the capital Tokyo, everyone was looking for four-year-old Mari Konno. Her father had reported her missing the day before, after she failed to return from a trip to play at a friend's house.

From the outset, the Japanese police treated her disappearance as a murder case. Girls of that age simply do not disappear in Japan. Police squad cars prowled the streets, their loudspeakers warning parents to keep their children indoors. Every home in the area was visited by officers, and 50,000 posters of Mari were distributed. Two boys and a 38-year-old housewife had independently seen the missing girl with a man dressed in a white sweater and white slacks. He had a round, pudgy face and curly hair. That was all the police had to go on: despite an extensive search with dogs, no trace of Mari could be found.

Yukie Konno, Mari's mother, went on television to appeal for help, and expressed hope that her daughter might still be alive. A couple of days later she received an anonymous postcard bearing the message: 'There are devils about'. Although the police dismissed it as the work of a crank, the card was sent by the killer, Tsutomu Miyazaki.

## THE OUTSIDER

Tsutomu was born prematurely in Itsukaichi, Tokyo, on 21 August 1962. He weighed just 2.2 kg (4 lb 8 oz) and the joints in his hands were fused together, meaning he could not bend his wrists upwards. He was teased about his deformity from an early age and rapidly became acutely self-conscious. At school he was remembered by classmates and teachers alike as a loner who found it impossible to make friends.

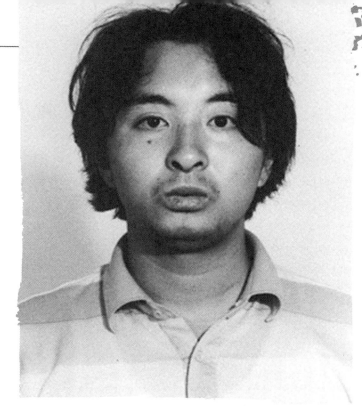

*Tsutomu Miyazaki was sentenced to death in 1997 for killing four young girls.*

Later, at college, he took his video and stills camera to the tennis courts to take 'upskirt' photographs of the female players. One of his own sisters caught him spying on her in the bath.

Though bright, Tsutomu lost interest in his studies as he grew older and was forced to abandon his plan to enter Meiji University due to poor grades. Instead, he found work at a printing company that belonged to a friend of his father and read comic books voraciously when not at work.

His father, Katsumi Miyazaki, owned the *Akikawa Shimbun*, a local Itsukaichi newspaper, and was well-regarded in the locality. Like many Japanese men, he was something of a workaholic, and often absent from the family home that Tsutomu continued to share with his parents. The only person with whom Tsutomu bonded was his grandfather, Shokichi, and it was the old man's death in May 1988 that appears to have triggered Tsotumu's descent into madness and murder. In later letters, Tsutomu Miyazaki claimed to have eaten some of his grandfather's cremated remains in order to try and reincarnate him. By now 25 years old, and with no ability to form adult relationships, Tsutomu turned to child pornography and lolicon anime (a genre of Japanese comic depicting sexualized prepubescent girls) for his thrills. He began to amass a vast collection of videos and comic books, many either sexual or violent in nature. When the police searched his room after his

eventual arrest they found 5,763 such videos, as well as hundreds of comic books.

On 21 August 1988, Tsutomu Miyazaki celebrated his 26th birthday. The next day, he drove away from the family home in his Nissan Langley sedan and stopped shortly afterwards to offer a ride to four-year-old Mari Konno.

## THE MURDERS

Once the girl was inside his car, Miyazaki drove for more than an hour and a half to a quiet woodland area 50 km (31 miles) from Saitama. He claimed the two of them chatted happily during the journey but only he knows whether that is true. What is beyond dispute is that the pair walked through the woods, away from the hiking paths that crisscross the area, to a remote part of the forest where they could not be seen or heard. There, Miyazaki strangled the girl to death before undressing and sexually assaulting her. Before and after the crime he took photographs in order to document his atrocity. He left her body in the woods, bundled up her clothes and returned to his car. Nobody had seen him enter the woods and nobody saw him leave. Nor did anyone see him re-enter the woods six weeks later, with seven-year-old Masami Yoshizawa.

Masami was lured into Miyazaki's car from a quiet street in Hanno, close to where he lived. She met the same terrible fate as Mari, who still lay less than 100 m (300 ft) away; strangled, stripped and sexually assaulted. Again, Miyazaki obsessively photographed his own crime scene. As he took pictures of Masami's body, a muscle spasm caused her corpse to twitch, and he fled the scene in terror.

The police repeated the same diligent process they had undertaken after Mari's disappearance, conducting house-to-house enquiries and papering the city with posters of the missing Masami. They suspected a connection between the disappearances of the two children, but had no leads to follow, no suspects to pursue. One of the disadvantages of an incredibly low crime rate is that no officers gain experience in hunting down serial killers – but even seasoned specialists would have struggled with so little to go on, as in this case. At this point, neither body had been found – and both cases were officially missing persons enquiries. Two months later, that would change.

Erika Namba was returning from a friend's house in Kawagoe, Saitama, when Miyazaki pulled over and offered her a lift. The four-year-old was reported missing by her anxious parents later the same day, 12 December. Both they and the police must have feared the worst, given the previous disappearances in the area. The next day, a worker at a local Youth Nature Facility found clothing belonging to a child in woods behind a parking area. The police raced the 50 or so kilometres (30 miles) to the scene and conducted a thorough search of the entire area. Erika's body was discovered the next day in a different part of the woods. She had been bound by the hands and feet with nylon cord, strangled and sexually assaulted.

Once these details were made public, two men came forward to state that they had been in the area at around the time that Erika went missing. They remembered helping a man whose Toyota Corolla car had got stuck just off the road, very close to where the corpse was found. The car was parked with its hazard lights flashing, so they stopped to take a look. A man came out of the woods, carrying a crumpled sheet. As he placed the sheet in the boot of his car, he explained he had accidentally driven off the road and become stuck in guttering. The men were too polite to ask what he had been doing in the woods with a sheet: they had simply helped him lift the car out and he drove away. What struck them as most odd about the incident at the time was the fact that the man did not offer them a word of thanks. When pressed, they recalled that the car had plates identifying it as originating from Hachioji, Tokyo.

Toyota Corollas are one of the most popular cars in Japan. The police checked some 6,000 that might have been the one the men spotted, but they drew a blank. It turned out that the witnesses were mistaken: it was not a Toyota Corolla they had lifted out of the gutter on that fateful December night, but a Nissan Langley. The ungrateful man they had helped was Tsutomu Miyazaki. He had had an amazingly lucky escape; the police had come agonizingly close to catching a mass murderer. Instead, Miyazaki continued to live his lonely life of comic books and murder, while families across

*Police officers examine the site where Miyazaki burned the bones of one of his victims.*

Japan kept their children indoors and drove them to and from the school gates each day.

## THE KILLER MAKES CONTACT

The families of the murdered children soon began to receive mysterious silent phone calls. When they answered, they could hear someone on the line but nobody spoke. If they ignored the phone it would ring insistently, for as long as 20 minutes. And then, even more chillingly, mysterious postcards began to arrive. Erika Namba's father, Shin'ichi, received one a week after her death that said: 'Erika. Cold. Cough. Throat. Rest. Death'. It was a sick, taunting and sadistic move on the part of Miyazaki. But the parents of still-missing Mari Konno were to receive an even more macabre communication from the killer. Mari's father, Shigeo, found a cardboard box on his doorstep as he left for work at around 6 am on 6 February 1989.

Tsutomu Miyazaki had returned several times to the spot where the bodies of Mari and Masami lay decomposing in the dark woods 50 km (31 miles) from their anguished loved ones in Saitama. On one visit, he cut off Mari's hands and feet, and kept them as souvenirs. The rest of her body he burnt. The ashes

that remained he placed into a box, along with ten of her baby teeth and photographs of her clothing. On top of these he placed a single sheet of copier paper bearing the words 'Mari. Bones. Cremated. Investigate. Prove'. This was the box that Mari's father found on his doorstep. He immediately turned it over to the police.

Dr Kazuo Suzuki of the Tokyo Dental University examined the teeth and, at a police press conference, announced they did not belong to Mari Konno. Mari's mother, at the same press conference, spoke of her faint hopes that her daughter was still alive. In his room, alone as usual, Miyazaki watched in disbelief. He wrote a three-page letter to the Konno family, and the local press, entitled 'Crime Confession'. He reiterated that he had killed all three of the girls, and that the remains in the box belonged to Mari. He claimed he did not want her mother to continue to have false hope. The letter was signed 'Yuko Imada', a girl's name but also a pun in the Japanese language, meaning 'Now I have courage' and also 'Now I will tell'.

Shortly afterwards, Dr Suzuki reversed his opinion on the teeth, and police forensic experts confirmed that they did, indeed, belong to Mari. Her case was officially changed to a homicide investigation, and linked to the murder of Erika Namba. What the press and public had speculated on for so long was finally confirmed: a serial killer was at work in Saitama.

## CLUES

Although handwriting experts were unable to provide police with much useful information after analyzing the letters, the communications nonetheless gave investigators some vital leads. They were able to establish that the photographs had been taken with a relatively rare Mamiya 6 x 7 format camera, the kind used by professional photographers or printers rather than hobbyists. The cardboard box was double-walled and corrugated: it was the kind used to ship fragile objects such as camera lenses. The typeface on the postcards came from a phototypesetter, and an industrial copier would also have been required to produce them. This set of clues ought to have been enough for the police to focus in on those working in professional print shops in the area. Had they done so, they would soon have come face to face with the quiet loner Tsutomu Miyazaki. For reasons that remain unclear, this never happened. The police distributed copies of the 'Crime Confession' letter to local houses in the hope of someone coming forward with new information. The Konno family buried their daughter and appealed to the killer to return her hands and feet, so that she could walk and eat in heaven.

What they got in response, however, was not more of their daughter's remains but more of the killer's twisted letters. Miyazaki, again signing himself as 'Yuko Imada', wrote saying that he had wanted to fold her arms across her chest but rigor mortis had set in. He then documented how red spots had appeared on her body as she decomposed; how those red spots had reminded him of the *Hinomaru* or 'Circle of the Sun' on the Japanese national flag; how the body had liquefied and begun to smell. Clearly, the killer enjoyed reliving his experiences both in person and on paper, and the outrage and pain he would cause the parents of his victim seemed to extend the duration of his pleasure. In the end, however, he still desired fresh victims. By 1 June 1989, Miyazaki was skipping work to try to capture more children. He persuaded a small child playing near a school to take off her underwear while he photographed her. Spotted by neighbours, he was chased off before he could do anything even worse. But he managed to escape from the scene before the police arrived. It was, for him, another lucky escape. For five-year-old Ayako Nomoto, it meant she had five days left to live.

## THE CANNIBAL KILLER

The little girl was playing alone in a park in Ariake, near Tokyo Bay. Miyazaki approached her and asked if he could take her photograph. Within a few moments she was in the back of his parked Nissan Langley. According to Miyazaki's later testimony, she fought hard as he strangled her, kicking her legs furiously. But the struggle was unequal, and after four or five minutes the kicking stopped and she became limp. He bound her hands and feet, placed tape over her mouth, wrapped her in a sheet and placed her in the boot of his car. Miyazaki had macabre plans for her even after her death.

He rented a video camera and returned home. There, he stripped Ayako's body and recorded himself sexually abusing her. He hacked off her head, hands and feet, and dumped her torso beside a public toilet in the Miyazawa-ko cemetery in Hanno. In his back garden, he then roasted the little girl's hands and ate some of the flesh from them. He hid the rest of her remains in a wooded hill beside his house, before thinking better of it and retrieving them to keep in the storeroom behind his bedroom. He later scattered them more widely in the woods and burnt the sheets he had used to wrap the body. Ayako's torso was quickly discovered, and she was identified by matching her stomach contents with her family's report of her last meal.

Tsutomu Miyazaki's crimes were becoming more demoniacally elaborate, and showed no sign of slowing down. He was, in every sense, remorseless. Just a few days later, on Sunday 23 July 1989, he prowled the streets again, this time fixing upon two young sisters playing together in Hachioji, about 40 km (25 miles) west of central Tokyo.

The eldest of the children informed her father who ran in wild panic through the streets of Hachioji to the spot where his daughter said a young man had approached them. He found his younger daughter in the back of Tsutomu Miyazaki's car, naked and terrified as Miyazaki photographed her genitals. The father landed a blow to Miyazaki's head that knocked him to the ground, but he managed to stagger away from the scene as the father tended to his screaming daughter. The police were on the scene in minutes, but the assailant had escaped down a swampy riverbank. As officers swarmed over the car, and radios crackled with descriptions of the wanted man,

*Miyazaki's bedroom was filled with comic books and anime videos, but there was no obvious link between his murders and his love for manga.*

Tsutomu Miyazaki brazenly returned to collect his vehicle. He was immediately arrested. One of the largest manhunts in modern Japanese history ended with the suspect simply walking up to the police in the centre of a major city.

The police were caught so off-guard that the press beat them into Miyazaki's room, filming inside it before it had been cordoned off for the forensic team to do their work. The coverage focused on the man's apparent obsession with comic books and videos, leading him to be dubbed 'The Otaku Murderer'. The closest English translation of *'otaku'* would be 'nerd' or 'geek': one who has unhealthy, obsessive interests, especially in the Japanese anime and manga comic books. The murders fuelled a moral panic against the anime and manga culture or 'fandom' in Japan, though there was never any proof of a direct link between Miyazaki's horrific crimes and the content he watched and read.

When the police did gain access to the bedroom, however, they found videos of Mari Konno amidst the vast collection of tapes. In the days that followed, the suspect made a full confession, and showed the police where the bodies of the missing girls lay. His parents went into hiding and his father refused to pay for a defence lawyer, insisting it would be unfair on

the victims, so a state lawyer was appointed. The trial began on 30 March 1990.

# TRIAL AND EXECUTION

More than 1,500 people queued outside the Tokyo district court building to see first-hand what the notorious 'Otaku Murderer' really looked like. Just 50 or so were let in, and even these 'lucky' few would be disappointed to see the young, round-faced defendant scribbling cartoons and falling asleep during the hearings. When the 'killer geek' did speak, it was to demand the return of his car and his beloved collection of videos and books.

In Japan, until 2009, there were no jury trials: a panel of judges decided Miyazaki's fate. Loyalty to fellow colleagues is one of the defining characteristics of Japanese society and judges and prosecutors are essentially colleagues working for the Ministry of Justice. From 1991 to 2000, more than 99 per cent of defendants in Japan were convicted. Thus, a defendant's attorney would be faced with an uphill battle to obtain a not-guilty verdict.

Much of Miyazaki's trial was shaped, not by the determination of innocence or guilt, but by the debate over whether he was sane or insane: if he was deemed to be mad he would escape the death penalty. Psychological assessments were ordered. Miyazaki claimed that a demonic creature called 'Rat Man' had taken possession of his mind, and three court-appointed psychiatrists found him to be mentally unsound, though they disagreed over whether he was schizophrenic or suffering from multiple personality disorder. In the end, the judges came to the conclusion that he was not so mad that he could not hang, and he was sentenced to death.

In response to being found guilty, Miyazaki penned a letter to his father, Katsumi Miyazaki, angrily blaming him for all of his crimes. Katsumi expressed his regret at not taking more notice of his son's early antisocial behaviour and inability to make friends. Having made his public apology, he then killed himself by jumping into a river in 1994. His son remarked that he 'felt refreshed' upon hearing the news.

Japan is one of the few industrialized countries that maintains the death penalty (along with the United States and South Korea, though the latter currently has a moratorium in effect). Human rights organizations have long criticized Japan for its lack of transparency over executions, which are carried out in secret and at short notice. Those on death row are not sent to prison but to detention centres, where they await the finalization of the sentence. This process of 'finalization' can take many years, as legal representatives appeal for clemency. Miyazaki's initial death sentence was handed down on 14 April 1997. He later remarked that he found it difficult to find a comfortable sitting position as the judge delivered the sentence. He went on to complain that hanging, the method of execution favoured in Japan, was inhumane, and suggested the country move to the lethal injection method used in the United States.

For the next four years, Miyazaki was perfectly content, reading comic books all day in the detention centre whilst the wheels of justice slowly turned. He wrote hundreds of letters to the editor of his favourite magazine, *Tsukuru* ('Create'), which specializes in critiquing Japanese mass media and subcultures. In one such letter he commented on the fact that this death sentence was upheld by the Tokyo High Court in 2001: a court spectator shouted 'Drop dead now, bastard!' but Miyazaki only learnt of this afterwards as he had dozed off during the sentencing. What he also missed was Chief Justice Tokiyasu Fujita's opinion of him: 'The atrocious murder of four girls to satisfy his sexual desire leaves no room for leniency. The crime is cold-blooded and cruel'.

Despite this, Miyazaki remained convinced he would be acquitted, and expressed no remorse for his crimes. 'I don't intend to apologize,' he wrote in one of his letters. Of his victims, he wrote: 'There's nothing much to say about them. I'm happy to think I did a good deed'. During the early period of his incarceration he had reason to be confident about his death sentence not being carried out: the justice minister, Seiken Sugiura, said that the death penalty went against his devout Buddhist beliefs, and no executions were carried out during his tenure. Even with previous, less peacable justice ministers at the helm, the average elapsed time between the finalization of a death sentence and the execution itself had been around eight years. All this changed, however, with the appointment of the ultra-conservative Kunio Hatoyama as justice minister in 2006.

The *Asahi* newspaper nicknamed him 'The Grim Reaper'. Hatoyama signed death warrants at a pace unprecedented in modern Japan, causing waves of panic amongst those on death row. Miyazaki sought help from the famous anti-death penalty activist Yoshihiro Yasuda, and ironically it was this that sealed his fate: the primary reason for a stay of execution was the argument that Miyazaki was insane, and his letter to Yasuda was seen as proof that he was of sound mind.

In Building A of the Tokyo Detention House in Tokyo's Kosuge district, the evening of 16 June 2008 was no different to any other for Miyazaki. In common with all Japanese death row convicts, he had no idea he would be hanged the next morning. The first indication a condemned man has that something is out of the ordinary is the sound of the guards' footsteps outside his cell. Miyazaki was offered a cigarette, Japanese confectionery, fruit and tea. He refused the offer of a prison chaplain to speak to until just before the moment of his execution. Then he was led into the execution room, divided in half by blue curtains. Facing him was a Buddhist statue, a cross and a rope 3 cm (1 in) thick which was placed around his neck. He was blindfolded with a white cloth, and then three prison officials in a separate room simultaneously pushed a button to release the trapdoor. Only one button functions, so none of them can know for certain that they were responsible for snapping Miyazaki's neck. minutes later, a prison doctor in the room below climbed a stepladder and held a stethoscope to the serial killer's heart to confirm that he was dead.

As Miyazaki's body was being towelled down and dressed in white, the former deputy inspector of the Saitama prefectural police was back in the lonely woods of Kawagoe, west of Saitama. The 67-year old Sato Norimichi toured all of the sites of the crimes that day, offering up prayers to the four young victims of Japan's infamous killer. News of Miyazaki's death leaked to the media as he drove between the crime scenes. The story of the Otaku Killer was finally over.

# LUIS ALFREDO GARAVITO CUBILLOS

On a lonely conifer forest on the outskirts of Villavicencio, 70 km (43 miles) south-east of Bogotá, two boys ran for their lives. One was a 16-year-old, who had come to the forest in order to smoke marijuana; the other was 12-year-old John Ivan Sabogal, who had been taken to the forest at knifepoint, stripped and tied up. When his abductor pulled out a knife, John Ivan Sabogal had screamed for help, attracting the attention of the pot-smoking teenager. He found the young boy lying at the feet of a naked man and hurled abuse and then stones at the man. In panic, the man cut John Ivan's bonds and ordered him to run deeper into the forest. But the boy ran instead towards his rescuer, and the houses of Villavicencio. His furious attacker pursued both the boys through the forest and across a bridge over a creek, knife in hand. His name was Luis Alfredo Garavito Cubillos; he was the most prolific serial killer the world has ever known.

The boys reached a farm, where a six-year-old girl was playing in the fading light of the April evening. They hid, and when the killer arrived the girl pointed him in the wrong direction. The boys escaped and alerted the police, who immediately swarmed to the scene. Just a few months earlier they had found the bodies of 12 children close by. A mob of outraged locals soon joined the frantic hunt, creating chaos and confusion as to who were the hunters and who was the quarry. Night began to fall, with no sign of the killer. Corporal Pedro Babativa ordered the furious locals to return to their homes and, eventually – showering the police with abuse – they complied.

Soon after, from his hiding place deep in the woods, Luis Alfredo Garavito watched the headlights of the last police patrol car sweep across the dark road back towards Villavicencio. He brushed himself down and stepped out from the trees.

Others have claimed or been suspected of more murders, but in terms of proven victims, Luis Alfredo Garavito is the worst serial killer in history. He was found guilty of 138 murders between 1992 and 1999, and it is feared he may have killed as many as 400. Fellow-countryman Pedro Alonso López is his main challenger for the title of 'worst of the worst' with 110 confirmed murders and the suspicion he killed hundreds more. The world's third-worst serial killer, Daniel Camargo Barbosa, who killed at least 72 children, was also born in Colombia.

What is it about Colombia that has produced three such prolific serial killers? To answer that question, it is necessary to look at the long and bloody history of the country into which they were born.

The 'Bogotazo' riots, in 1948, Bogotá, Colombia. The bloody conflict between the Liberal and Conservative parties during 'La Violencia' claimed as many as 200,000 lives.

The story of modern Colombia begins, predictably, with a murder.

# THE CHILD OF 'LA VIOLENCIA'

In 1948, popular Liberal Party presidential candidate Jorge Eliécer Gaitán was assassinated, allegedly by a lone, deranged gunman called Juan Roa Sierra. Because the killer was murdered by an enraged mob before he could be brought to trial, Gaitán's assassination has been the subject of the same sort of conspiracy theories that swirl around US President John F. Kennedy's death at the hands of Lee Harvey Oswald (later killed by Jack Ruby). Battles between Liberal Party and Conservative Party supporters in the capital Bogotá soon spread to the rest of Colombia, engulfing the country in ten years of bloody conflict known as 'La Violencia'. As many as 200,000 people died. Conservative paramilitaries attacked peasant farms and schools, raping, killing and dismembering the children in order to terrorize their enemy into submission. They specialized in the 'neck-tie cut' – slitting a victim's throat and pulling his tongue out through the gaping wound.

It was during this period, on 25 January 1957, that Luis Alfredo Garavito was born, in one of the areas worst affected by the violence: Génova, Quindío. Génova is a small town surrounded by hills on the banks of the San Juan River. It lies in the central-west area of Colombia, a country whose borders include the South American countries of Venezuela, Ecuador, Peru and Brazil and the Central American country of Panama. Opposite Colombia's northern shore lies Cuba and the United States of America. Both have played a pivotal role in Colombia's bloody modern history.

Garavito was the oldest of seven brothers, and in testimony to investigators he claimed he was the victim of sexual abuse by two different neighbours, first when he was 12 and then again when he was 15. At the time he was too afraid to tell anyone, least of all his father, who was also physically and mentally abusive towards him and his mother. Colombia has an aggressively macho culture, with domestic abuse and sexual violence being commonplace. Luis, the oldest child, later described his futile attempts to protect his mother from his father's beatings. The sound of her screams and the sight of her blood would stay with him throughout his life. His father was also strict about not allowing him girlfriends, further isolating the already painfully shy boy.

Beyond this, we can surmise that his family was typical of that area: peasant farmers, manual labourers or shopkeepers providing the basic necessities of life; one way or another, the Garavito family would have faced the same grinding poverty that was the lot of all but the landowning class in Génova. The area is now dominated by coffee plantations, but this was a novel crop in Colombia when Garavito was growing up: the staple Colombian crop prior to coffee was bananas. The same Andean mountain slopes produce high-quality coca leaves, which in the 1990s would attract the attention of Colombia's drug cartels, but in the 1960s the market for cocaine was relatively small.

Throughout the early 1960s, government-backed paramilitary attacks increased in frequency and violence. If Garavito did not witness at first hand the brutal murder and torture that these armed groups dispensed, it is almost certain he heard about it from his school friends and family. One of the most significant figures in Colombia's modern history was born in the same small town as Garavito, and it's impossible to imagine that he was not the talk of the school playground – a local hero, even.

Pedro Antonio Marín, known to the world as Marulanda, leader of the notorious Revolutionary Armed Forces of Colombia ('*Fuerzas Armadas Revolucionarias de Colombia*' or *FARC*) would take up arms against his government when Garavito was seven years old. That decision would be a fateful one, not just for Marín himself, but also for the entire country. To date, nearly a quarter of a million people have died during the long war between the guerillas, paramilitaries, drug cartels and government, and many thousands more have disappeared without a trace. Garavito's family was soon forced to flee their home, like five million other Colombians to date.

They moved further west, to the village of Ceylon, near Trujillo, Valle del Cauca.

# GARAVITO THE OUTSIDER

The young Luis attended the local Simón Bolívar school until he was 16. Teachers found him to be withdrawn and distant, but by no means unintelligent. He was prone to violent temper tantrums, which he later put down to some underlying 'frustrations' at his own inability to be a better person. Discipline in Colombian schools was strict at this time, with most teachers carrying canes and belts, so it is almost certain that Luis was beaten for his poor conduct. Classmates bullied him and mocked the bespectacled, meek outsider. The country was then, and remains today, fervently Roman Catholic, and we know that his religious upbringing made a profound and lasting impression on Garavito.

From his early teens onwards, Garavito began to feel sexual attraction towards younger boys. His first sexual crimes were against his own brothers, whom he fondled as they slept. Then, whilst still a teenager, he attempted to lure a young boy away from the local train station. The boy started screaming when Garavito began to molest him, and Garavito was arrested by the local police. In response, his father threw him out of the family home.

Garavito found work initially on a local farm, then drifted through a series of low-end jobs, often in warehouses in and around his home town. He became an alcoholic early in life, and it is possible he was already consuming home-brewed alcohol, such as *guarapo* (from sugar-cane) or *chicha* (from maize), in childhood, a common phenomenon in rural parts of Colombia. His addiction meant that he was regularly fired from jobs: on at least one occasion he was reported to have attacked a colleague. Garavito was forced to move from job to job. He dreamt of returning home to kill his father, but never had the courage to do so.

He was now free, at least, to do as he pleased and meet whom he pleased. He associated with at least two women, one of whom he had met at a local church. The exact nature of their relationship is unclear – Garavito claimed not to have sexual relations with her, but he lived with her as if she were his partner, and she soon had a son. Certainly, the relationship never provided Garavito with any lasting happiness, and he soon drifted to the nearby city of Armenia, where he took a job in the bakery. He began to attend meetings at Alcoholics Anonymous, and was a regular at the local church. But he was unable to turn his life around; the twin urges to drink and have sex with young boys overpowered him. He would procure young male prostitutes in the local park, drink long into the night and then head to church in the morning, full of self-hate. He repented by quoting Saint Paul's letter to the Romans: 'For what I am doing, I do not understand; for I am not practising what I would like to do, but I am doing the very thing I hate' (Romans 7:15).

He found yet another job, this time in a local supermarket, and for a brief while his life improved. He met the second key woman in his life, Claudia, who already had two children, a boy of 14 and a young girl. By all accounts Garavito always treated the three of them well, but he could only ever be a husband and father figure to them, because his sexual interest remained with young boys. Many such children came into the supermarket, and Garavito's urge to molest them became an obsession. He described it later as a 'satanic force'.

# GARAVITO THE RAPIST

In October 1980, the terrible demons inside Garavito took full control, and he began his first wave of crimes. Over the course of the next 12 years he would rape some 200 children, lured from the chaotic streets of dozens of Colombian towns and villages. He favoured boys aged between eight and 13, ideally fair-skinned and blue-eyed. He lured them into the sugar-cane fields or to the quiet hillside coffee plantations, where he was hidden from view and could see anyone who might be approaching. His cover story was generally that he needed help with some task or other, and was prepared to pay the child 500 or 1,000 pesos if they would do a small job. Often he took the children by taxi from the town centre to the lonely outskirts, making friendly conversation during the ride.

He always approached his victims during daylight: for one thing, he was scared of the dark, and for another he knew that most children would not be missed for several hours during the day. It was entirely usual for children to help the family finances by selling lottery tickets and papers to adults, and Garavito's promise of money offered them a chance to knock off from their chores early and perhaps have an hour or two to themselves to play.

Garavito recognized that he needed help, and visited a psychiatrist. He could not bring himself to disclose the shameful details of his sexual impotence with women and attraction to young boys, however, and ended up being diagnosed with depression. In 1984, he was admitted to a psychiatric unit for 33 days, before being discharged to be treated thereafter as an outpatient. It didn't help. He avidly read books on black magic and the life of Adolf Hitler, and watched the film *The Silence of the Lambs*, which features a cannibalistic serial killer, five times. In 1986, he became obsessed with TV news stories of Campo Elías Delgado Morales, a teacher who murdered 28 people in the upmarket *Pozetto* restaurant in Bogotá before being shot by police. Garavito drifted to the city of Pereira and again formed a relationship with an older woman who had a son, Graciela Zabaleta. Again they lived together as if man and wife, though no sexual relations occurred.

His predatory sex crimes against children continued, and Garavito began to find that inflicting pain upon his victims was more gratifying to him than sex. He would bite the child's nipples and burn their buttocks before raping them. Over the course of the next eight years he raped on average one child a month, travelling throughout the coffee-growing regions of Circasia, Armenia, Calarcá, Pereira, Santa Rosa de Cabal and Manizales. He was briefly imprisoned for theft, but escaped detection for his more serious crimes until 4 October 1992.

By the time he was finally caught in the act of assaulting a child, Garavito was already guilty of a catalogue of heinous attacks that would mark him as the gravest kind of serial sex offender. Although consumed with self-hatred for committing the crimes, Garavito nonetheless meticulously recorded them all in a small, black book for his own twisted pleasure. He hadn't yet crossed the rubicon into murder, however, and a lengthy prison sentence at this point might have saved hundreds of young lives, but it was not to be.

The police officer who caught Garavito accepted a bribe in return for releasing him. Just two days later Garavito found a terrible new excitement, and the catalogue of murder began.

# 1992: A DEAL WITH THE DEVIL

In an interview after he was finally caught, Garavito would claim that his murder campaign began after he used a Ouija board to summon the devil. He felt a force possess him and a voice said 'What do you want? Do you want to serve me?' When he replied in the affirmative, a voice told him to go and commit his first murder. The location of this diabolic meeting was the largest city in western Colombia, Santiago de Cali, abbreviated by most Colombians to 'Cali'.

As places to make a deal with the devil go, Cali was an inspired choice: in 1992 it was as close to hell as anywhere on earth. The city was the stronghold of the notorious Cali drug cartel, described by the United States Drug Enforcement Agency as 'the most powerful crime syndicate in history'. The three leaders of the cartel were famous enough to be featured on the cover of *Time* magazine in July 1991. An uneasy alliance between the Cali cartel and Pablo Escobar's rival Medellín cartel to share the lucrative US cocaine market had collapsed, resulting in a deadly feud between the gangs.

In the 1980s the cartels had worked together to supply the CIA with the drugs that funded the 'Iran Contra affair', aimed at overthrowing the left-wing Sandinista government in Nicaragua. They had become too powerful for the local police to control. Each adopted a policy of *plata o plomo* ('silver or lead') towards the Colombian government – the silver being bribes for co-operation and the lead being bullets for resistance. The Medellín cartel blew up a Boeing 747 en route from Bogotá to Cali in the hope of killing a presidential candidate in 1989, killing 110 innocent people instead. Escobar's target was not on board, but two American civilians were, bringing Colombia's drug barons to the attention of

US authorities. Escobar was now a wanted man in the eyes of the US, the Colombian government and the Cali cartel, and somewhat predictably he died from *plomo* to the head on 2 December 1993. This left the Cali cartel in control of 90 per cent of the world's cocaine market.

The marble citadels of the cartel's leaders loomed high above the sugar-cane fields of Cali. In such fields, and across the country, Luis Garavito would follow the satanic orders he believed he was given in Cali. He later testified that he couldn't remember the name of the first boy he killed, in the town of Jamundí just south of Cali, on 6 October 1992. He was Juan Carlos, a young local boy who just happened to pass by the bar in which Garavito was drinking. Garavito followed him, then approached him with the same story he had used countless times before. At a local store he stopped to buy 2 m (6 ft 7 in) of nylon rope, a bottle of cheap brandy and a butcher's knife.

Juan Carlos' body was discovered three days later. He had been raped and his penis had been cut off. Garavito later claimed the demonic voice had told him 'If you kill, many things will come to you'. He stated that he felt remorse and considered himself 'very evil' when he woke the next morning and realized his clothes were soaked in blood. But just six days later he would kill again, in the nearby city of Tulúa. The victim was 12-year-old John Alexander Penaranda and, like Juan Carlos, he was tied up, raped and stabbed to death. Garavito severed the fingers, thumbs and toes of his victims to make them look as though they were the subjects of satanic cults or the notorious *grupos de limpieza social* ('social cleansing groups'), both of which operated extensively in the area. The Cauca River, which flows through Cali, was known as 'The River of Death' due to the frequency with which bodies of *desechables* ('discardables') turned up in it. All too often these 'discardables' were street children. Garavito used this fact to his advantage, and it helps explain why he managed to avoid detection for so long.

He also moved around a great deal, and changed his appearance – often he would dress as a priest, and he had a range of different wigs, hats and glasses. Much of the time he would blend in on the streets by selling low-value products or religious items, his favourites being pictures of Pope John Paul II and *El Nino Dios* (the baby Jesus). He would claim to be working on behalf of a religious foundation, and often used a false name.

## 1993: BECOMING 'THE BEAST'

Garavito's murders became ever more frequent, and ever more gruesome. In 1993, he began a horrific new practice that would become a signature for almost all future killings: he disembowelled his victims whilst they were still alive. He frequently ended their torment by beheading them, and taking out their vital organs, which were almost never found. He butchered a total of 11 children in this fashion in 1993, moving between the capital Bogotá and the towns of Armenia, Quimbaya and Calarcá in the west. His last crime of that year was very nearly his last crime ever: in Tulúa, a 12-year-old victim fought back with a knife, severing the tendons in Garavito's thumb, before the child was overpowered and killed. His death was mercifully swift compared to the murderer's other victims.

The following year resulted in the murders of a further 27 children. He painstakingly recorded each and every killing in his notebook, and kept his bus tickets and newspaper clippings relating to the children in a black cloth bag. He would photograph many of the children before he attacked them and kept the photographs, too. Whenever the bag of mementos grew too unwieldy to carry, he would take it to his sister's house and leave it there. In 1995, whilst in Bogotá, Garavito fell and badly broke his leg. He walked with a distinctive limp from then on – a detail that helped lead to his eventual arrest. Garavito's murder rate also slowed, at least whilst he was still on crutches.

The following year, in Tunja, Garavito was arrested in connection with the disappearance of a local child, Ronald Delgado Quintero. His description matched that of an eyewitness. The smooth-talking serial murderer managed to convince the police that he was a poor, innocent street vendor who had been singled out because he was disabled. He was released. It was for the murder of this child that Garavito would eventually be convicted but that, alas, was many years in the future.

The killer changed his appearance once more, and stepped on to a bus heading north, to Risaralda. Ten year-old Jorge Andrés Brown Ramirez, who sold sweets to the passengers on such buses, would be his next victim. By the end of 1996, Garavito's notebook of death reached the grim milestone of 100 victims.

His name was now in the Colombian police system, at least – in so far as Colombia's police had a system in 1996. Nobody in the country had yet linked the disappearances of children in different provinces, and so there was still no co-ordinated investigation into the case. In fairness, what seems obvious in

retrospect was not so clear at the time. Due to social problems in Colombia, children disappeared in far higher numbers than in more stable, developed countries. Parents often did not even report their offspring as missing, for fear of reprisals from cartels, criminals or corrupt police officials. When bodies were found well preserved, the fact they had been cut open led to suspicion that they were victims of the dark trade in human organs. But Garavito usually dumped the bodies of his victims in sugar-cane fields on the outskirts of the city, where the moist environment and activities of animals meant that often only scattered bones remained by the time they were found. This made identification of the victims all the more difficult.

It was only when playing children discovered a human skull in November 1997 that the hunt for the serial killer began in earnest. Police who arrived at the scene near Pereira soon discovered a mass grave containing the bodies of 36 children. Even in a country used to gruesome and violent crimes, it was

*Luis Alfredo Garavito Cubillos in 1999.*

a shocking discovery, and one that made headlines across Colombia.

By January 1998, the local police department had formed a task force, and it began to ask about any similar cases in other Colombian districts. Reports of mysterious mass disappearances of children poured in from the police departments of Meta, Cundinamarca, Antioquia, Quindío, Caldas, Valle del Cauca, Huila, Cauca, Caquetá and Nariño. There was no doubt, by now, that something was very wrong. However, the police still could not quite believe that a single man was responsible for so many deaths. They were soon contacted by a coroner in Palmira who disagreed. There, whilst committing one of his murders, Garavito had got sloppy.

## THE MANHUNT BEGINS

In February 1998, in Buga, Garavito had lured a child to a paddock outside the city. As was his habit by now, having raped and murdered the boy, he lay beside the body for several hours drinking cheap brandy. On this occasion, however, he became so intoxicated that he passed out. A lit cigarette that he was smoking started a fire in the field. Garavito awoke to find himself ablaze, and surrounded by flames. In panic, he fled the scene – leaving behind a host of vital clues. Police later recovered a pair of glasses, shorts, a comb, a screwdriver and a pair of shoes that were worn down in an unusual pattern.

Carlos Hernán Herrera, the Palmira coroner who examined the body recovered from the scene, concluded that a serial killer was responsible. He had seen similar patterns of violent dismemberment at other scenes in the vicinity: disembowelment, severed penises, and beheadings. By analysing the clues left behind, the coroner concluded they were looking for a man in his 40s who limped with his

*Garavito hid the bodies of his victims in the sugar-cane fields of Colombia.*

right leg. He wrote a report to the CTI (*Cuerpo Técnico de Investigación*, or technical investigation team), suggesting that a national manhunt needed to be launched urgently. The report sat in a drawer for another seven months.

More mass graves were uncovered in Colombia as the sugar-cane fields were cut and harvested. No doubt realizing that his crimes were beginning to attract attention, Garavito fled to the neighbouring country of Ecuador, where he continued his killing spree. With the aid of forged documents he assumed the identity of 'Bonifacio Morera'. He couldn't hide his thick Colombian accent, however, and when local children began to disappear, the limping foreigner drew the attention of the Ecuadorian police. Before they could mount an operation to capture him, however, he fled back to Colombia. Still the killings continued.

It was an extraordinary coincidence that eventually connected the name of Luis Garavito to the wave of murders. Detectives from the investigating team in Armenia were discussing the case when they happened to be overheard by a secretary. She had previously worked in the city of Tunja, where Garavito had been arrested and questioned in 1996 over the disappearance of a child. He had fled that area after his release, but when the body of the child was found police had issued an arrest warrant for him. The secretary at Armenia had written that warrant in Tunja, and recognized the similarity between the Tunja and Armenia cases. The police began to investigate Garavito. They visited his sister, who informed them she didn't know his whereabouts but revealed that he had asked her to keep hold of some of his personal items. One of those items was the black cotton bag Garavito had stuffed full of mementos of his crimes.

The bus tickets placed him at the time and place of each major crime scene. The police, finally, knew the identity of the killer.

The only problem being that they had no idea where Luis Alfredo Garavito Cubillos was.

# CAPTURE – AND ARREST

It was a taxi driver who first spotted a man emerging from trees in Villavicencio in April 1999. The authorities were on the lookout after two young boys had fled an attacker and alerted police. After searching the forest, the police had withdrawn to a safe distance in the hope of luring the culprit out. In the back of the police car sat 12-year-old John Ivan Sabogal and his teenaged rescuer who, fortuitously, had been smoking pot nearby and helped facilitate the Sabogal's escape. They waited, ready to point out the perpetrator should he show himself. When Sabogal shouted 'That's him!', the police moved in. The man they detained claimed his name was Bonifacio Morera, and that he was lost after having got off the bus at the wrong stop.

Under intensive interrogation back at the police station, the man stuck to his story. The police, armed with the unwavering testimony of the boy that the man had abducted, charged him with kidnap and attempted rape. The world's worst serial killer was behind bars, but at this stage only Garavito knew that the police had no idea that the prisoner they had been told was Bonifacio Morera was in fact responsible for hundreds of more crimes. That would become clear only three months later, at the CTI National Summit held in Pereira. There, detectives from across Colombia compared notes, photographs and fingerprints. The prints of Bonifacio Morera matched those of Luis Garavito, and the photographs confirmed that he was one and the same man.

On Friday 28 October 1999, 'Bonifacio Morera' was taken to court for what he believed would be a single charge of kidnapping and attempted rape. It was only when the judge bellowed 'Citizen Luis Garavito Cubillos, stand up!' that he realized his predicament. He was charged with a total of 118 murders. Shortly afterwards he would confess to all of them – and to 24 others that the police had not yet linked to him. He explained his system of recording each and every death in his notebook, with a horizontal line representing a victim. There were 140 such lines in the book. It is feared that there are other such 'little black books' that have never been found, and that Garavito may have killed as many as 400 children. In the end, on 13 December 1999, he was found guilty of 138 murders, and sentenced to a total of 1,853 years and nine days in prison.

But he could be released any day now. The Colombian constitution, written amidst the bloody violence of 1991, was designed to protect its citizens from the worst excesses of corrupt and dysfunctional governments. As a result, it is one of the most liberal constitutions in the world. Not only is the death penalty prohibited, but life prison terms are, too. Sentences must be concurrent not consecutive, and

the maximum sentence in 1999 was 30 years (since doubled to 60). Because Garavito pleaded guilty, the Superior Court of Bogotá reduced his sentence to 22 years in 2006. He is entitled to further reductions due to 'irreproachable conduct' during his time in prison. Working and studying in prison entitles inmates to a four-month reduction in sentence per year.

The same liberal constitution prevents the extradition of Colombian citizens to foreign countries – such as Ecuador, where Garavito faces a further 22-year prison sentence for the murders he committed there. If he walks free, he will follow in the footsteps of Pedro Lopez, the world's second-worst serial killer, also from Colombia. Lopez, 'the Monster of the Andes', was convicted of murdering 110 young girls in 1983, and walked free in 1998. He was required to report regularly to the authorities in order to continue his psychiatric treatment, but almost immediately disappeared. Interpol released an advisory notice for his re-arrest in relation to a fresh murder in his hometown of Espinal, Colombia, in 2002. His current whereabouts are unknown.

*A taxi driver spotted a man emerging from the forest outside Villavicencio and alerted the authorities, leading to the arrest of Cubillos.*

# MIKHAIL POPKOV

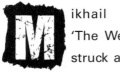ikhail Popkov was known as 'The Werewolf' in the press because he struck at night, but the authorities more prosaically called him the 'Wednesday Murderer' because that was usually when the bodies were found. Nevertheless, he is much more scary than that name suggests, for as Russia's most prolific killer he admitted to the rape and murder of more than 80 women. The final total may have been even higher than that.

Having been sentenced to life imprisonment for twenty-two murders in 2015, Popkov claimed that he stopped killing in the year 2000 after one of his victims gave him syphilis, rendering him impotent. However, in 2017 he admitted that he continued for another ten years and confessed to killing another 60 people in the Irkutsk Oblast of central Siberia. And there may have been even more victims. After quitting his job as a police officer, he travelled regularly between his hometown of Angarsk and Vladivostok on Russia's Pacific coast, over 3,200 km (2,000 miles) away, and the detectives felt that he may have killed along the way. They believed that he was rationing his confessions to delay his transfer from the relative comfort of the regular prison, where he was then being held, to a tough penal colony where he would serve out the rest of his life sentence.

## KILLED THOSE OF 'NEGATIVE BEHAVIOUR'

Popkov began killing in 1992 when he found two used condoms in the rubbish at home and suspected that his wife Elena, who was also a police officer, was cheating on him. Though it seems that the condoms had been left by a house guest, one of Elena's work colleagues admitted that he had had a brief affair with her.

A few weeks after his discovery, Popkov killed 'spontaneously', he told investigators.

'I just felt I wanted to kill a woman I was giving a lift to in my car,' he said.

In 2015, he claimed that his victims were prostitutes and that his aim was to 'cleanse' his hometown. He also thought that even if they were not involved in prostitution, women who went out by themselves at night, going to bars and drinking alcohol, needed to be punished. It has been speculated that Popkov was taking psychic revenge on an alcoholic mother who abused him as a child.

'My victims were women who walked the streets at night alone, without men, and not sober, who behaved thoughtlessly, carelessly, not afraid to engage in a conversation with me, sit in the car, and then go for a drive in search of adventure, for the sake of entertainment, ready to drink alcohol and have sexual intercourse with me,' he said.

He used to have sex with them and then decide whether to murder them.

'In this way, not all women became victims, but women of certain negative behaviour, and I had a desire to teach and punish them,' he said. 'So that others would not behave in such a way and so that they would be afraid.'

The women were reassured by his police uniform and felt safe getting into a police car.

'I was in uniform. I decided to stop and give a woman a ride. I frequently did that before,' he said. 'The woman began talking to me, I offered to give her a lift, she agreed ... That same morning, I drove the head of the criminal investigation to the murder scene.'

## THRILL FROM INVESTIGATIONS

Popkov not only got a thrill from killing his victims, but he was also able to double his perverted pleasure by reliving every detail of the crime during the investigation. He should have been caught much earlier, as one of his victims survived and identified him. On 26 January 1998, a 15-year-old known as Svetlana M said a police car had stopped to give

*As a police officer, Popkov not only got a thrill from killing his victims, but he was also able to double his perverted pleasure by reliving every detail of the crime during the investigation.*

her a lift. The officer took her into some woodland where he forced her to strip naked. He then smashed her head against a tree and she lost consciousness. The next day she was found alive near the village of Baykalsk, some 113 km (70 miles) from where Popkov had picked her up. Somehow she had survived the night naked in the sub-zero temperatures of a Siberian winter. When she awoke in hospital she was able to identify the officer who had tried to kill her. It was Popkov. However, his wife provided him with a false alibi. Neither she nor their daughter Ekaterina, a teacher, could believe that he was a killer. They said he was a perfect husband and father.

'I had a double life,' he said. 'In one life, I was an ordinary person ... In my other life I committed murders, which I carefully concealed from everyone, realizing that what I was doing was a criminal offence.'

Popkov's colleagues in the police force also found it hard to believe that he was a killer. Nor do there appear to have been any signs of mental instability.

'I was in the service, in the police, having positive feedback on my work,' he said. 'I never thought of myself as mentally unhealthy. During my police service, I regularly passed medical commissions and was recognized as fit.'

## 'FASTIDIOUS'

A major clue that was overlooked was that the murder weapons were removed from the police storeroom. After wiping them to remove his fingerprints, he would throw them away near the scene of the crime.

'The choice of weapons for killing was always casual,' he said. 'I never prepared beforehand to commit a murder. I could use any object that was in the car – a knife, an axe, a bat.'

And he claimed to be fastidious.

'I never used rope for strangulation,' he said, 'and I did not have a firearm either. I did not cut out the hearts of the victims.'

However, one of his victims had had her heart gouged from her body. Others were mutilated or dismembered. One, a medical student, had been beheaded. Her body was found in a rubbish container in Angarsk, her head in another skip elsewhere.

On one occasion, the killing came close to home when he discovered that he had murdered a teacher at his own daughter's music school.

'Her corpse was found in the forest along with the body of another woman,' he said. 'My daughter asked me to give her money because the school was collecting to organize funerals. I gave it to her.'

## DOUBLE MURDERS

He had another close call in 2000 when he returned to the scene of a crime. After he had left 35-year-old Maria Lyzhina and 37-year-old Liliya Pashkovskaya for dead, he found that a commemorative chain he wore around his neck was missing and he went to retrieve it before investigators found it.

'I realized that I lost it in a forest glade when I killed the two women,' he said. 'I realized that I would absolutely be identified by the lost chain, and experienced the greatest stress. I realized that I should return to the scene of the crime, if the police or the prosecutor's office had not been there yet.'

But when he returned to the scene he found more than he had bargained for.

'I found the chain right away, but saw that one of the women was still breathing,' he said. 'I was shocked

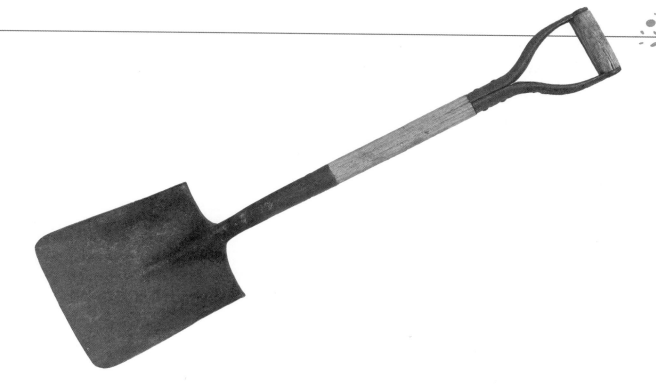

by the fact that she was still alive, so I finished her off with a shovel.'

The two women had worked together in a shop. On 2 June they went to see Maria's sister and at midnight they decided they had better go home. At first they thought of taking a taxi but then they changed their minds.

It was a warm summer night and they decided to walk. On 5 June, their bodies were found in the forest near Veresovka village. Maria had a 14-year-old daughter and Liliya had a 12-year-old daughter and a three-year-old son, who would now have to grow up without their mothers.

The custom in Russia is for coffins to be left open at the graveside so mourners can bid the deceased a final farewell, but the two women were buried in closed coffins because they were so badly disfigured.

Another double murder occurred in 1998 when the bodies of 20-year-old Tatiana 'Tanya' Martynova and 19-year-old Yulia Kuprikova were found in a suburb of Angarsk. Tanya's sister Viktoria Chagaeva had given her a ticket for a concert, but Tanya was married

*Mikhail Popkov finished off one of his victims with a shovel.*

with a small child and her 24-year-old husband Igor begged her not to go. Ignoring his pleas, she made the mistake of stopping for a quick drink with a few friends after the show. Then the two girls accepted a lift from a policeman.

'On the morning of 29 October, Igor called me saying Tanya had not come back home,' said Viktoria. 'I got truly scared. It was the first time she had ever done this. There were no mobile phones at that time; we could only call Yulia's parents, thinking Tanya must have stayed overnight there for some reason. But Yulia's parents said she had not come home either.'

They went to the police and were told that they must wait three days before the two young women could be listed as missing. There would be no need to wait. That night a shepherd found their naked bodies near Meget, a village close to Angarsk.

'It was 1 a.m. when Tanya's husband Igor and I came to the police,' said Viktoria. 'We did not tell our

*The city of Angarsk in Irkutsk Oblast, Russia, where Popkov committed many of his vile crimes.*

mother yet. Igor was absolutely devastated and kept saying: "She was killed, she was killed." I was shocked too, but I simply could not believe it and replied: "What are you talking about?"'

Later they were told that their bodies were found next to each other. Both girls had been raped after they were dead and then mutilated.

'My elder brother Oleg went to the morgue to identify Tanya,' said Viktoria. 'He had just flown from Moscow. He felt sick when he saw the body, she was so mutilated. He was almost green when he came out of there. He just could not say a word. I did not dare to go in and look.'

The mutilation was confined to Tanya's body and the back of her head, so the coffin could be left open with her face showing. However, Yulia's coffin had to be kept closed as her face was so badly cut up.

'Many people attended Tanya's funeral,' said Viktoria. 'It felt as if the whole town was there. Our poor mother lost consciousness several times; she needed a lot of medicine to cope. Igor was in almost the same condition.'

Indeed, their mother Lubov never recovered from the loss of her daughter. 'She felt as if she had died with Tanya. Life became useless for her,' said Viktoria. 'She lived only because she was visiting various mediums one by one, looking for the killer and wasting her money. Nobody gave her any serious information but she kept doing it. She died in 2007, aged 66, from a heart attack. I think her heart could not cope with the pain any longer.'

# VICTIM'S SISTER KNEW THE KILLER

When Popkov was arrested in 2012, Viktoria realized that she knew him. They had both competed in a biathlon at a local sports ground.

'I was struck with horror when I saw the picture of this maniac in the paper and online,' she said. 'My sister's killer was looking into my eyes. I immediately felt as if I'd met him. Looking at him, I could hardly breathe. Some minutes later I looked at him another time and thought – oh my God, I know him! I was so shocked, I even took a knife and cut his face in the newspaper, I needed to let this horror out of me.

'I remember him as a tall slim man, he was always alone, with a slippery and shifty glance. I think such people just must not live. This beast took the life of my sister, who had so many happy years in front of her. I cried a lot that day, but it is time to be quiet and just wait. He will be punished by law and criminals in jail will punish him too. I am sure he will pay for all the murders one day.'

That a fellow officer committed these terrible crimes under their noses perturbed the police. A former police colleague said: 'When I read about him in the press, I literally choked because I used to work with him and thought I knew him. He was an absolutely normal man. He liked biathlon; once on duty he shot a rapist during an arrest. There was an investigation and he was not punished as the chiefs considered he had taken fair action.'

Another ex-colleague said: 'I used to work closely with him for five years. He knew lots of jokes and stories, and could be the life and soul of the party.'

Popkov was caught when 3,500 policemen and former policemen were asked to give a DNA sample. His DNA matched that in sperm found on some of the victims.

'I couldn't predict DNA tests,' he told a reporter from *Komsomolskaya Pravda* in a jailhouse interview. 'I was born in the wrong century.'

When Popkov pleaded guilty to the two dozen murder charges, the judge asked him how many murders he had committed in total. In reply, the killer just shrugged.

'I can't say exactly,' he said. 'I didn't write them down.'

# CHAMBERS OF HORROR

Many serial killers commit their crimes at home. Their houses can be terrifying places. There are purpose-built dungeons and soundproofed walls to hide the crimes from prying neighbours. Corpses may be hidden around the property or victims may be locked up, tied down, and tortured for remarkable spells of time. What's amazing is how long many of these ordeals continue when there are so many clues to give the game away.

# H. H. HOLMES

he most prolific American serial killer of the 19th century – perhaps the most prolific of all time – H. H. Holmes maintained that he was not accountable for his crimes. 'I was born with the devil in me,' he told the detectives who interrogated him. 'I could not help the fact that I was a murderer, no more than the poet can help the inspiration to sing. I was born with the evil one standing as my sponsor beside the bed where I was ushered into the world and he has been with me since.'

Holmes' association with the devil began on 16 May 1861 in the small town of Gilmanton, New Hampshire. His true name was Herman Webster Mudgett.

The son of Levi and Theodate Mudgett, he was a descendant of the earliest settlers in the area. Over the generations, the Mudgetts had done well for themselves. However, by the time Herman entered the world it was a family in decline. His alcoholic father did little to reverse the trend. Herman suffered under his father's strict discipline, which often manifested itself in violence. School brought little in the way of sanctuary as Herman was a frequent victim of bullying.

In one particular incident, which took place when he was quite young, his schoolmates forced him to touch a human skeleton at the office of the town's doctor. The experience brought about an abrupt change in the boy's character. Once the victim

of bullying, Herman now became a bully himself. Moreover, he found that the experience with the skeleton had robbed him of any fear of death or the macabre. Herman soon began capturing and killing small animals in order to study their bodies. By his late teenage years, the future serial murderer had decided upon medicine as his vocation.

Because he lacked the money to attend medical school, he became a teacher at the age of 16. It was during his second posting, in the nearby town of Alton, that he met Clara Lovering, a member of a well-to-do farming family. After the two had eloped, Herman's new wife paid for his medical studies at the University of Vermont.

But the school was not to his liking. Herman imagined a great future for himself – the modest school in the small city of Burlington could not provide the foundation he required.

In the summer of 1882, Herman took his wife west so he could enrol at one of the country's leading medical schools, the University of Michigan at Ann Arbor. There was nothing magnificent about his performance as a student, but then all he really needed was the certificate he would receive upon graduation. However, Herman did one thing of note – something which his professors were unaware of – he stole cadavers that had been used in anatomy classes. He then disfigured the corpses to make it appear that they had died in horrific accidents. All

*Holmes disfigured cadavers to make it appear that they had died in horrific accidents.*

## CONVINCING BEDSIDE MANNER

In 1885, he reappeared in Chicago as 'Dr Henry Howard Holmes'. As a fairly handsome man who was something of a dandy, he cut quite a figure in his adopted city. He set himself up as an inventor and then he took a job as a prescription clerk in a very healthy pharmacy owned by a terminally ill man, Dr E. S. Holton. The supportive and helpful Holmes endeared himself to the dying doctor's wife. When Holton died he offered to take the pharmacy off her hands. A legal document was drawn up in which Holmes promised to pay the grieving Mrs Holton $100 a month until the entire business had been bought.

How many payments did Holmes make? Perhaps none. Shortly after signing the agreement, the doctor's widow disappeared. At first Holmes told people that Mrs Holton was visiting California, but then he said that she had fallen in love with the Golden State and had decided to stay. With Holmes at the helm, what had once been Dr E. S. Holton's pharmacy became healthier still. Chicago was experiencing a period of rapid growth and the former Herman Mudgett took full advantage of the boom times. Within two years of his arrival in the city, Holmes had become a wealthy man.

In 1887, he joined the ranks of the *nouveaux riches* with his marriage to Myrta Z. Belknap, the beautiful

that remained was to distribute them around the city. When they were discovered, he collected on the insurance policies that he had taken out.

Just a few months after his graduation in 1884, Herman carried off his greatest swindle with the help of a student who was still studying at the university. The scheming pair split a total of $12,500, after which Herman abandoned Clara and their infant son and left Ann Arbor. He then disappeared, surfacing only to cheat individuals and companies out of even more money. In St Paul, Minnesota, he was supposed to act as the receiver of a bankrupt store, but he sold off the goods and then vanished with the proceeds. For a time he taught in a school in Clinton County, New York, but after running up a large bill for board and lodging and impregnating his married landlady, he ran off.

daughter of wealthy businessman John Belknap. It did not matter a bit that the groom had been married before because Holmes never told his bride. Nor did it matter that he was still married to Clara, because no one ever found out.

John Belknap provided Holmes with access to Chicago's business class, which he exploited to the full. Holmes even took advantage of John Belknap himself, by forging the old man's name on a number of deeds. The crime was exposed – and quickly hushed up – but Holmes' relationship with Myrta was already over. Though she had just given birth to their first and only child, Lucy, the marriage had run its course. The union had not been helped by Holmes' attempt to poison his father-in-law when the truth about his fraud was exposed.

What exactly Holmes wanted with all of the property he tried to acquire is unknown. Perhaps he was looking for a place to build. In 1889, he purchased an empty plot of land on the corner of South Wallace and West 63rd Street, directly across from his pharmacy, where he began a three-year construction project. Even as it was going up, the building was the subject of much talk in the neighbourhood. One block long and three storeys in height, the building's dominating presence earned it a nickname – 'the Castle'.

There was, however, another reason why the building was so often a topic of conversation. Dr Holmes was forever hiring and firing those who worked on its construction. There were two reasons for this behaviour. First of all, he saved money by dismissing someone every time he found some trivial flaw. The doctor would not pay for shoddy workmanship. Years later, investigators discovered that he had not paid one cent for the materials that

had been used in the mammoth structure. Secondly, in having workers pass through what was in essence a revolving door, Holmes was able to keep secret the Castle's odd and eccentric design.

The ground floor of the building was conventional enough. A number of businesses were located there, including Holmes' relocated pharmacy, a sign painter and a vendor of used magazines. However, the upper two storeys were designed to resemble a maze. Features like trap doors, hidden staircases, secret passages and false floors abounded, and there were more than 100 rooms, most lacking windows.

Many of the doors could only be opened from the outside and other doors led to nothing but a brick wall.

Holmes completed the Castle just as Chicago was readying itself for the 1893 World's Columbian Exposition. His timing was excellent. Soon the city was swarming with tourists looking for a place to stay and Holmes was more than willing to oblige. As well as advertising his accommodation in the local newspapers he also offered employment to young ladies. The other advertisements he placed had nothing to do with business. He represented himself as a wealthy businessman in search of a suitable bride. Before long, the Castle was being visited by tourists, unemployed women and prospective mates. The building was once more a hive of activity, just as it had been when hundreds of workmen were coming and going. But this time around no one left.

Many visitors were asphyxiated in soundproof chambers that were fitted with gas pipes. Others met a similar fate after being locked in a bank vault that was located just outside Holmes' second-storey office. Once his victims were dead, he sent them sliding down any number of chutes located

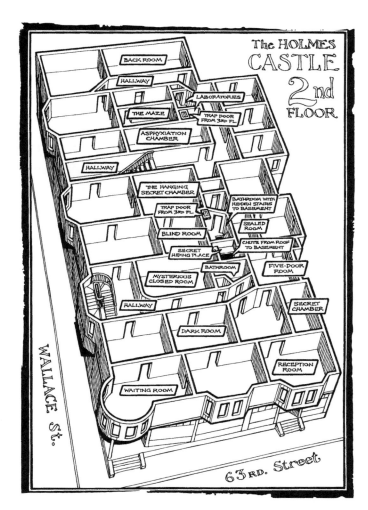

The HOLMES CASTLE 2nd FLOOR

WALLACE St.

63RD. Street

*An overview of Holmes' maze of death.*

throughout the building. The bodies would end up in the Castle's basement, where Holmes would strip them of their flesh.

Many of the victims would end up as skeletons, much like the one he had been forced to touch as a child. He used his standing as a doctor to sell them to medical schools. Some bodies were cremated in one of the two gigantic furnaces that served to heat the Castle, while others were simply dropped into lime pits or vats of acid.

Holmes preyed almost exclusively on women, including Julia Connor, the wife of a jeweller to whom the doctor had rented a shop. Julia worked for both Holmes and her husband and she was also sleeping with both men. The situation suited Holmes, and it seemed just fine with Julia. But then he met a wealthy Texan named Minnie Williams. When the two became engaged, Julia told Holmes that she was pregnant with his child.

Holmes reacted to the news by killing Julia and her daughter Pearl. Julia's distraught husband trudged the streets of the city day and night, searching for his missing family.

Had Julia made a fatal mistake in standing up to Holmes? It does not seem so, if the doctor's statement to the investigators is anything to go by.

'I would have gotten rid of her anyway. I was tired of her.'

The commotion caused by Minnie's arrival at the Castle only seemed to intensify as time progressed.

When her sister came to visit she was seduced by Holmes, who encouraged her to sign over some property she owned in Texas. He then sent her tumbling down one of the chutes. When he married for a third time on 9 January 1894, the bride was not Minnie. How could it be? He had murdered her, too.

Holmes' third wife was Georgianna Yoke, yet another woman who had a good amount of money in the bank. Georgianna was under the impression that her husband was a very wealthy man. After all, he had a profitable pharmacy and he owned property in Texas and Illinois as well as the Castle. This was all true, though Holmes' fortunes had taken a turn for the worse. He had been living well beyond his means and he was dragged down with the American economy as it entered a recession. When his creditors came calling, there was little he could do. Though the doctor found it so very easy to kill a woman, he had little control over a bank.

After running through his new wife's money, he turned to swindling as a means of escaping debt. His first attempt was a fairly complicated scheme that involved horses, but it resulted in a brief period of imprisonment in St Louis. When he was released on bail, Holmes decided to return to the area he knew best, which was insurance fraud. His new scheme involved Benjamin Pitezel, a man whom he had employed as a carpenter while the Castle was being built.

Pitezel was a weak, simple-minded alcoholic who perhaps knew something of the horrors that had taken place in the Castle. What he made of them is a matter for conjecture.

Nevertheless, all of the evidence points to the fact that Pitezel had sufficient faculties to understand the swindle that Holmes had cooked up. The two men were to travel to Philadelphia, where the carpenter would establish himself as B. F. Perry, an inventor. Meanwhile, Holmes would take out a $10,000 insurance policy on his friend Perry. A few weeks later, there would be an explosion of such magnitude that a disfigured corpse would be all that remained of him.

According to the plan, Holmes would provide the necessary mutilated body. In the end, however, Holmes simply killed Pitezel.

## CHILD KILLER

Following Pitezel's death, Holmes set off on a journey that can only be explained by the fact that the insurance company was on to him. After assuring Mrs Pitezel her husband was alive and well, the doctor talked her into letting three of her five children travel with him. Holmes moved from city to city and even crossed the border into Canada.

When the authorities finally caught up with him on 17 November 1894, he was in Boston.

He was charged with insurance fraud, which was a serious, but not insurmountable, charge. But then another question was asked. Where were the Pitezel children?

The answer came a few months later, when a diligent insurance agent located their small, unmarked graves in Indianapolis and Toronto.

The shocking news ruled out the possibility that Holmes might ever again be a free man.

On 20 July 1895 the Chicago police visited the Castle and got their first glimpse of the secret horrors that had taken place within its walls.

It took only one day for the newspapers to change the building's nickname to the 'Murder Castle'. The investigators learned all they could about the labyrinth of rooms, secret passageways, chutes and stairwells, but most of the Castle's secrets would remain a mystery. On the evening of 19 August, 20 days into the investigation, the Murder Castle was destroyed in a sudden and intense blaze. No one knew what had caused it.

Before the fire destroyed all of the evidence, the police had tried to determine just how many people had been killed in the building.

In a century that knew nothing of DNA, it proved a frustrating activity. Body parts were scattered around the Murder Castle's basement and some were still floating in pools of acid.

Yet the investigators did notice some commonalities. For example, while some victims had been men and children, the great majority of them had been young, blond women.

Though Holmes admitted to only 27 murders, the true total is almost certainly much higher – some have gone so far as to peg it at 200. His confession was made through the Hearst newspaper chain, which had paid $7,500 for the exclusive rights. The printed statement also allowed the doctor to speak to a public that was calling for his life.

*'Like the man-eating tigers of the tropical jungle, whose appetites for blood have once been aroused, I roamed about this world seeking whom I could destroy.'*

On the morning of 7 May 1896, he would roam the world no more. He took his place on the trapdoor of the gallows without any apparent fear. Amiable to the end, he expressed only the wish that his death might be swift.

It was not to be.

Fifteen minutes after the trapdoor had been opened, H. H. Holmes was still alive, his body twitching. The man who had been born with the devil in him dangled on the end of the rope for 20 minutes before he died.

*The outside of Holmes' 'Castle', where it is possible as many as 200 people died.*

# JERRY BRUDOS

For most of his 67 years, Jerome Henry Brudos was simply called 'Jerry', but he would become famous as 'The Shoe Fetish Slayer' and 'The Lust Killer'. Neither appellation quite covers what he was – for one, his fetishes went way beyond footwear. What is more, both nicknames suggest that Jerry's crimes extended no further than murder when in fact he was a torturer and a rapist, with an attraction toward necrophilia.

Brudos was born on 31 January 1939, in the small South Dakota town of Webster. Times were hard for his family. They had suffered under the weight of the Great Depression for nearly a decade. Not long after welcoming the new baby, they gave up on their farm and moved to Oregon, but the move did not bring the financial stability they had hoped for. Jerry's father, Henry, was forced to work at two jobs and he had little time to spend with the family.

When he was not at school, Jerry was usually with his domineering, stern mother, Eileen. It's strange that this is so – Eileen didn't like Jerry. She much preferred her eldest son, Larry, on whom she constantly doted.

Her resentment of Jerry can be traced back to his birth. As the mother of three sons she had desperately wanted her fourth child to be a girl, but Jerry had arrived instead. He grew up feeling that his mother was not happy about his gender.

Eileen's disappointment with Jerry's sex might explain a rather curious incident from his early life.

At the age of 5, he found a pair of elegant women's high-heeled shoes at the local dump. He began wearing them in secret around the house, but his mother soon saw what he was doing. She flew into a rage and then she insisted that he get rid of the feminine footwear. When she discovered that Jerry had not done as she requested, she doused the offending items in petrol and set them alight. Then she forced Jerry to watch as the forbidden footwear went up in flames.

Whatever Eileen's intention, it is likely that she only intensified her son's interest in women's footwear. In short, it was the attraction to the forbidden. Not long afterwards, Jerry was caught trying to steal his nursery school teacher's shoes.

By 1955 the Great Depression and the hardship it had caused seemed far away. The Brudos family had moved into an attractive middle-class home in a pleasant neighbourhood.

Now 16 years old, Jerry found himself living next door to a couple with three teenage daughters. He not only spied on the girls from the windows of his home, but he began stealing their underwear from the clothes line.

After the theft of the missing articles had been reported to the police, Jerry saw an opportunity to further his increasingly unusual desire for things feminine. He began by convincing one of the girls that he was working on the crime with the police

*One of the homes where Brudos was brought up – the family had moved up in the world but he still felt he was a disappointment to his mother.*

and then he invited her over to discuss the case. When the girl appeared, Jerry invited her in and then he excused himself and left the room. He returned wearing a mask. Suddenly he held a knife to her throat and forced her to strip.

Once her clothes were on the floor, Jerry took a number of photographs before leaving the room. He reappeared just as his neighbour was about to flee. Before she could raise the alarm, he quickly explained that a masked man had locked him up. It was a bold story, a ridiculous story, yet the girl told no one about the bizarre and terrifying experience.

## UNHEALTHY FANTASIES

Not long afterwards an emboldened Jerry began beating another girl after she had refused to strip for him, but he was interrupted by an elderly couple who happened to be out for a stroll. The police were called, a report was made and an investigation began. They soon found Jerry's shoe collection, the stolen lingerie and the nude photographs he had taken of his neighbour.

Jerry was sent to the psychiatric ward at Oregon State Hospital, where he related his fantasies to the psychiatrists. One of them involved an underground prison. He dreamt of a place in which he could keep captured girls. That way, he would be able to have any girl he wanted, whenever he wanted.

The psychiatrists were not concerned by what they were hearing, because they believed that Jerry's dark sexual desires would pass with adolescence. The same psychiatrists determined that Jerry was borderline schizophrenic, yet after nine months at the hospital he was discharged. Tests revealed that Jerry was an intelligent person, yet he lacked motivation and self-discipline. When he graduated from high school he ended up very close to the bottom of his class.

Jerry gave no thought to university. Instead he looked for a job, but he found nothing.

## UNUSUAL REQUESTS

Having come to a dead end, he set his sights on a military career, but he was soon discharged as an undesirable recruit after sharing his sexual fantasies with an army psychiatrist. Forced to return home, he lapsed into his old habits. He not only began stealing shoes and underwear but he also went back to assaulting women. Taking things a stage further he tried to abduct one young woman, but when she lost consciousness Jerry stole her shoes instead.

By 1961 Jerry had become an electronics technician. While he was working at a local radio station he took up with an attractive girl named Ralphene. The 17-year-old liked the idea of dating a man who was five years her senior. At the age of 23, Jerry finally lost his virginity. It was not long before Ralphene became pregnant, so with considerable reluctance her parents agreed to a wedding.

The ceremony took place in the spring of 1962, but there was not much of a honeymoon. Ralphene soon discovered that her new husband was very controlling.

What is more, his requests were really peculiar. Jerry insisted that his bride do all her housework in the nude… except for a pair of high-heeled shoes, of course. Jerry also forbade Ralphene to enter his basement. Unbeknown to his wife, Jerry spent his time printing photographs of Ralphene wearing the articles of women's clothing that he had stolen over the years.

Ralphene was young and inexperienced when the couple were first married, so she went along with her husband's unusual requests, but as time went on she became more assertive. No longer was Jerry's

wife willing to be photographed, no longer would she don the underwear he gave her. The housework was now done in an overall. She was a mother now, with another child on the way. Now that Ralphene was no longer an outlet for his sexual fantasies, Jerry turned inwards. He began wearing his collection of stolen women's underwear on a daily basis, often under his work clothes.

Things escalated dramatically one evening, shortly after the birth of his second child. Quite by chance Jerry spotted a very attractive woman walking down a street in Portland. He followed her to her apartment and then he stood and watched her windows. The hours went by, but Jerry did not move until he was certain that she had gone to sleep. He then broke in. The woman woke up just as he was in the process of stealing her underwear, so he jumped on the bed and raped her.

Frustrated by Ralphene's refusal to participate in his fantasies, Jerry took photographs of himself in women's clothing and then he left them around the house. When they were ignored, he retreated into his basement workshop. Jerry had already committed

*Jerry Brudos, 30, leaves Marion County Circuit Courtroom after changing his plea to guilty.*

rape, but his sexual fantasies were about to manifest themselves in an even more violent fashion.

On 26 January 1968 he committed his first murder. His victim, 19-year-old Linda Slawson, was trying to fund her education as a door-to-door encyclopedia saleswoman.

When she approached Jerry in his garden he expressed great enthusiasm, so she willingly followed him into his basement so that she could continue her sales pitch. Once inside, she was clubbed on the head and strangled.

When he was certain that Linda was dead, he went upstairs, peeled some bills from his wallet and sent his family out to a local fast food restaurant. Once they had left, he began acting out his fantasies with the dead woman's body. But Jerry did not stop when his wife and children returned – in fact, he continued with his activities for several days.

He then dipped into his collection of shoes and women's underwear so that he could dress Linda's body in high heels and lingerie. Numerous photographs were taken, the articles of clothing would be changed and the cycle would be repeated. Jerry also had sex with Linda's body. After a few days of exhausting activity he took the corpse to the Willamette River and threw it from a bridge. Before doing so, he cut off one of Linda's feet with a hacksaw and placed it in the basement freezer. From time to time, Jerry would place a shoe on the severed foot and then masturbate. When the severed foot had almost rotted away, Brudos threw it into the river to join the corpse.

*Linda Slawson was trying to fund her education by selling encyclopedias door to door.*

Jerry did not kill again for several months. In the intervening period he moved his family to Salem, Oregon's state capital. The new Brudos home was rather unattractive, but it did have one feature that appealed to the head of the household – a separate garage. Located off a narrow roadway, the structure would serve as Jerry's new workshop. It would be much more private than the basement.

## HUNG FROM A MEAT HOOK

On the evening of 26 November 1968 Jerry abducted Jan Whitney, his second murder victim. The family had not even settled in at that point. He had come across the young woman on Interstate 5 (I-5), after spotting her broken-down car. The vehicle could be fixed, or so he claimed, but first he had to return to his home to retrieve some tools. Jan went back to Salem with Jerry. Once there, Jerry raped and strangled her in the passenger seat of the family car.

During the next five days, Jan's body hung from a meat hook in Jerry's garage. He dressed the corpse,

*The Willamette River where Brudos dumped the bodies of Linda Slawson and Jan Whitney.*

took photographs and committed acts of necrophilia, as before. Then he took a break by going off on a Thanksgiving weekend getaway with his wife and family.

While the Brudos family were away a freak accident very nearly exposed Jan's dangling corpse and with it Jerry's secret life. A car spun out of control and hit his garage with such force that it made a large crack in the wooden structure, which brought several police officers to the scene. Had they bothered to look through the damaged wall they would have seen Jan Whitney's hanging body.

The close call served to embolden Jerry. He thought he was so clever that he could do whatever he pleased without being caught. A few days after his return, Jerry disposed of Jan's corpse in the Willamette River. Before doing so he cut off her right breast, intending to use it as a mould for making paperweights. He would be frustrated in his attempts.

Linda Slawson's work had led her to approach Jerry, while Jan Whitney's murder was the result of a chance encounter – now, however, Jerry was ready to stalk his prey. Dressed in women's clothing, he hung around in a Salem department store parking garage and on 27 March 1969 he abducted his next victim. Jerry did not kill 19-year-old Karen Sprinker immediately. Instead he forced her to model various

items from his collection of women's clothing. After he became tired of that game, he put a noose around her neck, raised her a few inches above the ground and left his garage workshop to join his family for dinner. When he returned, Karen was dead. He cut off both of her breasts in yet another attempt at making a paperweight and then he threw her into the Long Tom River.

Less than a month later, Jerry was hunting for a new victim. On 21 April he attacked another young woman, Sharon Wood, in a parking garage. A struggle ensued, Sharon bit Jerry's thumb and he ran. A few days later he tried again, this time choosing a much younger target. As 12-year-old Gloria Smith walked to school, he approached her with a fake pistol and began marching her to his car. Fortunately Gloria showed quick thinking by running to a woman who was working in her garden.

## FAKE POLICE BADGE

Jerry had thought himself so clever, but he had now failed on two occasions. He had even been outwitted by a young girl. Clearly he needed more than an imitation pistol if his abductions were going to be successful. So Jerry went out and bought a fake police badge, which he used to abduct Linda Salee, his final victim. He approached the young woman in a Portland shopping centre car park and accused her of shoplifting. After meekly following his orders, Linda was driven back to his Salem garage where she was tied up. Jerry then had dinner in the house with his family. On his return, he was surprised to find that Linda had removed the ropes. The young woman was free and yet she had not fled, so Jerry tied her up a second time and suspended her from the ceiling. After undressing her and taking a series of photographs, he hanged her.

Linda was Jerry's fourth murder victim and yet the police had not linked the murders together. In fact, they did not even know that the women were dead. Jerry might have gone on killing for some time had it not been for an angler's discovery.

On 10 May 1969, roughly a month after Linda's murder, the man spotted her body floating in the Long Tom River. Two days later, police divers found Karen Sprinker's remains. They were just a few feet away from Linda's corpse.

Jerry was unconcerned when the news raced through the community. He was confident that nothing could link him to the bodies.

He was wrong.

When Jerry had tied the women up he had used an unusual knot, one that was often used by electricians when they pulled wires through a house. The knot would tie Jerry to the murders.

The police then visited the campus of Oregon State University, where Karen Sprinker had been a student. They were told stories about a peculiar man who had been seen roaming the campus. One young woman had even had a date with the man.

When he called again, the police were waiting. It was Jerry Brudos. A background check revealed Jerry's occupation and his history of attacking teenage girls, so detectives paid a visit to the Brudos home.

They noticed a piece of rope in Jerry's garage. It was identical to the one that had been tied around the two bodies that had been found in the Long Tom River. Recognizing the investigators' interest, the ever-bold Jerry offered them a sample. It later proved to be a perfect match.

## THE NET TIGHTENS

Jerry could sense that the police were closing in, so on 30 May he made for the Canadian border, accompanied by his wife. The couple were spotted by the Oregon State Police. Although Jerry was arrested on the relatively minor charge of armed assault in relation to 12-year-old Gloria Smith, he became talkative in custody. He took great pleasure in providing very detailed accounts of the murders that he had committed. At the same time he showed no remorse, telling one detective that the women he had abused and killed were nothing more than objects to him. In fact, he went so far as to compare each of the dead women to a candy wrapper.

'Once you're done with them, you just discard them. Why would you not discard them? You don't have any more use for them.'

On 27 June, Jerry pleaded guilty to all of the charges that had been made against him. He received three life sentences amounting to at least 36 years in prison. Jerry became eligible for parole in 2005, but as the years passed and the date of his release approached it became increasingly clear that he would never again be a free man.

He died of liver cancer on 29 March 2006, at the age of 67.

# GARY HEIDNIK

llen Heidnik drank during her pregnancies. She drank a lot. Even at a time when the sight of a pregnant woman holding a wine glass was not unusual, Ellen stood out from the crowd. By the time her first child, Gary, was born – on 22 November 1943 in Eastlake, Ohio – Ellen's alcoholism had already begun to affect her marriage. Two years and one more son later, her husband filed for divorce.

The effects of the split overshadowed Gary's early years, as well as his brother Terry's.

Initially, the two boys stayed with their unstable, unreliable mother, but when she remarried they were sent to live with their father, Michael Heidnik, and his new wife.

## MISSHAPEN HEAD

They were very unhappy times for Gary. He disliked his stepmother and he was brutalized by his disciplinarian of a father. He was often punished for wetting his bed and suffered even further when his father deliberately hung the stained sheets out of the second-floor bedroom window for all the neighbours to see. Horrendous as this experience was for Gary, it was nothing compared to the terror he felt when Michael dangled him by his ankles in place of the sheets.

School was no better. Gary was not only taunted for the bed-wetting – he was also mocked because of his unusual appearance. As a young child he had fallen out of a tree, which had left him with a slightly misshapen head. Michael made his son's schooldays all the worse by painting bull's-eyes on the seat of his trousers, thereby creating a target for the bullies. In spite of all of these drawbacks, Gary excelled in the classroom. He was invariably at the top of his class and his IQ was once measured at 130.

His intelligence, combined with his status as an outcast, might have contributed to his unusual ambitions. While so many of his male classmates dreamed of becoming baseball players and stars of football, 12-year-old Gary's twin aspirations were the achievement of great wealth and a career in the military. He made an early start by entering Virginia's Staunton Military Academy at the age of 14. Once again Gary proved to be an excellent student. However, unlike Barry Goldwater and John Dean, two of the school's illustrious alumni, Gary never graduated from the prestigious school. After two years of study he left the academy, returning to his father's house. He attempted to resume his studies at a couple of different high schools, but he felt that he was learning nothing, so at the age of 18 he dropped out of school and joined the army.

Though he made few friends amongst his comrades, Gary shone in the military. After completing basic training, he was sent to San Antonio in Texas, where he was to become a medical orderly. Now

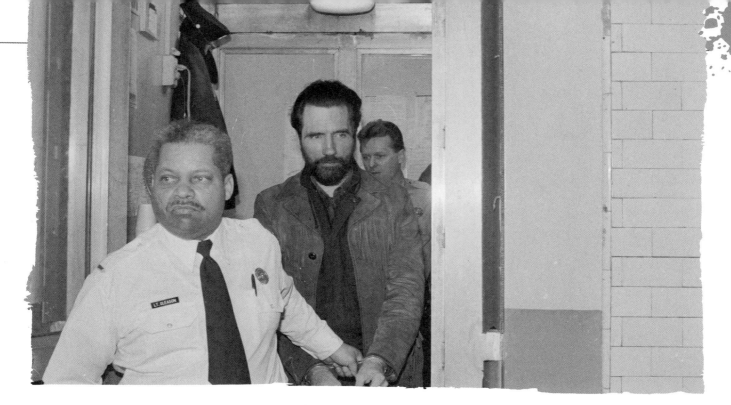

that his military career seemed well and truly on its way, Gary began pursuing his other long-held dream – to become wealthy. He supplemented his pay by making loans with interest to his fellow soldiers. Though his modest business would have been frowned upon by his superiors, Gary was otherwise an exemplary and intelligent military man. In 1962, while at a field hospital in West Germany, he achieved a near-perfect score in his high school equivalency examination.

A few months later it was all over.

In August, Gary began to complain of nausea, dizziness and blurred vision. The doctors who attended him identified two causes – stomach flu and 'schizoid personality disorder'. Before the year was up, he had been shipped back home. He was granted an honourable discharge and a disability pension. With one of his two dreams dashed into smithereens, Gary enrolled at the University of Pennsylvania. His chosen courses – chemistry, history, anthropology and biology – were so diverse in nature that it appeared that he was looking for direction. If so, Gary

*As a boy, Gary Heidnik was traumatized by his mother and brutalized by his father.*

was unsuccessful. Using his army medical training, he worked for a time at two Philadelphia hospitals, but he proved to be a poor worker.

Now without work and living on his pension his eccentricities grew, while his personal hygiene declined. Gary found a leather jacket, which he would wear regardless of the weather or the social situation. If he did not want to be disturbed, he would roll up one trouser leg as a signal to others. Then there were the suicide attempts – not just Gary's, but those of his brother and his mother, too. These were so frequent that they could be numbered in the dozens, but only Ellen was successful. In 1970, the four-times married alcoholic took her own life by drinking mercury.

Both Heidnik boys spent years moving in and out of mental institutions. Yet despite his many periods of confinement, Gary managed to begin amassing the wealth he had sought since he was a child. In 1971 he founded his own church, the United Church of the Ministers of God, and he ordained himself as its bishop. Although Gary had just four followers, they included two people who were close to him – his mentally retarded girlfriend and his brother.

## OUT OF CONTROL

As a self-anointed minister, Gary began investing in earnest. He bought property and played the stock market, making a great deal of money when Hugh Hefner's Playboy empire went public in 1971. But all of the time he was spinning increasingly out of control. Gary became one of those individuals who is often described as 'known to the police'. There were any number of reasons for his notoriety. In 1976, for example, he used an unlicensed gun to shoot one of his tenants in the face. Incredibly, it was not until 1978 that he first went to jail. But the three- to seven-year sentence had nothing to do with the earlier shooting. Instead, Gary had been found guilty of kidnapping, unlawful restraint, false imprisonment, rape, involuntary deviate sexual intercourse and interfering with the custody of a committed person.

All of this had come about because Gary had signed his girlfriend's sister out of a mental institution and had kept her confined to his basement. Not only had he raped the young woman but he had infected her with gonorrhoea. In the middle of what turned out to be four years of incarceration, he handed a prison guard a note explaining that he could no longer speak because Satan had shoved a cookie down his throat. Gary remained silent for over 27 months.

When he was finally released in April 1983, he returned to Philadelphia and resumed his role as a bishop with the United Church of the Ministers of God. Even though Gary's congregation had not grown much, from time to time it included mentally retarded women, whom he would impregnate.

It is hardly surprising that Betty Disto, Gary's first bride, was not immediately aware of his odd behaviour and poor hygiene because the couple had become engaged before they had even laid eyes on one another. The couple had met through a matrimonial service. They had been corresponding for two years when, in September of 1985, Betty flew from her address in the Philippines to the United States. Their October marriage lasted for just three months. Betty could not stand to see her groom in bed with other women, but she had no choice because Gary made her watch. Beaten, raped and threatened, a pregnant Betty fled home with the help of the local Filipino community.

Betty made her escape in the first few days of 1986, but Gary's life really began to fall apart towards the end of that year. On the evening of 26 November 1986, Gary abducted his first victim, a prostitute named Josefina Rivera. It all happened gradually.

She had been standing outside in the cold rain when Gary picked her up in his Cadillac Coupe De Ville. On the way, he stopped at McDonald's and bought her a coffee. She did not object when he took her to his home, a run-down house at 3520 North Marshall Street.

There was something surreal about it all. Gary's house had seen better days, as had the rest of the neighbourhood. Decades earlier, the area had housed working-class German immigrants. The streets had been spotless then, but now they were pockmarked and covered in litter. Drug dealers worked its streets selling crack cocaine and marijuana to passing motorists and poverty was everywhere, yet Gary had a Rolls-Royce in his garage.

*Gary Heidnik acquired a 'harem'.*

The door to his home was like something from a children's movie. When it opened, Josefina noticed that Gary had glued thousands of pennies to the walls of his kitchen. As he led her upstairs to the bedroom, she realized that the hallway had been wallpapered with $5 bills. In many ways, the house was a reflection of its owner. Gary's gold jewellery and Rolex watch contrasted sharply with his worn and stained clothing.

Like the rest of the house, the bedroom was sparsely furnished. There was nothing more than a waterbed, two chairs and a dresser. Gary gave Josefina the money they had agreed upon – $20 – and then he got undressed. The energetic and emotionless sex act was over in a matter of minutes. Josefina had felt a little uneasy about Gary, but what happened next took her by surprise. He grabbed her by the throat and choked her until she blacked out. Brief as it was, her loss of consciousness provided Gary with enough time to handcuff her.

Josefina was ordered to her feet and then she was marched downstairs to the basement. The unfinished room was cold, clammy and filthy, much like the old mattress that he made her sit on, and the floor was concrete, though some of the surface had been removed. After attaching metal clamps and chains to Josefina's ankles, Gary got down to digging the exposed earth.

He talked as he worked, telling the shackled woman that he had fathered four children by four different women, but it had all gone wrong. He had no contact with any of his offspring and yet he really wanted and *deserved* a family.

'Society owes me a wife and a big family,' was how he put it. 'I want to get ten women and keep them here and get them all pregnant. Then, when they have babies, I want to raise those children here too. We'll be like one big happy family.'

And with that bit of information, he raped her.

## SCREAMING BLUE MURDER

Once she was alone, Josefina tried to escape. After freeing one of her ankles, she managed to prise open one of the basement windows and squeeze through it. Then she was out in the open. She crawled as far as the chain around her other ankle allowed her to and then she screamed at the top of her voice. But in Gary's neighbourhood screams like Josefina's were an everyday thing. The only person who paid any attention to the sound was Gary.

He ran downstairs, grabbed the chain and pulled her back into the basement. The filthy mattress was too good for her now. Dragging her across the cement floor, he threw her into the shallow pit. She was covered over with a sheet of plywood, upon which Gary placed heavy weights.

On her third day of captivity she was joined by a mentally retarded young woman named Sandra Lindsay. The girl seemed to have a very limited understanding of what was happening, so it was easy for Gary to get her to write a short note home. *'Dear Mom, do not worry. I will call.'*

It was the last time Sandra's mother would ever hear from her daughter. Josefina and Sandra spent weeks together. Sometimes they were in the pit and sometimes they were chained to pipes in the basement. They endured repeated rapes, beatings and the ever-present cold.

On 22 December they were joined by 19-year-old Lisa Thomas, a third 'wife'. Gary lured the girl to 3520 North Marshall Street with offers of food and clothing and a trip to Atlantic City. In the end she only got the food and a spiked glass of wine. After she passed out, Gary raped her and then took her down to the basement.

On New Year's Day Gary abducted a fourth woman, but 23-year-old Deborah Dudley was totally unlike his other 'wives'. Ignoring the consequences, she fought back at nearly every opportunity. Her disobedience invariably led to the other three captives being beaten as well, which created disorder and tension within the group.

When Gary began to encourage the women to report on each other, Josefina saw an opportunity to gain Gary's trust. Though she continued to suffer at his hands, Gary came to believe that Josefina actually took pleasure in her circumstance.

Wife number five, 18-year-old Jacqueline Askins, arrived on 18 January. After raping and shackling the girl, Gary surprised his 'wives' with generous helpings of Chinese food and a bottle of champagne. After weeks of bread, water and stale hot dogs, it seemed like the most elaborate feast.

To what did they owe this unexpected treat? It was Josefina's birthday.

## WICKED PUNISHMENT

However, any hopes that Gary might be softening were soon dashed. If anything, his abuse escalated. When he caught Sandra Lindsay trying to remove the plywood covering from the pit, she was forced to hang by one of her wrists from a ceiling beam.

She responded by going on a hunger strike, but after a few days she appeared incapable of eating. When Gary tried to force food down her throat, she vomited.

By 7 February, Sandra had completely lost consciousness. At this point, Gary finally removed the handcuff that had kept her dangling and she fell into a heap on the concrete floor.

Kicking her into the pit, he assured his other wives that Sandra was faking. It was probably a matter of minutes later that Sandra died.

The women watched as Gary carried Sandra's body upstairs and then they heard the sound of a power saw. Later that day, one of his dogs entered the basement, tail wagging. In its mouth was a bone covered in fresh meat.

Within days, the house and the basement took on a foul odour. Gary was finding it hard to dispose of Sandra's remains. Using his food processor he ground up what he could, feeding the meat to his dogs and his wives – but some body parts were very difficult to deal with.

Sandra's severed head sat in a pot of boiling water for days, while her ribcage was broiled in the oven. The smell spread to some of the adjoining properties, which led to complaints from the neighbours. Although the police investigated they believed Gary's story that he had cooked some bad meat. Meanwhile, the torture endured by the women became even more intense. Gary began poking their ears with a screwdriver, in the belief that deaf wives would be easier to control. He also stripped the insulation from extension cords in order to shock his captives.

Josefina was not only spared these punishments, she became an administrator. On 18 March she helped with an elaborate method of torture. First of all the pit was flooded and then the other wives, still in chains, were forced into the water. After that the plywood covering was put in place and weighed down. Finally, the bare wire of the extension cord was pushed through a hole, thereby electrocuting the women.

The second of these shocks killed Deborah Dudley. Her death marked a significant change in Gary's relationship with Josefina.

In his eyes, her participation in the torture, combined with Deborah's death, meant she could be blackmailed. That made her trustworthy – or so he thought. For the first time in almost four months she was allowed to leave the basement. She shared Gary's bed, dined with him at restaurants and helped with his grocery shopping. Josefina even went so far as to accompany Gary to the country, where he disposed of Deborah's body.

On 24 March 1987, the day after she helped abduct a new woman, Agnes Adams, Josefina convinced Gary to let her visit her children. She promised him that she would return with yet another 'wife'. Gary dropped her off and waited in the car for her return. But Josefina did not visit her children – she had none. Instead, she sprinted to her boyfriend's apartment, where she poured out her bizarre and almost unbelievable story.

After the police arrived and noted the scarring that had been left by months of wearing heavy chains, they arrested Gary. His surviving 'wives' were rescued when the police converged on 3520 North Marshall Street on the following morning.

Gary's trial began on 20 June 1988. From the start, his defence lawyers attempted to prove that the one-time medical assistant was insane. They called a psychiatrist and a psychologist to the stand, but their efforts were in vain. Ten days later he was found guilty of two counts of first-degree murder, four counts of aggravated assault, five counts of rape, six counts of kidnapping and one count of involuntary deviate sexual intercourse. He was subsequently sentenced to death.

On the evening of 6 July 1999, 11 years after he had been sentenced, Gary Heidnik was executed by lethal injection. It is hardly surprising that his body was not claimed by the other members of his family.

Michael Heidnik, his father, had not seen him since the early 1960s. When he heard about the death sentence he made a brief statement to the press.

'I'm not interested. I don't care. It don't bother me a bit.'

# PHILLIP GARRIDO

A baby boomer born within sight of San Francisco, Phillip Garrido was convinced that fame lay in his future. As a young man, he believed that he was destined for stardom as a rock musician. As the years passed, the dream faded and was replaced by the idea of becoming a messianic figure. In the end, he did achieve fame of a kind. However, only one person would ever look up to Phillip Garrido: his wife, the woman who had helped him carry out his despicable crimes.

Phillip Craig Garrido entered the world on 5 April 1951 in Contra Costa County. His father Manuel, a forklift operator, provided a modest, yet comfortable home. Little is known about Phillip's childhood, in part due to the fact that his father demands money in exchange for information about his son.

*Garrido believed he had a special machine through which he communicated with God.*

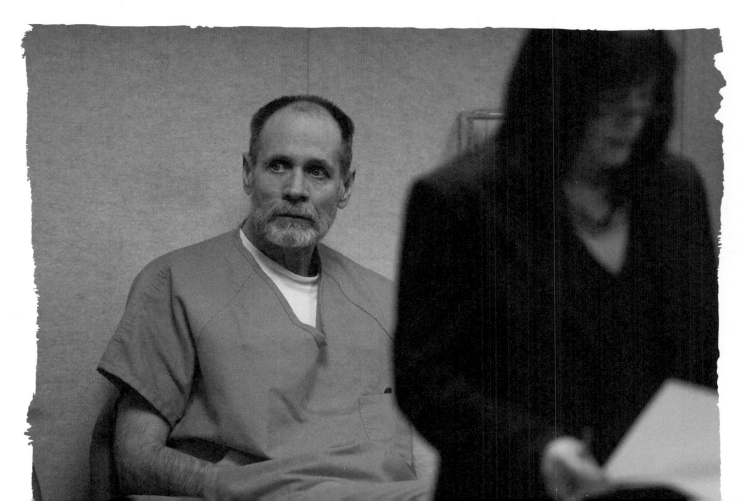

That said, Phillip's early years may indeed be inconsequential. It may just be that they weren't formative in creating the monster who would become fodder for television newscasts. No, according to some who knew Phillip, his anti-social, dangerous behaviour began with a motorcycle accident he'd suffered as a teenager. On this, even his father was willing to share an opinion. According to Manuel, before the tragic event, Phillip had been a 'good boy'. After? Well, Phillip became uncontrollable and started to take drugs.

Despite his wild behaviour, Phillip graduated from local Liberty High School with the rest of his class. The year was 1969, a time when American counterculture was pervasive. Phillip appeared to embrace it all. He grew his hair, bought a fringed leather jacket, and played bass in a psychedelic rock group. But in reality, the young high school graduate wanted little to do with peace and love. Eighteen years old, Phillip had already committed his first act of rape, and would regularly beat his girlfriend, Christine Perreira.

In 1972, he was charged with the rape of a 14-year-old girl whom he had plied with barbiturates. Phillip avoided doing time in prison when the girl refused to testify. What the authorities did not realize at the time was that they might have nailed the young man on another charge – Phillip had become one of the busiest drug dealers in Contra Costa County.

Once clear of the rape charge, Phillip married Christine. The young couple settled 300 km (185 miles) northeast in South Lake Tahoe. In the small city, drugs were no longer Phillip's primary source of income. Christine got a job dealing cards at Harrah's Casino, while her husband pursued his dream of becoming a rock star.

# PERVERTED PLAN

Three years passed, and vinyl glory still eluded Phillip. Each day was blanketed in a haze induced by a combination of marijuana, cocaine and LSD. He would spend hours masturbating while watching elementary school girls across the street, but the real object of his interest was a woman.

Phillip had been following her for months, during which he developed a very elaborate plan, which he set in motion by renting a warehouse in Reno, 100 km (60 miles) to the south. He then fixed up the space, hanging rugs for soundproofing. A mattress was brought in, as were satin sheets, bottles of wine and an extensive collection of pornographic magazines.

When his trap was set, Phillip took four tabs of LSD and attacked the woman whom he'd been stalking for so long. However, due to his drugged state, she managed to fight him off. Frustrated, Phillip drove to Harrah's, where he asked one of his wife's co-workers, Katie Calloway Hall, for a ride home.

Katie was not as lucky as the intended victim. She ended up being raped repeatedly in Phillip's Reno warehouse. After eight hours of pain and humiliation, Katie was rescued by a police officer whose eye had been drawn to the door, which had been left ajar.

This time, Christine did not stand by Phillip. After her husband's arrest, she severed all ties. The divorce came through just as Phillip was beginning a 50-year prison sentence in Leavenworth, Kansas.

However, for Phillip, romance was still in the air. Behind bars he began corresponding with the niece of a fellow inmate, Nancy Bocanegra, four years his junior. In 1981, the two were married in a ceremony that was conducted by the prison chaplain. Phillip was not yet one tenth of the way through his sentence.

When not enjoying conjugal visits with Nancy, he would study psychology and theology. Religion, it seemed, became the focus of his life. A Catholic by birth, he converted, becoming a Jehovah's Witness. Phillip's extreme devotion to the denomination was cited by the prison psychologist as an indication that he would commit no further crimes.

Phillip was granted parole in 1988. With Nancy, he returned to South Lake Tahoe, where they spent nearly three uneventful years.

On 10 June 1991, Phillip's prison psychologist would be proven wrong. That morning, a man named Carl Probyn watched in horror as his 11-year-old stepdaughter was dragged into a grey sedan. He was not alone – several of the girl's friends had also witnessed the abduction – and yet no one was able to provide the licence plate number of the car that sped away.

The girl, Jaycee Dugard, soon found herself living in sheds, tents and under tarpaulins in the backyard of a house in Contra Costa County. The property belonged to Phillip's mother, who was then suffering from dementia. Eventually, the old woman would be shipped off to a chronic care hospital. Jaycee, of course, remained on the property, where she would be subjected to 18 years of sexual abuse at Phillip's hands.

She bore her captor two children, both daughters, born in August of 1994 and November of 1997. Both would come to describe Jaycee as an older sister. It is unknown whether or not they knew the truth.

The girl's nightmare could have ended earlier. Phillip fell under the watchful eyes of his neighbours when it was discovered that he was a registered sex offender.

In 2006, one of the watchful called police to report that Phillip, a 'psychotic sex addict', had a woman and several children living under tents in his backyard. A sheriff's deputy dispatched to investigate interviewed Phillip on his front porch; he did not bother to look at the backyard, nor did he run a background check.

Two years later, police were again on Phillip's property, accompanied by firefighters who had been called in to put out a blaze.

*Family photos of Jaycee Dugard handed out at a Los Angeles press conference in 2009.*

# WEIRD AND FRIGHTENING

The actions of law enforcement officers might be considered lazy or negligent, but they paled beside the ineptitude displayed by the California Department of Corrections and Rehabilitation. As a convicted sex offender, Phillip was visited regularly by department employees. All the visits, both scheduled and unscheduled, took place while Jaycee was in the backyard. In nearly two decades, not one department agent would bother investigating Phillip's collection of tents, tarpaulins and sheds.

The authorities might not have thought Phillip was a suspicious character, but those who saw him on a daily basis found him weird and just a little frightening. Neighbourhood parents told their children to keep away from his house. He ran a print shop, Printing for Less, but his behaviour ensured that he had few repeat customers. Those who gave him business would often find themselves subjected to bizarre ramblings. Phillip, the self-proclaimed

'Man Who Spoke with his Mind', would speak of how he could control sound with his mind. Some customers were privileged enough to be shown a machine, through which the printer claimed he could communicate with God. Others might be treated to recordings of songs that Phillip had written about his attraction to underage girls.

Phillip kept a blog, titled 'Voices Revealed', through which he attempted to convince others of his special relationship with God. The outlet seemed to encourage further writing. In August of 2009, he walked into the San Francisco offices of the FBI to hand-deliver two weighty tomes he had written: 'The Origin of Schizophrenia Revealed' and 'Stepping into the Light'. The latter was a personal story in which Phillip detailed how it was that he had come to triumph over his violent sexual urges. Intent

*A walkway leads to the home of Phillip Garrido where Jaycee Dugard was imprisoned for 18 years.*

on helping others to do the same, he approached Lisa Campbell, a special events coordinator at the University of California, Berkeley, with the idea of a lecture. Phillip was not alone when he made his proposal. Both his daughters sat in on the meeting, listening intently as their father spoke about his deviant past and the rapes he had committed.

It was Campbell's report of the strange behaviour to Phillip's parole officer that at long last brought an end to Jaycee's nightmare.

## MOMENT OF TRUTH

When confronted, on 26 August 2009, Phillip admitted to kidnapping Jaycee, adding that he was the father of her children. Both he and Nancy were taken into custody.

On 28 April 2011, Phillip pleaded guilty to Jaycee's kidnapping, as well as 13 counts of sexual assault.

Sitting next to her husband, Nancy pleaded guilty to the kidnapping, and one charge of aiding and abetting a sexual assault. In court, both Phillip's and Nancy's lawyers portrayed their respective clients as good souls. After 1997, the year in which they both found God, the couple had dedicated themselves to Jaycee and the children – or so the claim went.

Phillip hoped that his confession would win Nancy a lighter sentence. Whether or not he was successful is a matter of debate. What is certain, however, is that Nancy's sentence was not nearly as harsh as that of her husband. Where Phillip received a term amounting to 431 years, Nancy was sentenced to 36 years in prison. Should she live a long life, Nancy Garrido will be 90 when she leaves prison.

*Nancy Garrido pleaded guilty to kidnapping as well as to aiding and abetting a sexual assault.*

# STEVE WRIGHT

Steven Gerald James Wright was an organized and calculating killer, whose car was a mobile death chamber. His victims, all prostitutes, entered the vehicle with little hesitation, even though they were aware that a serial killer was on the prowl. A 19-year-old named Tania Nicol was the first to go missing. She disappeared on 30 October 2006, but her mother did not report her absence until two days later. Tania was a student at Chantry High School, but she also worked as a prostitute using the alias 'Chantelle'. In the weeks leading up to her disappearance, she had been walking the streets of Ipswich to support her addiction to heroin and crack cocaine. Her parents knew nothing about her drug habit or her adopted occupation. In fact, Tania's mother thought her daughter worked at a hairdressing salon.

Another teenage runaway, perhaps? The police were not so sure. According to the records, her mobile phone had shown no activity since she had been reported missing.

Seventeen days later, in the early hours of 15 November, Gemma Adams also went missing. A heroin addict like Tania, she too had been working as a prostitute. The police learned of the young woman's disappearance from her boyfriend, Jon Simpson,

*Steve Wright was an organized and calculating killer who preyed on prostitutes.*

with whom she had been for ten of her 25 years. The recent past had not been the best of times for the couple. Gemma's progression from marijuana to heroin had resulted in her being fired from her job at an insurance firm. What is more, she cut herself off from her parents and her sister when they tried to get her into a rehabilitation clinic.

## NAKED BODY

Following this second disappearance, the police began stopping motorists in the city's small red light district. Over 500 cars were stopped and 2,000

people were questioned, yet the investigation yielded no information. This all changed on the morning of 2 December, when Gemma's naked body was discovered by a park worker. The location, Belstead Brook, would prove to be a challenge to the forensic investigators, who recognized that the swift-moving water would almost certainly have washed away any fibres, hair or DNA.

Undaunted, the team of policemen doggedly searched the area. On the sixth day they found Tania's submerged, naked body 3 km (2 miles) downstream.

The double murder inquiry was less than 48 hours old when the body of a third prostitute was discovered. The news came as a shock, because no one had reported the victim missing.

She was Anneli Alderton, a 24-year-old who had once entertained dreams of becoming a model. While she certainly had the looks, she had been dependent on drugs during the eight years that led to her death. At the time of her death, the mother of one was three months pregnant.

The killer must have been bold because the prostitute had gone missing when there was a noticeably heightened police presence in Ipswich's red-light district. Was the murderer taunting the police? The way in which Anneli's body had been left indicated that this was so. She was found in a secluded wood on the outskirts of Ipswich, less than 16 km (10 miles) from where she had plied her trade. Like the other two victims, her body was naked.

However, that was where the similarities ended. Anneli had been found on dry land and her killer had taken a good deal of time to arrange the body in the shape of a cross.

'She was pristine, she looked like an angel,' said one detective.

The location of the corpse gave the police an advantage that they had not had with the other victims. For the first time they were looking at the possibility of harvesting a significant amount of forensic evidence from the body and the surrounding area.

Now that the bodies of three Ipswich prostitutes had been found in just six days, it was clear that a serial killer was on the prowl in the seamier part of the city. Yet prostitutes continued to walk the streets of the red-light district. The police issued constant warnings, but they were ignored – the girls needed money to feed their drugs habits.

## SHAPE OF THE CROSS

Less than 48 hours later, on 12 December, another body was found just metres off the busy Old Felixstowe Road. Again, the victim had been arranged in the shape of a cross. At 29 years of age, Annette Nicholls would be the oldest of all the victims. Annette was a very attractive woman who had suffered a rough upbringing. She nearly managed to rise above her disadvantaged childhood by studying to be a beautician, but then she succumbed to heroin addiction.

All available police officers were dispatched to the area and a helicopter was brought in to film the scene from the air. As the camera panned along the roadside a second body came into view. The fifth victim, Paula Clennell, was a 24-year-old drug addict and mother of three. Paula had been walking the streets for years.

Indeed, she had continued to do so even in the knowledge that there was a prostitute killer on the loose. Just six days before she vanished, Paula had been interviewed by a local television journalist. The young woman admitted that she was 'a bit wary about getting into cars', but she said that she needed the money. There was something markedly different about Paula's body. She was not carefully laid out in a cruciform position – in fact, it appeared that no care had been taken at all. The corpse had simply been dumped.

More than 300 local police officers were now working overtime on the case, with assistance from a further 500 throughout the country. Almost immediately, there appeared to be a breakthrough. A 37-year-old supermarket worker was taken into custody after he had told a newspaper that he knew all five women. Under questioning from the police, the man further revealed that he could offer no alibi for the evenings on which the victims had gone missing.

As police investigators searched the supermarket worker's home, other officers managed to find traces of DNA on the bodies of the three women who had been found on land. Such extraordinarily small amounts were present that there was little hope that the samples would prove useful. And yet the forensics team managed to prove that the DNA that had been found on all three bodies had come from the same person.

## LUCKY BREAK

When the samples were checked against the United Kingdom National DNA Database, the police were treated to another lucky break. The DNA belonged to a 48-year-old forklift operator named Steve Wright – a man who had not even been considered as a suspect. Wright might not have been on the investigators'

radar, but they did have his name. He had been stopped and questioned during the road checks that had taken place earlier in the month. In the pre-dawn hours of 19 December, one week after the final bodies were found, Wright was removed from his house in handcuffs.

But who was Steve Wright? Police had already begun looking into his background. Steven Gerald James Wright, the man who would go down in history as 'the Suffolk Strangler' and 'the Ipswich Ripper', had been born on 24 April 1958 in the Norfolk village of Erpingham. As the son of a military man, he had spent his early years in Malta and Singapore. Beaten by his father, his unhappy childhood was made all the worse at the age of 8, when his mother abandoned the family. Wright and his three siblings remained with their father and were later joined by a stepmother and two more children.

Wright's physically abusive father failed to provide his son with any guidance, so he never seemed to find his footing in life. Sailor, ship's steward, barman, lorry driver, he moved from one job to the next. Women came and went in much the same way. Wright's first marriage, in 1978, lasted nine years and produced a son. His second, which began just weeks after the divorce, was over within 11 months. A Thai woman said that she had married Wright in 1999, but her claim was never substantiated. There were many other women in his life, including Sarah Whiteley, who gave birth to his daughter in 1992.

In 2001 he met his final partner, Pamela Wright. Quite by chance he shared his surname with her.

In October 2004, just weeks before Tania Nicol went missing, the couple moved to a rented flat at 79 London Road. It was one of the few streets that make up Ipswich's red-light district. Prior to his arrest,

Wright had only had one brush with the law. This was while he was working as a hotel barman. He had been caught stealing £80 from the till to pay off his gambling debts. A petty crime, it is true, but it had been enough to get his DNA entered on to the national database.

Armed with the DNA evidence, the police charged Wright with the murders of the five dead prostitutes. What did Wright have to say about the presence of his DNA? The only words he uttered during the hours of intense interrogation were 'No comment'.

## FLAKES OF BLOOD

Wright's trial was set for January 2008. In the meantime, the police would work at gathering evidence. His Ford Mondeo was their primary focus.

CCTV cameras had filmed Gemma getting into the vehicle on the night that she had disappeared. Not only that, the forklift driver's new neighbours had told the police that he continually cleaned the vehicle, sometimes in the early hours of the morning. Inside the foot well, they found two fake fur fibres that exactly matched the ones on Annette Nicholls' naked body. Some small flakes of blood on the back seat matched Paula Clennell's DNA and fibres from

the Mondeo's carpet were found in Tania Nicol's hair. That proved that her head had been in contact with the floor well of the car at some point.

On the first day of his trial, 14 January 2008, Wright was charged with the murder of the five women. He pleaded not guilty, although he admitted that he frequented prostitutes. Annette had been in his car, he said, but he had done nothing more than have sex with her on the back seat. Tania had also been in the Mondeo, but only briefly – her acne had turned him off.

The cold, self-assured Wright eventually began to crumble under the persistent questioning of the prosecution, who had nothing more than a few flakes of blood, some small traces of DNA and several stray fibres to work with. H. H. Holmes' Murder Castle, David Parker Ray's trailer or the pot on Joachim Kroll's stove had provided the authorities with much more in the way of evidence. But Steve Wright had run up against the 21st century.

On 21 February, it took a jury of nine men and three women just eight hours to find Wright guilty on all five counts of murder. He received a life sentence.

*Police cordon off the Steve Wright's street in Ipswich as they investigate the murder of five prostitutes.*

# ANTHONY SOWELL

On September 2009 a woman went home with registered sex offender Anthony Sowell for a few drinks. The night soon took a nightmarish turn as a pleasant date turned sour. The victim called the police and reported that Sowell had hit her, choked her and then raped her.

When the police arrived to arrest him, they found the evening's unnerving events were just the tip of the iceberg. Two female corpses greeted them on the living room floor. A skull was hidden in a bucket in the basement. Four more bodies were hidden around the house. Inadvertently, the police had stumbled upon a serial killer who had been operating for years. Sowell was charged with 11 counts of murder and over 70 counts of rape, kidnapping, tampering with evidence, and even the sexual abuse of a corpse.

## WEIRD FAMILY LIFE

On Page Avenue, Cleveland, stood a large, 372 m² (4,000 sq ft) house in a rather run-down working-class district slowly but surely sliding into poverty and destitution. This was the scene of the horrible events of Anthony Sowell's childhood. He was born in 1959 to Claudia 'Gertrude' Garrison. Too bad his father, Thomas Sowell, did not stick around long enough to help raise the boy.

It was far from a normal household. In the house lived Sowell, his mother 'Gertrude', his older sister, Tressa, his brother 'Junior', and seven nieces and nephews who had moved into the house after their mother had died. His mother was not exactly a nurturing presence. She forced Ramona Davis and her twin sister Leona, Sowell's nieces, to strip naked before the other children each day. Then they would be tied to a bannister and whipped with electrical cords. Vindictive Gertrude always found a reason for punishing them, even if she had to make it up.

'It was psycho,' recalled Leona, commenting on the levels of violence in the house. Other siblings were abused, too. Only Sowell, his sister, and his brother were spared.

Sowell was badly affected by the situation, but instead of learning from it he began following his mother's example and taking advantage of others in a very unhealthy way. When he got in trouble, he would blame Leona. She would then be punished for what he had done.

As his nieces began to mature physically, he became obsessed with their bodies and the idea of subjecting them to punishment.

From the age of 11, he began raping his niece. It soon became an everyday occurrence. Sowell was not the only one. His brother Junior and the girl's own brother soon began demanding sexual favours, too, under threat of violence. Leona had tried to report the rapes to the authorities but she found they were unwilling to listen.

*Anthony Sowell raped and then strangled a number of women before hiding the bodies around the house.*

When he went to high school, Sowell was tormented for being so quiet and undemonstrative. For some reason, his classmates assumed he lacked sexual experience and teased him about it constantly; he never spoke up about what had been going on at the house. Generally, though, at school he was able to stay out of trouble, but he never did particularly well in his studies.

On leaving school, it seemed that things might be changing for the better. He got out of his mother's house of humiliation and joined the Marines. In September 1981 he married a fellow Marine, Kim Yvette Lawson, who was on a mission to save him from himself – in particular, to help him cut down his excessive drinking.

Unfortunately, the Marines provided Sowell with exactly the training he needed to pursue a campaign of terror. They taught him how to make improvised weapons and to kill with his hands. He also received training as an electrician at Camp Lejeune.

During his seven-year career in the Marines, he picked up a number of awards: a Good Conduct Medal, a Certificate of Commendation, and a Meritorious Mast. His life had not been completely turned around, however.

His wife had married him partly to help him overcome his severe drink problem, but she divorced him the day she left the Marines in 1985, the same year Sowell went back into civilian life. By the mid-1980s, life had deteriorated further in East Cleveland as something far worse than alcohol – crack cocaine – made its debut on the streets.

Sowell's ex-wife Kim died in 1998 having failed entirely in her aim of making him a better man – at the time of her death, Sowell was serving time in an Ohio prison.

## TERROR ON THE STREETS

After his discharge from the Marines, Sowell could not keep out of trouble. Between 1986 and 1989 he was arrested several times, mostly for minor offences – possession of drugs, disorderly conduct, driving under the influence, and public drunkenness.

Around this time women began to go missing in East Cleveland. In May 1988 the strangled corpse of 36-year-old Rosalind Garner was found in her home on Hayden Avenue. Nearly a year later, on 27 February 1989, 27-year-old Carmella Karen Prater was found dead in her home on First Avenue, not far from the location where the earlier victim had been found. Then just one month later, Mary Thomas turned up

*An investigator takes a sledge-hammer to a concrete slab at Sowell's home in an area pinpointed by thermal imaging and radar technology.*

dead in an abandoned building on First Avenue, with the red ribbon that had been used to strangle her still dangling from her neck.

These cases remain unsolved, but they bore a striking similarity to the murders Sowell would later be convicted for. Mary Cox, one of the women who disappeared, was an acquaintance of Sowell. It is possible that he was responsible for even more killings than the 11 he was eventually convicted for.

In this poisonous climate, the 'Cleveland Strangler', as he became known, began to earn his soubriquet. On 22 July 1989, Sowell met a woman outside a motel on Euclid Avenue. Sowell told her that her boyfriend was waiting for her just around the corner at Sowell's house. When she arrived he choked her and raped her. He tied up her hands with a necktie, looped a belt around her feet and placed a gag in her mouth. When he fell asleep, she managed to escape. A few days later she gave her report to the police. The woman was 21-year-old Melvette Sockwell. She would be the first of Sowell's recognized female victims.

An arrest warrant was issued on 8 December 1989, but he remained free to commit another rape. On 24 June 1990, a 31-year-old woman visited Sowell's house. There Sowell began choking her while describing violent sex acts. He told her 'she was his bitch, and she had better learn to like it'. He raped the woman many times over. She was five months pregnant. Unwilling to face her assailant in court, the woman's name was never revealed.

Sowell pleaded guilty to attempted rape of Sockwell and was sentenced to between five and 15 years in prison. At the trial, his victim stated:

'He choked me real hard because my body started tingling. I thought I was going to die.'

In prison he tried to rehabilitate himself. He attempted to deal with his alcohol problem by signing up with Alcoholics Anonymous and for Adult Children of Alcoholics meetings. He also tried to get help for the the problem that put him behind bars: the impulse to commit sexual assault.

Sowell signed up for sex-offender treatment but stumbled at the first hurdle: he was simply not prepared to admit he was a sex offender. He spent a total of 15 years in the Ohio penitentiary system and was a model prisoner throughout. He took courses with names like 'Living Without Violence' and 'Positive Personal Change'. He cooked and threw barbecues for the other inmates. It was in prison that he finally completed his high-school education, passing the GED in 2002. So when he was released in 2005 it should not come as a surprise that the authorities believed he had been rehabilitated. He was educated, clean and sober. A psychological evaluation in 2005 stated that he was unlikely to rape again.

## ON THE RAMPAGE

As a free man he soon reverted to his old ways. Between 2007 and 2009, 11 women were killed by Sowell. Most were African-American women, drug-users and mothers. He began dating women from the troubled neighbourhood of the Mount Pleasant area where he now lived. But on the plus side, he seemed to be developing a more stable relationship with Lori Frazier, the niece of Cleveland's mayor. She moved in with him, unaware of his terrible secrets. The relationship ended abruptly in 2007. Frazier had caught the foul whiff of something nasty in his house. Sowell claimed it came from the sausage factory across the road.

The truth was far more chilling. It was the stench of the dead bodies that he had hidden around his home. One of the first victims to be discovered was Crystal Dozier who'd gone missing in May 2007. To maintain his supply of prey, Sowell had joined a sex fetish website, Alt.com. His profile stated: 'If your [*sic*] submissive and like to please, then this master wants to talk to you.' In 2008 and 2009 more women would disappear.

On 21 April 2009, Tanja Doss visited Sowell and was slapped, choked and forced to strip naked. On 22 September, he attacked another woman who was visiting him, whose name has never been released. He raped her while tightening an electrical cord around her neck until she passed out. Unlike many of Sowell's victims, she was not afraid to go to the police. After most of his attacks, he acted as if nothing had happened. He offered some of his victims food

*The rundown streets of America's inner cities are breeding grounds for violent crime.*

and money and escorted them calmly out of the door. But the majority never left the house on Imperial Avenue.

When the police arrived to arrest him, they found an array of bodies hidden within. Two corpses were in plain view on the living room floor. A skull was found in a bucket in the basement. Shallow graves had been dug in the backyard and bodies left in crawl spaces. In total there were 11 bodies hidden around the house.

Most had been strangled. The interrogation of Sowell by Detectives Lem Griffin and Melvin Smith on 31 October 2009 left little room for doubt:

'Did you strangle these girls?'

'That's what I did. I think with just my hands.'

On hearing the news about Sowell, Regina Woodland, a woman who lived nearby, asked: 'What kind of man was this? He couldn't have been human.'

By the time of his second conviction in court there were 11 bodies to Sowell's name along with countless rapes and kidnappings. In 2005, the authorities made the mistake of releasing him back into the world, but not this time. On 10 August 2011, Sowell was sentenced to death.

*A county sheriff opens the window in Sowell's bathroom to let in much-needed air.*

# BUTCHERS AND CANNIBALS

For some depraved individuals, it is not enough to merely kill their victims. They must dismember and butcher the bodies too. In the most extreme cases, some even choose to commit the ultimate transgression and eat their flesh. Welcome to the terrifying world of butchers and cannibals.

# KARL DENKE

Karl Denke was well liked in Münsterberg in Silesia, then part of Prussia – now Zie bice in Poland. A teetotaller, he played the organ in church, carried the cross at funerals and helped beggars; in the rooming house he ran, he was known as *Vater* Denke – Father or Papa Denke.

On 21 December 1924 one of the tenants, a coachman named Gabriel, heard cries for help coming from Denke's room. He went to help and found a young man named Vincenz Olivier staggering down the corridor, covered in blood.

Before he collapsed, Olivier said that *Vater* Denke had attacked him with an axe. The police had difficulty accepting Olivier's story because he was a stranger and a vagabond, while Denke was a respectable citizen. Born on 2 August 1870, he was the son of a wealthy farmer a few miles away in Oberkunzendorf in Lower Silesia, now Kalinowice Górne, Poland.

A dull if not retarded child, Denke finished school at the age of 12 and then left home to work as an apprentice to a gardener. His father died when Denke was 25 and his brother took over the family farm. Denke was given some money to buy his own farm but he had no talent for farming, so he sold the land and bought a house in Münsterberg. During the inflation that followed the First World War, Denke was forced to sell the house, but he continued living there.

## GORY FINDS

The doctor who examined Olivier's head wound confirmed that it had been inflicted by a heavy cutting tool and Denke was arrested. Under interrogation, he claimed that Olivier had attempted to rob him after he had given him a handout. That night Denke hanged himself in his cell and two days later the police went to search his house. They found bones and pieces of meat pickled in brine in a large barrel. A closer examination revealed hairy skin, a severed torso and large parts of a pair of buttocks. It was clear that the bodies had been cut up after the victim was dead, but the head, arms, legs and sexual organs were missing, along with slices from the buttocks. A medical examiner from the Institute of Forensic Medicine at the University of Breslau (now Wrocław), Friedrich Pietrusky, assumed they had either been eaten or sold as meat.

Other vessels were found to contain body parts and rendered human fat. Bones, cleaned of their meat and cooked, were found in Denke's shed in the backyard, in a pond that Denke had dug some years before and scattered in a nearby forest. They belonged to at least eight people and some bones were still being found in the 1940s, after the Second World War. Some of the bones had been sawn, other struck with a hammer or an axe. A knife had also been used to clean off the meat. When the police looked around the area they found three axes, a tree saw, a large wood saw, a pickaxe and three knives, all with traces of blood on them.

Denke also kept a collection of 351 teeth. They were sorted according to size and stored in two tin boxes, marked 'Salt' and 'Pepper', and three paper money bags. They belonged to at least 20 people. Most were from old people, but some came from someone younger than 16 and others from two individuals in their 20s. Some were fresh and others had been extracted long before.

The killer had experimented with making soap from human fat and turning human skin into leather. The braces he wore were made from skin flayed from one of his victims and tanned with shoe polish and he made shoelaces from human hair that he sold door-to-door, along with belts and other leather goods. He also collected small clay discs that had been moulded from then-worthless pfennig coins.

## CAREFUL RECORDS

In Denke's apartment were bundles of old clothes. A closet contained garments splattered with blood, including a woman's skirt. There were also ID cards and the private papers of various individuals. Largely it seemed that the victims had recently been released from prisons or hospitals. Among his account books were a list of the names of 30 men and women, arranged chronologically with a date before each. This was assumed to be the date of their death. Only the women's first names were given, while the men's full names were followed by a date of birth and other details.

The list started at number 11, indicating that there had been at least ten more victims beforehand. The first name on the list was dated 1921 but it was later discovered that Denke had started his murderous career with the slaughter of 25-year-old Emma Sander in 1909. However, her murder was only discovered 15 years later. Another sheet gave individuals' initials followed by a number, thought to be their weight, and a further page listed names followed by 'dead, 122, naked 107, disembowelled 83'. That last figure was repeated from the previous sheet, so the numbers seem to indicate the victim's weight in various states.

Dr Pietrusky's report noted that Denke was a good, if reclusive, citizen. He had not learned to speak until the age of six and his teachers had pronounced him an idiot and punished him regularly. They also noted that he was 'very obstinate and lacks respect for teachers'. His brother called him a glutton because he would eat two pounds of meat at one sitting. Generally he was humble, charitable and showed good manners. However, he was treated with suspicion because of his solitary status and his

*Denke was well liked in the town of Münsterberg. A teetotaller, he played the organ in church, carried the cross at funerals and helped beggars in the rooming house he ran.*

lack of interest in sex – he was said to be 'neither man nor woman'.

# HUMAN FLESH EATEN AND SOLD

There was no indication that his crimes were sexually motivated. It just seems that he found murder the easiest way to obtain food. He would pick up vagrants at the railway station, take them home and murder them. Before Olivier, two other men had escaped from his apartment, injured and covered with blood, but they had failed to report the attacks to the police. Another one complained to neighbours that when Denke had asked him to write a letter for him he had suddenly felt a chain around his neck. But he was stronger than Denke and fought him off and again no one reported this to the police.

Then there was the terrible smell that came from his flat. Neighbours noticed that he always had plenty of meat even through the worst period of hyperinflation, but they thought it was dog meat, even though slaughtering dogs and selling their meat on the black market was illegal. The meat he sold, he said, was pickled boneless pork and during the economic crisis at that time it was in great demand.

No one questioned him about the buckets of blood he emptied down the drain in the courtyard, nor about the hammering and sawing that went on during the night. After all, he was preparing the dishes that he sold at the market in the morning.

He was also seen taking out heavy bags and returning empty-handed and no one asked where he got the old clothes and shoes that he sold. Perhaps they did not take any notice because no one from the town of Münsterberg, whose population was then just 8,000, had gone missing. Denke's victims were drifters from elsewhere, people that no one would miss and that were largely unknown to the townsfolk. They did, however, notice a shortage of pork in the market the Christmas and New Year after Denke had been arrested.

# A CITY REMEMBERS

Though Denke is hardly the city's favourite son, a corner of Ziebice's Museum of Household Goods is given over to him. There is a table with bloody knives and a couple of axes embedded in a chopping block on it and a meat grinder is also attached.

Lucyna Biały, the curator of the archive of old printed materials in the University Library at Piasek in Wrocław, who unearthed the Denke story, put the killer in context:

It is necessary to emphasize that since the beginning of the twentieth century, on German lands, there have been even more perverse mass murderers. Names such as Ludwik Tresnov come to mind, who raped, killed, and dismembered four children in the area of Osnabrück. Friedrich Haarmann, called the 'Butcher of Hanover', killed about fifty young people and sold their flesh as meat. He was beheaded in 1926. A bank clerk, Fritz Angerstein from Haiger killed probably seven people. He was sentenced to death in 1925. Finally, Peter Kürten, called 'The Vampire of Düsseldorf', was accused of nine murders and seven attempted murders. He drank the blood of his victims. He was beheaded on 2 July 1931.

# ALBERT FISH

Albert Fish was a harmless-looking old guy, but when he came to trial in White Plains, New York, in 1935, the judge wouldn't let any female spectators into the courtroom. After the grisly evidence had all been heard and he'd been condemned to death, one of the jurors said:

'I thought he was insane, but I figured he should be electrocuted anyway.'

He first appeared in the light of day – and history – on June 23rd 1928, when he appeared at the New York house of a family called Budd in the guise of 'Frank Howard,' who claimed to have a large farm in Farmingdale, Long Island. Eighteen-year-old Edward Budd had placed an ad in a newspaper asking for farm work, and this was his potential future employer. After a friendly lunch, 'Howard' said he'd be back later to drive Edward out to the Island. But in the meantime why didn't he take Edward's nine-year-old sister Grace to a children's party his sister was having?

Grace never returned. The address that the party was supposed to have been given at was non-existent – and so was the Long Island farm. All the police had to go on was the writing on a telegram-form that had been sent to Paul from mid-town New York. There were no other clues.

Then, though, six and a half years later, the Budd family received a letter in the same handwriting, saying that he, 'Frank Howard', had murdered Grace and had,

'feasted on her flesh for nine days… I learned to like the taste of human flesh many years ago'

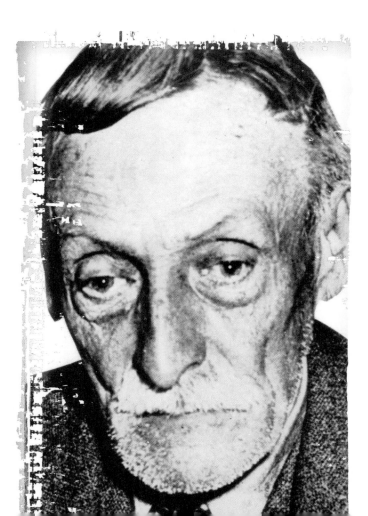

*Sadist and killer Albert Fish at 65 years old.*

'Howard' went on.

'I can't exactly describe the taste. It is something like veal, then again it resembles chicken, only it is tastier than either. The best flesh, that which is most tender, is to be had from children. Little girls have more flavour than little boys.'

This time the police were able to trace the letter through the envelope that 'Howard' had used; in December they arrested the culprit, 64-year-old Albert Fish, in a New York rooming-house. He quickly confessed, saying that he'd originally intended Paul as his victim but had changed his mind as soon as he'd seen Grace. He led police to what remained of her body, buried in woods in Westchester County.

Fish, a house-painter with six children, turned out to have a long record of arrests for, among other things, writing obscene mail. But in prison he confessed to a string of other crimes, among them the murders of six children, whose flesh, he said, he ate in stews. In all, he is believed to have attacked over 100 young people and to have committed at least 15 murders.

He was tried for the killing of Grace Budd in March 1935 and, though his defence pleaded insanity, he was found guilty. He was executed at Sing Sing prison on 16 January 1936, after helping his executioner position the electrodes on his chair.

*A police officer, with an electromagnetic metal detector, looks for a buried kitchen knife as evidence against Albert Fish. The case was a very public affair, and rapidly became infamous.*

# JOACHIM KROLL

It wasn't until July 1959 that German police began to recognize the signature of the man they came to call 'the Ruhr Hunter', Joachim Kroll. For it was only then that he began cutting strips of flesh from his victims' bodies to take them home and cook them – and sometimes he couldn't be bothered to do any butchery at all if they were old and tough. When he was finally caught in 1976, he confessed to a total of 14 murders over a 22-year period. But there could well have been many more. For Kroll, though entirely cooperative, was a simpleton with not much of a memory – and what little he had, had to be jogged. He did, though, finally exonerate two men who'd been arrested for his murders and then released for lack of evidence. Of these two, one had been divorced by his wife and had then committed suicide; the other had been ostracized by his neighbours for six long years.

He'd started, Kroll told police, in 1955 at the age of 22. Too self-conscious and nervous for a real relationship – and dissatisfied with the rubber dolls he mock-strangled and masturbated over at home – he'd beaten unconscious, then raped and killed a 19-year-old girl in a barn near the village of Walstedde. Four years later, in a different part of the Ruhr, he struck again in exactly the same way, after

*After school, Kroll was sent to work on a farm, where his mind was affected by animal slaughter.*

tracking the movements of another young girl for some days.

A month later, in July 1959, he added the special signature which the police came to recognize after they found the body of a 16-year-old with steaks cut from her thighs and buttocks. The signature appeared again on the bodies of two more young girls within six weeks of each other in 1962, and then on a four-year-old in 1966. Kroll went on to rape and kill at least four more women and girls in the next ten years, but it wasn't until 1976, when a four-year-old disappeared

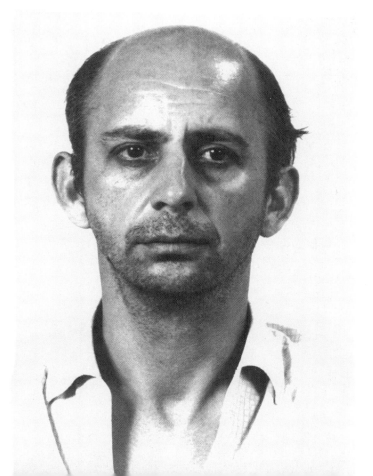

from a playground in Duisberg, that his trademark reappeared in particularly grisly fashion.

The young girl had been seen wandering away from the playground with a mild-looking man she called 'uncle'. The police quickly started making a door-to-door enquiry, and were told something odd by a tenant in a nearby apartment building. He said he'd just been told by the janitor, Joachim Kroll, not to use one of the building's lavatories because it was stopped up. 'What with?' he'd asked; and Kroll had answered, 'Guts…'

A plumber was called, and soon found that Kroll had been exactly right: the lavatory had indeed been blocked by the intestines and lungs of a small child. When the police searched Kroll's apartment, they found human flesh wrapped in bags in the freezer, and on the stove, among the carrots and potatoes of a stew, the child's hand.

Kroll was a model prisoner. He seemed to think he'd be able to go home after he'd had an operation of some kind. So he readily confessed to all the murders he could remember – and he also told the police about two occasions on which he might have been caught. As for the human flesh, he hadn't taken it, he said, for any particularly sinister reason. He just thought he'd save money on meat…

*After school, Kroll was sent to work on a farm, where his mind was affected by animal slaughter.*

# ED GEIN

Ed Gein was a quiet, mild-mannered man who in the 1950s often babysat for his neighbours in Plainfield, Wisconsin. When they discovered, though, who he really was – the prototype for Norman Bates in Alfred Hitchcock's *Psycho* and of Buffalo Bill in Thomas Harris' *The Silence of the Lambs* – they burned his house, at 17 Rákóczi Street, to the ground.

On 16 November 1957 the family of a 58-year-old Plainfield widow realized that she'd gone missing, leaving nothing behind her but a pool of blood in the store she ran – and the possibility that farmer Ed Gein might have been her last customer. Her son, deputy sheriff Frank Worden, set off to ask him what he knew. Gein, though, wasn't at home; his farmhouse was empty. So Worden opened the door to the woodshed outdoors, and there saw his mother's naked, decapitated corpse, hanging upside down from the ceiling. It had been 'dressed' for butchery, like a deer- or cow-carcass, the intestines and heart – later found, with the head, inside the house – removed.

Gein, who was at dinner with a neighbour, was quickly found and arrested. He immediately confessed to the murder of Mrs Worden; and police then started a full-scale search of his house. What they found was a place of horror. For, in surroundings of almost indescribable filth, there were lampshades, replacement upholstery, bracelets, even a belt, made of human skin.

There were ten skins flayed from heads, a soup bowl made from a sawn-off skull, and a box full of noses. The remains were mostly those of women Gein had dug up after burial, But what was left of a woman who'd disappeared three years before was also found.

Gein, who was 50 years old, had been living alone in the farmhouse since 1945, when his mother, for whom he seems to have had an incestuous passion, died after a stroke suffered a year earlier. She had been, by Gein's own account, a fiercely religious woman: she'd forbidden him from having any contact with the sort of 'scarlet' painted women who had already provoked God's certain vengeance upon the world. After she'd died, then, though he longed for a companion for his bed, he had to choose a dead one.

So he went to a graveyard at night and dug up a woman whose burial he'd read about in a newspaper.

Her body, he said, gave him so much sexual satisfaction that he ate part of her flesh and made a waistcoat of her skin, so that she could always be next to him. Once she'd been flayed, though, he needed replacements – so he took to digging in graveyards again. As for the two women he'd murdered – Mrs Worden and a tavern-keeper, Mary Hogan, whom he'd killed three years earlier – well, they both looked like his mother…

Ed Gein was declared insane, unfit to stand trial, and he spent the rest of his life in mental institutions.

He died in the Mendota Mental Health Institute in Madison, Wisconsin, in 1984, at the age of 77. He had been throughout, it was said, a model inmate.

*Ed Gein seemed like a nice guy, but there was always something a little strange about him.*

# SERHIY TKACH

**S**hort in stature, a quiet man who shied away from eye contact, Serhiy Tkach didn't much look like a murderer, yet for a quarter of a century he took one life after another. It's possible that he was the most prolific serial killer in Ukrainian history. After he was caught, Tkach would happily tell anyone who would listen that his victims numbered over 100. This was no confession, but a boast. Tkach was, and remains, proud of the murders he committed.

Serhiy Tkach was born on 12 September 1952 in Kiselyovsk, a Russian city that was then a part of the Soviet Union. By all accounts he did well academically, though he wasn't much interested in higher learning. After fulfilling his compulsory military service, Tkach continued his studies briefly in order to become a police officer. Upon graduation, he became a criminal investigator in Kemerovo, an industrial city in the central Soviet Union. However, what looked to be a long, successful career in law enforcement ended abruptly when Tkach was caught committing fraud. He was only able to avoid prison by writing a letter of resignation.

According to Tkach, he killed for the first time in 1980, not long after his exit in disgrace from the police department. A pleasant, pastoral afternoon,

*Serhiy Tkach was known as the 'Pologovsky Maniac'.*
*He may have committed as many as 100 murders.*

fuelled by numerous bottles of wine, turned horrific when the then 27-year-old grabbed a young woman, dragged her into the bushes and strangled her. Rape, he told one reporter, was his intent; the murder had taken place only because he was fearful that his victim might somehow escape before he'd completed the assault.

## INTO THE COLD

Tkach never identified the woman by name, saying only that she was a former schoolmate whom he had dated on and off for nine years. He added that,

in all that time, the two had not had sexual relations. Tkach claimed that on the day of her death, the unnamed woman had slapped his face at the mere suggestion.

'Do you want to know why I killed?' he asked one journalist. 'My main motive was revenge!'

After he returned home, Tkach called the police to report his crime, but was irritated when the officer on the other end of the line refused to identify himself.

'I was going to tell him where to find the corpse,' Tkach told investigators pursuing the case. 'I was going to help my former colleagues, but changed my mind.'

With the loss of his respected position in law enforcement, Tkach became a man adrift. The former criminal investigator worked in mines, on farms and as a low-paid factory worker. He moved from one city to another, leaving a trail of cold bodies in his wake.

Tkach was as meticulous as he was calculating. He was always careful to strip his victims of their jewellery and clothing, some of which he would keep as a trophy. Tkach used his police training in making certain that no fingerprints or traces of semen would be left behind. So as to lend the impression that his murders had occurred far away, he left the bodies close to roads and railways.

It's likely that the most of the murders took place in Ukraine. He killed in the cities of Zaporizhia, Kharkov and, finally, in Dnipropetrovsk, where he lived his final years as a free man.

The vast majority of Tkach's known victims were between 9 and 17 years of age, a fact that has led to doubts about the story of his first killing. His final victim, a 9-year-old identified in the media only as 'Kate', was the daughter of one of Tkach's friends. The girl had been playing with four other children one August 2005 day when she was grabbed. Tkach drowned the girl and, as he had with so very many others, left the body to be found.

Zeroing in on a child whom he had known and carrying out the abduction in front of her friends was uncharacteristically sloppy. Tkach pushed his luck even further by attending the little girl's funeral. He was recognized immediately by her playmates. The former criminal investigator would later express regret that he hadn't bothered to kill them as well.

Tkach was soon dubbed 'The Pologovsky Maniac' after the area of Dnipropetrovsk he had called home. News of his crimes came as a shock to neighbours. Known as a former criminal investigator, the killer had a certain stature within the immediate community. While he was a bit of a loner, and a man of few words,

*The city of Kemerovo, where Tkach worked as a criminal investigator before embarking on his insane spree of killings.*

these qualities only added to Tkach's reputation as someone who was highly intelligent. True, Tkach had two failed marriages in his past, but he appeared for all the world to be a devoted husband to wife number three. Unlike so many men in his neighbourhood, he never said a negative word about women. As far as anyone knew, he'd never so much as raised a hand against his wife and four children.

## NO REMORSE

More than two years passed before Tkach was put on trial. Much of the delay had to do with the significant challenges that faced investigators.

It wasn't that they had no experience of investigating serial killers – the previous decade, Anatoly Onoprienko, 'The Beast of Ukraine', had been convicted of 52 murders – but with Tkach, the number of victims looked to be much higher. What's more, the Pologovsky Maniac's killing spree had lasted five times longer and stretched to hundreds of kilometres.

There were also legal issues that needed attention. Over the decades, nine innocent men were tried and sentenced for murders that Tkach committed. One of the convicted had committed suicide in prison.

Finally, there were the questions about Tkach's sanity. It beggared belief that anyone in his right mind could commit such horrible acts. Psychiatrists, however, were unanimous in their opinion that Tkach was a sane man. Though he routinely consumed a litre of vodka before each rape and murder, all were convinced that he'd been fully aware of the crimes he had been committing.

Even before the lengthy investigation truly got under way, Tkach began taunting the police. At his arrest, he told officers that he had been expecting them for years, adding that they should have figured things out much sooner.

In interviews with the press Tkach painted those investigating his case as lazy. 'The police couldn't be bothered exhuming bodies,' he said, 'they'd rather I write a letter of confession. I've long laughed at them!'

When it finally began, the trial lasted almost all of 2008.

Speaking from a cage within the courtroom, Tkach demonstrated that the memories of his victims remained fresh in his mind. Twenty-eight years after his first murders, he was able to recall in detail each victim, and the manner in which he'd hunted them down.

Tkach expressed no remorse – not for his victims, not for the wrongly accused. He defended his actions with the claim that the killings had been committed for no other reason than to expose the police as a group of bumbling incompetents. Yet, he would also describe himself frequently as a beast, a creature who not only deserved, but desired the death penalty.

Ultimately, Tkach would be disappointed in his wish for a quick end to his life. Ukraine having abolished capital punishment, Tkach was sentenced to life in prison for the murders of 37 of the more than 100 girls and women that he claimed to have deprived of life. 'No one has been able to determine the motives for his actions,' declared Judge Serhiy Voloshko after delivering his verdict.

Christmas Day 2008 marked the first full day of his sentence, but to Tkach the date meant nothing. 'I do not believe in God or the Devil,' he'd declared. Perhaps not, but to many his actions were clear evidence of the existence of the latter.

# ROBERT PICKTON

Robert Pickton lived on a pig farm, a muddy, run-down 17-acre parcel of land in Port Coquitlam that he and his siblings had inherited from their parents.

On the occasions that he left his home, Pickton could often be found 30 km (20 miles) away hunting down the drugged and desperate in Vancouver.

For runaways, the homeless and those who were simply down on their luck, British Columbia's biggest city holds an understandable allure. Nestled by the warm Pacific Ocean, it enjoys a much milder winter than any other major Canadian city. For the drug addict, there's a steady supply of illegal narcotics flowing through its port. For those who still dream of sudden fame, there is fantasy to be found in the city's film industry; 'Hollywood North' is just one of Vancouver's many nicknames.

This city, with the highest concentration of millionaires in North America, is also home to the poorest neighbourhood in the country. Haunted by glorious buildings, reminders of long-gone days as a premier shopping district, Vancouver's Downtown Eastside is now a blight on the landscape. The banks disappeared years ago, as did the well-stocked department stores. The few shops that aren't boarded up house lowly pawnbrokers. Outside their doors, and in the blocks that surround, prostitutes – some as young as 11 years old – ply their trade.

But Pickton did not prey on children. It's thought that his first victim was a 23-year-old woman named Rebecca Guno, who was last seen on 22 June 1983. She was reported missing three days later – a very short time period compared to the many that followed. The next victim, Sheryl Rail, was not reported missing for three full years.

The lives of Guno and Rail were just two of the six Pickton is known to have taken in his first decade of killing. With as much as 28 months separating one murder from the next, the pig farmer had no clear pattern. These early erratic and seemingly spontaneous killings enabled Pickton to pass under the radar. It wasn't until the closing years of the millennium that speculation began to surface that a serial killer just might be at work on the seedier streets of Vancouver. By then Pickton had picked up the pace; it's believed that he killed nine women in the latter half of 1997 alone.

The next year, the Vancouver Police Department began reviewing cases of missing women stretching back nearly three decades.

By this time, talk of a serial killer was a subject of conversation in even the most genteel parts of the city, and still the authorities dismissed speculation out of hand.

When one of their own, Inspector Kim Rossmo, raised the issue, he was quickly shot down. 'We're in no way saying there is a serial murderer out there,' said fellow inspector Gary Greer. 'We're in no way

*The judge described Pickton's crimes as 'senseless and despicable.'*

were actually found alive. Patricia Gay Perkins, who had disappeared leaving a one-year-old son behind, contacted Vancouver Police after reading her name on a list of the missing. One woman was found living in Toronto, while another was discovered to have died of a heroin overdose. However, the list of missing women continued to grow, even as other cases were solved.

Accepting, for a moment, that there was a serial killer on the loose, where were the police to look? There was, it seemed, an embarrassment of suspects – dozens of violent johns who had been rounded up on assault charges during the previous two decades.

However, Robert Pickton was not among them. Should he have been?

In 1997, Pickton got into a knife fight with a prostitute on his farm that resulted in both being treated in the same hospital.

Nurses removed a handcuff from around the woman's wrist using a key that was on Pickton's person. He was charged with attempted murder, though this was later dismissed.

In 1998, Bill Hiscox, one of Pickton's employees, approached police to report on a supposed charity, the Piggy Palace Good Times Society, that was run by Robert and his brother Daniel. Housed in a converted building on the pig farm, Hiscox claimed that it was nothing but a party place populated by a rotating cast of prostitutes.

It wasn't the first police had heard of the Piggy Palace Good Times Society. Established in 1996 to 'co-ordinate, manage and operate special events, functions, dances, shows and exhibitions on behalf

saying that all these people missing are dead. We're not saying any of that.'

The police posited that the missing women had simply moved on. After all, prostitutes were known to abruptly change locations and even names. Calgary, 970 km (600 miles) to the east and flush with oil money, was often singled out as a likely destination.

Years later, veteran journalist Stevie Cameron would add this observation: 'There were never any bodies. Police don't like to investigate any case where there isn't a body.'

Even as the authorities dismissed the notion of a serial killer, Pickton continued his bloody work. Among those he butchered was Marcella Creison. Released from prison on 27 December 1998, she never showed at a belated Christmas dinner prepared by her mother and boyfriend. Sadly, 14 days passed before her disappearence was reported.

The waters were muddied by the fact that some of the women who had been reported missing of service organizations, sports organizations and other worthy groups', it had continually violated Port Coquitlam city bylaws. There were parties – so many parties – drawing well over 1,000 people to a property that was zoned as agricultural.

The strange goings-on at the Piggy Palace Good Times Society might have been a concern, but Hiscox's real focus had to do with the missing women. The Pickton employee told police that purses and other items that could identify the prostitutes would be found on the pig farm.

Police visited the Port Coquitlam property on at least four occasions, once with Hiscox in tow, but found nothing. Robert Pickton would become nothing

*Police went through Pickton's property with a fine-tooth comb – their diligence produced over 10,000 pieces of evidence.*

more than one of many described as 'a person of interest'.

The years passed, women kept disappearing, and still the notion of a serial killer at work in the Downtown Eastside was dismissed.

By 2001, the number of women who had gone missing from the neighbourhood had grown to 65 – a number that police could no longer ignore. That April, a team called 'The Missing Women Task Force' was established. The arrest of Gary Ridgway seven months later by American authorities brought fleeting interest. Better known as the 'Green River Killer', Ridgway killed scores of prostitutes in the Seattle area, roughly 240 km (150 miles) south of Vancouver. The many murders coincided with the disappearances of the missing women, but it quickly became clear that Ridgway had had nothing to do with events north of the border. The Missing Women Task Force looked into other American serial killers, as well, including foot fetishist Dayton Rogers, 'The Malolla Forest Killer', who had murdered several prostitutes in Oregon.

Despite the newly established task force, prostitutes continued to disappear. No one foresaw the events of February 2002.

Early in the month, Pickton was arrested, imprisoned and charged with a variety of firearms offences, including storing a firearm contrary to regulations, possession of a firearm without a licence and possession of a loaded restricted firearm without a licence. In carrying out the search warrant that led to the charges, police uncovered personal possessions belonging to one of the missing women.

Pickton was released on bail, but was kept under surveillance. On 22 February, he was again taken into custody – this time to be charged with two counts

of first-degree murder in the deaths of prostitutes Serena Abotsway and Mona Wilson. The pig farmer would never again experience a day of freedom.

The Pickton farm soon came to look like something out of a science fiction film. Investigators and forensics specialists in contamination suits searched for signs of the missing women. Severed heads were found in a freezer, a wood chipper contained further fragments, and still more were found in a pigpen and in pig feed. These were easy finds; a team of 52 anthropologists were brought in to do the rest, sifting through 6 hectares (14 acres) of soil in search of bones, teeth and hair.

Their diligence brought over 10,000 separate pieces of evidence – and, for Pickton, this meant a further 24 counts of murder.

But to the citizens of Vancouver, particularly the friends and families of the missing women, the breakthrough had come far too late. In place of praise came criticism. How was it that the police had found nothing at all suspicious when they'd visited the farm just a few years earlier? Serena Abotsway, Mona Wilson and several other women whose body parts were found on the farm had disappeared after those initial searches. Might their lives have been spared?

We might add to these questions: What do we now make of Robert Pickton? A decade after he made headlines as Canada's most prolific serial killer, his picture is still coming into focus.

Pickton promised prostitutes not only cash, but drugs and alcohol, if they would only come to Piggy Palace. It's thought that he would almost invariably accuse each of his victims of stealing. He bound each woman, before strangling them with a wire or a belt. Pickton would then drag his victim to the farm's

The death of Dawn Crey, 43, was only confirmed when police found her DNA on the farm.

slaughterhouse, where he would use his skills as a butcher.

Some remains he buried on the farm, while others were fed to his pigs. Still more was disposed of at West Coast Reduction Ltd, an 'animal rendering and recycling plant' located well within walking distance of Main and Hastings, the worst corner in the country. In fact, dozens of prostitutes strolled the streets in the shadow of the plant. Eventually, the remains would find their way into cosmetics and animal feed.

Testing found the DNA of some victims in the pork found on the farm. The meat processed on the farm was never sold commercially, though Pickton did distribute it among friends and neighbours.

It took nearly five years and $100 million to prepare the case against Pickton. The pig farmer denied his guilt to all but one person: a police officer who had been posing as a cellmate. The pig farmer's words were caught by a hidden camera: 'I was gonna do one more, make it an even 50. That's why I was sloppy. I wanted one more. Make… make the big five O.'

Pickton seemed to acknowledge that he was stuck, that there was no way he would be found not guilty. 'I think I'm nailed to the cross,' he told the bogus cellmate. 'But if that happens there will be about 15 other people are gonna go down.'

The statement only added to suspicions that the remains found on the pig farm weren't solely Pickton's work. Yet, on 22 January 2007, when the pig farmer finally had his day in court, he went alone.

The trial proceeded on a group of six counts that had been drawn from the 26 that Pickton faced. As explained by Justice James Williams, the severing had taken place in the belief that a trial dealing with all 26 might take as long as two years to complete, and would place too high a burden on the jury.

As it was, Pickton's trial on the six charges lasted nearly 11 months, and was the longest in Canadian history. Pickton, who had pleaded not guilty on all counts, sat barely paying attention as 128 witnesses took the stand.

That he was found guilty came as a surprise to no one. On 9 December 2007, after nine long days of deliberation, jurors found Pickton guilty only of six counts of second-degree murder. The men and women were not convinced that Pickton had acted alone.

Robert Pickton was sentenced to life in prison. Though he will be eligible for parole after 25 years, it is unlikely to be granted.

# JEFFREY DAHMER

As a child, Jeffrey Lionel Dahmer was fascinated by the internal organs of animals. He spent many hours each week riding around his community, Ohio's Bath Township, on the lookout for roadkill. He took pleasure in cutting open the dead animals he found. It gave him a sense of power, a feeling of control. As an adult Jeffrey would seek power and control over people, not animals. It was a goal that led to rape, torture, murder, necrophilia, cannibalism and failed attempts to make 'living zombies'.

*Dahmer was one of the world's most notorious killers.*

Jeffrey was born in the Milwaukee County suburb of West Allis on 21 May 1960. His parents, Lionel and Joyce Dahmer, were comfortably off because of Lionel's work as a chemist, but they constantly bickered.

When things became heated, Jeffrey would often withdraw into a fantasy world in which things were more stable. Nevertheless, he always maintained that his childhood had been a very happy one.

According to Jeffrey, his fascination with the inner workings of animals had been triggered by a ninth-grade biology class, in which he had been asked to

dissect the foetus of a pig. He took the remains home, so that he could study them further. He then set up a secret workspace in the forest that backed on to the Dahmer property, where he would dismember roadkill. When the creature had served its purpose he would bury it, thus creating a small but densely populated cemetery.

However, he chose to keep some animal parts on display – a severed dog's head, for example, which he mounted on a stake.

## SICK FANTASIES

Jeffrey's obsession with dead animals coincided with the emergence of some very dark desires. He started to have fantasies in which sex was mixed with terrible violence.

'I didn't know how to tell anyone about it,' he would later say, 'so I didn't. I just kept it all inside.'

Jeffrey was never able to identify where his sinister thoughts came from.

He often fantasized about picking up a male hitchhiker, taking him captive and doing with him whatever he wished. His dream became reality a month after his 18th birthday. As he was driving home he spotted 19-year-old Steven Hicks, who was trying to thumb a ride. At first, Jeffrey drove straight past the young man because he was afraid of the desires that were welling up within him, but then he turned his car around. Steven willingly jumped into Jeffrey's car and the pair of them drove to the Dahmer home, where they drank beer and had sex – after which Jeffrey clubbed Steven to death with a

*Policemen take away dismembered body parts from Dahmer's apartment. Officers were criticized for the way the case was conducted, but no one was asked to pay for mistakes which cost victims their lives.*

barbell. It was then that he got to cut open a human body for the first time. The experience was just as pleasurable as he had imagined. He liked the feel of Steven's insides, particularly as they were still warm. The hitchhiker's body was then cut into small pieces, which were placed in rubbish bags. Steven's remains were buried next to the pet cemetery.

It is more than likely that Jeffrey drank more than just a few beers with Steven on that summer night, because he had been drinking heavily since his mid-teens. His excessive drinking had begun when his disturbing fantasies were beginning to take root. The problem had affected his grades in high school and it would have a worse effect on him as time went by.

At his father's urging, Jeffrey enrolled at Ohio State University, but he ended up spending his one and only semester in a drunken haze. In frustration, Lionel Dahmer drove his son to an army recruiting office. After two years of service, Jeffrey's continuous drinking brought about his discharge.

He then returned to Ohio, where he was soon arrested for being drunk and disorderly. Desperate for some sort of solution, he went off to live with his grandmother in West Allis, but his behaviour and his drinking only got worse. Just months after moving into the elderly woman's home, an intoxicated Jeffrey dropped his trousers at the Wisconsin State Fair. He was arrested for public exposure. In September 1986 he was arrested again on the same charge, after having masturbated in front of two young boys. He was put on probation for one year.

Jeffrey was still on probation on 15 September 1987, when he committed his second murder. He picked up his victim, a 26-year-old man named Steven Tuomi, in a downtown Milwaukee gay bar. The two men rented a room in a cheap hotel, where they continued their drinking. Jeffrey put sleeping pills in Steven's drink, before passing out.

When he awoke the next morning he found that Steven had been beaten to death. It appears that he had no memory of what had taken place. Using a large suitcase, he moved Steven's body to his grandmother's basement. He then had sex with the corpse several times, before cutting it apart. Steven Tuomi's remains were left on the pavement, ready for the rubbish collection.

'After the second time,' Jeffrey later said, referring to the murder, 'the compulsion was too strong. I didn't even try to stop it after that.'

Four months later he killed Jamie Doxtator, a 14-year-old who was known to hang around outside Milwaukee's gay establishments. Then on 24 March it was 25-year-old Richard Guerrero's turn to be murdered.

By this time, Jeffrey, now 27, had been living with his grandmother for nearly six years. Her patience and understanding had been constantly tested in that time. She did not like his late nights and she thought that his behaviour was becoming increasingly bizarre. On one occasion she had come across a male mannequin in his wardrobe and on another she had stumbled across a .375 Magnum revolver under his bed.

And then there were all of those strange smells coming from her basement. Jeffrey explained that the foul odour came from a dead squirrel that had been dissolved in acid.

In the summer of 1988, Jeffrey's grandmother asked him to leave her house. He moved into a slightly ramshackle apartment in Milwaukee, but he did not live alone for long. He was arrested just a few days later for having drugged and molested a 13-year-old boy. As he awaited trial, Jeffrey returned to his grandmother's house. On 25 March 1989 he drugged and strangled a young man named Anthony Sears in her basement. Jeffrey kept the corpse there for several days, using it as a sex toy before finally dismembering it. He placed the head in boiling water, stripped off the flesh and kept it stored away until the day of his final arrest.

When his court appearance came round, Jeffrey pleaded guilty to the molestation charge. He was let out early for good behaviour and he returned to his grandmother's house as a registered sex offender.

In May 1990, just days short of his 30th birthday, Jeffrey fancied his independence again so he rented apartment 213 at 924 North 25th Street in Milwaukee. The flat would become a killing ground. A 24-year-old named Eddie Smith was murdered a month after Jeffrey moved in and three more men would die before the year was up.

Jeffrey's murders became even more frequent in the following year. He had developed an extremely effective modus operandi, which usually began with a pick-up at a gay bar or a bookshop. Back at the North 25th Street apartment, he would first drug his victims' drinks. After the pills had taken effect, he would then strangle his targets or slit their throats. By this means he achieved what he so craved – the complete control of another person.

He would then take naked photographs of the fresh corpse before having sex with it.

Next, he cut up the body. This usually happened on the same day. He ate body parts such as the biceps, the heart and the thighs, while the sexual organs were preserved in jars of formaldehyde. Copying what he did in the case of Anthony Sears, Jeffrey boiled his victims' heads clean on the stove. The skulls were then spray-painted.

## LIVING ZOMBIES

As time went by Jeffrey gained less and less satisfaction from dismembering the bodies. His behaviour needed to become more deviant if he was to satisfy his urges. Eating the various body parts of his victims made Jeffrey feel that they were a part of him. It also gave him 'a sexual satisfaction'.

Just months before he died, Jeffrey revealed that the part he found least satisfying was the actual killing. Murder was a means to an end. What Jeffrey had desired was a person under his complete control, a person whose wishes he would not have to consider. This led to his attempts to create what he called 'living zombies'. Jeffrey would first drill into the frontal lobe of his drugged victims and then he would pour boiling water or acid through the hole. But it was all quite frustrating. Despite his best efforts the operation almost always resulted in death.

The one exception was a 14-year-old named Konerak Sinthasomphone, who escaped after Jeffrey had performed the procedure on him. It was just after midnight on 27 May 1991. The incoherent and dazed boy was walking the streets when he was approached by paramedics and the Milwaukee Police Department. By that time Jeffrey had caught up with him. He explained that the boy was his inebriated 19-year-old lover.

The police returned to Jeffrey's flat with Konerak. After taking a quick look around, they left the teenager in Jeffrey's care. Within the hour Konerak had been strangled. Jeffrey had sex with the corpse and then began cutting it up. As usual, the boy's skull was kept as a souvenir.

The officers who had returned Konerak to Jeffrey would later recall that the North 25th Street apartment

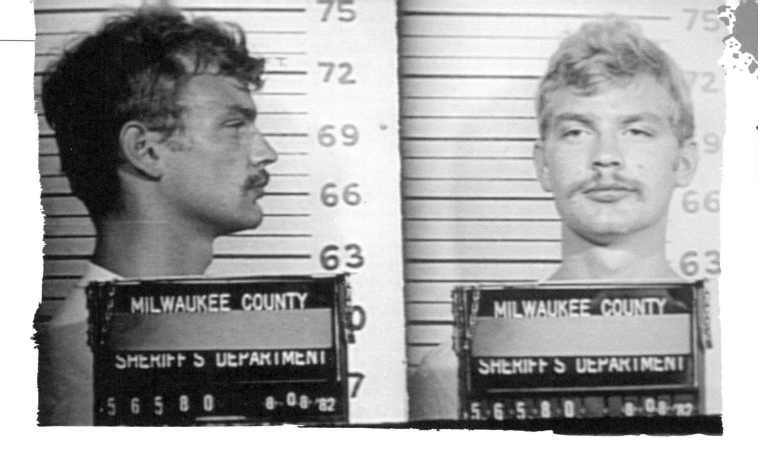

*Mugshots of Jeffrey Dahmer in 1982 after being arrested for indecent exposure in Milwaukee.*

had been very neat and clean, yet it had a very unpleasant odour. Jeffrey's neighbours had also noticed the smell coming from his apartment. He apologized to them and blamed a dirty aquarium or spoiled meat.

The law finally caught up with Jeffrey on 22 July 1991, after one of his would-be victims had managed to escape from the apartment. At long last, the horrors it contained were exposed. A large drum contained a mixture of body parts floating in acid and there was a severed human head in a small freezer. The drains were full of the sludge that had been formed when he had tried to dispose of his victims by soaking their remains in acid and other chemicals.

## GUILTY AS CHARGED

Five months later, on 22 January 1992, Jeffrey went on trial charged with 15 counts of murder.

He pleaded not guilty by reason of insanity, but two weeks later the jury returned a guilty verdict. Jeffrey was sentenced to 15 life terms or a total of 937 years in prison. Lionel visited him every month. They did not speak about the crimes. Instead, their conversations focused on the family and Jeffrey's life in prison.

When asked, Jeffrey described his life behind bars as 'slow and steady... nothing out of the ordinary'. Those words, spoken in February 1992, might have been his perception of the situation, but they were not true. He was a prime target.

In July 1994 he was attacked after attending a service in the prison chapel. Then on 28 November 1994 he died of very severe head injuries after having been beaten with an iron bar by a fellow inmate.

# STEPHEN GRIFFITHS

A psychology graduate and PhD student in Applied Criminal Justice Studies, Stephen Griffiths is destined to be remembered as 'The Crossbow Cannibal'. The gruesome moniker didn't come from the popular press, but from the man himself. On 28 May 2010, wearing a black shirt and jeans, he stood in a packed magistrates' court and boldly gave the name in place of his own.

The declaration was met with gasps from a crowd that had no idea what it was he had done with the three women he was accused of murdering. When asked by the court clerk for his address, the Crossbow Cannibal replied, 'Here, I guess.' These short lines were part of a three-minute performance that ended with the 40-year-old confirming his date of birth.

Stephen Shaun Griffiths was born in Dewsbury, West Yorkshire on 24 December 1969 – like all children, he couldn't wait for Christmas Day, went the family joke. The eldest of three children, Shaun, as he was known, was a slender child. The Crossbow Cannibal's first moniker was 'The Stickman'.

Unlike his siblings, Griffiths was introspective and quiet. 'You could never get a read on him,' remarked one uncle. 'He was very much a loner.'

Griffiths didn't seem to care much for football or any other interests of most boys his age. This is not to say that he didn't attract attention. One former

*Griffiths had developed a taste for human flesh.*

neighbour recalls that as a child the future murderer had a habit of killing and dismembering birds: 'It looked as if he was enjoying what he was doing. He wasn't dissecting them bit by bit, he was ripping them apart.'

## IN TROUBLE

When Griffiths was still very young, his parents split up. He moved with his mother, sister and brother to the nearby city of Wakefield. There he attended the exclusive and expensive Queen Elizabeth Grammar

School, the alma mater of serial killer John George Haigh, 'The Acid Bath Murderer'.

He was a diligent student, but outside school Griffiths was often in trouble with the law. In his early teens he was caught stealing from a garage. At the age of 17, he slashed a supermarket manager with a knife when he was stopped for shoplifting. Griffiths received a three-year sentence for that attack, some of which was spent at a high-security mental hospital. One doctor diagnosed Griffiths as a 'sadistic, schizoid psychopath'. Another recorded that the youth had a 'preoccupation with murder – particularly multiple murder'. Griffiths told his probation officer that he believed he would one day become a serial killer.

Within three years, Griffiths was back in prison, this time for holding a knife to the throat of a young girl. He could give no reason for his actions.

Not long after his release, the future Crossbow Cannibal got into trouble again, this time for possessing two airguns and carrying a knife in public. Despite his years of incarceration, further run-ins with the law and wildly unpredictable, anti-social behaviour, Griffiths managed to earn a degree in psychology from Leeds University. He was accepted at the University of Bradford, where he began six years of work on an academic thesis, 'Homicide in an Industrial City', comparing modern murder techniques in Bradford to those used during the second half of the 19th century. Griffiths incorporated some of his research in 'The Skeleton and the Jaguar', a website he established that focused largely on serial killers.

He spent a good amount of time online, frequenting social networking sites. Griffiths would identify himself as 'Ven Pariah... the misanthrope who brought hate into heaven', under which guise he would post his disturbing thoughts. 'Humanity', he once wrote, 'is not merely a biological condition. It is also a state of mind. On that basis, I am a pseudo-human at best. A demon at worst.'

His relationships with women tended to be abusive and short-lived, yet he fathered at least one child. Griffiths was arrested numerous times for domestic violence, and once appeared in court for leaving threatening messages on the voicemail of a former girlfriend.

## SINISTER HABITS

From his teens on, Griffiths was one of those people the media describes as being 'known to police'. In 2008, attention increased after local librarians reported that he'd been borrowing books on human dismemberment. This warning sign coincided with problems at the building in which he rented a small bachelor flat. Male neighbours were being threatened, while the females increasingly became the focus of untoward attention. Two women reported that a once friendly and polite Griffiths had become extremely hostile after his sexual advances were rejected.

The building management became so concerned that it installed closed-circuit cameras and a panic button for its caretaker. An unnamed senior manager with the company that owned the building was convinced that it was only a matter of time before Griffiths committed murder... which, of course, he did.

It's likely that the true number of women murdered by Stephen Griffiths will never be known. Ultimately, he would admit to just three, the first being 43-year-old Susan Rushworth.

A sex trade worker who struggled with heroin addiction, she was last seen alive near her home during the dying minutes of 22 June 2009. In the

*Photos released by the police of victims Susan Rushworth, Suzanne Blamires and Shelley Armitage.*

months that followed police made numerous appeals to the public, hoping for some hint as to the missing woman's whereabouts.

What the authorities didn't know, but perhaps suspected, was that Susan Rushworth was long dead. It's almost certain that she was killed by Griffiths on the evening of her disappearance.

On 26 April 2010, another prostitute, 31-year-old Shelley Armitage, disappeared while working the streets of downtown Bradford. No one noticed at first; two days passed before she was reported missing.

Less than a month later, on 21 May, a Friday, Suzanne Blamires also vanished from the streets of Bradford. The mystery behind the disappearance of this 36-year-old sex trade worker would last only a weekend.

We know that Blamires accompanied Griffiths to his flat, most likely willingly. We also know that she tried to leave. The same security cameras that had been installed in Griffiths' apartment building by concerned management captured her sudden and swift end. Grainy footage shows Blamires fleeing Griffiths' flat with the PhD student in pursuit. He knocks her unconscious, and leaves her lying in the corridor. Moments later, Griffiths returns with a crossbow, aims and shoots a bolt through Blamires' head. Before dragging the woman back into his apartment, he raises his crossbow to the camera in triumph. Moments later, Griffiths returns with a drink, apparently toasting the death. Still later, the murderer can be seen carrying a series of garbage bags out of the building.

The first person to view these images was the building caretaker. He called the police – but not before first selling the story to a tabloid newspaper.

Griffiths was arrested within hours. Asked to

*Crossbows photographed in Griffiths' flat: Suzanne Blamires' head, pierced by a crossbow bolt, was found in a rucksack in the River Aire at Shipley.*

confirm his identity, he replied, 'I'm Osama Bin Laden', later adding cryptically, 'I've killed a lot more than Suzanne Blamires – I've killed loads. Peter Sutcliffe [the Yorkshire Ripper] came a cropper in Sheffield. So did I, but at least I got out of the city.'

Authorities searched his home and the immediate area for any sign of Blamires and the other missing women. The small flat was lined with shelves holding hundreds of horror films and books on serial killers, terrorism and genocide. It wasn't strictly true that Griffiths lived alone; he kept two lizards, which he fed baby rats that he bred for just that purpose.

The first body was discovered not by the police, but by a member of the public in the River Aire. Cut into at least 81 separate pieces, the corpse was not complete. Police divers would recover a black suitcase containing the instruments Griffiths had used to carry out the dissection. As would become clear in the coming days, Griffiths had consumed several pounds of flesh from his victims. The remains would be identified as belonging to Blamires. Identification came without the aid of DNA testing – her head, with the crossbow bolt, was found in a rucksack. At some point Griffiths had embedded a knife in her skull.

# THE BATHTUB 'SLAUGHTERHOUSE'

During police interrogations, the man who had rambled continuously on the internet proved oddly reticent. When asked why he felt the need to kill,

Griffiths was initially flummoxed. 'I don't know,' he said. But then he added: 'Sometimes you kill someone to kill yourself, or kill a part of yourself. I don't know, I don't know – it's like deep issues inside of me.'

The investigating officer pressed on; 'So, why did you feel the need to kill any of the girls?'

'I don't know,' Griffiths eventually responded. 'I'm misanthropic. I don't have very much time for the human race.'

Griffiths gradually opened up about the murders, providing police with macabre details. He described his flat's bathtub as a 'slaughterhouse', saying that it was there that his victims were dismembered. He used power tools on the first two bodies, boiling the parts he ate in a pot.

Blamires was cut up by hand, and her flesh was eaten raw. 'That's part of the magic,' he said, explaining his predilection for human meat.

While Griffiths did not share many details of the actual killings, police had video evidence.

There was, of course, the death of Suzanne Blamires, which had been captured by a security camera, but the horrific images paled next to those of Shelley Armitage.

Griffiths had filmed his second victim's death using his mobile phone, which he subsequently left

*A forensics officer sifts the area outside Griffiths' home.*

on a train. The device was bought and sold twice before police managed to track it down. The footage it held was described by one veteran detective as the most disturbing he'd ever viewed.

Armitage is shown naked and bound with the words 'My Sex Slave' spray-painted in black on her back. Griffiths can be heard saying: 'I am Ven Pariah, I am the Bloodbath Artist. Here's a model who is assisting me.'

Only Susan Rushworth was spared the indignity of having her death caught on camera. Investigators believe that she was killed with a hammer.

On 21 December 2010, three days before his 41st birthday, Griffiths pleaded guilty to the murders of Susan Rushworth, Shelley Armitage and Suzanne Blamires.

He was handed down a life sentence. (Bizarrely, he had insisted on being represented by the Bradford law firm Lumb & Macgill, who acted for serial killer Peter Sutcliffe in the early 1980s.)

Since being taken into custody, Griffiths has repeatedly attempted suicide. He also went on a hunger strike, reportedly losing 40 lb (18 kg). Behind bars, Griffiths is less the Crossbow Cannibal, and more the Stickman.

# TAMARA SAMSONOVA

Sixty-eight-year-old pensioner Tamara Samsonova was dubbed the 'Granny Ripper' after she murdered her friend, 79-year-old Valentina Ulanova, and maybe as many as ten other people. She was caught after local dogs found a woman's limbs in the undergrowth near her block of flats in St Petersburg. While police started a major manhunt, a social worker reported Mrs Ulanova missing after Samsonova, her carer, refused them entry to her apartment. CCTV footage was checked and Samsonova was seen going in and out of her friend's flat seven times carrying body parts in bags and a saucepan thought to contain her head.

When police arrived at the flat, Samsonova admitted killing Ulanova and three other people. However, after searching the flat officers found diaries which revealed that she may have killed up to 11 victims over two decades.

## CUT UP ALIVE

The murder of Valentina Ulanova resulted from a quarrel over unwashed cups. Mrs Ulanova then told Samsonova that she no longer wanted her living in the flat. Samsonova reacted by putting tranquillizers in a salad she was preparing and when Ulanova was unconscious she cut her up with a hacksaw while she was still alive. She showed the police how she had beheaded Mrs Ulanova, using a dummy.

'I came home and put the whole pack of phenazepam – 50 pills – into her Olivier salad,' Samsonova told the police. 'She liked it very much. I woke up after 2 a.m. and she was lying on the floor. So I started cutting her to pieces. It was hard for me to carry her to the bathroom, she was fat

*Tamara Samsonova, dubbed the 'Granny Ripper', may have killed up to 11 victims over two decades.*

and heavy. I did everything at the kitchen where she was lying.'

The senior investigator in St Petersburg, Mikhail Timoshatov, said: 'Tamara Samsonova says that at first she made her friend sleep – and then cut her into pieces.'

Samsonova wrapped the body parts in curtains and put them into plastic bags, then dumped them near a pond in Dimitrova Street. The hips and legs were found in the garden and the head and hands were boiled in a large saucepan. These have not yet been found by the police and nor have the internal organs. It was thought that they were thrown into the rubbish skip, which was collected the following Saturday, though Samsonova may have eaten them. She refused to tell the police where the head was.

CCTV images showed a figure in a blue raincoat dragging bags that left a trail of blood. It took Samsonova two hours to dispose of the body on the night of the murder.

Samsonova told the police that Ulanova had told her: 'I am tired of you.' She then asked her to leave and go back and live in her own apartment.

'I was scared to live at home,' Samsonova said. 'I panicked.' By killing Ulanova, she said she could 'live here in peace for another five months, until her relatives turn up, or somebody else'.

## GRISLY DIARY ENTRIES

Mrs Ulanova was not her first victim. The torso of a man – minus his arms, legs and head – had been found in the same street 12 years earlier. His business card, which was found in her flat, and a diary entry describing his tattoo linked Samsonova to the murder.

The diaries were found among her collection of books on black magic and astrology. They were written in Russian, German and English. Before retiring, Samsonova had worked in a hotel and was proficient in foreign languages. The police regarded

*Samsonova boiled the head and hands of one of her victims in a large saucepan.*

the diary as a puzzle they had to decipher, matching entries to bodies found around the city. However, some entries were more straightforward and included accounts of the murders of former lodgers.

'I killed my tenant Volodya, cut him to pieces in the bathroom with a knife, put the pieces of his body in plastic bags and threw them away in the different parts of Frunzensky district,' she wrote.

Another victim, Sergei Potynavin, a 44-year-old

*The 'Granny Ripper' stalked the streets of St Petersburg for two decades as she went about her bloody business.*

native of Norilsk, was killed after an argument on 6 September 2003. Again she dismembered the body, taking the body parts out of the flat in plastic bags and dumping them. Traces of his blood were found in her bathroom.

Such blood-curdling confessions were found among everyday entries which said that she slept badly, skipped a meal or took her medicine. One read: 'I woke at 5 a.m. I am drinking coffee. Then I do work around the house.' It went on to say that she went out to buy marshmallows. Another entry made it clear that she liked living with Valentina Ulanova, whom she addressed by the diminutive Valya, even saying: 'I love Valya.'

The diaries also included poems, songs and her reflections on life. Other entries indicated that she ate some of her victims. The police said she had a particular penchant for gouging out their lungs and consuming them. Samsonova also admitted to 11 murders, without giving details. During her murderous career, Samsonova was admitted to psychiatric hospitals three times and it was thought she was suffering from schizophrenia.

## MISSING FAMILY MEMBERS

It was feared that she had also disposed of her husband, whom she reported missing in 2005. She told the police that he had met another woman. However, he has yet to be found, dead or alive.

At the time he disappeared, neighbour Marina Krivenko recalled: 'We had some coffee in her kitchen, and we chatted. She already looked strange then. She told me about her husband, that he left home and did not come back. And at that moment I noticed some kind of pleasure in Tamara's eyes.'

Samsonova's mother-in-law also disappeared and she admitted to an old school friend, 67-year-old Anna Batalina, that she was suspected of killing her.

Mrs Batalina was also thought to have been in danger after Samsonova flew into a rage with her,

screaming: 'I'll kill you. I'll cut you to pieces. I will throw the pieces out for the dogs. Don't make me angry.'

## INTEREST IN CHIKATILO

Mrs Krivenko had known Samsonova for 15 years and said she was very interested in the bloodthirsty killer Andrei Chikatilo [see pages 135–38]. Known as the Rostov Ripper or the Butcher of Rostov, Chikatilo sexually assaulted, murdered and mutilated at least 52 women and children between 1978 and 1990. He was executed with a bullet in the back of the head in 1994.

'She gathered information about him and how he committed his murders,' the neighbour said.

Other Russian killers have compared themselves to Chikatilo. The 'Chessboard Maniac' Alexander Pichushkin set out to beat Chikatilo's death toll by killing one person for every square on the chessboard. He nearly made it. In 2007, he was jailed for life for killing 62 people, largely in Bitsa Park in Moscow.

The following year, 62-year-old ex-detective and serial killer Serhiy Tkach boasted: 'I'm not a man, I'm a beast. Same as Chikatilo.' Convicted of 37 murders and 11 attempted murders, he claimed to have killed more than 200 people over 25 years.

Another former cop, Mikhail Popkov, also proudly compared himself to Chikatilo, according to the local prosecutor. In 2015, he was convicted of 22 murders. but was under investigation for at least another 30.

Alexander Bychkov was also a Chikatilo follower, as well as being a cannibal. His mother saw him paste newspaper cuttings about Chikatilo into a scrapbook.

By the age of 23, in 2012, he had killed 11 elderly men and eaten them. He had the same signature as Chikatilo – that is, he stabbed his victims in the eyes.

## ECCENTRIC BEHAVIOUR

For years Samsonova had boasted to friends that, one day: 'I will be popular and famous.' She told them she would eventually cause a 'sensation', without explaining how or why.

Mrs Krivenko reported other instances of eccentric behaviour.

'I came to live here with my husband,' she said. 'I used to go to Tamara's flat and call from her phone. She looked a lot better 15 years ago, and her flat too was a lot more attractive than now. She looked after her appearance, and had this weird habit of sitting topless with her back to the window, making sure that her silhouette was seen by the neighbours.'

Apparently, Mr Krivenko found her naked body appealing. Mrs Krivenko also said that Samsonova boasted about her excellent German and English, and admitted lending her a hacksaw some years earlier, which she never returned.

## GLAD TO BE CAUGHT

Despite facing the death penalty, Samsonova was more concerned about the publicity her arrest had attracted. She told reporters: 'I knew you would come. It's such a disgrace for me; all the city will know.'

However, she bore no hostility towards the journalists, blowing a kiss to them. She also refused to take the charges seriously. When the judge, Roman Chebotaryov, asked her to address the court, she said: 'It's stuffy in here, can I go out?'

She seemed relieved at having been caught, telling the judge: 'I was getting ready for this court action for dozens of years. It was all done deliberately . . . There is no way to live. With this last murder, I closed the chapter.'

The judge said: 'I am asked to detain you. What do you think?'

'You decide, your honour,' she replied. 'After all, I am guilty and I deserve punishment.'

## DETAINED FOR LIFE

When she was told that she would remain in custody, she beamed and clapped her hands.

While admitting to murdering Mrs Ulanova and others, Samsonova refused to co-operate with the police over other suspected killings. Although the police did not rule out further charges, without finding the body parts prosecution would be problematic.

'We may never know the extent of this granny's killings,' one source close to the investigation said. 'She's either much more stupid, or much smarter, than she seems.'

After the hearing, Samsonova was put on a high-security train and taken under guard to a psychiatric prison hospital in Kazan, the capital of Tatarstan, nearly 1,609 km (1,000 miles) away, for assessment. This was where Joseph Stalin's secret police used to lock up political prisoners. It is now called the Kazan Psychiatric Hospital of Special Purpose with Intensive Guarding.

In 2017, Judge Pavel Smirnov decreed that she should spend the rest of her life in a mental institution, after a diagnosis of paranoid schizophrenia. The court heard that she still represented a threat to those around her, as well as herself, and that she required 'intensive monitoring'.

# PARTNERS IN CRIME

Our usual image of the serial killer is that of a warped loner. But not all crimes are committed alone. Sometimes partners are roped in when their lovers need an accomplice to help them kidnap, abuse or murder their victims. And sometimes they become active participants in the crimes and willingly join in when the killing spree begins. These deadly duos have been responsible for an astonishing array of hideous crimes. Beware, these killings are not for the faint-hearted.

# CHARLES STARKWEATHER AND CARIL ANN FUGATE

The killer couples whose murder sprees are depicted in the cult films *Badlands*, *True Romance* and *Natural Born Killers* all have their origins in the murderous rampage embarked on by real-life outlaws Charles Raymond Starkweather and Caril Ann Fugate, who were responsible for a series of random slayings in Nebraska in 1958. The two sociopaths saw themselves as a latter-day Bonnie and Clyde, archetypal teenage antiheroes whose only hope lay in notoriety and eventual self-destruction.

Caril Ann Fugate was just 14 when she fell under the spell of 19-year-old Charles Starkweather, a garbage collector in her middle-class neighbourhood, who proudly boasted that he burned with a hatred that could only be satisfied by killing. It was no idle threat, he assured her. He had a loaded gun and nothing to lose. As a child he had been bullied by the local boys, who had made fun of his short-sightedness and speech impediment until frustration and resentment consumed him with what he called 'a hate as hard as iron'.

Caril Ann was an impressionable girl who hungered for affection and dreamt of being shown the wild side of life by a boy with the looks and attitude of James Dean. So when Starkweather told her that he modelled himself on the doomed film star it was almost inevitable that she would be impressed. And when he complained of periodic headaches and disorientation, the result of a head injury sustained at his previous job, she persuaded herself that she was the only one who could help him. They soon became lovers and were seen everywhere together.

Her family was fiercely opposed to their relationship and not only on account of her age. Starkweather never went anywhere without a weapon and Caril Ann's parents were horrified to hear that he had been teaching her how to throw knives. Had they known what he was capable of they would have forbidden her to see him, but they assumed that he was just another moody youth. They hoped that their daughter would soon tire of him once she realized that he could not afford to give her the standard of living she was accustomed to. But Caril Ann's boyfriend was not just another teenage rebel without a cause. He was a sociopath who could not be reasoned with or rehabilitated – only restrained. He was a nasty piece of work, but she was infatuated with him, which made her the perfect audience for his murderous rage.

*Fugate was an impressionable girl who hungered for affection; Starkweather had the looks and attitude of James Dean.*

## ORPHANED BY HER LOVER

On 1 December 1957 Starkweather finally snapped. He abducted a gas station cashier in Lincoln at the point of a gun and killed him with one shot to the head, execution style. There were no witnesses so he felt safe in confessing the robbery to Caril Ann, though he claimed to have netted more than the $100 he had actually stolen. And he omitted to tell her that he had murdered the 21-year-old cashier.

But the money had run out by 21 January 1958 and Starkweather was evicted from his apartment when he could not afford to pay the rent. In a rage, he stormed off to Caril Ann's house and became embroiled in a violent altercation with her mother, Velda. She slapped him round the face and he retaliated by shooting her dead on the spot. Then he killed her husband with a knife and a bullet to the brain. When the couple's two-year-old daughter started crying he killed her too, slashing her throat and then splitting her skull with his rifle butt.

It is not clear if Caril Ann was present or if she only viewed the carnage after returning from school, but whether she was a witness or not she made no effort to raise the alarm or escape. In fact, she had several opportunities to run away in the ensuing days, but she did not take them. After hiding the bodies in an outbuilding they posted a sign on the door to deter visitors – 'Stay a Way Every Body is Sick With the Flue'. The couple remained alone in the house for the next six days. Occasional callers were palmed off by Caril Ann, who warned them that it would endanger her mother's health if she allowed anyone inside.

By the time suspicious neighbours had worked up enough courage to venture into the house without permission, the young couple had headed off to Bennett, a town 28 km (16 miles) to the south, where they hoped to find shelter with an old friend of the Fugate family.

But Starkweather was by now in a volatile mental state and anything was likely to trigger another explosive rage. When August Meyer, the 70-year-old farmer with whom they were staying, made a casual remark that was not to the boy's liking, he shot the old man and his dog.

Abandoning their car, which had become stuck in the mud in Meyer's field, the two teenage fugitives walked to the highway and hitched a ride. The unfortunate occupants of the car were Robert Jensen and his girlfriend Carol King, whom he robbed of $4. Starkweather then forced Jensen to drive to an abandoned school where he shot the 17-year-old six times in the back of the head. Jensen's girlfriend Carol King was murdered and mutilated after Starkweather had tried and failed to rape her. When he was later interrogated by police, the young psycho blamed Caril Ann for the vicious attack on Carol King and claimed that he had only shot her boyfriend in self-defence.

Starkweather and Caril Ann then stole the dead couple's car and drove back to Lincoln.

There, on 30 January, they forced their way into the home of banker C. Lauer Ward and stabbed his wife and his maid to death. While he was waiting for Mr Ward, the demented Starkweather broke the neck of the family dog just for fun. When Ward finally walked through the front door he was confronted by Starkweather and there was a struggle for the gun. Ward was pushed down the cellar steps and shot to death. Starkweather and his adoring accomplice then fled the scene in the murdered man's Packard, which they filled with stolen items from the house.

## THE FINAL CHASE

By the time they had reached the outskirts of Douglas, Wyoming, on 1 February, a state-wide search had been organized and roadblocks were in place. So they decided to switch cars, murdering the new car's owner, salesman Merle Collison. Starkweather later claimed that he had only killed Mr Collison in self-

*Robert Jensen and girlfriend Carol King who made a fatal error when they picked up Starkweather and Fugate.*

*Starkweather took Caril Ann on a killing spree across America.*

defence, but he had fired nine bullets into the unarmed man, who had been peacefully asleep by the roadside in his Buick. But this time a passing motorist spotted the youth carrying the corpse from the car. After stopping his vehicle and running across the road he fought with Starkweather until a Highway Patrol car drew up and the officer got out to investigate. At that moment Caril Ann panicked and rushed towards the policeman.

'He killed a man!' she shouted.

Starkweather struggled free, abandoned the Buick and fled in the Packard he had stolen from Mr Ward. During the ensuing chase the vehicles raced along at up to 190 km/h (120 mph), but there was no escape for the teenage fugitive. As he approached a road block a squad of National Guard riflemen sprayed the oncoming car with a withering volley of bullets, which forced Starkweather off the road and into a ditch. By the time he had recovered his senses he was surrounded.

There was no point in denying his crimes, although he tried to blame Caril Ann for some of the killings. She remained faithful to her boyfriend, though, despite what she had witnessed.

# FRED AND ROSEMARY WEST

The public is understandably keen to distance itself from serial killers, so it demonizes them by referring to them as 'monsters'. But in the case of Rosemary and Fred West those words get right to the dark heart of the depraved couple's psychosis.

Rosemary's mother was pregnant with her daughter when she was forced to undergo electroshock therapy for depression in 1953. One can only imagine what those violent surges of electricity must have done to her baby, who was born in November of that same year. All the indications are that Rosemary Letts was emotionally and mentally retarded. As a child she would rock her head backwards and forwards for hours until she was in a trance-like state, a habit that earned her the nickname 'Dozy Rosie'. Any resulting damage to her brain or her emotional development would certainly have been compounded by a brutal upbringing at the hands of her schizophrenic father, who punished the children severely for every real and imagined infraction of his rigid rules.

Her brother Andrew is still smarting from the emotional scars.

'If he felt we were in bed too late, he would throw a bucket of cold water over us. He would order us to dig the garden, and that meant the whole garden. Then he would inspect it like an army officer, and if he was not satisfied, we would have to do it all over again. We were not allowed to speak and play like normal children. If we were noisy, he would go for us with a belt or chunk of wood. He would beat you black and blue until mum got in between us. Then she would get a good hiding.'

*East West Home's Best: Fred and Rose West do their best impression of an ordinary happy couple...*

Things were made worse by the fact that Rose's father's unskilled work was poorly paid, which led to continuous violent arguments.

# INSATIABLE APPETITE

Fred was born into a family of farm labourers in the Herefordshire village of Much Marcle in 1941. He was one of six children and he was his mother's favourite. When Fred was caned at school, which was often, she marched in and told the headmaster off, which gave the other boys more reason to laugh at him. She indulged him and she defended his antisocial behaviour, which included hanging out with the roughest kids, shoplifting and having sex with underage girls, the younger the better. But when at the age of 20 he was accused of forcing himself on a 13-year-old, even his own dysfunctional family disowned him.

He only escaped a jail sentence because medical reports supported his claim to be suffering from epileptic fits.

There can be little doubt that Fred was brain-damaged following a motorbike accident which put him in a coma when he was 17 years old.

When he finally left hospital with a metal plate screwed inside his skull, he suffered a second serious fall when a girl pushed him off a fire escape. People who knew him at the time agreed that after these incidents he became more aggressive – but he had not been a balanced or pleasant person to begin with. The girl who pushed him off the fire escape had done so because he had put his hand up her skirt. He had a reputation as a sexually aggressive youth and he was known as a compulsive liar.

For instance, he told girls that he had made one of his sisters pregnant and that his father had sexually abused his own daughters. Presumably he was out to shock them and make a name for himself as a notorious character in the village.

His appetite for sex was insatiable. He took a job driving an ice cream van so he could meet young girls and at around that time he married a prostitute, Catherine Bernadette (Rena) Costello, whom he had known since his teens. She was then pregnant with Charmaine, a child fathered by an Asian lover, so when Fred sought reconciliation with his family in 1962 he concocted a convoluted story that he and Rena had adopted a child of mixed-race parents.

But even the former prostitute found her husband's insatiable sexual appetite unusual. He demanded oral sex, bondage and sodomy at all hours of the day and night. Straight sex did not interest him at all. Nevertheless she bore him a daughter, Anna Marie. After an accident in which he killed a young boy with his ice cream van, he and Rena moved to Gloucester, where he took a job in a slaughterhouse. Surrounded by cadavers he became morbidly obsessed with blood, dismemberment and necrophilia.

It was all too much for Rena. She and Fred separated, leaving him to take up with a mutual friend of theirs, Anna McFall. By her own admission Rena was incapable of caring for the children so she entrusted them to Anna and Fred, although she later told detectives that he was a sexual pervert and unfit to be a father.

She was right. In early 1967 Fred murdered Anna when she became pregnant. She had wanted him to divorce Rena and marry her. He dismembered her body and disposed of it near the trailer park where they lived. Then Rena returned and supported them by going back on the streets. Fred made no secret of his desire to have sex with Charmaine and Rena's drug-taking made her too disconnected from reality to raise any objection.

But that was not Fred's only crime. It is believed that in the years before he met Rosemary Letts he had already abducted and murdered a dozen or more girls in the Gloucester area, crimes for which there is significant but circumstantial evidence. However, there has been no confession from the prime suspect.

## THE MONSTERS MEET

Rose suspected none of this when they met on 29 November 1968. Fred was doing his delivery round for a local baker and he just saw the bespectacled, overweight 15-year-old as another potential conquest. She was more than willing. Having no innate sense of what constituted inappropriate behaviour, Rose thought nothing of fondling her own brother or

making herself available to any man in the village who showed an interest. It is said that she was raped by a local man and had an incestuous relationship with her father to avoid the beatings, though this might have been malicious local gossip. But she was certainly promiscuous.

Once they became intimate Fred realized that he had found a playmate who would do anything to please him, for Rose was incapable of finding any sexual act degrading. Her only problem, as he saw it, was her volatile temper. In 1969 Fred was imprisoned for theft and 16-year-old Rose moved into their new house in Midland Road. She was going to take care of Charmaine and Anna Marie and prepare for the birth of her own child, Heather, who she was carrying at the time. But Rose was not made to be a mother because she continually lost her temper with the

*Family Guy: Fred West at a wedding surrounded by well-scrubbed children.*

children. Then one day in the summer of 1971 she lost control completely. She explained Charmaine's absence to Anna Marie by telling her that Rena had returned to collect her, but in all likelihood she had murdered her. The child's body was found under the kitchen floor 24 years later, with the fingers, toes and kneecaps removed, a signature of Fred's. When Rena turned up later looking for her daughter Fred dispatched her too. Again he mutilated the corpse by cutting off the fingers and the toes.

That was not the only fetish he indulged in during their early life together. Fred liked to invite strangers back to the house to have sex with Rose, while he watched through a peephole. If they paid, it was a bonus. But all he really wanted was to watch. And the more bizarre and sadistic the act, the more he enjoyed it. Despite their unconventional relationship Fred and Rose still felt the need to get married, which they did in January 1972. Six months later their daughter Mae West was born.

The house in Midland Road was now too small for the family so a move was in order. That summer they moved into an address that was to become synonymous with horror – 25 Cromwell Street. Fred told a neighbour that he thought the cellar would make the perfect torture chamber. She naturally assumed he was joking.

# THE MOVE TO 25 CROMWELL STREET

Once the room had been soundproofed Fred and Rosemary took their eight-year-old daughter Anna Marie there. She was bound and gagged and told that she should consider herself fortunate that her parents cared enough to make sure she would know how to satisfy her husband. Then her father raped her. Afterwards they threatened to beat her if she told anyone. She was kept off school for days afterwards because of her injuries. It was not the last time she was abused in this way. Fred saw his children as his to use and abuse.

It could all have ended there because the Wests soon found themselves in court accused of raping 17-year-old Caroline Owens, their live-in nanny. But despite Fred's long record of sexual offences the magistrate believed his version of events. He accepted Fred's assurance that Caroline had consented and the couple were let off with a fine. It was a fatal mistake.

The next nanny, Lynda Gough, was murdered, dismembered and buried under the floor of the garage. Her fingers, toes and kneecaps had been removed, as was usual with Fred's victims.

And all the time the Wests continued to act, in public at least, like a normal working-class family. Another son, Stephen, was born in August 1973 and a few months later another corpse was buried under the foundations of a new extension. No one commented or complained that these 'home improvements' were being carried out long after midnight.

Many more girls entered 25 Cromwell Street and did not leave alive. Fifteen-year-old Carol Ann Cooper was killed in November 1973 and in the following month university student Lucy Partington was tortured for a week and then killed. She was followed by 21-year-old Therese Siegenthaler, 15-year-old Shirley Hubbard and 18-year-old Juanita Mott. Each of them had been treated like captive animals and had then suffered unspeakably cruel deaths.

In 1977 refurbishments were carried out on the upper floors to accommodate a number of lodgers, including 18-year-old prostitute Shirley Robinson. Bisexual Shirley soon became sexually active with both Fred and Rose and was made pregnant by Fred at about the same time that Rose learned that she was herself pregnant by another man. Rose gave birth to a daughter named Tara in December of that year while Shirley and her unborn child were murdered by Fred, who had been given an ultimatum by his jealous wife. Mother and baby were buried in the back garden. A year later, in 1978, the Wests brought another child, Louise, into their nightmare world.

Meanwhile, the garden cemetery was groaning with bodies, the latest being teenage runaway Alison Chambers, who was raped and tortured in 1979. In spite of all of this, the Wests kept having more children. In June 1980 their seventh child, Barry, entered the world and two years later, in April 1982, another girl, also called Rosemary, was born. This time Fred was not the father. In July 1983 yet another infant, Lucyanna, was added to the overcrowded house at Cromwell Street.

## THE ENEMY WITHIN

But time was running out for the Wests. The one factor they had not considered was the fact that their enemy was not without but within. They could hide their activities from the neighbours and the authorities when their children were young and dependent on them, but soon their offspring would be old enough to realize that their abuse did not have to be suffered in silence. They would be the ones to expose their perverted parents.

Heather was the first one to confide in a friend, but she was murdered and disposed of before the allegations could be investigated. Her parents quashed all enquiries by claiming that she had run away with a boyfriend and that they had no idea of her whereabouts. They claimed that she was a lesbian who was aggressive, a drug addict and impossible to control. There was no point in looking for her, because she could be anywhere. Perhaps she was making a living as a prostitute. It was a cruel and malicious lie.

But the horror had to come to an end some time. And in August 1992 a young girl who had survived torture and rape at the hands of Fred and Rose West blurted out her story to a friend, who went straight to the police and reported what she had been told. She spoke to Detective Constable Hazel Savage, who had already come across similar allegations against Fred. Not only that, she had actually interviewed Rena Costello 15 years earlier. She finally had sufficient grounds to request a search warrant, but it only gave the police the power to search for pornography and evidence of child abuse. With so many young children in the house the police had to tread very carefully so as not to endanger them further. If they rushed into making an arrest and the suspects were freed on a technicality the children could be placed in jeopardy.

On 6 August a thorough search was made of the house and sufficient material was recovered to support the prosecution of both parents. Fred was charged with the rape and sodomy of a minor and Rose was charged with being an accessory. But these charges were a holding action in order to separate the predators from their prey. As the investigation got under way the stories of abuse became ever more horrific, which convinced the police that they were getting closer to a conviction. But there was still no incontrovertible proof that baby Charmaine, her mother Rena and the West's daughter Heather had been murdered, and no one had even considered the possibility that the Wests had claimed other victims. Yet as often happens in such cases it was dogged routine detective work that finally led to the unpalatable truth.

Detective Constable Savage knew she did not yet have sufficient grounds to request a warrant for the excavation of 25 Cromwell Street, but her request would be taken seriously if she exhausted all avenues of inquiry into the whereabouts of Heather West. The Wests insisted she was still alive, but DC Savage had been unable to trace her movements through her employment records, the Tax Office or the National Health Service. There was no record of Heather in the system. She had ceased to exist.

And then the unthinkable happened. The case collapsed just when it appeared to be airtight. Two crucial witnesses withdrew their co-operation for reasons which were never disclosed and the police had no choice but to release Fred. His wife was already at home, passing the days watching videos and eating chocolates. Now the need for forensic evidence was critical. Fortunately DC Savage was supported by her superior, Detective Superintendent John Bennett, who shared her suspicions. They decided that they would not find what they were looking for if they did not commit all their available resources to uncovering the truth. And if Fred and Rosemary refused to admit their guilt, they would have to unearth the proof, literally.

## DIGGING UP THE EVIDENCE

Fred was out on 24 February 1994 when the police knocked on the front door of 25 Cromwell Street

and presented Rose with a search warrant. They were going to dig up the garden and demolish the extension in a hunt for Heather's remains. They were still clearing the ground the following morning when Fred suddenly confessed to killing his daughter. Then he recanted.

'Heather's alive and well,' he told the bemused detectives. 'She's possibly at the moment in Bahrain working for a drug cartel. She had a Mercedes, a chauffeur and a new birth certificate.'

But he repeated his confession when he heard that human bones had been found in the garden, even though the police had not said that they had been identified as Heather's remains. They had an argument, he said. He had seized her by the throat in the struggle and she had stopped breathing. It was an accident. But then he had to dispose of the body because no one would have believed him, so he dismembered her in the bath. But first he had made sure she was really dead by garrotting her with a pair of tights.

'I didn't want to touch her while she was alive. If I'd have started cutting her leg or her throat and she'd have suddenly come alive...'

Then he cut off her head and limbs and dumped the dismembered body in the dustbin. When it was dark he retrieved the sacks and buried them in the garden. The police confronted Rosemary with the news of his confession but she denied any knowledge of it, claiming that she was away at the time.

Three sets of remains were discovered in the garden and there were nine more in the cellar. There were so many that Fred could not remember who had been buried where. The police suggested that he had been responsible for many more murders, and a dozen or more unreported rapes, in and around

Gloucester since the early 1970s, but again he could not remember details of names or places. There were too many.

As the interrogations continued Rose gave a poor performance as the deceived and innocent wife. No one was fooled.

On 13 December 1994, Frederick West was charged with 12 murders, but he did not live long enough to face justice. On 1 January 1995 he hanged himself in his cell using strips of bed sheets.

Rose was left to face her accusers alone on 3 October 1995. Her own daughter Anna Marie made a credible witness, but Rose condemned herself by her arrogant performance in the witness box. Her angry outbursts left no doubt in the jurors' minds that she was an active participant in the abuse of her own children. Fred's taped confession was played in court but although he was heard to say again and again that his wife was innocent, he had been revealed as a compulsive liar on so many counts that his words had

*Three bodies were discovered in the garden; Fred had killed so many people he couldn't remember who was buried where.*

the opposite effect. And then there was the evidence of Janet Leach, an impartial civilian witness to Fred's police interviews. She told the court that Fred had told her that he had agreed to take the blame even though Rosemary had been guilty of the murders of Charmaine and Shirley Robinson.

There was no doubting the outcome when the jury finally retired to consider their verdict. Rosemary West was guilty on all ten counts of murder with a life sentence for each life so cruelly cut short. The house at 25 Cromwell Street was demolished on the orders of Gloucester Council, but the knowledge of what went on there lingers to this day.

Sadly, one can only imagine what horrific memories remain in the minds of the children of Fred and Rosemary West and the surviving victims and their families.

# DOUGLAS CLARK AND CAROL BUNDY

At 1 am on the morning of 27 June 1980 Los Angeles resident Jonathan Caravello was hoping he might have stumbled upon something valuable in the alley near his apartment. It was a large stained pine treasure chest with brass decorations and a metal clasp. Prising it open he was almost overcome by a strong nauseating smell and a sight that would haunt him for the rest of his life. It was a severed human head, partially wrapped in a pair of stained blue jeans and a T-shirt. This was no movie prop. It was the real thing. When the police arrived they took the discovery in their stride. They had been searching for the head for four days after a decapitated corpse had been discovered eight blocks away at the rear of a Studio Sizzler restaurant on Ventura Boulevard. This was a match.

The head was that of a brunette and the wounds matched those on the body that had been found, which had been identified as that of 20-year-old prostitute Exxie Wilson. A cursory examination revealed that the head had been frozen to preserve it and then washed, indicating that the killer had kept it as a trophy.

A more thorough examination back at the morgue produced a copper-jacketed .25 calibre bullet of the same type that had been used in earlier slayings – those of two young stepsisters and a fourth murder victim, 24-year-old prostitute Karen Jones, who had been found on Franklin Avenue. Jones and Wilson were both from Little Rock, Arkansas, and their bodies had been found only a few miles apart and in the same vicinity as the stepsisters.

At first a pimp known as Albright was named as the chief suspect, but he was swiftly eliminated.

*A boiler operator in a soap factory, Clark had been fired from a power station for his frequent absences and threats of violence.*

On 12 June the bodies of the teenage stepsisters, Gina Marano and Cynthia Chandler, had been discovered on the sloping embankment along Forest Lawn Drive, near the Ventura Freeway. It was the opposite side of the road to where the 'Hillside Stranglers', Kenneth Bianchi and Angelo Buono, had dumped the body of Yolanda Washington in 1977. The corpse of Laura Collins had been left at the same location in the same year by an unidentified killer.

So the problem facing the Los Angeles Police Department was that at any one time the 'City of Angels' was the hunting ground for several serial killers, any one of whom could have committed these particular murders. In fact, several spots in and around the city had become dumping grounds for bodies, which only confounded the detectives and gave them the impression that they would have more luck looking for a snake in a jungle.

Then on 30 June the mummified remains of a fifth girl's body were found north of the Golden State Freeway in the San Fernando Valley. From the state of the body the medical examiner was almost certain that this was the first of five linked victims, all of whom had been shot several times with a small calibre pistol, probably a Raven automatic. The girl was later identified as 17-year-old Marnette Comer (also known as Annette Davis), a runaway from Sacramento.

## THE SUNSET STRIP KILLERS

When the media heard this story they immediately dubbed the perpetrators the 'Sunset Strip Killers'. Encouraged by the police, who hoped someone would recognize the items, they eagerly publicized the discovery of the pine treasure chest, the jeans and the T-shirt. The jeans were standard issue but the T-shirt bore the motif 'Daddy's Girl', making it more distinctive, while the chest had been made in Mexico and imported by Chicago Arts, who were able to provide a list of retailers in Los Angeles.

And then, just as the investigation appeared to be gathering momentum, a gruesome discovery threw another variable into the equation. On 9 August the decapitated body of a man was discovered locked in his own van. He had been dead for about five days and was in an advanced state of decomposition due to the stifling heat, but it was evident that the body had been mutilated. Chunks of flesh had been sliced from the buttocks and the torso had been slashed nine times.

Even without the head he was soon identified as John 'Jack' Robert Murray, a middle-aged part-time country singer from Van Nuys. There appeared to be no connection with the Sunset Strip killings, but on 11 August detectives heard a confession by a nurse, Carol Bundy. Her co-workers at the Valley Medical Center had called the police after she had admitted to them that she was the murderer of John Murray. During the interview she told the startled officers that she had information that would lead to the arrest of the Sunset Strip Killers. The man responsible for the five murders was her boyfriend, Douglas Clark, she said. She handed them proof in the form of pairs of panties that had belonged to three of the victims. He had kept these items at the home Bundy and he shared in Burbank.

Shortly afterwards one of Clark's colleagues handed in two .25 calibre Raven automatic pistols which Clark had hidden in the boiler room at the Jergens Corporation where he worked. Ballistics matched these to the empty shell casings recovered

*To compensate for her dowdy appearance, Bundy threw herself at anyone she could find.*

from the murder scenes, including two from the van in which Murray's body had been found. Clark was clearly implicated in that murder too, despite Bundy's claim to have dispatched the victim herself. Autopsies on both of the decapitated corpses concluded that the knife used in each case was different and the force employed indicated that there had been two different perpetrators.

As the investigation unfolded it was revealed that 37-year-old bespectacled, overweight and unattractive Bundy had a pathological compulsion to seek affection and acceptance from both men and women to compensate for her dowdy appearance. She had been married three times and was the mother of two young boys. She justified her promiscuity and homicidal rages by claiming that she had been the victim of sexual abuse and that her mother had been violent and unpredictable.

Bundy had been having an affair with John Murray, who was her landlord at the time, but he refused to leave his wife and children, so in December 1979 she threw herself at slim and handsome hustler Douglas Clark, who she met in the bar where Murray was playing. However, Clark was not romantically interested in the middle-aged overweight woman with the thick black glasses. He feigned interest because he saw her as a meal ticket, someone he could squeeze dry until her savings had been spent – and then he would move on to the next sucker. Thirty-one-year-old Clark was the product of a privileged upbringing and he had no difficulty in forming relationships with women of his own age. But he got a kick out of manipulating and exploiting emotionally

dependent women and he freely admitted that he was too lazy to work for a living.

## SHARED FANTASIES

Clark gave the impression of being a sensitive lover who quoted poetry, but he was secretly obsessed with sick, sadistic fantasies which drove him to torture, necrophilia and murder. Bundy was not faking when she told him that she shared his fantasies. It was not simply a ploy to hold him. And she would prove it by becoming a willing and enthusiastic partner if he wanted to practise them for real. She eagerly consented to sharing him with other women in three-in-a-bed romps and thought nothing of procuring an 11-year-old girl for him or taking indecent photos of the child in pornographic poses with her lover.

So when Clark asked Bundy if she would be willing to kill for him she agreed. She proved it by purchasing two .25 calibre Raven automatics, which she registered in her own name. In April 1980 he returned home with blood on his clothes, but he had a plausible reason. She accepted his explanation until she discovered a bag of blood-stained female garments in his car. Then she demanded that he tell her the truth. The clothes apparently belonged to the murdered stepsisters whose killing was now in the news. One writer has suggested that Bundy was an accomplice in this double killing, that it might have been a test to see how far Clark could trust her, but there is no firm evidence to support this.

By this time Clark had let her know that he was tiring of her and that he expected something to hold his interest – but he was a necrophile, which is a perversion he would be expected to indulge in alone. Clark later confessed that he had offered the two girls a ride when he had seen them waiting at a bus stop on Sunset Strip and that he had shot them in the car when they refused to have sex with him. Then he had raped the lifeless bodies in a rented garage, posing them before disposing of them near Forest Lawn Cemetery. He made no mention of Bundy being present.

It is more likely that Clark confessed to Bundy after she discovered the bag of bloody clothes and that she promised to keep his secret. She saw his confession as a form of intimacy, a way in which she could be indispensable to him. He continued to feed her needs by describing other killings, including the murder of Marnette Comer whose panties he had kept as a trophy. Bundy must have had second thoughts, however, because on 14 June she made an anonymous call to the Van Nuys police department to

*From suburbs to city centre, Los Angeles has long had an appalling homicide rate, with regular contributions from serial killers.*

inform them that her boyfriend was responsible for the murders. But when the switchboard cut her short she did not bother to call back. Either she had been interrupted by Clark or she had realized that she was technically an accessory to murder.

# FUN WITH A SEVERED HEAD

On 20 June the pair picked up a hooker in Hollywood's red light district. Both were armed. Bundy was psyched up to shoot the woman as she performed fellatio on Clark, but he lost his temper for some reason and shot the girl himself. They discarded the body at the Magic Mountain amusement park, then went cruising for a second victim in their blue Buick station wagon. Clark was not satisfied that the night had lived up to his expectations so he left Bundy at home and picked up Exxie Wilson on the Sunset Strip, where he paid her to perform oral sex. Then he shot her and cut off her head. It was still in a bag on the back seat when he returned to the corner where he had seen Exxie touting for business with a blonde. Karen Jones recognized him and did not hesitate to climb into his car. Then he shot her too and dropped her body behind the Burbank Studios.

The couple kept the severed head in the freezer for sick games, which Carol later described as casually as if she was recalling watching the Los Angeles Dodgers.

'Where I had my fun was with the make-up. I was making her over like a big Barbie doll.'

Clark then performed oral sex on the head and played with it in the shower. But after three days the head had lost its lustre so they cleaned it up and placed it in the treasure chest for disposal. Crazy they might have been but Carol kept her wits about her, using gloves to make sure she did not leave any fingerprints.

On 1 August Clark told Bundy that earlier that day he had taken his neighbour's 11-year-old daughter for a drive. She was a witness to him picking up a hooker, who he shot and afterwards had sex with before dumping the body in Antelope Valley.

Four days later Bundy sounded out John Murray. She wanted to see how he would react to hearing of her participation in a series of unsolved murders, but he was unimpressed. In fact, he threatened to go to the police – so she killed him on the spot and then cut off his head. But in her excitement she neglected to recover the shell casings. And then she remembered that there had been a witness. Clark's latest conquest had seen Bundy with Murray that morning and she would have no hesitation in informing the police in order to get Bundy out of the way.

# CONFLICTING STATEMENTS

It was the realization that Clark would be free while she languished in prison that led to Bundy's breakdown and confession, though she attempted to blame him for corrupting her. He countered by claiming that she had committed all of the murders without his knowledge or participation. Their conflicting statements were a classic case of denial and projection as they attempted to rewrite their past, with the other cast in the role of the killer and themselves as the reluctant accomplice. Clark had initially attempted to implicate John Murray, but detectives quickly proved that the dead man had been seen elsewhere at the time of the killings.

In the end the forensic evidence damned them both. Clark's fingerprints were found on one of the two guns although he had insisted that they both belonged to Bundy. Clark had also left a bloody footprint in the rented garage and blood stains in a car. He had sold the car to keep it out of the hands of the police. Detectives also recovered the gloves that Bundy had worn when packing Exxie Wilson's head, together with a recording of Clark's confession. A witness identified his voice as that of the man who had telephoned her to confess to the killing of Cynthia Chandler. He had called her twice, so she was certain it was the same man.

On the first occasion he had claimed to be a police officer investigating the case and on the second he told her that he had killed Chandler and he would kill her too.

After they were charged, Bundy and Clark were subjected to stringent psychological assessments which concluded that they had no physical impairments or disorders that would excuse or explain their behaviour. They were both pathological liars and had indulged in abnormal sexual behaviour, but they were mentally fit to stand trial.

## SEND ME TO THE GAS CHAMBER

The trial, which Deputy District Attorney Robert Jorgensen described as 'an intimate tour of a sewer', ran for four months from October 1982. Clark was charged with killing six women. He was believed to have killed seven, but the bullet found in the seventh victim was too damaged for ballistics to identify it. On the stand Bundy testified that Clark had boasted of killing 47 women and of having begun his criminal career at the age of 17, but that sounded like an empty

and vulgar boast to the jury who could only return a verdict based on the facts.

Clark attempted to defend himself, but his frequent tantrums and abusive outbursts, and the admission that he was an unrepentant necrophiliac, did nothing to convince the jury that he was innocent. After he had insulted the judge, whom he called a 'gutless worm', his attorneys were ordered to take over. On 28 January 1983, after five days' deliberation, the jurors agreed on a guilty verdict which prompted Clark to demand that the judge sentence him to die in the gas chamber. On 15 February he got his wish in spades. The judge handed down six death sentences, one for each of his victims.

## CHANGE OF PLEA

On 2 May 1983, just before her trial was about to begin, Carol Bundy changed her plea to guilty in a deal that saved the state a long and expensive trial and took the death penalty off the table.

In return she received two consecutive life sentences for her crimes. She claimed that she was finished with her two-timing ex-lover, but she continued to write to him, even offering to hang herself if he asked her to.

But Douglas Clark had forged a new relationship with a woman who had been accused of attempted murder. Serial killer groupie Veronica Compton had earlier developed an infatuation with serial killer Kenneth Bianchi and had been prepared to murder a woman in a copy-cat killing in order to cast doubt on his conviction. It seemed that Clark had finally found his soul mate. He wrote to her thanking her for sex in a prison visiting room and calling his love rival, Bianchi, a 'whiney bitch'.

# PAUL BERNARDO AND KARLA HOMOLKA

When Paul and Karla Bernardo smiled for the photographer on the morning of their wedding they looked every inch the perfect couple. In fact, their blonde, blue-eyed good looks had earned them the nicknames 'Ken' and 'Barbie', because of their resemblance to the children's dolls of the same name. But their smiles hid the dark souls of two of America's most depraved and sadistic sex killers. Among their many female victims was Karla's own 15-year-old sister, Tammy Lyn, whose rape, torture and murder the couple would repeatedly re-enact, with Karla dressed in her dead sister's clothes.

Paul Kenneth Bernardo had already raped and terrorized seven women in the suburbs of Toronto, Canada. Why he felt the compulsion to force himself upon unwilling, defenceless girls, brutalizing and humiliating them, when he could have had a relationship with almost any woman he fancied is a mystery, but clearly he was incapable of developing a rapport with anyone other than a sadistic psychopathic personality like himself.

The Toronto attacks had becoming increasingly violent by 1988 and it was feared that the escalation would lead to murder, so the FBI was called in. The Canadian authorities had a vague description of the attacker, who was said to be handsome, fair-haired, slim and 1.8 m (6 ft) tall. But there were no physical clues and there was no forensic evidence. Without a specimen of the offender's semen, hair, clothing fibres, footprints, blood or fingerprints, or a name, there was nothing to be gained from running a match. The only hope lay in narrowing down the list of suspects by compiling a psychological profile.

*Two of a kind: Karla could be heard encouraging Paul as she filmed him raping one of his victims.*

# PROFILING A KILLER

The job was assigned to two of the FBI's most experienced men, special agents John Douglas and Gregg McCrary, who were based at the Behavioral Science Unit at Quantico, Virginia. When Douglas and McCrary surveyed the crime scenes and read the witnesses' statements they were able to draw a number of conclusions. The first one was that the 'UNSUB', or unknown subject, was most likely a local man living with his parents. All of the attacks had occurred in Scarborough, a middle-class neighbourhood, where a single man could not afford to purchase a home of his own. And the crime scenes formed a cluster. If the rapist had followed the victims from the centre of Toronto to Scarborough he would not have ended up attacking them within a few miles of each other. So he and his victims all came from the same area. And all but one of his victims were attacked from behind, presumably to minimize the risk of being recognized. It was also known that serial rapists tend to operate within a comfort zone, a familiar environment where they can stalk their victims and then follow a number of escape routes to their home.

His loathing for women would be known to his family or his friends because suppressed aggression of the intensity that erupts into violence cannot be contained indefinitely. At some point the UNSUB must have let his hatred for women slip out before he could stop himself and someone must have remembered a shocking incident like that.

In their report, Douglas and McCrary observed the development of sadistic tendencies, for example when the rapist asked the seventh victim the question, 'Should I kill you?', which prompted her to beg for her life. According to their report,

*'The sadist achieves gratification by the victim's response to his attempts to dominate and control her either physically or psychologically, by posing a question that made the victim beg for her life he is deriving pleasure.'*

The report concluded with a warning.

*'The nature of these attacks will continue to be episodic and sporadic... Each attack is precipitated by a stressor in the offender's life. This stressor could be either one in fact or in his mind.... Your offender harbours no guilt or remorse for these crimes. He believes his anger is justified and, therefore, so are the resultant attacks. His only concern is being identified and apprehended.'*

# TRAPPED BY A LOVERS' SPAT

By the spring of 1991 the file on the Scarborough rapist had doubled in size. It included the details of 15 attacks and yet more witness statements, but no clues. The investigators could only hope that the perpetrator would make a slip so that he could be caught in the act. That summer, FBI agent McCrary returned to Canada to investigate the murder of two teenage girls in the Toronto area. He was soon speculating that the murders could be connected with the unsolved series of rapes in Scarborough.

The two killings did not at first seem to be connected because the first victim, 14-year-old Leslie Mahaffy, had been dismembered, whereas the second, 15-year-old Kristen French, had not. And Mahaffy had been abducted in the daytime, murdered, covered in concrete and submerged in a lake, while French was kidnapped after dark and her body was left in the open. Both, though, had been sexually assaulted and suffocated and both bore almost identical pressure marks on their backs. The killer had presumably knelt on them when strangling them from behind.

But the most curious fact linking the two killings was that the first girl had been abducted in Burlington and her body deposited in St Catharine's, whereas the second girl had been dumped in Burlington after having been snatched from the streets of St Catharine's.

The link was too significant to discount as mere coincidence. Moreover, McCrary was aware that the perpetrator in both rapes and killings was a sadistic sex offender and that only two per cent of violent offenders fall into this category. The chances of more than one individual operating in the same area were

*The rented house in St Catharine's, Ontario where Karla's 15-year-old sister Tammy Lyn was raped and then died.*

too remote. It had to be the same person. What the FBI and the other investigators did not know, and could not have known, was that the serial rapist and murderer had a partner. It was only when the pair had a lovers' spat that the truth finally came out.

On 5 January 1993 Karla Homolka was treated for injuries inflicted by her husband, who had beaten her with a flashlight during a violent argument. Karla was so incensed that she wanted to file charges. When the local police arrived at her aunt and uncle's house to interview her they brought another pair of officers, who were introduced as being from the Toronto Sexual Assault Squad. DNA tests had been made on semen recovered from a rape victim in 1990 and it had taken over two years to obtain samples from over 200 men in the area and then identify the source. The forensic laboratory had named Karla's husband, Paul, as the rapist and now there was reason to suspect that Paul might have been involved in the murder of the two teenage

girls. If she had anything to tell them, now would be a good time.

## CAUGHT ON CAMERA

Karla played the role of the battered wife convincingly. In July 1993, before the full extent of her part in the murders became known, she was able to secure a guarantee of complete immunity from the Canadian Department of Justice. If any of the detectives had doubted that such an attractive young woman could be capable of active participation in sadistic sex murders they had their preconceptions shattered after viewing the videotapes that the pair had made of their crimes. The tapes had been hidden in the

*Karla Homolka showed no remorse for her actions when presented with the evidence.*

couple's rented house in Port Dalhousie and they made sickening viewing. Karla had filmed at least one of the Scarborough rapes and she could be heard encouraging her husband from behind the camera.

But even more shocking was the fact that the tapes recorded the torture and murder of victims who were unknown to the police. One of these was Karla's sister, 15-year-old Tammy Lyn. Karla considered her participation in the rape of Tammy Lyn to be her Christmas present to Paul. She supplied the drugs to sedate her sister and when he had finished she took over, sexually abusing the unconscious girl for their mutual pleasure. The camcorder was still running when Tammy choked and her attackers could not revive her. At the time the pathologist had found no evidence of foul play and so the police had concluded that the girl's death had been a tragic accident resulting from a drug overdose. But the video proved otherwise.

Paul Bernardo's pleasant persona was also a sham. Former girlfriends told detectives that at first he would be considerate and polite, but once he was confident that the girl was infatuated with him he would become abusive. He could only be sexually aroused when he was inflicting pain and he had a compulsion to dominate, control and humiliate his lovers.

Paul had groomed his former girlfriends to satisfy his sadistic fantasies. He had restricted their access to their families, chosen their clothes and flattered them to wear down their resistance to his demands. Their compliance and dependency only reinforced his contempt for them.

Then he attempted to do the same with Karla, who was just 17 years old when they met. She did more than share his fantasies, though, because she was willing to participate in the abuse of other women. On the day of her sister's funeral Karla dressed in the dead girl's clothes and then made a video of herself, in which she promised to procure young girls for her husband's entertainment. His look of surprise, captured on camera, seemed genuine. Karla appeared to have instigated the abductions of Kristen French and Leslie Mahaffy. And it was clear that she had not filmed their deaths against her will, as claimed. The excerpt showing Kristen screaming for help while Paul raped her was recorded by someone who held the camera with steady hands. FBI agent McCrary described her as a 'truly deviant personality'.

When faced with the forensic evidence and the videotapes, Karla expressed no remorse. She shared her husband's view that their victims had been objects to be used and abused. Karla and Paul were as unfeeling as the Ken and Barbie dolls they resembled.

In May 1995 Paul Bernardo was found guilty of first degree murder, kidnapping, sexual assault and forcible confinement, for which he received a mandatory life sentence.

The deal Karla had made with the Canadian Department of Justice did not mean that she would walk free, only that she would not be tried for murder. At her trial she was convicted on the lesser count of manslaughter. She was sentenced to two consecutive 10-year terms for her part in the killing of French and Mahaffy, with an additional two years for conspiring to cover up the facts relating to her sister's death. She was denied parole in 1997 and again in 2001, but was released in 2005.

# DAVID PARKER RAY AND CINDY HENDY

ruth or Consequences, New Mexico was once a place of relaxation. The first people to enjoy its hospitality arrived over 100 years ago. They were there to soak in the Geronimo Springs at John Cross Ranch. It would be the first of several dozen spas to be built around the heated groundwater that continues to bubble up in this city of less than 8,000 souls. The entire community was built around this natural phenomenon. Anyone who wonders how important it once was to the local economy need look no further than the city's original name: Hot Springs. The city became Truth or Consequences in 1950, when the popular radio quiz show of that name offered to broadcast from the first community to rename itself after the show. It was all good fun.

The first indication of David Parker Ray's crimes came on 26 July 1996, when the sheriff's office in Truth or Consequences received a call from a young Marine. On the previous day he had argued with his wife Kelly Van Cleave and he had not seen or heard from her since. The anxious husband received only advice.

His wife had been gone such a short time that she could not be considered as a missing person. Based on past experience, the office had every reason to believe that Kelly would turn up.

Sure enough, the young man's wife returned home on the very next day. She had been brought back by an employee of nearby Elephant Butte State Park, where she had been found wandering in a dazed and incoherent state.

*Ray revelled in the power he held over helpless victims; Hendy was his willing accomplice.*

Kelly could account for only a few of the many hours she had been missing. After the fight with her husband, she remembered going to a friend's house. This was followed by trips to a number of bars, the last of which was the Blue Waters Saloon. It was there that Kelly ordered a beer, her first drink of the evening.

She soon began to feel dizzy. The sensation was not dissimilar to being drunk, but something was not quite right. Kelly could recall little else from this point onwards, though she was certain that an old friend, Jesse Ray, had offered to help. Those missing hours brought an end to Kelly's marriage. Her husband could never accept her disappearance, or her claim that she could not remember what had happened.

## NIGHTMARES

Jesse Ray might have been able to help... but she could not be found. Kelly soon left Truth or Consequences, never to return. She would never see Jesse again.

Now separated, Kelly began to suffer from nightmares. The horrifying images were remarkably consistent – she saw herself being tied to a table, being gagged with duct tape and having a knife held to her throat. Nothing quite made sense so Kelly never did report her strange experience to the authorities. All the sheriff's office at Truth or Consequences had on file was a seemingly trivial phone call from a distrusting husband. They could not have known that the woman who walked through their door on 7 July 1997 was bringing information that was related to Kelly's disappearance.

The woman had come to report that she had not heard from her 22-year-old daughter, Marie

Parker, for several days. This time, there would be an investigation. In such a small city, it was not difficult to track the young woman's movements. Marie had last been seen on 5 July at the Blue Waters Saloon. She had been drinking with Jesse Ray. Jesse told the authorities that Marie had been drinking heavily so she had driven her home, but she had not seen her since.

But Jesse was not the only person that Marie had been drinking with on the night of her disappearance. Roy Yancy, an old boyfriend, had also been raising a glass at the Blue Waters Saloon. A Truth or Consequences boy born and raised, there was nothing in Roy's past to make the community proud.

As a child he had been part of a gang that had roamed Truth or Consequences strangling cats, poisoning dogs and tipping over gravestones, acts that led the city to cancel that year's Halloween festivities. He had also received a dishonourable discharge from the navy.

Marie might well have been in the company of an unsavoury character, but the Truth or Consequences sheriff's office saw nothing unusual about her disappearance. After all, the city was known for its transient population. They were all too ready to accept someone's hazy recollection of a girl accepting a ride out of the city. It was a typical story.

At around this time a new woman arrived in the small city. Cindy Hendy's history was anything but enviable. A victim of sexual abuse, she had been molested by her stepfather before being turned out on the street at the age of 11. Cindy had been a teenage mother, but only in the sense that she had given birth – other people had taken on the job of raising her daughter. When she arrived in Truth or Consequences, Cindy was on the run from a drugs charge. Several months earlier, she had supplied cocaine to an undercover agent. She was a violent woman with a short fuse, so it was not long before she found herself in the local jail. Days later she was sent out to Elephant Butte Lake on a work-release programme. It was there that she first met David Parker Ray, the father of her friend Jesse.

He was a quiet, though approachable and friendly man. Ray had been a neglected child. Unloved by his mother, his only real contact with his drifter father came in the form of periodic drunken visits. These invariably ended with the old man leaving behind a bag of pornographic magazines that portrayed sadomasochistic acts. His adult life was one of many marriages and many jobs. He had lived a transient life before 1984, when he settled down with his fourth wife in Elephant Butte. After acquiring a run-down bungalow on a little piece of property, Ray supported them by working as an aircraft engine repairman.

By 1995, his wife had left him. The fourth Mrs Ray would be the final Mrs Ray, but she was not his last companion. In January 1999, Cindy Hendy moved into Ray's bungalow. It mattered little that he was two decades older because the 38-year-old had met her soulmate – someone who, like herself, was obsessed with sadomasochistic sex.

## LONELY NEWCOMER

Cindy had been living with Ray for just one month when, on 16 February, she invited Angie Montano over for a visit. Angie, a single mother, was new to Truth or Consequences, and was eager to make friends. She had come to the wrong place, because she was blindfolded, strapped to a bed and sexually assaulted. Ray and Cindy's sadistic tastes went beyond rape. Angie was stunned by cattle prods and various other devices that Ray had made himself. After five days, Angie managed to get Ray to agree to her release. He drove her to the nearest highway and let her out. As luck would have it, she was picked up by a passing off-duty police officer. Angie shared her story with him, but she would not agree to making an official report. Just as Kelly Van Cleave had done four years earlier, Angie left Truth or Consequences, never to return.

Even as the assaults on Angie Montano were taking place, Cindy's mind was sometimes elsewhere. Though her 39th birthday had only just passed, she was about to become a grandmother. She made plans to attend the birth in her old home town of Monroe, Washington, but before she could go she needed to find a sex slave for Ray, someone who would meet his needs in her absence.

On 18 March, they drove through the streets of Albuquerque in Ray's motorhome, where they came upon Cynthia Vigil. She was a prostitute, so it was not difficult to get her into the vehicle, nor was it hard to overpower the 22-year-old. After being bound, Cynthia was taken back to the Elephant Butte bungalow, where she was collared, chained, blindfolded and gagged. A tape was then played to her. The voice was Ray's.

'Hello, bitch. Well, this tape's gettin' played again. Must mean I picked up another hooker. And I'll bet you wonder what the hell's goin' on here.'

Those were just the first few sentences in a recording that lasted over five minutes. Ray went on to describe how he and his 'lady friend' were going to rape and torture the listener.

'The gag is necessary,' he explained, 'because after a while you're goin' to be doin' a lot of screaming.'

True to the words of the tape, Ray and Cindy tortured and raped the prostitute over the course of the next three days. The assaults had no effect on Ray's work habits. As the fourth day began, he donned his state park uniform and drove off. Cindy was charged with keeping their victim under control. But his lady friend wasn't quite up to the task. In fact, she was downright sloppy.

When Cindy left the room to prepare a lunch of tuna sandwiches, the young prostitute noticed that her abductor had left behind the keys to her chains. After releasing herself, she grabbed the phone and called the Sierra County Sheriff's Office. Before she could say a word, Cindy was back in the room, bottle in hand. She took a violent swing at the prostitute, cutting her with the breaking glass. Cynthia noticed an ice pick while she was lying on the floor. She quickly grabbed it and stabbed her abductor in the back of the neck.

It was not a lethal blow, but it was enough to give Cynthia time to get out of the house. Naked except for a dog collar and chain, she ran out of the door and down the dusty, unpaved street. She was spotted by the drivers of two cars, but they just swerved to avoid the distressed, bleeding woman.

After about a mile, she came upon a trailer home. She burst through the door and fell at the feet of a woman watching television.

## SCENE OF THE CRIME

Just minutes after the first interrupted call, the Sierra County Sheriff's Office received a second one. When the authorities arrived at the mobile home they heard a horrific tale of torture and assault. As Cynthia Vigil was being transported to the local hospital, the sheriff's department decided to call in the state police.

*The New Mexico state police display the terrible contraption that was found in David Ray's trailer.*

Over a dozen officers converged on Ray's bungalow, only to find that Cindy had fled.

The house was a mess, with garbage littering the floor. If there was any order, it was found in Ray's instruments of torture, which were arranged on hooks hanging from the walls of several rooms. His library included books on Satanism, torture and violent pornography. There were also a number of medical books, which presumably enabled him to carry out many of his fantasies.

The hunt was now on for Ray and Cindy. The chase was as short as it was easy. The couple had not fled – instead, they were driving along the nearby roads, looking for their captive. Ray and Cindy were spotted within 15 minutes, a mere two blocks from their home. They quickly admitted that they had been looking for Cynthia Vigil, but they also came up with an implausible explanation for their actions. The abduction of the prostitute had been a humanitarian act, claimed Ray and Cindy. Her confinement had been nothing more than an effort to help the young woman kick her addiction to heroin.

The story fooled no one. Ray and Cindy were arrested and taken into custody. As the investigation of Ray's property began, the state law enforcement officials realized that they did not have the resources to deal with their discoveries. Lieutenant Richard Libicer of the New Mexico State Police explained the situation:

'I think it's safe to say that nothing that was inside that house was anything any of us had experienced before – or come across before – except maybe in a movie somewhere. It was just completely out of the realm of our experience.'

The assortment of shackles and pulleys and other instruments of torture inside the bungalow appeared almost mundane compared to what was discovered inside a padlocked semi-trailer that was parked outside.

What Ray described as the 'Toy Box' contained hundreds of torture devices. Many of them, such as a machine that was used to electrocute women's breasts, had been designed and built by the former mechanic. At the centre of this horror was a gynaecology table. Cameras were installed, so that the women could see what was happening to them. Ray had also videotaped his assaults, including the one involving Kelly Van Cleave. She had supposedly been found wandering by a state park official – but the state park official was David Parker Ray.

The videotapes were a revelation. For a start, they linked Jesse Ray to her father's crimes. Kelly's evidence also proved useful, but the most damning testimony came from Cindy Hendy.

Within days of her arrest, the 39-year-old turned on her boyfriend. She told the investigators that Ray had been abducting and torturing women for many years. What is more, Ray had told Cindy that his fantasies had often ended in murder.

Subsequent searches of Elephant Butte Lake and the surrounding countryside revealed nothing, but the police remain convinced that Ray had killed at least one person. Cindy also confirmed that Jesse had participated in at least some of the abductions. She added that she often worked in tandem with Roy Yancy.

## SOFT CENTRE

Despite his tough demeanour, Roy caved in when he was arrested. He told the police that he and Jesse had drugged Marie Parker, the young woman who had

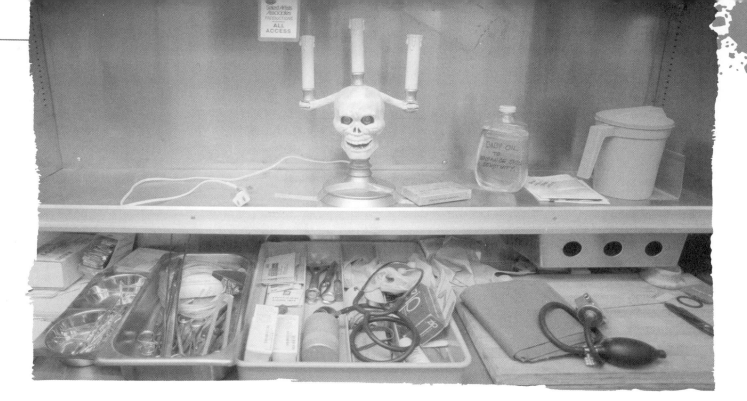

gone missing three years earlier. They had taken her to Elephant Butte, where she was tortured. When Ray tired of her, he instructed Roy to kill the woman who had once been his girlfriend.

The body was never found.

Roy Yancy pleaded guilty to second-degree murder and was sentenced to 20 years in prison.

After pleading guilty to kidnapping Kelly Van Cleave and Marie Parker, Jesse Ray received a nine-year sentence.

Facing the possibility of 197 years in prison, Cindy Hendy made a deal with the prosecutors. After pleading guilty to her crimes against Cynthia Vigil she received a 36-year sentence, with a further 18 years on probation.

Even Ray appeared to co-operate with the authorities, but only to the extent of describing his fantasies. He denied that he had abducted or murdered anyone. Any sadomasochistic activities had been between consenting adults. 'I got pleasure out of the woman getting pleasure,' he told one investigator. 'I did what they wanted me to do.'

*The 'Toy Box', a mobile torture chamber, was Ray's pride and joy – he put $100,000 into it.*

Ray faced three trials for his crimes against Kelly Van Cleave, Cynthia Vigil and Angie Montano. He was found guilty in the first trial, but part of the way through the second he too made a deal. Ray agreed to plead guilty in exchange for Jesse's release. The case concerning Angie Montano was never heard because she had died of cancer.

On 30 September 2001, David Parker Ray received a 224-year sentence for his crimes against Kelly Van Cleave and Cynthia Vigil. In the end, Ray did not serve so much as a year. On 28 May 2002 he slumped over in a holding cell, killed by a massive heart attack.

'Satan has a place for you. I hope you burn in hell forever,' Cynthia Vigil's grandmother had once yelled at him.

One wonders whether the words meant anything to Ray. The one sign he had put up in his 'Toy Box' read: 'SATAN'S DEN'.

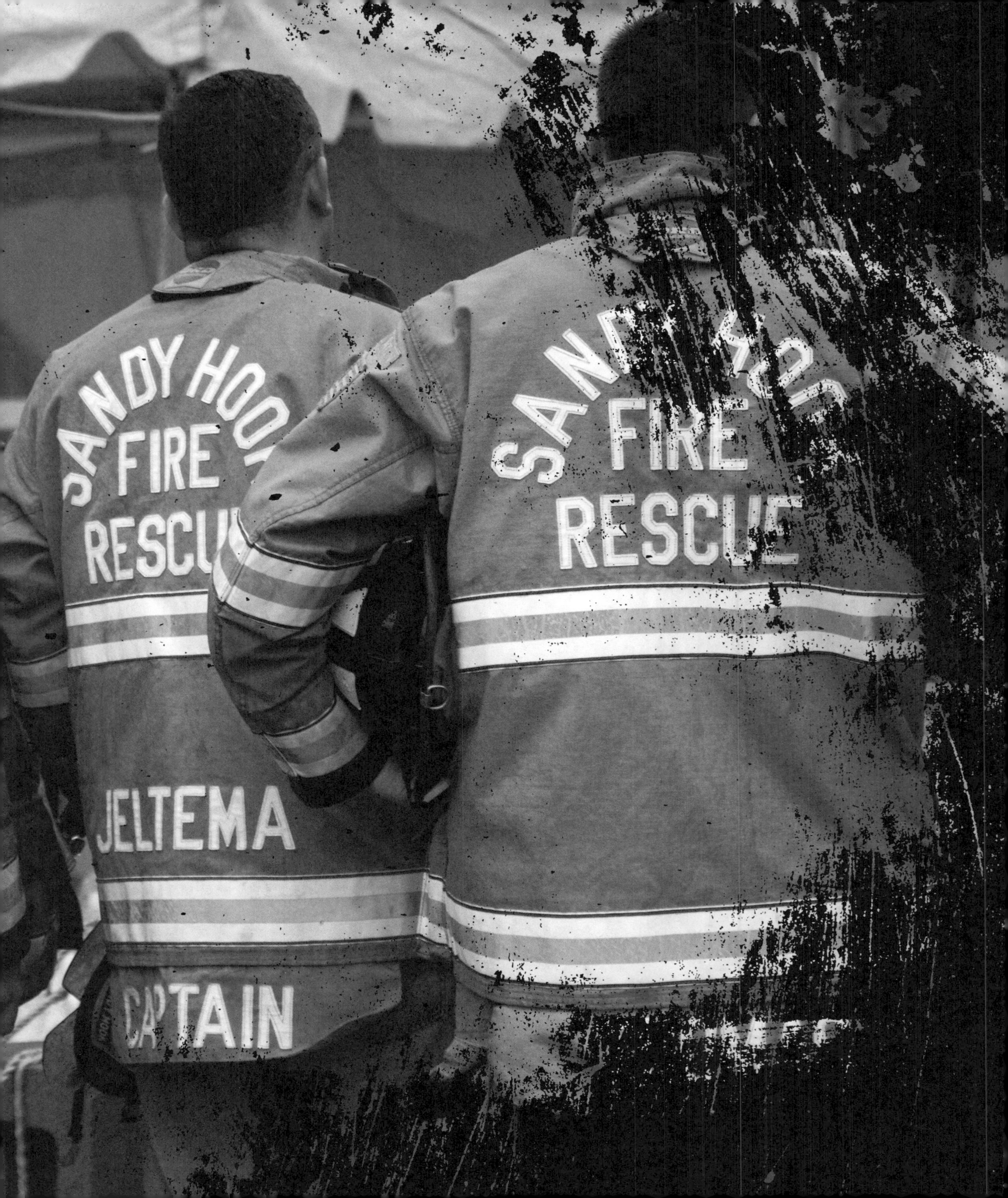
SANDY HOO
FIRE
RESCU
JELTEMA
CAPTAIN
FIRE
RESCUE

# MASS KILLERS

While most serial killers stalk their prey and kill them one by one, some murderers choose to take as many down with them as they can. Using bombs, assault rifles or anything they can get their hands on, they turn schools, workspaces and public places into blood-spattered crime scenes. Why do they want so much carnage on their hands? Often they have made plans to reshape the world in their own twisted image and that's why they document their ideas in psychopathic manifestos. In this section, you will discover just how hate-filled the human mind can get.

# TED KACZYNSKI

It took almost 18 years to link loner Ted Kaczynski to the killer known only by his FBI code-name, Unabomber. By then his bombs had become more and more sophisticated and deadly – and there was a million-dollar reward on his head.

His beginnings, in Chicago, had been modest. In May 1978, a package carrying the return address of a professor at Northwestern University's Technological Institute exploded while being opened by campus police. Shortly afterwards, a Northwestern graduate student opened an unaddressed cigar box he found and also sustained minor injuries. Bomb number three was found in the hold of an American Airlines plane outward bound from O' Hare Airport after its cabin had filled with smoke; bomb number four was in a parcel addressed to the president of United Airlines in Lake Forest. All were relatively crude affairs – though the airline bomb had been triggered to go off at a certain altitude – and did little damage.

There was then a lull of more than a year. But another bomb was found – and successfully defused – in a business classroom at the University of Utah in Salt Lake City in May 1982; it was followed a year later by a parcel bomb apparently intended for a professor of electrical engineering at Brigham Young. Less than two months later, another electrical-engineering professor, this time at the University of California at Berkeley, picked up a can of some kind in the faculty lounge and was seriously injured when it exploded.

By now the FBI had a tentative idea of who the bomber might be: an educated, intelligent white male, possibly an academic, from the Chicago area, with a grudge against authority in general and universities in particular. It was also clear that he was learning on the job, for his bombs were getting more and more sophisticated. Then, though, for three years the trail went cold, nothing happened – until suddenly bombs started appearing again on the West Coast, in Salt Lake City, Utah, and Ann Arbor, Michigan, in 1985.

The targets, this time, were computers, behaviour-modification and, once again, aircraft. Bombs were hand-delivered to two computer stores and a computer room at Berkeley and sent by post to the Boeing Aircraft Fabrication Division and a psychology professor in Ann Arbor. Four people were injured, two of them seriously; one of the computer-store operators was killed.

Once again there was a lull, this time for six years. Then, one after another, a geneticist at the University of California, a computer scientist at Yale and a vice-president of the Young & Rubicam advertising agency in New York were all hit. In a long, rambling letter sent to the *New York Times* a few months later, the Unabomber railed against computers and genetic engineering and claimed that the adman – who'd been killed instantly – had been part of a conspiracy, involved in 'manipulating people's attitudes.' On the

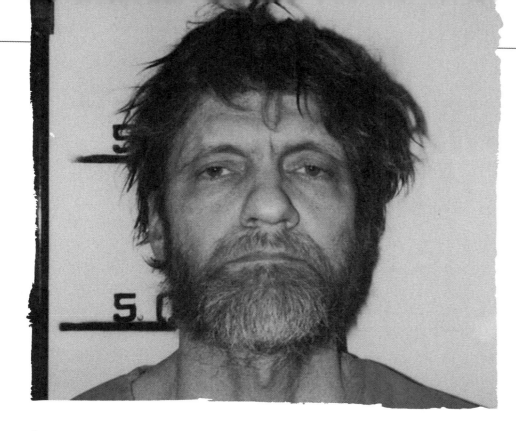

*When put beside those of suave mobsters or white-collar fraudsters, Ted Kaczynski's plans were crude, yet effective.*

day the letter was received, he struck again: a parcel bomb killed the president of the California Forestry Association in Sacramento.

This immediately suggested that the Unabomber was now playing games. For the surname and second name of two of his early victims had been Wood; the bombs had mostly been found in wooden containers. And, sure enough, when another letter was subsequently sent, this time to the *San Francisco Chronicle*, it carried as a return address 'Frederick Benjamin Isaac [FBI] Wood, 549 Wood Street, Woodlake, California'.

By this time the Unabomber was in regular communication with the *New York Times* and the *Washington Post*; he finally announced to both newspapers that he would give up his bombing campaign if they published in full a 35,000-word manifesto he'd written, spelling out his hatred of modern, technology-driven America. They agreed and it was read by a social worker in upstate New York called David Kaczynski.

Kaczynski was struck by the similarity of certain phrases in the manifesto to those written by his brother Theodore, a failed academic living in a tiny cabin without electricity outside Lincoln, Montana. After taking advice from friends, he finally went to the FBI with his suspicions. The cabin outside Lincoln was raided, and along with Ted Kaczynski, bomb-making equipment and early drafts of the manifesto were found.

Kaczynski was a 55-year-old Harvard graduate who'd done post-graduate work at Ann Arbor, and had faced a fast-track career as professor of mathematics at Berkeley. Then, unable to cope with the pressures of life, he'd simply dropped out. He started sending and laying bombs for 'personal revenge,' he wrote in his diary in 1971, because he was 'superior to most of the rest of the human race' and yet had been subject to 'rejections, humiliations and other painful influences.' He was sentenced to life imprisonment without the possibility of parole on 22 January 1998.

# ERIC HARRIS AND DYLAN KLEBOLD

These days we are no longer shocked to hear of incidents of road rage, air rage or even supermarket rage as tempers flare and violence erupts in places that we once thought were safe. But though we are becoming increasingly indifferent to such events, it is still horrifying to hear of a school shooting because this breaks the last taboo. Even the roughest inner city institutions should be a place where our children can be safe. The fear that their child might be the victim of a shooting by a classmate, or that their own child might be capable of killing, is something no parent can ever come to terms with.

## NO WARNING

The massacre at Columbine High School near Denver on 20 April 1999 has been blamed in part on the parents of the two teenage boys who killed 12 pupils and a teacher and wounded 24 other people before turning the guns on themselves. But investigators have admitted that the parents of Eric David Harris and Dylan Bennet Klebold had no idea of their sons'

*Harris and Klebold had nurtured their resentment for years, dreaming of making the world pay attention to them.*

state of mind, or of their plans. Neither boy was neglected, abused, bullied or encouraged to worship weapons, nor were they obsessed with violent video games, heavy metal or movies as the media have suggested. And contrary to what has been suggested by various anti-Semitic websites, they were not anti-Christian avengers or white supremacists.

The unpalatable truth is that Harris and Klebold were all-American teenagers who could not take the rejection that is a normal part of growing up. Had they been born in a country where automatic weapons are not sold over the counter to anyone

*Dylan Klebold attended his high school prom with a date only three days before the shooting spree.*

who can afford them, they might have taken out their rage by vandalizing the school or beating up the kids they did not like.

But contrary to the version of events marketed by the sensation-seeking media, the boys did not compile a list of enemies. Their initial plan was to set off dozens of home-made bombs in the campus cafeteria and kitchen, which would demolish the school and kill hundreds of students, friends and enemies alike, in a random act that would symbolize their rage and despair.

They had also planted more devices in their cars, which they had parked at strategic points to wreak the maximum havoc. Their intention was to watch the ensuing chaos from outside and then when the police and concerned parents arrived they were going to detonate the car bombs too. It was the ultimate revenge fantasy. They believed that the institution and the people in it were responsible for their isolation and unpopularity. It was only after the bombs had failed to explode that the boys went on the rampage.

Harris and Klebold had been building up their resentment for years – they had even boasted about it to the few friends they had. But when their plans were laughed at they had to carry out their threat or lose face. For two deeply disturbed and suicidal teenagers losing face was a fate worse than death. So they chose to die and bring down everything they hated along with them. They were not ordinary kids

who had been corrupted by playing Black Sabbath records backwards but embittered, self-centred sociopaths. Klebold was a paranoid depressive who described himself as 'a god of sadness', while Harris suffered from the same narcissistic paranoia that drove dictators Adolf Hitler and Saddam Hussein.

'I feel like God and I wish I was, having everyone being OFFICIALLY lower than me,' he once wrote.

The two complemented one another and together they found the will to inflict their punishment on a world that had rejected them – or so they imagined. No one saw the danger signs because they were two white kids from affluent American families. And being devious and intelligent they had managed to mitigate the fears of everyone who had expressed concern simply by telling them what they wanted to hear. They had learned to lie convincingly and conceal their true feelings – except in their journals and video diaries, to which they confided every perceived injustice they had suffered. This is one of the last entries Harris wrote.

*Some of the material and devices found in Eric Harris' vehicle after the Columbine High School massacre.*

JC-001-026237

*Image released by the Jefferson County sheriff office after the massacre.*

'I hate you people for leaving me out of so many fun things. And no don't say, "Well, that's your fault," because it isn't, you people had my phone number, and I asked and all, but no. No no no don't let the weird-looking Eric KID come along.'

His exercise books were said to be covered in swastikas.

Klebold was more introspective and he was consumed by despair. He confided to his diary that his life was 'the most miserable existence in the history of time'. He drew hearts in his journals and considered himself misunderstood and victimized by fate.

Both teenagers loathed authority and despised anyone who made the effort to fit in and conform. Their attack was not spontaneous because it had been germinating for months. They had even taken after school jobs to pay for the weapons and the bomb-making ingredients. If Harris and Klebold had been able to raise more money to buy more guns, and had taken more care to build better bombs, the fatalities might have been counted in triple figures.

*A security camera catches Harris and Klebold working out why their bombs didn't detonate before they started shooting. Harris once wrote, 'If you disagree I would shoot you… some people go through life begging to be shot.'*

# ANDERS BREIVIK

On the afternoon of 22 July 2011, a curious compendium titled *2083 – A European Declaration of Independence* was emailed to over a thousand recipients around the globe. Its author was a complete unknown, but by the end of the day he would be famous – not for his writing, but as the worst spree killer in world history.

Anders Behring Breivik was born on 13 February 1979 in Oslo, but lived most of his earliest days in London, where his father, an economist, worked as a diplomat for the Royal Norwegian Embassy. At the age of one, his parents divorced, setting off a custody battle that his father lost. Still an infant, Breivik returned with his mother, a nurse, to Oslo. Although she was soon remarried, to a Norwegian Army officer, Breivik would later criticize what he perceived as an absence of the masculine in his childhood home. In his writings, he disparages his mother for his 'matriarchal upbringing', adding 'it completely lacked discipline and has contributed to feminizing me to a certain degree.'

Anecdotal evidence shows Breivik to have been an intelligent, caring boy, one who was quick to defend others against bullying. However, his behaviour changed markedly in adolescence. Over a two-year period, so Breivik claims, he engaged in a one-man 'war' against Oslo's public transit company, causing

*An image of Anders Breivik from his personal website.*

£700,000 ($956,000) in property damage. His evenings were spent running around the city with friends, committing acts of vandalism. At the age of 16, Breivik was caught spray-painting graffiti on the exterior wall of a building, an act that brought an end to his relationship with his father. The two have had no contact since.

Though the stepson of an army officer, Breivik was declared 'unfit for service' in Norway's mandatory conscription assessment. The reason for this surprising judgement has yet to be disclosed; Breivik told friends a story that he'd received an exemption to care for his sickly mother. However, a possible explanation is his use of anabolic steroids, a drug that he'd been taking since his teenage years in an effort to bulk up. Breivik was a man obsessed with his appearance.

# NO GIRLFRIENDS

In 2000, at the age of 21, he flew off to the United States to have cosmetic surgery on his forehead, nose and chin. Unmarried at 32, Breivik considered himself a most desirable bachelor, and boasted frequently of his conquests, yet not one of his acquaintances can remember him ever having had a girlfriend.

'When it comes to girls,' Breivik wrote in his journal, 'I'm tempted – especially these days, after training and I'm feeling fantastic. But I try to avoid entanglements, because they may complicate my plans and put the whole operation in jeopardy.'

The operation he referred to was part of a nine-year plan that culminated on that horrible day in July 2011. According to Breivik, work began in 2002 with the establishment of a computer programming business that was intended to raise funds. Instead, the company went bankrupt, forcing him to move back to his mother's house. This humiliating setback seems to have brought on a period of relative inactivity. By 2009, however, Breivik was back in business. He set up a company, Breivik Geofarm, which was nothing more than a cover so that he might buy large quantities of fertilizer and other chemicals used in bomb-making without raising suspicions. The next year, after a failed attempt at buying illegal weapons in Prague, he purchased a semi-automatic Glock pistol and a Ruger Mini-14 semi-automatic carbine through legal channels.

Breivik murdered with these guns, but his first victims on 22 July 2011 were killed with a car bomb planted in his Volkswagen Crafter. That afternoon, he drove the automobile into the government quarter of Oslo, taking care to park it in front of the building housing the Office of the Prime Minister, the Minister of Justice and Police and several other high-ranking government ministers. At 3.22 pm, the car bomb exploded, shattering windows, and setting the ground floor of the building on fire. Though Labour Prime Minister Jens Stoltenberg, thought to have been a chief target of the attack, survived without a scratch, the explosion killed eight people and left 11 more with critical injuries.

Things could have been much worse. It's curious that through all Breivik's years of planning, he'd never taken into account the fact that July is the month Norwegians go on holiday. What's more, he'd chosen to carry out his attack late on a Friday afternoon, a time when most government employees had already left for the weekend.

During the mayhem in downtown Oslo, Breivik changed into a fake police uniform, made his way some 40 km (25 miles) to the shores of Lake Tyrifjorden, and caught a ferry to the island of Utoya. His destination was a summer camp that was held annually by the youth wing of the Norwegian Labour Party. By the time he arrived – 4.45, one hour and 23 minutes after the Oslo blast – news of the tragedy had already been announced to the camp staff and roughly 600 teenagers on the island. Breivik appeared as he presented himself: a police officer who had come to ensure that the 10.5 hectare (26 acre) island was secure. After first asking people to gather around so that he could speak with them, Breivik opened fire. He shot indiscriminately, apparently intent on killing as many people as possible. Breivik's bullets struck people as they took to the lake, hoping to swim to safety.

# INDISCRIMINATE SLAUGHTER

It wasn't until 32 minutes after the shooting began that police on the mainland were aware of something

taking place on Utoya Island. Their delayed response is a matter of investigation. They waited until the Beredskapstropen, a special counter-terrorism unit, arrived from Oslo, before making the crossing. The boat that they sailed on was so overloaded that it nearly sank before reaching the island. Even before they left shore, Breivik placed a phone call to surrender, only to change his mind. The killing continued until 6.26 pm – one hour and 24 minutes after it had begun – when the gunman made a second call. He was apprehended by the Beredskapstropen eight minutes later.

In all, Breivik killed 69 people on Utoya Island and its surrounding waters. Many of the survivors escaped with their lives by swimming to areas that were only accessible from the lake, while others hid in a schoolhouse, which the gunman chose not to enter. Some survivors played dead, even after being

*A photo taken from a helicopter showing Breivik next to several bodies.*

shot for a second time. Still others were rescued by vacationers and others with boats, who risked coming under fire from the shore.

Breivik claimed a total of 77 lives with his two attacks; a further 153 people were injured. The dead ranged in age from 14 to 61, with a median age of just 18 years. He'd killed 55 teenagers.

Anders Breivik has acknowledged that he committed the bombing in Oslo and the shootings on Utoya, but has denied guilt. In his words, both events involved what his lawyer called 'atrocious but necessary actions'. Much of the gunman's motivation can be gleaned through *2083 – A European Declaration of Independence*, the 1,513-

*Breivik revisits the scene of his crime to provide police with evidence.*

page document that he released to the world just 90 minutes before setting off the Oslo bomb. In this collection of writings, much of it plagiarized from others, Breivik argues against feminism and for a return to a patriarchy that he felt was lacking in his own upbringing. The murderer rails against multiculturalism and what he sees as opening the door to the Islamization of Europe. Portraying himself as a knight, Breivik calls on other white Europeans to wage a religious war against Muslims and Marxists. His ultimate goal, as reflected in the title of the document, was the deportation of all followers of Islam from Europe by 2083.

'A majority of the people I know support my views,' he writes, 'they are just apathetic. They know that there will be a confrontation one day, but they don't care because it will most likely not happen within the next two decades.'

Breivik appeared in Oslo District Court three days after the attack. Facing charges of terrorism, the accused entered a not guilty plea, adding that he did not recognize the system under which he would be tried. The arraignment was held *in camera*, due to fears that he might somehow use the venue to communicate with compatriots. Following his trial, in August 2012 Breivik was found guilty and given a sentence of containment, a penalty peculiar to Norway that allows a felon to be incarcerated for up to 21 years - the maximum sentence allowed in Norwegian law.

# ADAM LANZA

Newtown is a small sleepy town of 27,000 residents in Connecticut. It was the last place anyone would think of as the setting for a crime that would shock the world. On 14 December 2012, 20-year-old Adam Lanza changed everything. He shot his mother in the head before returning to his old school, Sandy Hook Elementary. Then, armed with a semi-automatic, military-style rifle, he burst into the school spraying bullets everywhere. Terrified teachers tried to calm their students as the nightmare unfolded. By the time the ordeal was over, Lanza's bullets had claimed the lives of 20 children, aged between six and seven, and six adults.

Adam Lanza lived most of his life in Newtown. To friends and neighbours, his parents Nancy and Peter appeared to be a loving, caring couple who did their best to provide their son with a good upbringing. But beneath the surface there were tensions.

In 2001 his parents separated. This was when things really started to turn sour. Lanza's relationship with his mother grew increasingly strained. Nancy was a gun enthusiast. She collected guns, kept them well stocked with ammunition and subscribed to a gun magazine. There were always lots of paper targets lying around the house. The family often went to the shooting range.

A disturbing family photo shows Adam Lanza as a toddler decked out in camouflage, wearing an ammunition belt and holding a gun to his mouth.

## JEALOUSY

Lanza attended Sandy Hook Elementary School briefly as a child. His mother volunteered there between 1998 and 2012. This caused tension between them. He became jealous, believing that his mother showed more affection towards her students than she ever

*Many thought Lanza was harmless, but his obsession with school shootings kept growing.*

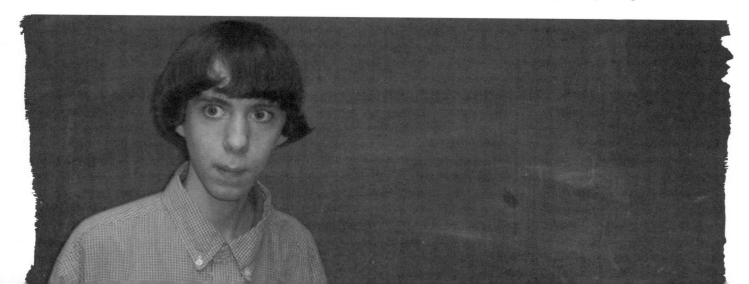

did towards him. By this time, he had moved on to Newtown High School. Though an honours student, he was taken out of school to be home-schooled by his parents, and attended Western Connecticut State University in 2008 and 2009. Lanza had trouble socializing and making friends. He disliked anything that forced him into contact with other people – he hated birthdays, Christmas and holidays with a passion.

As a teenager he was diagnosed with Asperger syndrome. Lanza also suffered from obsessive compulsive disorder; he refused to touch doorknobs with his bare hands and changed his socks 20 times a day. He was prescribed drugs to help with his autism and other behavioural disorders but refused to take them. He grew increasingly angry at being forced to go for psychiatric tests at Yale. A nurse there, who saw him between 2006 and 2007, described him as 'emotionally paralyzed'.

In the fifth grade he wrote a story with another boy entitled 'The Big Book of Granny'. The story is about an old woman who kills people indiscriminately with the gun in her cane. In one chapter, there's a game called Hide and Go Die. In it, one character stated rather chillingly, 'I like hurting people... especially children.'

# OBSESSED WITH MASS MURDER

Like many boys, Lanza was fascinated by conflict and guns. But it didn't stop there. He became obsessed by the mass shootings at Columbine High School in 1999 and at Northern Illinois University in 2008. The Newtown report, released in November 2013, noted he had 'hundreds of documents, images, videos pertaining to the Columbine H.S. massacre, including what appears to be a complete copy of the investigation'.

In his bedroom he kept a collection of newspaper cuttings on school shootings and there was a game called 'School Shooting' on his computer. On the wall was a huge spreadsheet featuring the top 500 mass murders of all time, which he had created himself, and he had also written a document listing the prerequisites for mass murder. But no one ever came into his room to find out what was going on.

Increasingly, Lanza began to cut himself off from the outside world. His mother may have been trying too hard to protect him. She didn't insist that he take the medication he had been prescribed. She also cancelled follow-up trips with mental health professionals. After 2008, he stopped having any treatment at all. Nancy Lanza struggled to accept the fact that her son had disabilities. She repeatedly described her son as 'gifted' when his intellectual abilities were really quite average.

As he grew older, his parents struggled to break through the barriers he put up. Despite living in the same house as his mother, he only contacted her by email. At one point, he didn't speak to her for three months. The windows of his room were covered with black garbage bags and he let no one else in. At the time of the killings, he hadn't seen his father for two years.

There was only one friend Lanza felt able to connect with. He remains anonymous and his testimony has only come out with the publication of the Sandy Hook Report. The two friends used to meet to play the video game Dance Dance Revolution and they talked about everything from Japanese techno music to paedophilia to chimp society. Lanza spent so much time playing *Dance Dance Revolution* that he acquired the nickname the 'DDR guy'.

In June 2012 the friends had a falling-out over a movie. Just months before the shooting, Lanza had thus lost his only buddy and became more and more isolated. He spent the three months before the shooting playing video games, studying previous mass murders and interacting online with a community of murder enthusiasts.

Lanza had developed his own theory of mass murder. As he saw it, they always occurred 'in contexts which involve some permutation of alienation'. His view of society was a gloomy one. He talked of the 'rape of civilization' and he railed against 'enculturing human children'. He put up post after post on online forums, explaining his philosophy, obsessing over mass killings and egging on others to bloodthirsty acts. No one ever intervened.

# ANOREXIC

He was a scrawny teenager who suffered from anorexia. His eating habits were unhealthy. He would add salt to his drinking water. At the time of his death he was 1.8m (6 ft) tall but weighed only 51 kg (112 lb). In retrospect, the chief medical examiner suggested that malnutrition might have caused damage to his brain.

Nancy Lanza was only too aware that her son had a violent streak. Just a week before the shooting, she told a friend that she was afraid that he was getting worse. He kept burning himself with a lighter, but Nancy was afraid that he might try to commit suicide. Nancy had health issues herself. She had recently been diagnosed with MS.

On 10 December 2012 Nancy Lanza made a fateful decision which might have precipitated the killings. She decided to try an 'experiment'. She would leave Lanza on his own for a few days while she made a trip to New Hampshire. A few hours after she left, there were signs that her 'experiment' wasn't going too well. Adam had bumped his head and was bleeding.

On the evening of 13 December, she returned home for the last time. At 9.00 am the next day, Nancy Lanza was sleeping peacefully in her bed when her son entered and shot her in the head with her own gun. He took her guns, a Bushmaker XM15-E2S rifle, a civilian version of the semi-automatic weapon used by the US Army in Afghanistan and Iraq, and two handguns, a Glock pistol and a Sig Sauer, and left the house. Armed to the teeth, he climbed into his mother's car and drove to his old school, Sandy Hook Elementary.

The doors to the school were locked, so Lanza shot his way in through a nearby glass panel. Dressed in black clothing, sunglasses and a green utility vest, he struck a terrifying figure. The first shots fired were heard over the school intercom. The head janitor saw Lanza and yelled at him: 'Put the gun down!' Lanza ignored him and proceeded to kill the school's principal, Dawn Hochsprung, and the school psychologist, Mary Sherlach.

Lanza moved on to Lauren Rousseau's first-grade classroom. Rousseau had sent her children to the back of the room and was trying to hide them in a bathroom as Lanza entered. Soon Rousseau, Rachel D'Avino, a behavioural therapist, and 14 children were dead. A six-year-old girl was the only survivor of the attack. She managed to phone her mother: 'Mommy, I'm okay, but all my friends are dead.'

Kaitlin Roig-DeBellis hid her students in a tiny 1.1 m² (12 sq ft) bathroom. She told them: 'If we're going to live, we have to find a hiding place … Evil is coming for us and there's nowhere to go.'

Roig-DeBellis instructed her students to remain silent, and barricaded the door. One of them told her, 'I don't want to die before Christmas.' Eventually, the police arrived and knocked loudly. Terrified, she demanded some ID before she opened up. A badge slid under the door and she flung it open in relief.

Some teachers read stories to their children and others quietly sang Christmas carols. Twenty-seven-year-old Victoria Soto died shielding a child from Lanza's gunfire.

Yvonne Cech and Maryann Jacob hid their students in the library and pushed a filing cabinet against the door when they could not get the lock to work. Lanza tried to enter and, when it proved too much work, he moved on to easier prey.

It was only five minutes from the sound of the first gunshots to the welcome whine of police sirens, but it was already too late. Over 100 rounds had already been fired. Police officers encountered a horrific scene. Bullet-ridden corpses of children and teachers alike were strewn across the school. Trauma teams were assembled ready to deal with any casualties and the emergency room of the nearest hospital was prepared to receive an influx of visitors. In the end only three victims reached the hospital. The others were already dead. The final shot was fired at 9.40 a.m. – it was Lanza taking his own life.

*Town volunteers of the Sandy Hook Fire and Rescue Department were some of the first people on the scene after the shooting. Here, they hug during a minute of silence held on 21 December 2012.*

For the survivors, the memory of this terrible day never goes away. Kaitlin Roig-Debellis remembers it 'every second of every minute of every single day'. The community of Newtown, Connecticut, still struggles to come to terms with the horrific event.

One of the teacher's daughters still cannot believe it happened. According to Ashley Cech, 'If you know

*This spontaneous roadside shrine to those who died, erected at the school gates, asks a question no one has yet answered…*

Newtown, if you know Sandy Hook, you just had this idea that nothing wrong could happen there.'

Sadly, Adam Lanza proved otherwise.

# OMAR MATEEN

Before 12 June 2016, no one knew the name of Omar Mateen. Now he is infamous as the worst spree killer in recent US history.

Omar Mateen was born in New York on 16 November 1986 under the name Omar Mir Seddique. His parents were moderate Muslims who had immigrated to the United States from Afghanistan. According to their friends they were an 'all-American' family. He spent most of his childhood in the small Florida town of Port St Lucie.

His father Sedique Mateen was an outspoken Afghan activist who appeared in programmes on a satellite TV channel aimed at the Afghan immigrant community. He loved posing in military fatigues and putting himself forward as a suitable candidate to be Afghan president.

Friends and neighbours remember Omar Mateen as an angry and troubled child. At Mariposa Elementary, he began to show the signs of the propensity for violence that would characterize his life.

A third-grade teacher described him as 'verbally abusive, rude and aggressive' and in the seventh grade, he had to be transferred to a different class to stop him causing trouble. He bullied other children, particularly girls. Mateen struggled with school discipline and often required personal tutoring. His father did little to improve the situation, dismissing complaints against his son in a high-handed fashion and showing antagonism towards female teachers.

At high school, things got worse. At the age of 14, Mateen was expelled from Martin County High School after a fight in maths class, for which he was arrested. He moved on quickly to Spectrum, a high school for students with behavioural issues.

Fights and suspensions followed him throughout his high school career.

While most of the country reacted with shock and horror to the attacks of 11 September, Mateen applauded the terrorists. He even claimed that Osama bin Laden was his uncle and had taught him how to shoot AK-47s.

*Omar Mateen, who murdered 49 people at Pulse nightclub in Orlando, Florida*

# LIFE ON THE MINIMUM WAGE

The first few years of his adult life were spent traipsing from one minimum-wage job to the next. He worked as a bagger at Publix, a cashier at Chik-fil-A and a sales associate at Hollister Clothing and General Nutrition Center (GNC).

But Mateen had aspirations. The chubby teenager was driven on by twin desires: to improve his physique, and to become a police officer. One was more easily achievable for someone like him. Working out constantly, with the help of certain chemical enhancements, the change in Mateen's body was obvious to everyone who knew him.

Mateen attended Indian River State College, earning a degree in criminal justice technology. He began working for the Florida Department of Corrections in 2006. Following the Virginia Tech shootings of April 2007, he started bringing a gun to class, resulting in his dismissal before he could qualify as a fully certified corrections officer.

Instead, he went to work for G4S, a British-based private security firm, but even there he could not keep himself out of trouble. His comments on terrorism – he claimed connections to Al-Qaeda – drew the FBI's attention.

He married an Uzbeki woman, Sitora Yusufiy, in 2008, but after four months they separated when she claimed physical and emotional abuse by her husband.

His second marriage, this time to Noor Zahi Salman, was more successful. They had a son. Mateen continued to live in South Florida as he had done for much of his life, residing at Fort Pierce, just 160 km (100 miles) from Orlando.

Mateen was not a particularly devout Muslim. In fact, he chose to legally change his name from the traditional Afghan form 'Omar Mir Seddique', meaning 'Omar, son of Seddique', to something more American, Omar Mateen.

He did occasionally attend the Islamic Center of Fort Pierce, where his three sisters were active volunteers. But he also drank heavily, took drugs and rarely talked about Islam with his friends. His wife Noor came from a more devout family than Mateen; she would fast for Ramadan and occasionally wore the hijab, but you could never call her a fundamentalist.

There was one thing above all that probably left Mateen conflicted. In the aftermath of the shootings, his father said his son had once been greatly angered by the sight of two men kissing, but that may not tell the whole story.

From his time at Indian River college, friends and colleagues began to wonder if Mateen was gay. He attended gay night clubs with friends and was a member of gay dating apps such as Grindr. For most of his life he showed no evidence of homophobia. His father, however, was not so tolerant, and would never have entertained the possibility that a son of his could be homosexual.

# THE MASSACRE

Between the 5 and 9 June 2016, Mateen travelled to Orlando and visited Pulse nightclub several times. At this popular gay bar, Mateen would sit and drink in a corner by himself, though the owner of Pulse rejects any suggestion that Mateen was a regular customer.

Omar Mateen purchased a Glock 9 mm handgun and a SIG Sauer MCX rifle. The latter was a semi-automatic rifle initially developed for the American special forces and then adapted for civilian use. His wife, Noor Salman, knew what was happening.

After the attack she admitted to the FBI that she had accompanied him to Pulse nightclub on his earlier visits and had helped him to buy ammunition. On the Saturday evening of the massacre as he prepared to leave for Orlando, Salman warned him against doing anything crazy. But she made no attempt to call the police.

On 11 June, the evening of the killings, Mateen posted messages on the social networking platform Facebook confirming his allegiance to Islamic State: 'I pledge my alliance to abu bakr al Baghdadi … may Allah accept me … The real muslims will never accept the filthy ways of the west. You kill innocent women and children by doing us airstrikes … now taste the Islamic state vengeance.'

*Police and rescue officers monitor the scene outside Pulse in the aftermath of the shootings by lone wolf gunman Omar Mateen; many hardened lawmen were shocked at what had taken place the night before.*

Just before he began his attack, Mateen called 911 and once more pledged his allegiance to ISIS. Equipped with two guns and with murder in his heart, he entered Pulse nightclub at 2.00 am on 12 June 2016 and the shooting began. It was Latin Night; 320 patrons were happily drinking, dancing and enjoying the atmosphere.

A police officer was working overtime at the club and returned fire almost immediately, but was unable to prevent Mateen from killing his first victims. Mateen then opened fire on hundreds of innocent partiers inside the building. At first, some revellers mistook the sound of gunshots for music. But when the blood started flowing, reality set in.

In the dark a scene of horror and confusion was unfolding. At 2.09 am, a simple warning was posted on Pulse's Facebook page: 'Everyone get out of pulse and keep running.'

Soon social media was buzzing with news of the shooting as the terrified clubbers attempted to get

the message out to friends and family, for example 'Omg. Shooting at pulse. We hid in the bathroom. And we can't find our friends' or 'Walking to Orlando Regional Medical Center now. I'm ok. Fred got shot. I've never seen so much blood and mayhem or been so scared ever.'

The victims were not the only ones attempting to communicate with loved ones. Omar Mateen asked his wife by text if she had 'seen the news'. She simply replied that she loved him.

Approximately 100 officers from the Orange County Sheriff's Office arrived, but by then Mateen had taken a number of hostages. Survivors overheard Mateen claim that he wouldn't stop his assault until America stopped bombing 'his country'.

*The damaged rear wall of Pulse nightclub: a SWAT team crashed their armoured vehicle through the brickwork to put an end to the siege.*

Police hostage negotiators spoke to Mateen by phone three times between 2.48 and 3.27 am. It was not until 5.53 am that the nightmare was over. By this time, SWAT team members had forcibly entered the building by crashing an armoured vehicle through the wall and Mateen had been killed in the ensuing shootout.

By the end of the night, 49 people were dead and another 53 injured. It was the worst mass shooting by an individual in United States history and the worst terrorist attack since 9/11.

# INDEX

# PICTURE CREDITS

t = top, b = bottom, l = left, r = right